PERGAMON GENERAL PSYCHOLOGY SERIES

Editors: Arnold P. Goldstein, *Syracuse University*
Leonard Krasner, *SUNY, Stony Brook*

STUDIES IN
DYADIC COMMUNICATION

PGPS-7

STUDIES IN
DYADIC COMMUNICATION

Editors

Aron Wolfe Siegman
University of Maryland

and

Benjamin Pope
The Sheppard and Enoch Pratt Hospital, Towson, Md.

Pergamon Press

New York/Toronto/Oxford/Sydney/Braunschweig

PERGAMON PRESS INC.
Maxwell House, Fairview Park, Elmsford, N.Y. 10523

PERGAMON OF CANADA LTD.
207 Queen's Quay West, Toronto 117, Ontario

PERGAMON PRESS LTD.
Headington Hill Hall, Oxford

PERGAMON PRESS (AUST.) PTY. LTD.
Rushcutters Bay, Sydney, N.S.W.

VIEWEG & SOHN GmbH
Burgplatz 1, Braunschweig

Printed in the United States of America

08 015867 6

Contents

Acknowledgments

We are grateful to the following agencies and institutions for financial assistance in organizing the research conference on which this book is based: The Psychiatric Institute, University of Maryland; Social Rehabilitation Service, Department of Health, Education and Welfare; and Merck Sharp & Dohme Products.

Aron W. Siegman, Ph.D.
Benjamin Pope, Ph.D.

Baltimore, Maryland

The Authors

HARRIET ARONSON, Ph.D. is an Associate Professor of Psychology in the Department of Psychiatry, Health Sciences Center, Temple University, Philadelphia.

ALLEN T. DITTMANN, Ph.D. is a Research Psychologist in the Section on Personality of the Laboratory of Psychology, National Institute of Mental Health, in Bethesda, Maryland.

STANLEY FELDSTEIN, Ph.D. is currently Associate Professor of Psychiatry in the Division of Biological Psychiatry of the Department of Psychiatry of New York Medical College, New York City.

URIEL G. FOA, PH.D. is a Professor of Psychology and Behavioral Research at the University of Missouri, Columbia.

EDNA B. FOA, Ph.D. is a Research Associate in The Center for Research in Social Behavior at the University of Missouri, Columbia.

NORBERT FREEDMAN, Ph.D. is both Professor in the Department of Psychiatry and Director of Psychology at the University Hospital at the Downstate Medical Center, Brooklyn, New York.

HERBERT S. GROSS, M.D. is an Assistant Professor of Psychiatry at the Psychiatric Institute, University of Maryland School of Medicine, Director of the Division of Adult Outpatient Psychiatry, and candidate in The Washington Psychoanalytic Institute.

KENNETH HELLER, Ph.D. is Professor of Psychology at Indiana University in Bloomington. He is co-author with Arnold P. Goldstein and Lee B. Sechrest of the book *Psychotherapy and the Psychology of Behavior Change.*

ADAM KENDON, Ph.D. is associated with the Project on Human Communication, Bronx State Hospital, New York City, where he is doing research on various aspects of human communicative behavior.

GEORGE F. MAHL, Ph.D. is Professor of Psychology in the Departments of Psychiatry and Psychology, Yale University, and Instructor in the Western New England Institute for Psychoanalysis.

BENJAMIN POPE, Ph.D. is now the Director of Psychology Services at The Sheppard and Enoch Pratt Hospital, Towson, Maryland, and Professor of Clinical Psychology (p.t.) at the University of Maryland School of Medicine.

ARON WOLFE SIEGMAN, Ph.D. is Professor of Psychology at the University of Maryland, Baltimore County Campus, and Research Professor of Clinical Psychology (p.t.) at The Psychiatric Institute, University of Maryland School of Medicine.

JAMES T. WEBB, Ph.D. is Assistant Professor of Psychology at Ohio University, Athens, Ohio.

WALTER WEINTRAUB, M.D. is Professor of Psychiatry and Director of Adult Inpatient Psychiatry at The Psychiatric Institute, University of Maryland School of Medicine. He is a psychiatric consultant to the Perry Point Veteran's Administration Hospital, Perry Point, Maryland, and the Crownsville State Hospital, Crownsville, Maryland.

Chapter 1

Introduction

Aron Wolfe Siegman and Benjamin Pope

ALL BUT the last two chapters in this volume were papers presented at a conference on interview research which took place at The Psychiatric Institute of the University of Maryland, April 22nd and 23rd, 1968. Herbert Gross, the author of Chapter 12, participated in the conference but did not make a formal presentation, and Uriel Foa and Edna Foa, the authors of Chapter 13, were unable to attend.

The purpose of the conference was to provide investigators of the interview with an opportunity for extensive discussions of mutual research concerns. In keeping with this objective, formal presentations were followed by discussion periods. These discussions dealt with the technicalities of the research studies, such as different experimental designs and measuring instruments. For the participants this may very well have been the most valuable part of the conference. Nevertheless, it was decided not to include the verbatim transcripts of these discussions as their value to a broader readership was considered to be minimal.

This volume does not pretend to be representative of all the major research programs concerned with the interview. Financial limitations restricted the geographical range from which participants could be recruited, and some who were invited could not attend. Moreover, not all the studies discussed in this volume are based on interviews, experimental or naturalistic. Some studies utilize experimental dialogue; others, free speech samples. In each case, however, the focus of the study is relevant to a central issue in interview communication. Even when data are not obtained from psychotherapeutic interviews, the emphasis is not on the therapeutic outcome, but rather on the verbal or non-verbal interaction between the participants, i.e., on communication.

1

Implicit in the title of this book is the assumption that the interview is best understood if it is conceptualized as an interpersonal communication system. Of course, one must also consider those features of the interview which make it into the specialized kind of communication system which it is. The distinct roles of the interviewer and the interviewee, with one asking questions and the other giving information, create an asymmetrical relationship between the participants. Furthermore, the professional status and the specialized skills of the interviewer contribute to the asymmetrical status and power relationships which characterize the interview dyad. While some of the contributors to this volume focus on problems which characterize interpersonal communication in general, others focus on problems which arise from the specialized nature of the interview system.

Chapter 2, by Heller, begins and concludes with some general observations on interview research. These observations set the stage for many of the subsequent contributions, most particularly for Chapters 3 and 4. To begin with, Heller makes a plea for conceptualizing that which transpires in the interview in general psychological terms. Early attempts in this direction were dominated by learning theory (Dollard and Miller, 1950; Mowrer, 1950; Shoben, 1949). Heller, on the other hand, draws primarily on recent theoretical developments and research findings in social psychology, including game theory as applied to small group behavior. Similarly, the interview studies reported by Pope and Siegman in Chapter 4 are cast in a social-psychological framework. Their research on the role of interviewer warmth and status in facilitating interviewee communication draws conceptually on Foa's (1962) work on the dimensionality of dyadic relationships, while their earlier study on the role of intervieweee-interviewer attraction in facilitating communication derives from the ideas formulated by Festinger and Thibaut (1951) and Newcomb (1956) pertaining to the relationship between attraction and communication within small groups.

Chapter 3, by Siegman and Pope, deals with the effects of interviewer ambiguity and anxiety on interviewee productivity and fluency. Here the theoretical framework is information theory for the effects of interviewer ambiguity, and drive theory for the effects of anxiety.

Heller's work illustrates some of the advantages that can occur when one conceptualizes that which happens in the interview in general psychological terms. One immediate benefit is the opening up of new lines of research, such as Heller's studies on interviewer remarks that deliberately disagree with or challenge the interviewee. A long-range benefit, implicit in his findings on disagreement as an interviewer strategy, is the development of new techniques for the use of the clinician. It should be pointed out that not all benefits go in one direction. The interview can provide an excellent testing ground for general psychological theories as well. Thus, in Chapter 3, Siegman and Pope used the interview in order to test some of the implications of a drive approach to anxiety.

The primary emphasis in Heller's research is on the *structure* of the interviewer's messages and the interviewer-interviewee relationship rather than the *content* of the communications. A similar emphasis is found in the other two chapters in this section and in the remaining contributions to this volume. To be sure, content is not completely ignored. For example, a major independent variable in the paper by Siegman and Pope is interviewer topical focus (family relations vs. school history). They are concerned with the relationship between *what* is said and *how* it is said, and with the interaction between structural variables and content in the communication process. Moreover, many of the dependent variables, such as problem admissions (Heller), self-references (Heller), superficiality, and resistiveness (Pope and Siegman) are certainly content-oriented. Nevertheless, it is true that the major focus of most of the research reported in this volume is on formal and structural rather than content variables.

The studies reported by Heller and most of the studies discussed by Pope and Siegman are based on experimental analogues of the initial interview. The advantages of this research strategy are self-evident. Yet it has a serious limitation, namely, that the relationships which are noted in the experimental situation may not necessarily obtain in naturalistic settings. It should be pointed out, however, that experimental and naturalistic interviews vary on a number of specific dimensions, which are themselves subject to experimental investigation.

The reader will note some apparent contradictions between the results reported by Heller and those reported in the subsequent two chapters. For example, Heller found that the level of structure in an interviewer's remarks (referred to as "interviewer ambiguity level" by Siegman and Pope) had no significant effect on students' speaking time. This is opposite to the results obtained by Siegman and Pope in Chapter 3. Discrepancies of this kind were taken up in the discussion periods which followed the formal presentations. When inconsistencies between studies occurred they could be related to differences in experimental procedure, differences in measuring instruments or techniques, and to differences in subject characteristics.

Temporal parameters of speech have received considerable

research attention over recent years in investigations dealing with the verbal interaction within the interview and in dyadic conversation. Such temporal indices as reaction time, silent pauses, and articulation rate have served as dependent variables in a number of studies discussed in the present volume (Siegman and Pope, Chapter 3; Pope and Siegman, Chapter 4; Aronson and Weintraub, Chapter 11). However, only the studies of Feldstein (Chapter 5) and Webb (Chapter 6) are primarily concerned with certain temporal aspects of speech as central foci of study. It seemed appropriate, therefore, to include these in a separate section.

Feldstein employs three speech duration variables and two pause duration variables. He tells about the instrument he has used for automatically "detecting and recording the sound-silence patterns of dialogue in computer-readable form." He then discusses two studies that investigate the reliabilities of the duration variables that he uses and the interspeaker influences that occur both within the interview and dyadic conversation. He concludes that "the two studies suggest that the temporal patterning of an individual's conversational behavior is a stable characteristic of that individual and, in addition, is capable of modifying and being modified by the temporal patterning of other individuals with whom he interacts." Feldstein ends with a recursive model for temporal aspects of speech in the dyadic interaction.

The relevance of Feldstein's findings about interspeaker influence to the work that has been done with the synchrony effect is apparent (Matarazzo, Weins, and Saslow, 1965). Webb (Chapter 6) deals with the synchrony phenomenon. His temporal variables are two indices of rate of speech, rather than duration as in the case of Feldstein. Synchrony is defined as a phenomenon in which the S varies his own interview behavior, e.g., activity level, to match the variations of the E. The experimental procedure used is based on an automated interview. Webb finds that synchrony does indeed occur in one of his two indices of rate. He continues with a comprehensive consideration of different explanatory models for the synchrony phenomenon, and concludes with a brief excursion into the futuristic realm of automated clinical interviews.

The papers written by Dittmann (Chapter 7), Freedman (Chapter 8), and Kendon (Chapter 9) constitute a cohesive section encompassing three different approaches to the study of body movements in dyadic communication. Thus Dittmann writes of the relevance of body movements to emotional expression and to psycholinguistics. The former is of no concern in his present paper. The latter, the subject of Chapter 7, is sought in the relationship between body movement and the rhythmical characteristic of speech, its "prosodic nature." Dittmann did not attempt an evaluation of possible meaning associated with specific body movements. Instead he grouped movements together and related their frequency to their positions in the phonemic clauses into which he analyzed speech samples. In this sense, he is very much concerned with the speech relatedness of body movements. In general, he found a significant "but not very close relationship between speech rhythm and body movement. Both hesitations in speech and body movements tend to appear early in phonemic clauses and, in addition, movements tend to follow hesitations whenever they may appear in clauses" (see p. 141). He infers that hesitations occur at moments of decision, when lexical and syntactical choices are being made. One may regard the occurrence of body movements at moments of decision as instances of the spill-over of tension into the motor system. In brief, Dittmann's interest is in the relationship of body movement to certain rhythmic aspects of speech production. This relationship is contained within the speech units emitted by each individual while he is participating in a dyadic exchange.

By contrast, Freedman's interest (Chapter 8) is centered in certain aspects of the dyadic interaction and more particularly in the communicative functions performed by body movements. Freedman divides body movements into two broad categories, designated as "object-focused" and "body-focused." In his view, object-focused movements reflect a high intent to communicate while body-focused movements reflect an autistic orientation. "More specifically, it can then be hypothesized that under conditions of high communication intent, where object-focused movements predominate, we can observe behavior signifying an approach to the listener and more fully articulated verbal representations. Conversely, under conditions of low communication intent, where body-focused movements predominate, we can note a withdrawal from the listener and more impoverished and global verbal representations" (see p. 169).

Kendon (Chapter 9) regards his work as a descriptive analysis of the patterning or the organization of body movement and its articulation with the flow of speech. If his results appear to point to functional relationships between movement and speech, such indications must be taken to be "preliminary." Kendon's concern is with gesticulations defined as "complex movements of the hands and arm and head. . . ." The categories selected for the analysis of both speech and body motion are particularly well-adapted to the tracking of the flow of speech and of movement. The findings are given in terms of the analogous flow of communication in both the verbal and body movement channels. The following are some of his results in very brief summary: "Each speech unit is distinguished by a pattern of

movement and of body part involvement in movement. The larger
the speech unit, the greater the difference in the form of movement
and the body parts involved. Prior to each speech unit there is a change
in position of one or more body parts. The larger the speech unit, the
more body parts there are that are involved in this movement. . . ."
(see p. 205). Like Dittmann, Kendon emphasizes the interrelationship
between body movement and speech rhythms. Unlike Dittmann
and like Freedman, he attributes communicative functions to body
movement.

If the preceding papers separate themselves into topical clusters,
the Mahl (Chapter 10) and Aronson and Weintraub (Chapter 11)
studies are topically unique within the context of the present collection,
and as such they are grouped together in a "special problems" section.

Mahl's contribution (Chapter 10) "concerns the role of auditory
feedback in the control of spontaneous speech and interaction, and in
determining subjective experience" (see p. 211). He discusses several
models for the role of feedback in the control of behavior and
presents a comprehensive summary of the research literature on the
feedback regulation of speech. Mahl regards the study reported here
as essentially exploratory; the method used is primarily clinical-
observational in character, and only secondarily quantitative. The data
consist of taped series of three interviews obtained from seventeen
college students and conducted under control and masked auditory
feedback conditions.

While the results speak for themselves, a brief statement of some
of Mahl's findings will be given at this point. Under conditions of
masked auditory feedback his Ss spoke more loudly than they did
under control conditions, with flattened intonation and with a
tendency to lengthen the enunciation of syllables. A particularly
interesting finding was a "regressive" sort of shift in social class
dialect. There were also several general behavioral changes including
increased affective expression, freer associative response, increased
cognitive confusion, and some "thinking aloud." Out of several
possible mechanisms considered, Mahl selected that of "feedback
deficit" and concluded that "normal auditory feedback plays an
important role in the regulation of many *vocal* dimensions of
language behavior, in the control of the vocal expression of affects and
thoughts, and in the maintenance of a sense of self and of reality"
(see p. 261).

The second paper in the "special problems" group by Aronson
and Weintraub (Chapter 11) continues an old tradition in psycholinguistic investigation. This tradition dates back to the 1940's
when Sanford (1942) published his work on the relationship between

personality and speech. The Aronson and Weintraub study deals with the association between certain pathological personality conditions and speech. It differs from other investigations in the present collection in its use of free speech monologues, rather than dyadic interactions, as its source of data.

The concluding section of this volume consists of two theoretical contributions. The usual procedure is to place such work at the beginning of a book, preceding the empirical studies. We have reversed this procedure for the following two reasons. First, the focus of the conference, of which this volume is a product, was research rather than theory. Second, the implications for the interview of theoretical models presented in these two chapters have yet to be tested in the crucible of empirical research. They were included, however, because both represent fresh theoretical approaches to the interview, with a strong potential for generating meaningful research.

After a very brief summary of his research on the relationship between encoding and decoding skills, Gross proposes a psycholinguistic model for the psychotherapeutic interview. In contrast to the model proposed by Feldstein which deals with the structure of the interviewer-interviewee exchanges, that suggested by Gross emphasizes the content of their interactions. Gross believes that the criterial attribute of what psychoanalysts call "insight" is represented by or reflected in increments in the skill with which the interviewee describes his experiences. "The interviewee and interviewer dyad monitors the text of the interviewee with implicit psycholinguistic criteria of adequacy. When they note departures from a shared baseline expectation they restrict their attention to the 'relatively inadequate text', and the curiosity of the dyad is satisfied when the account returns to baseline." Clearly, this model was formulated with the psychoanalytic interview in mind.

A number of behavior theorists have found it useful to apply the economist's concept of resource exchange to social behavior. The concluding chapter by Uriel Foa and Edna Foa is a comprehensive statement of exchange theory and its implications for social communication. While proposing a model for social communication in general, they also spell out specific implications for both the therapeutic and the information-gathering type of interview.

References

DOLLARD, J. and MILLER, N. E.   *Personality and Psychotherapy: An Analysis in Terms of Learning, Thinking, and Culture*. McGraw-Hill, New York, 1950.

FESTINGER, L. and THIBAUT, J. W.   Interpersonal communications in small groups. *J. Abnorm. Soc. Psychol.*, 1951, **46**, 92-9.

FOA, U.   Convergencies in the analysis of the structure of interpersonal behavior. *Psychol. Rev., 1961*, **51**, 341-53.

MATARAZZO, J. D., WIENS, A. N., and SASLOW, G.   Studies in interview speech behavior. In L. Krasner and L. P. Ullman (Eds.), *Research in Behavior Modification: New Developments and Their Clinical Implications*. Holt, Rinehart & Winston, New York, 1965.

MOWRER, O. H.   *Learning Theory and Personality Dynamics*. Ronald Press, New York, 1950.

NEWCOMB, T. M.   The prediction of interpersonal attraction. *Amer. Psychol.*, 1956, **11**, 575-86.

SANFORD, F. H.   Speech and personality. *Psychol. Bull.*, 1942, **39**, 811-45.

SHOBEN, E. J.   Psychotherapy as a problem in learning theory. *Psychol. Bull.*, 1944, **46**, 366-92.

Part I

Experimental Manipulations
of
Interviewer Variables

Chapter 2

Interview Structure and Interviewer Style in Initial Interviews[1]

Kenneth Heller

INTERPERSONAL influence is a frequent component of social interaction. It is sometimes easily recognized and socially sanctioned as, for example, in the socialization and education of children. At other times the influence component in social interaction may be disguised. However, if by the term "influence" we mean *the transmission, by a sender, of information designed to change the psychological state of a listener,* it becomes difficult to conceive of an active interpersonal interaction that does not involve influence.

Most often, influence is thought of as a one-way process, akin to propaganda, in which a communicator is invested with considerable exploitative power to do something exploitative to a passive audience (Bauer, 1964). But even in the field of propaganda, the exploitative model does not provide an accurate conceptualization, for as Davison (1959) has noted:

> . . . the communicator's audience is not a passive recipient—it cannot be regarded as a lump of clay to be molded by the master propagandist. Rather the audience is made up of individuals who demand something from the communications to which they are exposed, and who select those that are likely to be useful to them. In other words, they must get something from the manipulator if he is to get something from them. A bargain is involved (p. 360).

INFLUENCE IN PSYCHOTHERAPY

We have been steadily moving toward a transactional model of the influence process in which influence attempts are seen to be reciprocal in nature in that both parties expect to give to and take from the interaction. Our view of psychotherapeutic influence has also been

---

[1]Research reported in this paper was supported by Research Grant No. NH-10225 from the National Institute of Mental Health, United States Public Health Service.

9

moving toward a transactional model (Heller, 1963). Early conceptualizations of psychoanalysis described what could be called a "non-contingent interaction" (Jones and Thibaut, 1958) for the behavior of one participant was not thought to be a determinant of the behavior of the other. Patients were said to be engaged in inner-determined free association which when unraveled would lead to a causal trauma, while what therapists said or did had little effect in determining the nature of the associations. Beginning with Sullivan (1954), contemporary clinical theory has viewed psychotherapy as involving a "reciprocally contingent interaction" (Jones and Thibaut, 1958) with each participant acting as a partial cause of the other's behavior. In Sullivan's view, psychotherapy is a situation of influence and counter-influence. The therapist is cautioned to remember that he is engaging in a performance of *two* persons (Davis, 1968).

The study of psychotherapeutic influence provided the impetus for our earlier research efforts (summarized in Heller, 1968) and the Sullivanian analysis of the therapeutic interaction in terms of reciprocal influence attempts still impresses us as being essentially accurate. We would agree that patients want and expect help but resist change; that is, many patients expect relief from the discomfort of symptoms while resisting attempts to change their values or behavior. For their part, therapists accept patients hoping to exert beneficent influence, while at the same time, either not recognizing counter-influence attempts initiated by the patient or expecting to remain immune to them.

THE EXPERIMENTAL STUDY OF INTERVIEWS

One of the difficulties confronting investigators who view social influence as a transactional phenomenon is that it is difficult to study and experimentally control a reciprocally contingent interaction. Processes of influence and counter-influence are not easily identifiable in a transaction where both participants are variable responders, each alert to incoming cues from the other and each, in turn, acting as a partial cause of the other's behavior. One approach to this problem is to reduce the interaction to an "asymmetrical contingency" (Jones and Thibaut, 1958) by appointing one of the members involved in the interaction as an experimental accomplice who behaves as a standard responder in accordance with a fixed operating procedure supplied by the experimenter (Davis, 1968; Heller, 1963). The advantage of such an approach is that it brings the behavior of one member of the interaction under the experimenter's control so that its effects on others involved in the interaction can be systematically investigated. While this procedure is fairly well accepted in social psychology, particularly in studies of group interaction, it has only recently been adapted to the study of interview behavior. For example, it is possible to program interviewers to operate according to standardized roles and measure their effects on the behavior of interviewees (Heller, Davis, and Myers, 1966). Or, the interviewee, as an experimental accomplice, may be programmed to operate according to a set of specified behaviors so that the responsivity of the interviewer can be measured (Heller, Myers, and Kline, 1963). Depending upon the ingenuity and interest of the experimenter, the behavioral program can be relatively simple or fairly complex; for example, ranging from interviewer silence (Berman, 1968) or statements of approval and disapproval (Heller, 1965) to more complex win-lose contingencies (Davis, 1968) or programs that vary instructional set (Jacobson, 1968; Ohnesorge, 1966; Treffts, 1966) or amount of information presented to subjects (Marlatt, 1966, 1968).

INTERVIEW AND THERAPY DYADS

The dyad has a special place in the study of influence processes. In our culture, the two-person group is the most frequent interpersonal structure for the transmission of *private* information and specific dyadic roles have been developed to facilitate the communication of intimate messages. Of these, the husband-wife dyad is perhaps the most prominent, but other examples of dyads that facilitate private communication might include the relationships that exist between two friends, between priest and parishioner, doctor and patient, or therapist and client. In the past, researchers concerned with dyadic interactions tended to emphasize differences between situations rather than highlighting possible commonalities. For example, those whose work was concerned with friendship pairs almost never extended their work to doctor-patient dyads; students of priest-parishioner relationships rarely published studies of husband-wife interactions. Similarly, researchers concerned with psychotherapeutic interactions have been notorious for their emphasis on the uniqueness of the phenomena they have been investigating. But this parochial orientation is now changing. There is now a growing rapprochement between research in learning, social, and clinical psychology (Ford and Urban, 1967; Heller and Marlatt, 1969; Lennard and Bernstein, 1960; Strupp and Bergin, 1969). Psychologists interested in social influence are now looking toward a convergence of factors involved in behavior change (Goldstein, Heller, and Sechrest, 1966).

Although the new emphasis is on the similarities in human interactions, situational determinants of behavior must also be studied. In other words, general "principles" of behavior do not operate in a vacuum. Variance associated with particular settings can be a powerful determinant of behavior. What is needed are more attempts at "bridging" research which test the conditions under which particular experimental findings might apply (Goldstein and Dean, 1966; Heller and Marlatt, 1969; Hovland, 1959).

The orientation we have taken to this research may be summarized at this point by the following set of assumptions:

1. Social influence is a transactional process in which the intent of the communicator, the manner in which his message is presented and the needs of the communicant interact in determining the final outcome.

2. The interview represents an appropriate structure for the study of social influence, particularly if one is concerned with conditions that facilitate the transmission of private messages.

3. One promising technique for studying reciprocal interview interactions is to standardize the role behaviors of one of the participants while allowing the behavior of the other to vary freely.

4. The outcome of an interview is a joint function of its content and its structural characteristics. Although dyadic interviews may differ in content, they often share common structural characteristics.

5. The role relationships developed between the participants, the interpersonal style with which each defines his role, and the informational properties of the interview task are primary determinants of the structural characteristics of an interview.

TYPICAL PROCEDURE

Subjects, who for the most part have been introductory psychology students, typically volunteer for an experiment which requires them to talk about themselves to an interviewer. Subjects are told about the nature of the task on the sign-up sheets on which they indicate their willingness to participate.

The independent variables in these experiments consist of either (1) aspects of the interviewer's overt behavior that are standardized and controlled, or (2) varying amounts of structure assigned to the subject's task, or (3) some combination of the two.

Examples of interviewer behavior studied include: the interviewer's interactive style as presented verbally and non-verbally (e.g., friendly, reserved, or hostile behaviors), the activity level of the interviewer in interaction with his affective style (e.g., a comparison of active hostility and passive hostility), specific evaluative statements of approval or disapproval, agreement or disagreement, or the effects of ambiguous interviewer feedback.

Examples of how the structure of the subject's task has been studied vary from instructions which are purposely left vague such as simply telling the subject to talk about himself, to instructions that specify fixed topics for discussion.

Instructions may be oriented toward a discussion of personal concerns or problems. Problem structure may be given either through direct instructions ("Your task in the interview is to talk to the interviewer about your problems.") or may be implied by requiring the subject to complete a personality test prior to the interview. Problem structure may also be given by providing the subject with a prior experience of hearing another subject (a "model") perform the task. The model usually has been presented on tape but may also be presented live (Marlatt, Jacobson, Johnson, and Morrice, 1966) or in the format of a written transcript (Duke, Frankel, Sipes, and Stewart, 1965). Consequences to the model as well as consequences to the subject may be pre-arranged. A subject may hear a model receive positive, negative, neutral, or no interviewer feedback for specific behaviors, and then enter an interview in which his own interviewer is likewise programmed (Marlatt, 1968). The results of the above studies have been summarized in two previous papers (Heller, 1968; Heller and Marlatt, 1969).

SOME EXPERIMENTAL RESULTS

Two interrelated findings appear in several of these experiments:
1. Subjects respond to challenging interview conditions with attempts to meet and overcome the challenge.
2. Subjects whose defensive style allows them to be more open in admitting personal concerns do so more frequently in moderately stressful interview conditions than in more subjectively pleasant and less threatening conditions.

The above points may be illustrated with some specific studies. In the context of a personal interview in which subjects were requested to speak about themselves, Heller, Brahlek, and Morris (described by Heller, 1968) found that interviewer disagreements presented as one word verbalizations ("no", "uh-uh") decreased the frequency of the response on which conditioning was attempted (past-tense verbs), but more active and longer disagreements in which the interviewer stated the exact subject remark with which he disagreed, produced an increase in the frequency of past-tense verbs. A second study by Heller, Marlatt, and Bailey (in Heller, 1968) replicated the finding that subjects would persist in talking on those topics marked by interviewer disagreement. In this experiment, subjects whose instructions were to talk about themselves were required to press a key in front of them in order to hear from an interviewer who was hidden from view behind a wooden screen. Subjects persisted in requesting responses from interviewers who disagreed with them. When confronted with interviewer agreement, subjects requested the interviewer to speak much less often and changed topics more frequently following an interviewer remark. In both of the above experiments, subjects indicated on a postinterview questionnaire that they felt more comfortable with and liked the positive, agreeing interviewers. Yet despite this preference, subjects persisted in discussing those topics which met with interviewer disagreement or disapproval. We interpret our results as indicating that when the interviewer controls the conversation by producing few orienting cues by which the subject can monitor his own responding, the subject is forced to follow the only cues available as best he can. But when the subject is provided with enough information so that he himself can judge the adequacy of his own response and postulate possible reasons for the interviewer's disagreement, he feels much more free to persist in the same topic, argue with the interviewer and attempt to convert him. In this latter case, rather than remaining the passive recipient of influence, the subject attempts to exert counter-influence.

In a doctoral dissertation, Davis (1968) confirmed and extended these results in a series of two experiments designed to test the proposition that subjects are motivated to place themselves in a more favorable status differential with respect to the interviewer. Davis proposed that the optimal strategy for a subject who receives a negative evaluation is to attempt a rescindment of that evaluation. In response to positive evaluation, the subject's best strategy is to avoid further evaluation on that topic, since the interviewer's agreement indicates that there is no longer any contest and that it is best to move to another topic.

In Davis' first experiment there were five interviewer programs, in each of which evaluations were non-contingent with the content of the subject's remarks. The sequence of evaluations received by the subjects were strictly predetermined and could not be influenced by them. The five programs represented five levels varying the relative frequency of positive and negative evaluations. In program 1, evaluations were all positive; in program 2, 25 percent were negative; in program 3, 50 percent were negative; in program 4, 75 percent were negative; and in program 5, all evaluations were negative.

Davis found that although subjects in the positive programs liked their interviewers better, the frequency of requests for interviewer messages increased as a function of the percentage of negative interviewer evaluations, being lowest in program 1 and highest in programs 4 and 5 (Fig. 1). In program 5, requests for interviewer evaluations increased steadily as the interview progressed while they decreased steadily in program 1.

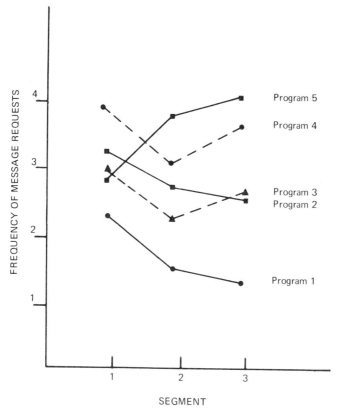

Fig. 1. Frequency of message requests as a function of interview segment for five interviewer programs (from Davis, 1966).

Davis' second experiment compared two programs that were contingent upon the subject's persistence on topic. In the "Lose" program, the interviewer's first evaluation was positive, but then he gave only negative evaluations if the subject remained on topic (PNNN). The only way a subject could receive another positive evaluation was to switch topics. He could never win within a topic because persistence on topic could only lead to further negative evaluation.

In the "Win" program, the interviewer's first evaluation was negative. Thereafter, he gave positive evaluations as long as the subject stayed on topic (NPPP), but gave a negative evaluation for each topic switch. Thus the subject could win on each topic (i.e., have a negative evaluation rescinded by a positive evaluation) by persisting through two message requests.

Davis hypothesized that the subject would persist on topic in the "Lose" program, hoping to convert the interviewer which, of course, could never occur. He also hypothesized that subjects would choose *not* to receive positive evaluations for topic switches since abandoning a topic was equivalent to losing. In the "Win" program, the optimal strategy would be for subjects to switch topics frequently, electing to receive negative evaluations for topic switches since these could easily be rescinded by a slight persistence in topic. Davis' hypotheses were confirmed in that subjects persisted on topic significantly longer in the "Lose" program than the "Win" program, a finding significant at the .001 level.

It should be noted that the results of the Davis experiments are not easily predicted from a simple reinforcement or verbal conditioning model. Such a theory would predict that in experiment I, the frequency of message requests should be a direct function of the proportion of positive evaluations. The converse was found to be true. In experiment II, a reinforcement theorist might suggest that the high frequency of topic switch behavior in the "Win" program occurred because a negative evaluation followed by a positive evaluation is a stronger "reinforcer" than a positive evaluation alone. Hence, subjects might be willing to accept a temporary negative evaluation that would soon be rescinded by a positive evaluation. However, such a theory would leave unexplained the subjects' persistence on topic in the face of negative evaluation in the "Lose" program.

Several of our studies are concerned with the conditions that facilitate verbal expression and the transmission of private information. The dependent variables in these studies are taken from content analyses of the taped interviews. We are concerned with the openness with which subjects can talk about themselves and score three variables that lie along a dimension of self-concern or self-disclosure. The specific variables are: *talk time*, taken directly from manually operated chronographs that are activated whenever the subject is speaking; *self-references*, scored as the number of 15-second intervals containing a reference to the subject; and, *problem references*, scored as the number of 15-second intervals containing a statement that refers to an inadequacy, weakness, concern, or worry of the subject.

In addition to the content variables listed above, at the termination of their interviews, subjects are asked to evaluate their experience indicating their degree of comfort in the interview, and their evaluation of the interviewer.

The study that initiated our concern for the conditions that facilitate personal self-disclosure was one in which we found that subjects with a prior disposition for admitting personal problems (i.e., subjects with high scores on the Mooney Problem Checklist) talked less but gave more problem references when confronted with interviewer silence compared with some conditions of greater interviewer responsivity (Heller, Davis, and Myers, 1966).

A further study by Heller, Marlatt, Bailey, and Silver (reported by Heller, 1968) confirmed that problem-admitting subjects would exhibit this behavior more characteristically in interviews involving moderate stress. In this study, positive, negative, and ambiguous interviewer evaluations were presented to subjects so that they could be clearly understood or were mechanically distorted. Speech distortion was produced mechanically by a throat microphone and a voice-distorting machine used in combination. The result was muffled speech, the relative clarity of which could be adjusted. In our use of the apparatus, we allowed subjects in the distorted conditions to hear occasional words and sometimes whole sentences so that they would continue to attend to the interviewer. Subjects and interviewers sat in separate rooms on opposite sides of a one-way mirror. The lighting of the rooms was controlled so that subjects could see the interviewer when he talked but at no other time.

The results of the experiment indicated that subjects interviewed by positive interviewers, both clear and distorted, rated their interviewers as more friendly and more comfortable to be with than subjects interacting with negative or ambiguous interviewers. Subject talk time was higher in the clear conditions than in the distorted conditions and male subjects in all conditions talked more than females (a surprising finding, since females sign up for interviewing experiments much more readily than males). But self-references were higher in the distorted than in the clear conditions although the groups could not be distinguished on problem statements. However, when subjects were divided into high and low problem admitters (on the basis of the Mooney Problem Checklist administered just prior to the interview), a significant interaction between subjects' personality and condition was found for both self-references and problem statements. Subjects with high Mooney scores emitted the most self-references when confronted with ambiguous evaluation, both clear and distorted, and when confronted with distorted negative interviewers. They emitted the greatest number of problem statements when talking to distorted ambiguous interviewers.

From the above we can see that not all subjects react to interviewer conditions in a similar fashion, and indeed there is no reason to expect subject uniformity. Some of the experiments we have conducted have involved attempts to track down the bases for differential subject responsivity to various interviewer styles.

In a college student sample, Berman (1968) found that subjects scoring in the upper third of a distribution of creativity test scores, but in the lower third of a distribution of intelligence test scores, are best able to maintain their levels of verbal productivity despite drastic changes in interviewer responsivity. The high creativity-low intelligence group was least affected by interviewer silence when compared with less creative subjects *or* with subjects high on both creativity and intelligence.

In the Davis (1968) study outlined above, it was found that repressors are better interpersonal game players than sensitizers. Repressors adopt more optimal strategies and seem more willing to accept negative evaluations.

DEPENDENCY AND INTERVIEWER STYLE

In a further study of differential subject responsivity to various interviewer styles, Heller and Jacobson (1967) asked 96 male and female subjects, chosen on the basis of dependency scores derived from the Edwards Personal Preference Schedule, to talk about themselves in thirty-minute personal interviews. Interviewers were either "friendly" or "reserved," or there was no interviewer.

In the *friendly* condition, interviewers were trained to respond at one-minute intervals with a restatement that best captured the essential message in the subject's previous remarks. In addition, they were to appear friendly, expressive, and encouraging by smiling appropriately, nodding, leaning toward the subject, and maintaining eye contact. Subjects in this condition were told that the interviewer's job was to be encouraging and interested.

In the *reserved* condition, interviewers also responded at one-minute intervals with their best restatement of content but were trained to maintain a reserved, non-responsive demeanor. They refrained from smiling or nodding and were generally non-expressive, leaning away from and often looking away from the subject except when speaking. Subjects in this condition were told that the interviewer's job was to be a good listener.

In the *no-interviewer* condition, subjects sat next to a desk and talked without anyone else in the room. Subjects were told that the absence of an interviewer was "to see how well people can do this task on their own."

Results (Table I) indicated that friendly interviewers were again best liked by all subjects. High dependent males talked longer than any other group. They talked about themselves most often in the reserved and the no-interviewer conditions; they talked about problems most often in the reserved condition. In contrast, low dependent males talked less than any other group. They talked about themselves least in the reserved condition and rarely spoke about problems in any of the conditions. The scores for the female groups were typically between those of the two male groups.

We had expected that independent subjects would speak about themselves most freely when no interviewer was present and would be most uncomfortable and inhibited with friendly interviewers. The assumption was that close expressive interviewer behavior would be most threatening to their typical interpersonal style of remaining aloof from interpersonal contact. This hypothesis received only minimal support from the independent females in that they did emit the most problem references in the no-interviewer condition. But the friendly condition was a close second, while their poorest scores on this variable were in the reserved condition. The hypothesis was completely unsupported in the case of the independent males, essentially because no condition proved facilitative for them. Similarly unexpected was the tendency for high dependent males to be most open with reserved interviewers.

That a moderately stressful condition, such as a reserved interviewer style, again proved facilitative for a specific sample of college students (high dependent males), increased our conviction that we had to test the generality of this finding on a non-college population. We chose a most extreme comparison group—chronic, hospitalized mental patients.

TABLE I.

Condition Means for Subjects According to Personality and Sex Groups

Interviewer Condition	Subject Personality	Sex	Post-Interview Reaction Checklist[1]	Talk-Time	Self-References[2]	Problem References[3]
Friendly	Dependent	M	9.75	17.10	91.25	14.62
		F	10.62	18.02	97.88	16.00
	Independent	M	11.75	18.96	86.75	9.50
		F	16.00	19.70	97.50	16.38
Reserved	Dependent	M	-3.38	20.00	102.75	18.75
		F	-5.88	15.65	91.88	18.62
	Independent	M	4.12	13.70	69.38	8.25
		F	-0.50	17.12	84.12	7.38
No-Interviewer	Dependent	M		20.18	98.00	13.88
		F		16.69	87.38	15.12
	Independent	M		13.43	80.12	9.50
		F		18.48	96.25	21.62

Note—From Heller and Jacobson, unpublished research.

[1]Not administered to subjects in the no-interviewer condition.
[2]Computed as the number of 15-second intervals containing a self-reference.
[3]Computed as the number of 15-second intervals containing a problem statement.

PATIENT REACTIONS TO INTERVIEWER STYLE

Friendly and reserved interviewer styles, similar to those of the previous study, were varied within the time span of a single interview and were presented to both college student and patient groups. In this study, Heller, Silver, Bailey, and Dudgeon developed two style sequences, friendly-reserved-friendly (FRF) and reserved-friendly-reserved (RFR), with the changes in style being made every ten minutes during a thirty-minute interview. The amount of structure provided by the interviewer was also varied. In the *structured* interviews, subjects were provided with a fixed sequence of five topics and were given a specific problem probe within each topic. In the *unstructured* interviews, subjects were simply encouraged to speak about themselves. Interviews were conducted by either a male or a female graduate student in psychology.

The data revealed that the non-verbal style changes presented within an interview by the interviewers affected the college students less than the patients. The students talked longer over the duration of the interview in the RFR sequence than the FRF sequence and were least disturbed by the reserved condition when it came first (Table II).

TABLE II.

Mean Talk Time for Patients and Students

| Group | Style | Structure | Time Block Means | | | Total Interview Means |
			1	2	3	
Patient	FRF	Str.	4.82	3.30	4.08	12.20
		Un.-Str.	6.06	5.14	5.54	16.75
		Combined	5.44	4.22	4.81	14.48
	RFR	Str.	3.75	3.49	2.80	10.04
		Un.-Str.	3.60	3.59	3.04	10.23
		Combined	3.68	3.54	2.92	10.14
Student	FRF	Str.	4.95	4.27	4.96	14.18
		Un.-Str.	4.91	3.87	4.27	13.05
		Combined	4.93	4.07	4.61	13.62
	RFR	Str.	5.30	5.11	5.13	15.54
		Un.-Str.	4.87	4.82	4.29	13.98
		Combined	5.08	4.96	4.70	14.76

Note—From Heller, Silver, Bailey, and Dudgeon, unpublished research.

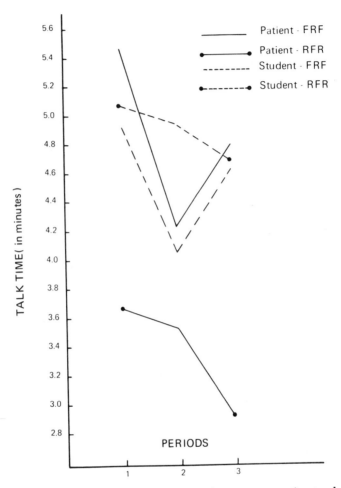

Fɪɢ. 2. Talk time for patient and student groups reacting to changes in interviewer style (from Heller, Silver, Bailey, and Dudgeon, unpublished research).

In terms of content, the degree to which the students talked about themselves or their problems was not significantly affected by the within-interview changes in interpersonal style.

In contrast, the patient group was very responsive to nuances in interviewer style. The friendly style was most facilitative, with patients talking more in the FRF than the RFR sequence. When the interviewer started with the reserved style in the RFR sequence, response inhibition was immediate and did not recover when the interviewer became friendly (Fig. 2). In their best condition, patients talked as much or more than the college students, but their worst performance was much lower than that of the student group. Not only did patients talk more in the friendlier (FRF) style but they also talked about themselves more in this condition than in the more reserved (RFR) condition (Table III). While the student group was more likely to maintain their level of self and problem discussion in the structured

Table III.

Mean Self-References for Patients and Students[1]

Group	Style	Structure	Time Block Means			Total Interview Means
			1	2	3	
Patient	FRF	Str.	38.75	32.50	37.75	109.38
		Un.-Str.	41.75	36.62	31.88	110.25
		Combined	40.25	34.56	34.82	109.82
	RFR	Str.	32.25	32.62	27.25	92.12
		Un.-Str.	28.88	28.38	20.62	77.88
		Combined	30.56	30.50	23.94	85.00
Student	FRF	Str.	41.50	38.38	41.75	121.62
		Un.-Str.	42.50	36.38	32.50	111.38
		Combined	42.00	37.38	37.12	116.50
	RFR	Str.	43.50	44.50	44.12	132.12
		Un.-Str.	40.75	40.38	34.25	115.38
		Combined	42.12	42.44	39.18	123.75

Note—From Heller, Silver, Bailey, and Dudgeon, unpublished research.
[1]Computed as the number of 15-second intervals containing a self-reference.

interviews as compared with the unstructured ones, no style or structure condition appeared to influence the problem admission of the patients (Table IV). This content variable started low and continued to decrease through the interview regardless of condition.

The patient group was chosen as an extreme comparison group and the demographic differences between the students and the patients were so great that speculation concerning the differential performance of the two groups is unwarranted at this time. Subject characteristics will need to be systematically studied in future research before we can hope to answer the question "What type of relationship is most facilitative to the open discussion of personal concerns—when and for whom?"

TABLE IV.

Mean Problem Admission for Patients and Students[1]

Group	Style	Structure	Time Block Means			Total Interview Means
			1	2	3	
Patient	FRF	Str.	4.12	2.88	3.75	10.75
		Un.-Str.	4.62	3.12	3.38	11.12
		Combined	4.37	3.00	3.56	10.94
	RFR	Str.	3.50	2.88	2.50	8.88
		Un.-Str.	5.12	3.12	1.88	10.12
		Combined	4.31	3.00	2.19	9.50
Student	FRF	Str.	4.12	2.62	4.88	11.62
		Un.-Str.	7.38	4.62	2.88	14.88
		Combined	5.75	3.62	3.88	13.25
	RFR	Str.	5.50	4.75	3.88	14.12
		Un.-Str.	6.12	3.88	2.12	12.12
		Combined	5.81	4.32	3.00	13.12

Note—From Heller, Silver, Bailey, and Dudgeon, unpublished research.
[1]Computed as the number of 15-second intervals containing a problem statement.

OVERVIEW AND CONCLUSIONS

This work has focused on the factors facilitating the verbal expression of private messages in a dyadic interaction. Partly motivated by clinical concerns, we have been interested in the communication process because it is the primary means through which one person helps another in our society. But the thrust of our research orientation is also social-psychological in nature. Human interactions are seen as sharing common properties determined by the setting in which the communication occurs and the structural relationships existing between the participants. The study of social influence would be incomplete without a careful focus upon these mediators of the communication process.

The messages that clinicians often transmit have to do with their interpretations of the internal states of their patients. Even here a social-psychological framework is useful and does not necessarily imply an abandonment of intrapsychic formulations. For example, a therapist's message may have an intrapsychic content but, presented in an interpersonal field, the reception of that message will be influenced by factors independent of the internal states of either patient or therapist.

Despite its deceptive simplicity, the variables influencing how one person talks about himself to another are, in reality, quite complex and the research problems associated with studying this phenomenon are formidable. We chose to study interview behavior within a controlled experimental setting in which the behavior of one of the interview participants could be programmed to occur according to a set of pre-established contingencies. This research strategy should help isolate the specific effects of factors which would be difficult to eliminate in naturalistic settings. But moving to the simplification and control of the laboratory and then back again is not without complication, and is particularly acute in applied settings where there are practitioners waiting to take action on the basis of research findings. This problem has been discussed elsewhere as it has applied to such fields as education (Hilgard and Bower, 1966), social psychology (Hovland, 1959), and clinical psychology (Bordin, 1965; Ford and Urban, 1967; Heller and Marlatt, 1969).

The findings of our research imply that mild to moderate stress and challenge, and the opportunity to overcome that stress are important ingredients in helping subjects perform a task involving the admission of personal concerns and worries. If these results are placed within the context of motivational theory, they do not appear too surprising. Subjects in psychological experiments want to do well and any suspicion that their performance is not meeting expectations should motivate them to work harder.

These research findings become provocative when we speculate about the possibility that a similar process may also occur in psychotherapy. Some psychotherapy theorists would declare that the opposite to our findings should be the case. For them, progress in therapy is facilitated when the patient feels comfortably accepted and understood. Therapist variables, such as unconditional positive regard, genuineness, and empathy, constantly presented throughout therapy are considered sufficient to effect client change (Rogers, 1957). Other therapy systems employ moderately stressful procedures but do not consider these to be primary factors in therapeutic change. For example, the Freudian method of free association increases the ambiguity of the therapeutic situation. The patient is unsure of what he should be doing; he is never certain when he is performing as expected, and is in constant doubt concerning whether the therapist thinks well of him. In this system the "good" patient is the one who can master his uncertainties and perform, thereby learning the subtle standards expected of him.

Finally, there are those therapy systems that clearly recognize elements of challenge in the interview interaction. The challenge may be interpersonal and involve the patient in a struggle to best the therapist (Berne, 1964; Haley, 1963) or at least convert him to a non-threatening ally (Sullivan, 1954). In some systems, the challenge may be cognitive, associated with the presentation of a new point of view by the therapist which, until assimilated, threatens the already established cognitive structure of the patient (Kelly, 1955; Levy, 1963). The cognitive group and the Sullivanians suggest procedures for dealing with the unavoidable stress and challenge of therapy. The interpersonal game theorists (Berne, 1964; Haley, 1963) take the more extreme position that the struggle to overcome challenge and be "one up" is the primary factor around which therapeutic progress revolves.

Our findings underscore the potential importance that mastery of interview-induced stress may have on the facilitation of self-disclosure. At this point, however, the results cannot be used to support any of the theoretical positions described above without more extensive follow-up. For example, our data indicate that a reserved interviewer style inhibits the performance of chronic psychotics although such is not the case for college students. Thus, interview stress may be facilitative only with fairly stable, high ability individuals.

Our work was started with college students because our methodology was essentially untried and we felt an ethical responsibility not to harm possibly vulnerable persons. Procedural unknowns were faced: Could programmed interviewer roles be developed that would appear natural in an ongoing interview? Could these roles capture important aspects of an interviewer's interpersonal behavior? Are subjects damaged by interview stress? These issues have been successfully resolved. It is now time to turn our attention to research that investigates the interaction of subject personality characteristics with setting, task, style, and message variables.

References

BAUER, R. A. The obstinate audience: The influence process from the point of view of social communication. *Amer. Psychol.*, 1964, **19**, 319-28.

BERMAN J. R. The effect of creativity on interview speech behavior. Unpublished master's thesis, Indiana University, 1968.

BERNE, E. *Games People Play: The Psychology of Human Relationships.* Grove Press, New York, 1964.

BORDIN, E. S. Simplification as a strategy for research in psychotherapy. *J. Consult. Psychol.*, 1965, **29**, 493-503.

DAVIS, J. D. The interview arena: A model for interviewee strategies in standardized interviews. Unpublished doctoral dissertation, Indiana University, 1968.

DAVISON W. P. On the effects of communication. *Pub. Opin. Quart.*, 1959, **23**, 343-60.

DUKE M. P., FRANKEL, A. S., SIPES, M., and STEWART, R. W. The effects of different kinds of models on interview behavior and feelings about an interview situation. Unpublished research, Indiana University, 1965.

FORD, D. H. and URBAN H. B. Psychotherapy. In P. R. Farnsworth (Ed.), *Annual Review of Psychology*, 1967, **18**, pp. 333-72.

GOLDSTEIN, A. P. and DEAN, S. J. *The Investigation of Psychotherapy: Commentaries and Readings.* Wiley, New York, 1966, pp. 369-73.

GOLDSTEIN, A. P., HELLER, K., and SECHREST, L. B. *Psychotherapy and the Psychology of Behavior Change.* Wiley, New York, 1966.

HALEY, J. *Strategies of Psychotherapy.* Grune & Stratton, New York, 1963.

HELLER, K. Experimental analogues of psychotherapy: The clinical relevance of laboratory findings of social influence. *J. Nerv. Ment. Dis.*, 1963, **137**, 420-6.

HELLER, K. A broader perspective for interview therapy. Presented at Midwestern Psychological Association, Chicago, 1965.

HELLER, K. Ambiguity in the interview interaction. In J. M. Shlien (Ed.), *Research in Psychotherapy.* Vol. III, American Psychological Association, Washington, D.C., 1968, pp. 242-59.

HELLER, K., DAVIS, J. D.; and MYERS, R. A. The effects of interviewer style in a standardized interview. *J. Consult. Psychol.*, 1966, **30**, 501-08.

HELLER, K. and JACOBSON, E. A. Self-disclosure and dependency: The effects of interviewer style. Unpublished research, 1967.

HELLER, K. and MARLATT, G. A. Verbal conditioning, behavior therapy and behavior change: Some problems in extrapolation. In C. M. Franks (Ed.), *Assessment and Status of the Behavior Therapies.* McGraw-Hill, New York, 1969, pp. 569-88.

HELLER, K., MYERS, R. A., and KLINE, L. V. Interviewer behavior as a function of standardized client roles. *J. Consult. Psychol.*, 1963, **27**, 117-22.

HELLER, K., SILVER, R., BAILEY, M., and DUDGEON, T. The interview reactions of patients and students to within-interview changes in interviewer style. Unpublished research, 1968.

HILGARD, E. R. and BOWER, G. H. *Theories of Learning*, Third edition. Appleton-Century Crofts, New York, 1966.

HOVLAND, C. I. Reconciling conflicting results derived from experimental and survey studies of attitude change. *Amer. Psychol.*, 1959, **14**, 8-17.

JACOBSON, E. A. A comparison of the effects of instructions and models upon interview behavior of high-dependent and low-dependent subjects. Unpublished doctoral dissertation, Indiana University, 1968.

JONES, E. E. and THIBAUT, J. W. Interaction goals as bases of inference in interpersonal perception. In R. Tagiuri and L. Petrullo (Eds.), *Person Perception and Interpersonal Behavior.* Stanford University Press, Stanford, 1958, pp. 151-78.

KELLY, G. A. *The Psychology of Personal Constructs.* Vol. 1. Norton, New York, 1955.

LENNARD, H. and BERNSTEIN, A. *The Anatomy of Psychotherapy.* Columbia University Press, New York, 1960.

LEVY, L. H.   *Psychological Interpretation.* Holt, Rinehart & Winston, New York, 1963.

MARLATT, G. A.   Exposure to a model and task ambiguity as determinants of verbal behavior in an interview. Unpublished research, Indiana University, 1966.

MARLATT, G. A.   Vicarious and direct reinforcement control of verbal behavior in an interview setting. Unpublished doctoral dissertation, Indiana University, 1968.

MARLATT, G. A., JACOBSON, E. A., JOHNSON, D. L., and MORRICE, D. J.   Effects of exposure to a model receiving varied informational feedback upon consequent behavior in an interview. Paper presented at Midwestern Psychological Association, Chicago, 1965.

OHNESORGE, J. P.   Interviewee verbalization of personal problems as a function of face-to-face interaction and experimenter's evaluation of pathology. Unpublished undergraduate honors thesis, Indiana University, 1966.

ROGERS, C. R.   The necessary and sufficient conditions of therapeutic personality change. *J. Consult. Psychol.,* 1957, **21**, 95-103.

STRUPP, H. H. and BERGIN, A. E.   Some empirical and conceptual bases for coordinated research in psychotherapy. *Internat. J. Psychiat.,* 1969, **7**, 18-90.

SULLIVAN, H. S.   *The Psychiatric Interview.* Norton, New York, 1954.

TREFFTS, J.   Problem admission and experimental evaluation as determiners of interview behavior. Unpublished master's thesis, Indiana University, 1966.

Chapter 3

The Effects of Ambiguity and Anxiety On Interviewee Verbal Behavior

Aron Wolfe Siegman and Benjamin Pope

FOR THE PAST several years we have been conducting an experimental research program on the initial interview.[1] Its major objective is to investigate the factors which facilitate interviewer-interviewee communication. Before embarking on a detailed presentation of these studies, it may be useful to state some of the basic assumptions underlying this research program.

SOME BASIC ASSUMPTIONS

First, the interview is conceptualized as a dyadic communication system in which one of the participants, the interviewer, has as his major objective to obtain information from the other participant, the interviewee. Consequently, it is assumed that certain formal characteristics of the interviewer's messages—such as, their intelligibility, ambiguity-specificity, etc.—will influence the flow of information within the system. These message characteristics are referred to as "communication variables." Second is the assumption that the social-interpersonal context within which this informational exchange takes place also influences the flow of information between the participants. By social-interpersonal context is meant the structure of the interviewer-interviewee relationship and the participants' feelings and attitudes towards each other. We refer to these variables as

[1]This research was supported by Grant No. 1728 from the Social and Rehabilitation Service, Department of Health, Education and Welfare, and by Grant No. 4287 from the National Institute of Mental Health, Department of Health, Education and Welfare.

We are grateful to Dr. Thomas Blass, a senior research associate in our laboratory, for a critical reading of this chapter and for his valuable suggestions.

"relationship variables." This distinction between communication and relationship variables was found to be conceptually useful, although it is understood that some variables can be legitimately assigned to either category. Third, a reciprocal relationship is assumed between the social-interpersonal context and communication. It is assumed that social-interpersonal configurations (i.e., relationships) which are socially reinforcing are associated with a productive flow of information free of strain. Conversely, productive informational exchanges free of strain are socially reinforcing and, consequently, produce mutual liking and attraction. These are the basic assumptions which guided the choice of variables in our major investigations.

The present chapter deals primarily with message variables, while the next one focuses on relationship variables. This chapter will begin with studies on the effects of ambiguity on interviewee's verbal behavior, to be followed by others on the effects of anxiety on interviewee's communications. The pairing of these two variables (i.e., ambiguity and anxiety) is not altogether arbitrary. It is based on the hypothesis advanced by some investigators (Bordin, 1955; Dibner, 1953; Kenny and Bijou, 1953) that the effects of ambiguity are, in fact, mediated by anxiety. It is hoped that later in this chapter, after having presented our findings on the effects of each of these variables, it will be possible to evaluate the validity of this hypothesis.

INTERVIEWER AMBIGUITY

It is widely assumed among practitioners of the interview that general probes (i.e., ambiguous remarks) are more effective than specific ones. This judgment is probably related to the fact that much in current interviewing practice is based on psychoanalytic technique, a point discussed at length by David Riesman (1964). In classical psychoanalytic practice, ambiguity characterizes the very structure of the analyst-patient relationship, as well as the analyst's communications to his patient. Psychoanalysts are enjoined to remain as much as possible in the background, not to emit any cues which may signify approval or disapproval of their patients' communications and not to reveal their own feelings and values. "Just say anything that comes to your mind" is a typical analyst message to his patient. The rationale for this emphasis on ambiguity is that it facilitates free association and transference, two basic features of the psychoanalytic process. As pointed out earlier, however, the primary objective of the interview is not to encourage free association or to establish a transference relationship, but rather to obtain a maximum amount of information about specified areas. The question to be asked, then, is whether ambiguous interviewer remarks, in contrast to specific ones, facilitate this objective. It is to this question that the following research on interviewer ambiguity is addressed.

PREVIOUS FINDINGS ON
AMBIGUITY AND PRODUCTIVITY

Our research on the effects of interviewer ambiguity was preceded by the work of Lennard and Bernstein (1960), although their study focused on psychotherapeutic interviews rather than on information-gathering type interviews. Lennard and Bernstein regard the psychotherapeutic dyad as an informational exchange system and they postulate a reciprocal relationship between the information put into the system by each of the participants. According to these authors, the crucial variable of the therapist's informational input is the ambiguity-specificity level of his message. The crucial variable of the patient's informational input is his productivity. According to the principle of informational reciprocity, high therapist informational input (i.e., a high specificity remark) is likely to be followed by low patient input (i.e., low productivity). On the other hand, high patient input (i.e., a productive response) is likely to be followed by low therapist input (i.e., an ambiguous remark). Lennard and Bernstein were able to demonstrate that specific interviewer remarks, in contrast to ambiguous ones, are indeed followed by relatively less productive interviewee responses. They were also able to show that relatively unproductive patient responses tend to be followed by specific therapist statements, and relatively productive patient replies by ambiguous therapist remarks.

Our first interview study (Pope and Siegman, 1962), based on twelve naturalistic initial psychiatric interviews, was essentially an attempt to replicate Lennard and Bernstein's findings. We obtained significant positive correlations between interviewer ambiguity level and subsequent interviewee productivity in eight out of the twelve interviews. No support was found, however, for an inverse relationship between interviewee productivity and subsequent interviewer ambiguity level. Thus the results of this study indicate that ambiguous interviewer messages, in contrast to specific ones, elicit more productive interviewee responses, but the findings fail to support Lennard and Bernstein's informational reciprocity model. Of course, other explanations besides the principle of informational reciprocity can account for the relationship between interviewer ambiguity and interviewee productivity. An ambiguous interviewer remark, by definition, is one which permits the interviewee to reply with a number of alternate responses. The interviewee, uncertain which of the response alternatives is the most appropriate, is likely to respond with several alternatives. According to this explanation, then, interviewee uncertainty is the mediating factor in the positive correlation between interviewer ambiguity and interviewee productivity. Another explanation is in terms of anxiety. As pointed out earlier, it has been suggested that ambiguity is anxiety-arousing. There is some evidence that anxiety tends to enhance verbal productivity (Davids and Eriksen, 1955). According to this explanation, then, anxiety is the mediating factor in the positive correlation between interviewer ambiguity and interviewee productivity. That anxiety may have been a factor is suggested by the finding (Pope and Siegman, 1962) that interviewees' responses to the ambiguous interviewer remarks, in contrast to the specific ones, contained significantly more speech disruptions as measured by Mahl's (1956) Speech Disturbance Ratio (SDR)[2]. This ratio has been shown to covary with fluctuations in anxiety level (Kasl and Mahl, 1960).

NATURALISTIC vs. EXPERIMENTAL INTERVIEWS

A topical classification of interviewer's messages in our naturalistic interview study (Pope and Siegman, 1962) revealed a thorough confounding between interviewer topical focus and ambiguity-specificity level. As the interviewers moved from one topic to another, they changed their interviewing strategy. They were specific in their questions concerning patients' work history and relatively ambiguous in their inquiries about patients' family relations. The greater the anxiety-arousing potential of a question, the greater the likelihood that the interviewer would phrase it in an ambiguous, rather than a specific fashion. This finding, that interviewers tend to modulate the ambiguity level of their remarks as a function of topical focus and its anxiety-arousing potential, casts doubt over all the results of our naturalistic interview study. The results in regard to both interviewee productivity and SDR may have nothing to do with interviewer ambiguity-specificity level. Instead, they may reflect variations in interviewer topical focus and its anxiety-arousing potential.

This type of confounding, which is inevitable in naturalistic interviews, has led us to base all our subsequent major studies on experimental analogues of the initial interview. In these studies, the

---

[2]In our naturalistic study, the SDR was based on "Ah" and "Non-Ah" speech disruptions. More recent findings (Kasl and Mahl, 1965), however, indicate that the "Ah" category should be excluded from the determination of the SDR. Consequently, we recalculated our data with essentially identical results.

interviewer's remarks are prepared ahead of time. This makes it possible to manipulate one or more variables (such as, interviewer ambiguity level and topical focus) while keeping all other known relevant variables constant. Additionally, the interviewers are trained to behave in a consistent manner. Early in the research program there was concern that such interviews may appear contrived and artificial. We are now satisfied, however, that it is possible for an interviewer to limit himself to rehearsed remarks and to behave in a fairly systematic fashion, and yet to leave interviewees with the impression that they were participating in a spontaneous exchange. Of course, experimental interviews differ from naturalistic interviews in a number of ways, some of which may be significant. One obvious difference is the motivations of both interviewers and interviewees for participating in the interview. The stakes involved in the two types of interviews are quite different. But, then, this variable, like others which distinguish experimental from naturalistic interviews, is itself subject to experimental investigation.

That experimental interviews are not the same as naturalistic ones is obvious. We only claim that our experimental interviews are analogous to naturalistic interviews and that the discovery of the lawful relationships which regulate communication in these experimental interviews are relevant to an understanding of interviewer-interviewee behavior in naturalistic interviews. Furthermore, such understanding should help fashion the interview into a more effective instrument.

THE EFFECTS OF INTERVIEWER AMBIGUITY ON INTERVIEWEE PRODUCTIVITY AND VERBAL FLUENCY: FIRST EXPERIMENT

A major objective of this study was to test in a controlled experiment the finding previously obtained in naturalistic settings, that ambiguous interviewer remarks, in contrast to specific ones, are associated with greater interviewee productivity. Additionally, we hoped to obtain evidence bearing on the hypothesis that anxiety is a mediating variable in the positive correlation between interviewer ambiguity and interviewee productivity. According to this hypothesis, the association between interviewer ambiguity and interviewee productivity should be more pronounced in anxious, than in non-anxious subjects. To assess this expectation, we included a measure of subjects' predisposition to anxiety, namely, the Taylor MAS. Also, the anxiety-arousing potential of interviewer's messages was systematically varied, with one half of each interview designed to be anxiety-arousing and the other half to have no such effect. If anxiety is indeed the mediating variable in the relationship between interviewer ambiguity and interviewee productivity, then this association should be more pronounced in the anxiety-arousing segment of the interview than in the neutral one.

A second major objective of this study was to ascertain the effects of interviewer ambiguity on interviewee verbal fluency. It will be recalled that in our naturalistic study (Pope and Siegman, 1962) the ambiguous interviewer probes, in contrast to the specific ones, had a disruptive effect on interviewees' verbal fluency as measured by Mahl's SDR. As has been pointed out, however, in that study there was a confounding between interviewer ambiguity-specificity level and topical focus. Consequently, we do not know whether the findings which were obtained in that study are a result of the ambiguity-specificity variable or a result of topical focus.

Disruptions in the normal flow of speech, such as speech disturbances or long silent pauses, are usually interpreted by clinicians as signs of anxiety. There is considerable evidence, however, that cognitive factors can also have a disruptive effect on speech. Uncertainty, for example, has been shown to be associated with a variety of non-fluency indices. Most prominent among the studies on the effects of uncertainty on speech are those of Goldman-Eisler. In one of these studies (Goldman-Eisler, 1961b), subjects were asked to describe and then to formulate the meaning or moral of a series of New Yorker cartoons. The basic assumption of this study is that the meaning of these cartoons is not immediately apparent and that, therefore, the formulation of meaning involves considerably more uncertainty than their description. She found that subjects' interpretations (i.e., the formulations of meaning) were associated with longer reaction times and longer silent pauses than their descriptions. She concludes that "pausing indicates that information is being generated at the time of speech and signalizes that verbal planning of some sort is actually and at present taking place" (Goldman-Eisler, 1964b, p. 103). Brenner, Feldstein, and Jaffe (1963) asked subjects to read passages varying in their degree of approximation to written English and monitored the occurrence of speech disturbances (as measured by Mahl's SDR). They found a negative correlation between a passage's level of approximation to written English and its elicitation of speech disturbances. Assuming that the lower a passage's approximation to written English the greater the reader's uncertainty, the authors conclude that uncertainty produces speech disturbances as measured by Mahl's ratio. Maclay and Osgood (1959) found that "ahs" and allied hesitation phenomena, or "filled pauses" as they designate such non-fluencies, occur more frequently before lexical words than before functional words. They attribute this finding to the greater uncertainty involved in the choice of lexical words as opposed to functional ones. We see, then, that uncertainty is associated with a variety of non-fluencies although the precise manifestations, apparently, vary as a function of the speaker's task and response conditions. Thus Goldman-Eisler (1961a) reports that uncertainty, as she manipulated it, did not increase the occurrence of filled pauses although in other studies uncertainty did promote such hesitation phenomena (e.g., Maclay and Osgood, 1959). The second major objective of our first experimental interview study, then, was to ascertain the effects of interviewer ambiguity on interviewee verbal fluency. Whether the effects of uncertainty on verbal fluency are mediated by anxiety is another question. However, the design of our experiment which calls for an orthogonal manipulation of both uncertainty and anxiety should shed some light on this question, too. Moreover, by focusing on a variety of extralinguistic measures it may be possible to identify a pattern of non-fluencies associated with uncertainty distinguishable from that associated with anxiety arousal.

EXPERIMENTAL PROCEDURE

Subjects. Fifty junior and senior students at the University of Maryland School of Nursing, all female, were selected. They were a rather homogeneous group in regard to age and intelligence, but somewhat less so in regard to socio-economic background. Subjects' ages ranged from 20 to 22. Their mean Mental Age score as determined by the Shipley Institute of Living Scale was 17.80, SD = .88. Their socio-economic background as determined by Hollingshead's (1957) two-factor index was as follows: upper class, 10 subjects; upper-middle class, 10 subjects; lower-middle class, 19 subjects; upper-lower class, 6 subjects; and lower-lower class, 5 subjects. Subjects received 4 dollars each for participating in the study.

Several weeks prior to the interview, all junior and senior nursing students participated in a group testing session. At this time, they were administered a background information questionnaire, an intelligence test, several standard personality questionnaires (including the Taylor MAS) and a specially constructed questionnaire dealing with school experiences. The latter provided the basis for the selection of interviewees. All respondents who reported any difficulty with school at any time were eliminated, so that, for those who remained in the study, school experiences would indeed be a neutral topic, in contrast to family relations, the anxiety-arousing topic. Because of the nature

of the interview questions, one other requirement was that subjects'
parents be alive.

TABLE I.

Experimental Interview

	Specificity Rating

A. Neutral Topic

Low Specificity

1. "Now would you please tell me something, anything you would like, about the schools you attended before coming to the School of Nursing." — 4.1
2. "Tell me something about the elementary school you attended (junior high school, high school—whichever was not emphasized in response to Question No. 1) and how you got along there." — 6.3

High Specificity

1. "In which of these schools did you get along better?" — 10.9
2. "Which of these schools was a better school?" — 10.9
3. "Did you participate in many extra curricular activities?" — 10.9
4. "Would you say that you participated more than the average student?" — 10.9

Low Specificity

1. "Now I'd like you to tell me something, just anything that occurs to you about your first two years in the School of Nursing at College Park." — 6.3
2. "I know very little about schools of nursing. Tell me some more about the School of Nursing, anything that occurs to you." — 6.3

B. Anxiety-Arousing Topic

Low Specificity

1. "Would you please tell me something about your immediate family and how you got along with them." — 4.1
2. "Tell me more about your father (mother—whichever was not emphasized in response to No. 1), just anything you can think of." — 6.3

High Specificity

1. "With whom did you get along better, with your father or with your mother?" — 10.9
2. "Did your father and mother get along well?" — 10.9
3. "Did your mother tell you about menstruation?" — 10.9
4. "Did your father treat all his children equally?" — 10.9

Low Specificity

1. "Tell me more about your brothers and sisters." — 6.3
2. "We've talked about you and your parents when you were younger. Tell me something about you and your parents now." — 6.3

The interview. A standard, prearranged interview was used with all subjects (Table I). The interview was divided into two topical areas: an anxiety-arousing topic, consisting of eight questions in the area of family relations, and a neutral topic, consisting of eight questions in the area of school history. Within each topic, two ambiguous questions were followed by four specific questions and then, again, by two ambiguous ones. The ambiguity-specificity distinctions were made on the basis of an empirical scale developed by us for the measurement of interviewer specificity level (Siegman and Pope, 1962). The questions in the two topical areas were equated for specificity. Sequence of topical focus was alternated between subjects.

In order to enhance the anxiety-arousing potential of the family relations topic, the interviewer preceded his questions in this area with the following remarks: "You remember taking a number of personality tests? Several of the questions dealt with family relations. I am interested in talking about this area further with you, because from past experience we know that even when a person is not aware of problems in this area and, therefore, does not express them in her responses to the test, such problems may actually exist." Where appropriate the interviewer concluded: "Of course, in your case you are aware of such problems and you have indicated them in your responses to the test."[3] The effectiveness of our topical manipulation is suggested by the interviewees' postinterview self-ratings on two 6-point bipolar scales: comfortable-uncomfortable and tense-relaxed. The ratings indicate that our interviewees were significantly more uncomfortable and tense during the family relations topic than during the school topic, although in relation to both topics, subjects felt more comfortable than uncomfortable and more relaxed than tense.

Dependent variables. The dependent variables were productivity and the following indices of verbal fluency: Mahl's SDR, the Ah Ratio or Filled Pauses Ratio, Reaction Time, Speech Rate, Silence Quotient, and Articulation Rate.

Productivity is the number of words per response. In earlier studies, the number of clause units per response was used as an index of productivity. We have since determined, however, that the simpler word count correlates very highly, about .96, with number of clause units.

The SDR was scored according to Mahl's (1956) scoring manual. Briefly, the ratio is obtained by counting all the incompletions, corrections, incoherent intrusions, stutters, repetitions, and tongue slips in a

---

[3]This sentence was added if subjects admitted to having problems in this area, according to their MMPI responses.

given response and dividing them by the total number of words in the response.

The Filled Pauses Ratio (FPR) or *Ah Ratio* is computed by taking all ahs and allied hesitation phenomena in a response and dividing them by the total number of words.

Reaction Time (RT) is simply the length of time in seconds between the end of the interviewer's question and the beginning of the interviewee's response (i.e., his first utterance).

Speech Rate (SR) is obtained by taking the total number of words in a response and dividing it by total response time. As pointed out by Goldman-Eisler (1961c), SR is a compound measure based on the speaker's articulation rate and the silences between utterances.

Silence Quotient (SQ) was obtained by taking the sum of all silences of two seconds and over within a response and dividing it by the total duration of the response. We decided on two seconds for the lower limit because shorter pauses could not be scored with sufficiently high reliability. Moreover, pauses of two seconds and over tend to be perceived as interruptions in the normal flow of speech, especially if they occur within a sentence.

Articulation Rate (AR) was computed by taking the total number of words in a response and dividing it by the total response time minus the silences of two seconds and over. Actually, Articulation Rate is a misnomer because, like Speech Rate, it is a compound measure based on subject's articulation rate and silent pauses of two seconds and less. This appellation is retained because it has been used in previous publications summarizing the studies discussed in this and the next chapter.

Goldman-Eisler (1956, 1961c, 1964a) has stated that if one removes all silent pauses of .25 seconds and over, there remains no significant interindividual or intraindividual variation in speech rate. Thus, according to this investigator, variations in speech rate are caused by variations in pausing, but actual articulation rate remains constant. If this is so, then our two indices of SQ and AR are actually measures of long and short pauses respectively.

The scoring of the SDR and the FPR is done from verbatim transcripts while simultaneously listening to the tape recording of the interview. For the scoring of the temporal indices, the tapes were played back and the relevant time readings were made with a stopwatch. Interscorer reliability (percentage of agreement) was 74 percent for the SDR and 89 percent for the FPR. For reaction time, response time, and silent pauses, the basic data from which all temporal indices were derived, the interscorer reliabilities (*r*s) were respectively, .99, .99, and .96.

RESULTS

Reliability of verbal indices and their intercorrelations. It will be recalled that each experimental condition (e.g., high ambiguity neutral remarks) consisted of four questions. It was, therefore, possible to divide the interview in two and to calculate split-half reliability correlations (r). The following results were obtained: Productivity, .707; SDR, .585; FPR, .707; SQ, .672; AR, .654; and RT, .461.

TABLE II.

**Intercorrelations (Pearson's rs)[1] Between
Six Verbal Indices in Interviewee Speech**

Variables	2	3	4	5	6
Productivity	-.08	.30°	-.27	.20	-.45°°
Filled Pauses Ratio		.22	.14	-.60°°	.25
Speech Disturbance Ratio			-.09	-.08	-.06
Reaction Time				-.08	.58°°
Articulation Rate					-.22
Silence Quotient					

° $p < .05$ level (.28); °° $p < .01$ level (.36); [1]N=50.

TABLE III.

Rotated Factor Matrix (Orthogonal) for Six Verbal Indices

	Factor			
	I	II	III	h[2]
Productivity	-.345	-.401	-.278	.357
Filled Pauses Ratio	.654	.145	-.325	.553
Speech Disturbance Ratio	.144	.008	-.504	.275
Reaction Time	.050	.624	.008	.392
Articulation Rate	-.702	-.086	.076	.506
Silence Quotient	.122	.695	-.069	.503
Σa^2	1.076	1.062	.448	2.586
% Total Variance	17.9	17.7	7.5	43.1

Productivity and the fluency measures were intercorrelated and factor analyzed in order to obtain some clues about the patterning of these verbal indices. The results suggest three factors (Table II and III). The variables with significant loadings on Factor I are the FPR with a positive loading, and Articulation Rate with a negative loading. Thus Factor I appears to describe cautious and hesitant speech. The variables with significant loadings on Factor II are Reaction Time and Silence Quotient, the latter a measure of relatively long silent pauses. Factor III is primarily a speech disturbance factor.

Assuming that Silence Quotient is a measure of relatively long pauses and Articulation Rate a measure of relatively brief pauses, the results of the factor analysis suggest that these two kinds of pauses represent distinct psychological processes rather than merely different points on the same variable.[4]

Effects of ambiguity on productivity. As expected, the ambiguous interviewer remarks, in contrast to the specific ones, were associated with significantly greater interviewee productivity (Table IV). The magnitude of the correlation between the two variables, as estimated by ε,[5] is .92.

TABLE IV.

Subjects' Mean Scores on the Verbal Indices in the Ambiguous and Specific Segments

Verbal Indices	Ambiguous Mean	Specific Mean	F^1	p
Productivity	382.91	129.32	217.93^2	< .001
Speech Rate	2.47	2.63	10.04	< .005
Articulation Rate	2.70	2.91	25.88	< .005
Silence Quotient	.1031	.1032	1.00	n.s.
Reaction Time	2.26	2.36	1.00	n.s.
FPR	.02596	.01857	14.16	< .005
SDR	.02531	.02375	1.00	n.s.

[1]$df = 1/48$.
[2]*Analysis of covariance with duration of interviewer remarks held constant:* $F = 46.01, p < .01$.

After completing this study, it became apparent that we failed to control for the duration of the interviewer's remarks. A statistical analysis showed that the ambiguous remarks were significantly longer than the specific ones ($t = 25.57$, df 48, $p < .001$), and the anxiety-arousing remarks significantly shorter than the neutral ones ($t = 11.25$, df 48, $p < .001$). This is a serious defect in the present study because, according to Matarazzo and his associates (1965), duration of

---

[4]In a recent study we obtained an identical factorial structure, lending further support to the distinction between the two types of silent pauses.

[5]*Epsilon* is an unbiased estimate of the correlation ratio, *eta*, and may be computed by the formula

$$\varepsilon = \sqrt{\frac{(F-1)\,df_1}{(F)\,df_1 + df_2}}$$

where:

df^1 = degrees of freedom associated with the numerator of the F ratio;
df^2 = degrees of freedom associated with the denominator of the F ratio.
In terms of its magnitude, ε may be interpreted in much the same way as r. Unlike r, ε does not presume a linear relationship (Cohen, 1964).

interviewer remarks is a highly significant source of variance in interviewee productivity. Long interviewer remarks elicit more productive interviewee responses than short ones. This finding, first noted by Matarazzo and his co-workers, was successfully replicated in our own laboratory (see Chapter 4 and Siegman and Pope, 1969). It is clear, therefore, that interviewer duration must be controlled in any study in which interviewee productivity is the dependent variable. Since the present study failed to do so, the data were submitted to an analysis of covariance in which the effect of interviewer duration was partialed out. The resulting F value for the effect of ambiguity on productivity was 46.01, with $\varepsilon = .49$. Thus the findings continue to show a significant relationship between interviewer ambiguity-specificity level and interviewee productivity, even with the duration of interviewer remarks held constant.

There was no significant interaction between interviewer ambiguity and topical focus, nor between interviewer ambiguity and interviewee anxiety level. There was no support for the hypothesis that the effect of interviewer ambiguity on interviewee productivity would be more pronounced in anxious than in non-anxious subjects, or for an anxiety-arousing topic than for a neutral one.

Effects of ambiguity on verbal fluency. The ambiguous interviewer remarks, in contrast to the specific ones, were associated with a significantly higher Filled Pauses Ratio and a significantly slower Articulation Rate in interviewees' speech. None of the other differences were significant (Table IV). The results of this study suggest, then, that uncertainty is associated with cautious and hesitant speech.

There was no support for the hypothesis that the effects of interviewer ambiguity on interviewee verbal fluency are more pronounced in anxious than in non-anxious subjects, or for an anxiety-arousing topic than for a neutral one. Thus there is no evidence for the hypothesis that anxiety is a mediating factor in the effects of interviewer ambiguity on interviewee speech. This conclusion is buttressed by the finding that the pattern of extralinguistic correlates of ambiguity or uncertainty is different from that of anxiety. The complete results of the topical manipulation are presented in the second half of this chapter, which deals with the effects of anxiety on speech. For the purposes of the present discussion, suffice it to say that anxiety arousal was associated with an acceleration, rather than a slowing down of speech. Also, unlike uncertainty, anxiety arousal was associated with speech disturbances. We conclude, therefore, that the effects of ambiguity or uncertainty on speech are a result of cognitive processes and are independent of anxiety.

THE EFFECTS OF INTERVIEWER AMBIGUITY ON INTERVIEWEE VERBAL BEHAVIOR: SECOND EXPERIMENT

Two methodological considerations led us to conduct a second experiment on the effects of interviewer ambiguity-specificity level on interviewee speech. First, in the previous experiment interviewer ambiguity was confounded with the duration of his remarks (i.e., his speaking time). Although we succeeded in partialing out interviewer speaking time by means of an analysis of covariance, it was felt that another study in which this variable would be experimentally controlled was indicated. Second, in the previous study the interviewer always initiated the interview with two ambiguous probes, followed by four specific questions which, in turn, were followed by two ambiguous remarks (i.e., a high-low-high sequence). While this provided a partial control for possible sequence effects, a more complete control for ambiguity sequence is in order (e.g., a high-low sequence alternating with a low-high one).

There is another issue of a substantive rather than a methodological nature which was overlooked in our first interview study. Granted that ambiguous interviewer probes, in contrast to specific ones, elicit more productive interviewee responses, what is the informational value of such longer responses? Or stated somewhat differently: What is the effect of interviewer ambiguity level on the noise-to-information ratio in interviewee's responses? Certainly, the practicing clinician who has to make a diagnostic or dispositional decision about his client is not interested in interviewee productivity per se, but rather in information that is relevant to his decision-making process.

While it is difficult to formulate general criteria for measuring the informational value of an interviewee's response, it should be possible to identify some of the variables which are relevant to such a determination. According to a widely held assumption among practicing clinicians, ambiguous interviewer probes, in contrast to specific ones, elicit more psychologically meaningful information (i.e., information which is relevant to a person's motivations, his values, his conflicts, and how he resolves them). Presumably, this type of information is more relevant to the interviewer's decision-making processes than factually descriptive, non-psychologically oriented, non-evaluative data. This second experiment, then, was addressed to the following question: What is the effect of interviewer ambiguity level on the ratio of psychologically meaningful to superficial information in interviewee's responses?

A number of studies have focused on a similar question in

regard to projective tests. A widely held assumption based on the "projective hypothesis" states that the greater the ambiguity of projective test stimuli (i.e., the less structured their stimulus properties), the greater the likelihood that they will elicit psychologically meaningful information rather than objectively descriptive and stereotyped responses (Kenny and Bijou, 1953). This assumption was tested in a number of studies, mostly within the context of the TAT. It has been stated that the results of these studies provide an empirical basis for the use of ambiguity in the interview (Bordin, 1955). In fact, however, the evidence indicates that if ambiguity in the TAT is defined as lack of structure, then its effects are opposite to those stated in the projective hypothesis. The findings consistently show that the greater the clarity of a card and the easier it is to identify its various figures, the greater its potential to elicit fantasy and personality-relevant material. (For a summary of this literature see Murstein, 1963.) Some investigators, proceeding from an information theory point of view, argue that ambiguity of projective test stimuli is more appropriately defined in terms of response variability (Kenny, 1954, 1961; Kenny and Bijou, 1953; Murstein, 1963, 1964). Thus, in the TAT, an ambiguous card is one which elicits a variety of responses (i.e., different themes or stories), while a non-ambiguous card is one which elicits a stereotyped response. (It will be noted that this conceptualization of stimulus ambiguity is analogous to the one which we used for interviewer ambiguity-specificity level.) If ambiguity in projective stimuli is defined in this manner, the empirical evidence provides some support for the projective hypothesis, but only at a marginal level. Thus Murstein (1966) obtained a significant positive correlation between the ambiguity level of TAT cards and their capacity to elicit personality-relevant themes, but only in a male and not in a female group. A study by Kenny and Bijou (1953) suggests that the relationship is a curvilinear one, with medium ambiguity cards eliciting the richest stories. Siegman and Pope (1966a), using female subjects, found that the ambiguous cards elicited less anxious and less depressed themes than the unambiguous cards. Contrary to the implications of the "projective hypothesis," this finding suggests that the greater the subject's response alternatives, the easier it is to suppress potentially anxiety-arousing themes and to replace them with relatively neutral ones.

We conclude that the projective test literature on this question is ambiguous and contradictory. To cite this literature in support of ambiguity in the initial interview is unwarranted. The present study, therefore, is an attempt to test the "projective hypothesis" within the context of the interview.

Hypothesis 1. Ambiguous interviewer remarks, in contrast to specific ones, are associated with a higher ratio of pyschologically meaningful to superficial statements in interviewee's responses. The other two hypotheses which were tested in this experiment are based on the results of the previous interview study.

Hypothesis 2. Ambiguous interviewer remarks, in contrast to specific ones, are associated with more productive interviewee responses.

Hypothesis 3. Ambiguous interviewer remarks, in contrast to specific ones, are associated with more hesitantly articulated interviewee responses.

PROCEDURE

Subjects. Thirty-two junior and senior female nursing students at the University of Maryland School of Nursing were selected. Their backgrounds were similar to those who participated in the first experiment. Subjects in this study were volunteers and they were paid for their participation.

Experimental design. Each subject was interviewed twice, each time by a different interviewer. Two analogous, prearranged interviews were used for the two sessions (see Table II in the next chapter). Each interview consisted of four questions in the area of family relations followed by four questions in the area of school history. Within each topical area, two questions were ambiguous and two were specific, as measured by our empirically derived Specificity Scale (Siegman and Pope, 1962). Interviewer speaking time was controlled by making all remarks eight or nine words long.

To counterbalance specificity sequence, there were two interview series. One followed a high ambiguity-low ambiguity sequence within each topic, the other a low ambiguity-high ambiguity sequence. Subjects alternated between the two sequences.

The design of this study called for two interviews, so that each subject could be interviewed by a "cold" and a "warm" interviewer. The details of the warm-cold manipulation and its effects on interviewees' verbal behavior is the concern of the next chapter. The fact that subjects participated in two interviews made it possible to compare the effects of interviewer ambiguity in the first, as opposed to the second, interview. (For one-half the subjects the first interview was "cold" and the second "warm"; for the others, the reverse was true.)

Dependent variables. As in our first experiment, the dependent variables consisted of productivity (word count) and the following verbal fluency measures: Filled Pauses Ratio, Articulation Rate, Reaction Time, Silence Quotient, and Mahl's Speech Disturbance Ratio. Additionally, this study included the Superficiality Ratio, which is the ratio of superficial to meaningful clause units in interviewee's response. To obtain this score, a subject's response is first divided into clause units according to the criteria of Dollard and Auld (1959). Each clause unit is then rated as either superficial or meaningful. Clauses which are factually descriptive or trivial, rather than evaluational or psychologically analytical, are scored as superficial. The Superficiality Ratio is then obtained by dividing the number of superficial clauses by the total number of clauses. In our laboratory the interscorer reliability (r) values for this index have ranged from .90 to .96. Regarding its validity, we have the following data. There is a clear-cut tendency for the meaningful clauses to be associated with more speech disruptions as measured by the SDR, and with more qualifying phrases than the superficial clauses. In one recent study, 30 out of 32 subjects showed this tendency. Furthermore, within this group the correlation (r) between subjects' Superficiality Ratios and their SDRs was -.35 ($p < .05$); between their Superficiality Ratios and their Qualification Ratios, -.42 ($p < .05$). These findings suggest that the meaningful statements, in contrast to the superficial ones, are associated with more conflict and anxiety (SDR) and with greater efforts to attenuate such feelings (Qualification Ratio). Of course, this would be expected if the Superficiality Ratio is a valid measure of superficial vs. psychologically meaningful clauses.

RESULTS

The first hypothesis was not confirmed. The ambiguous, rather than the specific, probes were associated with a significantly higher Superficiality Ratio. This finding obtained in the first and in the second interview (Table V).

The hypothesis that ambiguous interviewer remarks, in contrast to specific ones, are associated with more productive interviewee responses was confirmed. This relationship, too, obtained in both interviews (Table V).

The hypothesis that ambiguous interviewer remarks, in contrast to specific ones, are associated with less fluently articulated interviewee responses was also confirmed. Interviewees' responses in the ambiguous segments of the interview were associated with significantly higher FPRs, SQs, and RTs than their responses in the specific

TABLE V.

Subjects' Mean Scores on Verbal Indices in the Ambiguous and Specific Segments of the Second Ambiguity Experiment

Verbal Indices	First Interview			Second Interview		
	Ambiguous Mean	Specific Mean	F^2	Ambiguous Mean	Specific Mean	F^2
Productivity	120.30	40.57	31.52°°°	89.34	42.52	62.50°°°
Superficiality	11.48	5.68	4.64°	13.24	3.65	9.44°°
FPR	.0138	.0141	11.51°°	.0186	.0118	20.51°°°
AR	1.33	1.20	3.27	1.32	1.28	1.05
RT	2.90	2.05	6.62°	2.57	2.00	4.49°
SQ	.0617	.0430	5.56°	.0566	.0409	7.41°
SDR	.0168	.0139	1.84	.0169	.0166	.02
RT (Group A)[1]	3.25	1.94	7.69°	3.13	2.06	9.90°°
RT (Group B)[1]	2.54	2.17	.82	2.02	1.94	.08

$°p < .05;$ $°° < .01;$ $°°°p < .005.$
[1]Group A followed an ambiguous-specific interview sequence;
Group B, a specific-ambiguous sequence.
[2]df is 1/30, except for RT (Group A)[1] and RT (Group B)[1] where df is 1/15.

segments. The latter difference, however, was significant only if the interview was started with ambiguous, rather than specific, probes (Table V). All differences were equally apparent in both interviews (Table V).

Specificity sequence was not a significant source of variance in any of the dependent variables and the interaction between specificity and specificity sequence was significant only in relation to RT.

DISCUSSION

The relationship between interviewer ambiguity and interviewee productivity has now been successfully replicated in a more adequately controlled experiment than our first interview study. The improvements of the present study were: (a) the interviewers were "blind" in regard to the ambiguity-productivity hypothesis; (b) the interviewers' remarks in the two experimental conditions were of equal duration and (c) ambiguity-specificity sequence was counterbalanced. The relative increment in interviewee productivity in response to ambiguous interviewer probes, as opposed to specific ones, was remarkably alike in the two studies: 50 and 47 percent, respectively.

The finding that interviewer ambiguity sequence was not a significant source of variance in interviewee productivity is of interest. In clinical practice, it is customary to begin an interview, or the exploration of a new topic within an interview, with a moderately ambiguous probe, followed, if necessary, by more specific ones. The results of the present study indicate that the reverse procedure has no inhibiting effect on interviewee productivity.

In the present study as in the preceding one, interviewer ambiguity was associated with hesitant and non-fluent interviewee speech. There is, however, a discrepancy between the two studies. In the previous experiment, interviewee uncertainty had no significant effect on SQ; in the present study, it did. In regard to SQ, then, the findings of the present study are consistent with those reported by Goldman-Eisler (1961b).

In the present study as in the preceding one, interviewer ambiguity level had no significant effect on interviewees' speech disturbances. This finding, as pointed out earlier, is inconsistent with the hypothesis that the effects of interviewer ambiguity on interviewee verbal behavior are mediated by anxiety arousal.

The one major new finding of the present study was that the ambiguous interviewer probes, rather than the specific ones, were associated with a higher percentage of superficial clauses. This relationship is in the opposite direction of that which we hypothesized. It will be recalled that a similar disconfirmation occurred in our TAT study (Siegman and Pope, 1965c). Contrary to hypothesis, the unambiguous cards, rather than the ambiguous ones, were associated with more anxious and depressed themes. It was suggested that because the ambiguous stimuli, in contrast to the non-ambiguous ones, provide subject with a wider range of response alternatives, it is easier to suppress or repress unpleasant associations and to replace them with innocuous responses. Similarly, because the ambiguous interviewer probes, in contrast to the specific ones, permit the interviewee to respond with a wider range of response alternatives, it may be easier to suppress or repress psychologically meaningful and potentially anxiety-arousing associations and to replace them with superficial statements. We also considered an alternate explanation. Perhaps the finding that the Superficiality Ratio was higher in the ambiguous rather than the specific interview segments is related to the fact that the former elicit longer responses than the latter. It has been demonstrated that the ratio of different words to the total number of words spoken (i.e., vocabulary diversity or richness) is inversely proportional to the number of words spoken. Perhaps there is a similar inverse relationship between the ratio of meaningful statements and productivity. In a recent study, however, such a negative correlation was not found, either as between subjects or within subjects, which has led us to reject this as a possible explanation for the positive association between ambiguity and the Superficiality Ratio.

Although the *ratio* of meaningful clauses was lower in the ambiguous than in the specific segments of the interview, it should be pointed out that the *total* number of meaningful clauses was substantially higher in the former than in the latter. All 32 subjects responded with more meaningful clauses to the ambiguous probes than to the specific ones. It can be concluded, therefore, that ambiguous interviewer remarks, in contrast to specific ones, elicit not only more productive, but also more informative interviewee responses.

RELATIONSHIP AMBIGUITY AND INTERVIEWEE
VERBAL BEHAVIOR: TWO EXPERIMENTS

The preceding studies dealt with ambiguity in the interview arising from the way in which the interviewer formulates his communications or, as referred to here, message ambiguity. There are, however, other sources of ambiguity. One deals with the nature of the interviewer-interviewee relationship. The interviewer's feelings and attitudes about the interviewee are encoded primarily in such non-verbal cues as smiling, head nodding, and other body movements. By monitoring these non-verbal interviewer cues, the interviewee obtains information about the adequacy of his responses and the impression he is making upon the interviewer. Interviewer unresponsiveness is likely to be interpreted by the interviewee as rejection. If, however, some of these non-verbal reinforcing cues were eliminated by placing a screen between interviewer and interviewee, it is likely to merely increase interviewee's uncertainty about the interviewer's attitudes and feelings toward himself (i.e., the interviewee). The two experiments to be discussed in this section concern the effects of such reduced interviewer informational input on interviewee productivity and verbal fluency. Thus, while our previous studies dealt with message ambiguity, those to be described in this section focused on relationship ambiguity. On the basis of previous findings, we formulated the following hypotheses:

Hypothesis 1. The presence of a screen between interviewer and interviewee, in contrast to its absence, is associated with greater interviewee productivity.

Hypothesis 2. The presence of a screen between interviewer and interviewee, in contrast to its absence, is associated with more hesitant and more slowly articulated interviewee responses.

METHOD

Subjects. Thirty-two female junior nursing students participated. Their backgrounds were similar to those in the two previous experiments and, like the subjects in the preceding study, they volunteered and were paid for their participation.

The interviews. Each subject was interviewed twice: once with a screen separating interviewer and interviewee and once without a screen. There were two parallel, prearranged interview schedules for the two interviews. Each interview consisted of two low-specificity questions in the area of family relations and two low-specificity questions in the area of school history and professional experiences (Table VI). There was an interval of one week between interviews. The sequence of experimental conditions (i.e., screen vs. no screen, interview schedules, and order of topics within each interview) was alternated between subjects.

TABLE VI.

Interview Questions in Relationship-Ambiguity Studies

Interview 1
1. I would like you to tell me something about your father and how you get along.
2. Now tell me something about your friend X, and how you get along.
3. Tell me something, anything you wish, about your experiences in high school.
4. Now tell me something about your reasons for choosing nursing as a profession.

Interview 2
1. I would like you to tell me something about your mother and how you get along.
2. Now tell me something about your friend X, and how you get along.
3. Please tell me something about your experiences in the school of nursing.
4. Now tell me something about your professional experiences here at University Hospital.

Dependent variables. These were productivity and the following indices of verbal fluency: the Filled Pauses Ratio, Articulation Rate, Reaction Time, Silence Quotient, and the SDR.

RESULTS

The effect of the screen on interviewee productivity. The first hypothesis was disconfirmed. The presence of the screen between interviewer and interviewee, in contrast to its absence, was associated with significantly lower, rather than higher, productivity (Table VII). We now have a clear-cut reversal in the effects of two types of ambiguity. While message or informational ambiguity is associated with an increase in interviewee productivity, the opposite is true in regard to relationship ambiguity. Perhaps by eliminating interviewer non-verbal feedback (such as smiling, head nodding, and other social reinforcers), we are eliminating the very conditions which sustain interpersonal communication. The results, therefore, suggest that we cannot speak of interview ambiguity in general, but that we must distinguish between different sources of ambiguity. While one type of ambiguity (namely, message ambiguity) tends to promote communication, another type of ambiguity (namely, that which involves the interviewer-interviewee relationship) has the opposite effect.

The effect of the screen on interviewee verbal fluency. The second hypothesis was confirmed. The presence of the screen between interviewer and interviewee, in contrast to its absence, was associated

TABLE VII.

**Subjects' Mean Scores on Verbal Indices
in Screen and No Screen Conditions**

Verbal Indices	Screen	No Screen	F^1
Productivity	170.46	269.66	6.18°°
Articulation Rate	3.03	3.12	5.09°
FPR	.0322	.0270	6.48°°
Reaction Time	1.57	1.55	1.51
Silence Quotient	.1567	.1554	.01
SD Ratio	.0289	.0294	.04

$^1 df = 1/28;$ °$p < .05;$ °°$p < .025.$

with a higher FPR and a slower Articulation Rate (Table VII). Thus, relationship ambiguity, like message ambiguity, is associated with cautious and hesitant speech. It can be argued, of course, that the findings of this study have nothing to do with ambiguity or uncertainty, but are simply a result of the fact that a screen was interposed between interviewer and interviewee. Facing this screen may have been uncomfortable and distracting, and hence the reduced productivity and the hesitant speech. In order to rule out this explanation, another experiment followed in which the reduction of interviewer reinforcing cues was achieved without placing a screen between interviewer and interviewee.

SECOND RELATIONSHIP-AMBIGUITY EXPERIMENT

In this study, a reduction of interviewer informational input was achieved by manipulating subjects' seating position vis-a-vis the interviewer. In one interview, subjects faced the interviewer; in the other, they faced away. In the latter condition, subjects were seated at an angle so that they could not see the interviewer, but the interviewer was able to see them. In this manner, we reduced the interviewer's non-verbal reinforcing responses without instituting other potentially distracting cues.

It should be pointed out that in the preceding study, with a screen between interviewer and interviewee, we not only eliminated interviewer non-verbal feedback, but at the same time we also restricted the interviewee to the verbal channel. For example, we noticed a distinct reduction, although not a complete elimination, of interviewee body movement in the screen, as opposed to the no-screen interview condition. Of course, this restriction on the interviewee's normal encoding behavior may have affected his verbal behavior, independent of the effects produced by the lack of interviewer feedback. However, in the present study, we avoided this confounding by allowing the interviewer to see and watch the interviewee.

Subjects. These consisted of 16 female nursing students and 16 female graduate nurses. The students were selected from the same population as were the subjects of our previous study. The graduate nurses were somewhat older than the students (about two years), but otherwise of a comparable background. All subjects volunteered and were paid for their participation.

The procedure. This study was identical with that of the last experiment, with the one exception that this time there was no counterbalancing for topical sequence.

Results. The findings of this study were also comparable with those of the preceding experiment. Subjects were less productive and showed greater hesitation (FPR) in the facing-away condition than in the control interview (Table VIII). In contrast to the previous study, the experimental manipulation in the present one had no significant effect on the AR index; instead, it had a slowing down effect on subjects' reaction time (Table VIII).

Considering the comparable findings of the two studies, it is not likely that the findings of the previous experiment were simply a

TABLE VIII.

Subjects' Mean Scores on Verbal Indices
in Control and Facing-Away Conditions

Verbal Indices	Control	Facing-Away	F^1
Productivity	252.36	193.34	12.61°°
Articulation Rate	3.14	3.09	.81
Filled Pauses Ratio	.0326	.0374	6.03°
Reaction Time	1.74	2.23	5.11°
Silence Quotient	.171	.175	.78
Speech Disturbance Ratio	.0343	.0361	.70

$^1df = 1/30;$ °$p < .05,$ °°$p < .01.$

result of distraction produced by the screen. Instead, we attribute the results of both experiments to a reduction of interviewer informational feedback or relationship ambiguity.

The relationship between interviewee uncertainty and non-fluent or hesitant speech has now been demonstrated in four different studies and is apparently independent of the particular source of ambiguity; i.e., informational or relationship ambiguity. The one non-fluency index which was associated with uncertainty in all four studies is the FPR: the greater the speaker's uncertainty, the greater the occurrence of ahs and allied hesitation phenomena. The four studies are also consistent in that uncertainty had no significant effect on subjects' SDRs.

ANXIETY AND SPEECH

While there has been considerable research interest in the effects of anxiety on perception and learning, research on its effects on language and speech is of relatively recent origin and limited in scope. During the early work on ambiguity-uncertainty, when we were inclined to explain its effects in terms of the mediating role of anxiety, it became apparent that the empirical data in regard to anxiety and speech are not only sparse, but also, at least superficially, inconsistent.

PREVIOUS FINDINGS

Already referred to is the work of Mahl (1956), who found that anxiety is associated with flustered speech. The following explanation is suggested by Mahl and Schulze for the positive relationship between anxiety and the SDR. "It is well known that anxiety has a disruptive effect on finely coordinated behavior, and speech is an instance of finely coordinated behavior, par excellence. Speech disturbance may be a purely automatic, generalized consequence of anxiety in the same way that general changes in muscular coordination or attention span, for example, are brought about by anxiety" (Mahl and Schulze, 1964, p. 88). Mahl then proceeds to point out that speech disturbances may reflect not only the direct effect of anxiety per se, but also the indirect effect of defensive maneuvers against anxiety. Speech disturbances, like incomplete sentences, omissions, stutters, and tongue slips, may reflect the speaker's attempt to inhibit feared material. On the basis of this conceptual approach, i.e., that anxiety has a disruptive and inhibiting effect on speech, Mahl predicted that anxiety would be associated with long silent pauses in speech. This he was able to demonstrate in one study (Mahl, 1956), but he could not replicate this finding in a subsequent study (Mahl, 1961).

In contrast to Mahl's findings, there are other studies suggesting that anxiety has a facilitating effect on verbal productivity and fluency. Thus Davids and Eriksen (1955) found a positive correlation between manifest anxiety, as measured by the Taylor Manifest Anxiety Scale, and productivity in a word association task. Kanfer (1958, 1960), investigating the effect of anxiety on verbal rate, found that verbal rate accelerates in response to shock-conditioned tones and in response to anxiety-arousing interview topics.

These findings can be most parsimoniously explained in terms of a drive approach to anxiety as advocated by Spence and Spence (1966). If anxiety is regarded as a drive state, then it is to be expected that with an increase in anxiety level there would be an increase in verbal output both in terms of number of words and rate of speech. Moreover, the activation of different response tendencies may also produce an increase of speech disturbances (such as corrections, repetitions, etc.). Thus, functionally speaking, anxiety may have both a facilitating and a disruptive effect on speech. However, the aforementioned effects of anxiety were noted in different experiments, each defining anxiety differently and using different response conditions. It remains to be shown that similar results could be obtained within the conditions of a single study. This, then, was a major objective of our first experimental interview study: to ascertain the effects of anxiety on a variety of verbal indices.

THE EFFECTS OF ANXIETY ON INTERVIEWEE
VERBAL BEHAVIOR: AN EXPERIMENTAL INVESTIGATION

It will be recalled that in our first experimental study of the interview, the interviewer's remarks were equally divided between anxiety-arousing and neutral messages. This made it possible to ascertain the effects of anxiety on a wide variety of verbal indices.

Conceptualizing anxiety in terms of drive and taking note of previous findings, we hypothesized a positive correlation between anxiety and productivity, speech rate and speech disturbances as measured by Mahl's SDR. Also of interest was the effect of anxiety on vocabulary diversity as measured by the Type Token Ratio (TTR), which is the ratio of different words (i.e., types) to the total number of words in a given speech sample (i.e., tokens).

Mahl and Schulze (1964), who take the position that anxiety has a disruptive effect on the normal flow of speech, predict that anxiety is likely to reduce a speaker's TTR; i.e., increase his redundancy. The very opposite prediction, however, follows from a drive approach to anxiety. According to Hullian theory, a rise in drive level has the effect of activating previously below-threshold response tendencies. We should, therefore, obtain a positive association between anxiety and productivity. By the same token, we should also obtain a positive association between anxiety and vocabulary diversity as measured by the TTR.

At this point, one may question the appropriateness of investigating the effects of anxiety on speech within the context of the initial interview, where the non-verbal aspects of interviewer's behavior, no matter how well-controlled, are likely to be confounding factors. The answer to this criticism is that we consider speech essentially an interpersonal activity. Even when speaking to oneself there is an implied audience. Consequently, we consider the dyadic interview situation eminently suitable for an evaluation of the effects of anxiety on speech.

METHOD

A detailed account of the subjects and the design of this study was presented earlier in this chapter. Briefly, the subjects were 50 female nursing students. The interviewer asked eight questions, four ambiguous and four specific, in the area of school experiences and another eight questions in the area of family relations. Subjects were selected so that school experiences would not be an anxiety-arousing topic. Moreover, the questions pertaining to family relations were preceded by remarks designed to make subjects anxious about this topic. Postinterview ratings indicated that interviewees were, indeed, more tense and anxious when responding to the family relations inquiries than to the school questions.

The design of this study made it possible to determine the effects of anxiety-arousing interviewer messages on interviewee speech, both independently and in interaction with interviewer ambiguity-specificity level. Additionally, all subjects were administered the Taylor Manifest Anxiety Scale, which made it possible to ascertain the effects of predispositional anxiety on interviewee speech.

Dependent variables. The major dependent variables were productivity, the TTR, the SDR, and the various temporal indices (SR, SQ, AR, and RT). We also concluded the FPR in order to check Kasl and Mahl's (1965) contention that anxiety increases the SDR, but not the FPR.

Unfortunately, it was not possible to use all 50 subjects for the TTR analysis. Johnson (1944) has demonstrated that the TTR of any given speech sample is a function of the magnitude of the sample; the longer the sample, the lower the TTR. He suggests that it is possible to correct this distortion by dividing a given speech sample into equal segments of, say, 100 words each, obtaining the TTR of each segment separately, and then computing the mean segmental TTR. Jaffe (1956) has established the comparability of mean segmental TTRs obtained from 100-, 75-, 50-, and 25-word segments. We decided, therefore, to base our mean segmental TTR on 25-word segments, which forced us to eliminate all subjects who responded with less than that number to any one of the interviewers' 16 questions. This left us 16 usable subjects.

RESULTS

The effects of anxiety-arousing interviewer messages on interviewee speech. The anxiety-arousing topic, in contrast to the neutral one, was associated with greater productivity, a higher TTR, a higher SDR, a higher Speech Rate, and a shorter Reaction Time (Table IX). However, the latter two are only of borderline significance. Moreover, while the other differences are not significant, they are all in the direction of less hesitant and more quickly articulated speech in the anxiety condition.

Additionally, there were two significant interactions. First, there was a significant interaction between topical focus and specificity in relation to Speech Rate. The interaction was such that the anxiety-

TABLE IX.

Subjects' Mean Scores on the Verbal Indices in Two Topical Areas

Verbal Indices	Anxiety-Arousing Mean	Neutral Mean	F^1	p
Productivity	265.44	231.96	5.85^2	< .05
Type Token Ratio	85.20	83.95	12.03	< .005
Speech Rate	2.58	2.51	2.98	< .10
Articulation Rate	2.83	2.78	1.66	n.s.
Silence Quotient	.0977	.1085	2.59	n.s.
Reaction Time	2.14	2.45	3.54	< .10
SDR	.0262	.0231	7.56	< .05
FPR	.0212	.0233	2.42	n.s.

[1] $df = 1/48$ except for TTR where $df = 1/222$.
[2] Analysis of covariance with duration of interviewer remarks held constant: $F = 7.64$, $p < .01$.

arousing topic was associated with a significantly higher Speech Rate than the neutral topic, but only in the specific segment of the interview. The second significant interaction was between topical focus and specificity in relation to the FPR. The interaction was such that the anxiety-arousing topic was associated with significantly fewer ahs than the neutral topic, but only in the specific segment of the interview.

These findings are most parsimoniously explained either in terms of a drive approach to anxiety, as espoused by Spence and Spence (1966), or in terms of an activation-arousal approach to anxiety, as proposed by Duffy (1962) and Malmo (1966). The findings of this study also suggest that the activation effect of the anxiety-arousing interviewer messages is most pronounced when the interviewer zeroes in with specific questions. This is probably so because highly specific anxiety-arousing questions, in contrast to ambiguous ones, do not permit the interviewee to respond in an avoidant, defensive manner.

The effects of predispositional anxiety on speech. The correlations between subjects' MAS scores and their scores on the various verbal indices were determined separately for the two topics (Table X).

In the emotional topic, subjects' MAS scores correlated positively with productivity ($p < .025$) and Articulation Rate ($p < .05$) and negatively with the FPR ($.05 > p < .10$). It should be noted that there was no significant correlation between subjects' MAS scores and their SDRs.

In the neutral topic, there were no significant correlations between

TABLE X.

Correlations (r) Between Ss MAS Scores and Verbal Indices
in Anxiety Arousing and Neutral Topics

Verbal Indices	Anxiety-Arousing Topic	Neutral Topic
Productivity	.319°	.248+
FPR	-.240+	-.117
Articulation Rate	.337°	.191
Reaction Time	-.058	.011
Silence Quotient	.015	.047
SDR	-.059	.110

°$p<.05$; +$p<.10$.

subjects' MAS scores and their scores on the various verbal indices. This is not especially surprising since it has been suggested that the MAS is not a measure of chronic anxiety, but rather a measure of the anxiety level with which individuals respond to anxiety-arousing situations.

To summarize, then, we find that the pattern of verbal behavior associated with intersubject variations in predispositional anxiety is strikingly similar to that associated with intrasubject variations in anxiety arousal. In both instances anxiety is associated with an increase in productivity and speech tempo. There is borderline evidence that both types of anxiety are associated with a decrease in hesitation as measured by the FPR. The only discrepancy is in relation to the SDR. While experimental anxiety arousal was associated with an increase in subjects' SDRs, there was no similar relationship between subjects' MAS scores and their SDRs. It should be pointed out, however, that on other occasions significant positive correlations between these two measures were obtained in our laboratory.

A NATURALISTIC STUDY ON THE EFFECTS OF ANXIETY ON SPEECH

Exponents of the activation-arousal approach to anxiety have suggested that its effects are not monotonic, but take the shape of an inverted U. Very high arousal has the same effect as very low arousal. Of course, the results of our experimental anxiety study cannot shed any light on this hypothesis since there was only a minimal arousal of subjects' anxiety level. Even in the anxiety condition, subjects rated themselves as more calm than anxious and more relaxed than tense. It was decided, therefore, to study the effects of anxiety on speech in patients, who do experience relatively high anxiety levels.

Unlike the previous anxiety study which was based on the experimental arousal of subjects' anxiety level, the present investigation is based on the daily vicissitudes of anxiety in a group of hospitalized patients. Monologues which were taped on their most anxious days were compared with monologues taped on their least anxious days.

METHOD

Subjects. Six patients on a research ward of a psychiatric hospital— four females and two males, ranging in age from 17 to 39—were the subjects of this study. They all had psychosomatic diagnoses and they all occasionally manifested extreme anxiety. None was overtly psychotic. All had completed high school.

Anxiety. The daily vicissitudes of anxiety in the six patients were determined by two nurses with research training, utilizing a method described by Bunny and Hamburg (1963). These authors had developed a rating scheme "for the systematic observation and quantification of behavior in psychiatric patients, utilizing a relatively untapped source of observational data, namely, the nursing research team" (p. 293). The measure they developed is used for the evaluation of anger, anxiety, depression, and psychotic behavior in hospitalized patients. There are three global scales (one each for depression, anger, and anxiety) and 21 specific behavioral scales relevant to these attributes and the fourth one, psychotic behavior. Each global trait or specific behavior is rated on a 15-point scale, with a score of 15 indicative of a very high degree or level of the trait or behavior, and a score of one, its total absence. The specific behaviors are defined in concrete language; e.g., "verbalized thoughts about death or suicide." A consensual definition of the global terms is arrived at during a period of training in the use of the scale through discussion by the members of the rating staff.

Bunny and Hamburg (1963) provide the following reliability data. Fourteen consecutive admissions to a psychiatric ward were rated on the 24 scales by three or more members of the nursing team for the first day of hospitalization. Intraclass correlations were significant for 23 out of 24 scales. For anxiety, the scale which concerns us in the present study, the intraclass correlation was .567 ($p < .001$). In the present study, interobservational reliability (r) between two nurse observers on the day shift was .81, based on 35 daily ratings of one patient.

Verbal samples. The six patients taped daily, 10-minute, free speech monologues during the entire duration of their hospitalization. Each morning subjects spoke for about 10 minutes about any of their experiences during the preceding day. Subjects were alone in a room when they made their recordings. For the purpose of the present study, speech samples for each patient were selected over a three-month period to represent eight high- and eight low-anxiety days. The data, then, consisted of 96 taped monologues, 48 high-anxious and 48 low-anxious.

Dependent variables. Speech Rate, Articulation Rate, Silence Quotient, the SDR, and the FPR were the dependent variables. The nature of the speech samples (i.e., time-limited free monologues) precluded the use of productivity and RT as dependent variables.

RESULTS

High-anxiety, rather than low-anxiety, speech was characterized by a high speech rate and low SQs (Table XI). There was no

TABLE XI.

**Patient'[1] Mean Scores on Verbal Indices
on High- and Low-Anxiety Days**

Verbal Indices	High-Anxiety Days	Low-Anxiety Days	F^2
Speech Rate	1.3161	.9723	18.64**
Articulation Rate	2.80	2.67	1.85
Silence Quotient	.52	.63	13.58**
Filled Pauses Ratio	.0141	.0121	1.00
Speech Disturbance Ratio	.0224	.0178	4.17*

[1]$N = 6$; [2]*Analysis of variance for repeated measures: $df = 1/84$.*
*$p < .05$; **$p < .005$.

significant difference between the two conditions in relation to Articulation Rate. It is, therefore, clear that the finding in regard to Speech Rate is a consequence of fewer long silent pauses (two seconds and more) during the high-anxiety than during the low-anxiety days. Anxiety was also associated with a significant increase in subjects' SDRs (Table XI).

These findings, like the results of our previous study, are most parsimoniously explained in terms of a drive or an activation-arousal approach to anxiety, although they fail to support the inverted U hypothesis. The activating effect of anxiety on speech tempo has now been documented in three different types of situations: the experimental arousal of anxiety, predispositional anxiety, and naturalistic variations in anxiety. Also, we can now say, on the basis of replicated findings, that anxiety arousal is associated with speech disturbances, as measured by the SDR. However, the relationship between predispositional anxiety, as measured by the MAS, and the SDR requires further clarification.

A GENERAL DISCUSSION

The preceding pages have presented in some detail the results of a number of experiments. Let us now discuss these findings in terms of the following general questions: 1. What are the effects of ambiguity in the initial interview? 2. What are the effects of anxiety on interviewee speech? 3. Can one distinguish between uncertainty and anxiety in terms of their extralinguistic correlates? A related question is: Can one explain the effects of ambiguity on interviewee speech in terms of anxiety? 4. What, if any, are the clinical implications of the findings on ambiguity and anxiety?

AMBIGUITY AND INTERVIEWEE
VERBAL BEHAVIOR

We have been able to demonstrate repeatedly that ambiguous interviewer remarks, in contrast to specific ones, are associated with more productive (i.e., longer) interviewee responses. This relationship is independent of the sequence of the interviewer's ambiguity-specificity level; i.e., it occurs when the interviewer begins the interview with ambiguous remarks and proceeds to specific ones, as well as when he reverses the procedure. Moreover, this relationship is not restricted to the first of a series of interviews, but persists in the second interview as well. Finally, this relationship between interviewer ambiguity and interviewee productivity has been replicated in an economically deprived population and in a group of schizophrenic patients (Hirschler and Nutt, 1967).

A second finding is that ambiguous interviewer remarks, in contrast to specific ones, are associated with a higher *ratio* of superficial to meaningful interviewee statements (or to be precise, interviewee clauses). We believe that this is so because ambiguous interviewer inquiries provide the interviewee with a choice of response alternatives, and hence with the opportunity to substitute super-ficialities for potentially anxiety-arousing material. It should be remembered that this finding notwithstanding, the total number of meaningful interviewee clauses is greater in response to ambiguous than to specific interviewer inquiries.

A third finding is that ambiguous interviewer remarks, in contrast to specific ones, are associated with less fluent and more hesitant interviewee responses.

No necessity was found to invoke affective processes, such as anxiety, in order to explain the effects of interviewer ambiguity on interviewee speech. In fact, our findings contraindicate such an explanation. First, there is the finding that the relationships between interviewer ambiguity and interviewee verbal behavior are in-dependent of the latter's anxiety level, either as measured by the Taylor MAS or as manipulated via topical focus. Second, the effects produced by interviewer ambiguity on interviewee speech are distinct from those produced by anxiety. Ambiguity is associated with a slowing down of interviewee's speech, but anxiety, if anything, is associated with an acceleration of speech. Anxiety arousal is associated with speech disruptions as measured by Mahl's SDR, while inter-viewer ambiguity level has no such effect.

The finding that ambiguous interviewer remarks, in contrast to specific ones, are associated with more productive interviewee responses, led us to conclude in earlier reports (Pope and Siegman, 1965; Siegman and Pope, 1965a, 1966b, 1966c) that ambiguity or uncertainty per se enhances productivity. We argued that this was the case because the subject who is uncertain about what to say tends to exhaust the various response alternatives at his disposal. We now know, however, that uncertainty is not always associated with an increase in productivity. First, we have the screen study and the follow-up investigation, in both of which a reduction in interviewer feedback (one way, presumably, of producing interviewee un-certainty) was associated with a decrease in interviewee productivity. These findings, then, suggest that as far as productivity is concerned, it is necessary to distinguish between message ambiguity and relationship ambiguity. While the former is associated with an increase in productivity, the latter is associated with a decrease in productivity. Second, is the TAT study (Siegman and Pope, 1965c) in which the high-ambiguity cards, rather than the low-ambiguity ones, were associated with low productivity. This finding, of course, needs replication. If it is sustained in subsequent studies, it would emphasize at the very least that situational factors are most important in determining the relationship between ambiguity, or uncertainty, on the one hand, and productivity, on the other hand.

The above, however, should not lead to abandoning uncertainty as an explanatory construct for our findings. Throughout these studies it was found that ambiguity, no matter what operations are used to achieve it, is associated with hesitant and non-fluent speech. The construct of uncertainty provides a parsimonious explanation for this relationship between ambiguity and verbal non-fluency. At the same time, there is evidence that the particular manifestations of non-fluency are situationally determined. For example, Goldman-Eisler (1961a) reports that uncertainty is associated with long silent pauses, but not with filled pauses (ahs). In our four studies on the effects of uncertainty on speech, interviewee uncertainty was always associated with an increase in the FPR, but only once with an increase in SQ. This discrepancy may be a result of situational or task differences. It will be recalled that in Goldman-Eisler's study, subjects were required to describe a series of cartoons and then to formulate their meaning. In this type of situation, a subject can be silent and decide what to say next without the risk of "losing the floor." In the interview, however, the subject does run this risk when he is silent. Consequently, if an interviewee is uncertain about what to say next, he will be more prone to slow down his speech rate and to fill in the silences with "ah" rather than lapse into long silent pauses.

ANXIETY AND SPEECH

Anxiety-arousing interviewer messages, like ambiguous interviewer remarks, are associated with productive interviewee responses. We believe that this is a genuine anxiety effect and not merely a result of the fact that in our study the anxiety-arousing interviewer messages had greater associative pull than the neutral ones. We believe this for the following two reasons. First, predispositional anxiety as measured by the Taylor MAS was also associated with productivity. Second, in a recently completed and as yet unpublished anxiety study, we used the identical interviewer messages in both an anxiety-arousing and a control interview and, again, anxiety arousal was associated with productive interviewee responses. Neither of these findings can be explained in terms of the differential associative pull hypothesis.

The anxiety studies reported here confirm Mahl's findings that anxiety arousal is associated with speech disruption as measured by the Non-ah or Speech Disturbance (SD) Ratio. Here, however, a distinction has to be made between anxiety arousal, or moment-to-moment fluctuations in anxiety level, on the one hand, and pre-dispositional anxiety as measured by the Taylor MAS, on the other hand. The latter was not associated with the SDR. A similar negative finding is reported by Kasl and Mahl (1965), although positive findings have also been obtained in our laboratory.

Finally, we found that anxiety, experimentally manipulated as well as predispositional, is associated with an acceleration in in-terviewee speech tempo. In contrast, ambiguity has the opposite effect. It should, therefore, be possible to distinguish between anxiety and ambiguity on the basis of their extralinguistic correlates. Nev-ertheless, as will now be shown, there are factors which complicate an easy distinction between anxiety and ambiguity on the basis of their verbal correlates.

As pointed out earlier, our findings on the effects of anxiety on speech are most parsimoniously explained in terms of a drive or an activation-arousal approach to anxiety. Exponents of the latter have suggested that the effects of anxiety are not monotonic, but take the shape of an inverted U (Duffy, 1962; Malmo, 1966). According to this hypothesis, one can expect that a very high level of anxiety arousal would be associated with low productivity and slow speech. It should be noted that some of our data are inconsistent with this hypothesis. It will be recalled that in the naturalistic study we used hospitalized patients and compared speech samples obtained during their most and least anxious days. It is reasonable to assume that this study tapped relatively high-anxiety levels, and yet the results were similar to those obtained with low anxiety arousal. But even if our data do not support the hypothesized inverted U effect, it is clear that certain factors can attenuate, and perhaps even reverse, the relationships which were noted in our anxiety studies. Thus Levin and his associates (1960) found that subjects with high audience anxiety are less productive in front of an audience than in a two-person situation. This is probably so because the less a subject speaks, the more quickly he brings to an end the anxiety-arousing situation. If a subject can terminate or even reduce his anxiety by speaking less rather than more, he is likely to do so. A similar reversal may occur in relation to the temporal indices. There is evidence that repression or suppression is associated with silent pauses (Goldenberg and Auld, 1964; Siegman and Pope, 1965b). Consequently, if a person is made sufficiently anxious so that defensive operations (such as repression or suppression) are called into play, there is likely to be a slowing down rather than an acceleration of speech. True, no evidence for such a reversal was found in our naturalistic study, despite the subjects' relatively high-anxiety levels; but then, these were hospitalized patients who may not show the usual defensive reactions against anxiety.

In conclusion, then, we find that in "normal" subjects low anxiety arousal is associated with productivity, speech disruptions, and an accelerated speech tempo. In patients, even relatively high-anxiety levels seem to have a similar effect. Further research, however, is necessary in order to ascertain the effects of high-anxiety arousal in non-patient populations.

CLINICAL IMPLICATIONS

Some of our findings have obvious clinical implications. For example, they suggest that productive interviewee responses are more likely to follow ambiguous rather than specific interviewer remarks, and mildly anxiety-arousing interviewer messages rather than neutral ones. Of course, these findings will not come as a surprise to the clinician for he appears to observe them on a pragmatic basis in his interview practice. Somewhat more of a surprise may be the finding that from the point of view of interviewee productivity it does not matter whether the interview is started with specific or with ambiguous inquiries.

These findings have other less obvious, but perhaps more important, clinical implications. It has been said that affective processes are encoded or expressed primarily in the extralinguistic channel of speech (Pittenger, 1958). This view is widely shared by psychotherapists and by interviewers in general. Sullivan (1954), for example, has noted that "much attention may profitably be paid to the telltale aspects of intonation, rate of speech, difficulty in enunciation. . . ." Clinicians usually interpret such changes in the extralinguistic channel as telltale signs of anxiety and its defense mechanisms. If, however, our research findings contain a single important implication for the practicing clinician, it is that such changes in the extralinguistic channel do not necessarily indicate that the speaker is anxious, or that he is defending against anxiety, or that he is otherwise affectively aroused. The slowing down of speech, or hesitant speech, or silent pauses may simply reflect the speaker's uncertainty associated with cognitive decision-making. Of course, even those changes in the extralinguistic channel which are, in fact, associated with affective arousal may reflect cognitive processes. Thus, the speech disturbances associated with anxiety may result from the fact that anxiety arousal complicates the decision-making process involved in the generating of sentences. However, other extralinguistic correlates of anxiety, such as accelerated speech, are probably a direct effect of affect arousal.

While it is important to point out that the extralinguistic channel is not restricted to the encoding or expression of affect, it should also be remembered that in our studies anxiety arousal was associated with a specific pattern of extralinguistic indices, distinguishable from that associated with interviewee uncertainty.

Among clinicians, it is widely assumed that anxiety is associated with speech disturbances, silent pauses, hesitations; i.e., that anxiety has a disruptive effect on speech. In part, this view may be based on the implicit assumption that since anxiety is "bad," all its consequences must be "bad." Our findings, however, consistently show that anxiety, at least mild anxiety arousal, has a facilitating effect on speech.

References

BORDIN, E. S.   Ambiguity as a therapeutic variable. *J. Consult. Psychol.*, 1955, **19**, 9-15.

BRENNER, M. S., FELDSTEIN, S., and JAFFE, J.   The contributions of statistical uncertainty and test anxiety to speech disruption. *J. Verbal Learn. Verbal Behav.*, 1965, **4**, 300-05.

BUNNY, W. E. and HAMBURG, D. A.   Methods for reliable longitudinal observation of behavior. *Arch. Gen. Psychiat.*, 1963, **9**, 280-94.

COHEN, J.   Some statistical issues in psychological research. In B. Wolman (Ed.), *Handbook of Clinical Psychology.* McGraw-Hill, New York, 1965.

DAVIDS, A. H. and ERICKSEN, C. W.   The relationship of manifest anxiety to association productivity and intellectual attainment. *J. Consult. Psychol.*, 1955, **19**, 219-22.

DIBNER, A. S.   The relationship between ambiguity and anxiety in a clinical interview. Unpublished doctoral dissertation, University of Michigan, 1953.

DOLLARD, J. and AULD, F., Jr.   *Scoring Human Motives: A Manual.* Yale University Press, New Haven, 1959.

DUFFY, E.   *Activation and Behavior.* Wiley, New York, 1962.

GOLDENBERG, G. H. and AULD, F., Jr.   Equivalence of silence to resistance. *J. Consult. Psychol.*, 1964, **28**, 476.

GOLDMAN-EISLER, F.   The determinants of the rate of speech and their mutual relations. *J. Psychosom Res.*, 1956, **2**, 137-43.

GOLDMAN-EISLER, F.   A comparative study of two hesitation phenomena. *Language and Speech*, 1961, **4**, 18-26. (a)

GOLDMAN-EISLER, F.   Hesitation and information in speech. In C. Cherry (Ed.), *Information Theory.* Butterworths, London, 1961. (b)

GOLDMAN-EISLER, F.   The significance of changes in the rate of articulation. *Language and Speech*, 1961, **4**, 171-4. (c)

GOLDMAN-EISLER, F.   Discussion and further comments. In E. H. Lennberg (Ed.), *New Directions in the Study of Language.* MIT Press, Cambridge, Mass., 1964. Pp. 109-30. (a)

GOLDMAN-EISLER, F.   Hesitation, information, and levels of speech production. In A. V. S. de Reuck and M. O'Connor (Eds.), *Disorders of Language.* Churchill, London, 1964. Pp. 96-111. (b)

HIRSCHLER, H. and NUTT, J. W.   Interviewer specificity and client productivity: Schizophrenic and culturally deprived populations. Unpublished M. S. W. dissertation, University of Maryland School of Social Work, 1967.

HOLLINGSHEAD, A. B.   Two-factor index of social position. Unpublished manuscript.

JAFFE, J.   The comparability of small speech segments of different lengths in the calculation of the Type-Token-Ratio. Unpublished manuscript, 1956.

JOHNSON, W.   Studies in language behavior: I. A program of research. *Psychol. Monog.*, 1944, **56**, 1-15.

KANFER, F. H.   Effect of a warning signal preceding the noxious stimulus on verbal rate and heart rate. *J. Exp. Psychol.*, 1958, **55**, 73-86.

KANFER, F. H.   Verbal rate, eye blinks, and content in structured psychiatric interviews. *J. Abnorm. Soc. Psychol.*, 1960, **61**, 341-7.

KASL, S. V. and MAHL, G. F.   The relationship of disturbances and hesitations in spontaneous speech to anxiety. *J. Personality Soc. Psychol.*, 1965, **1**, 425-33.

KENNY, D. T.   Transcendence indices, extent of personality factors in fantasy responses, and the ambiguity of TAT cards. *J. Consult. Psychol.*, 1954, **18**, 345-8.

KENNY, D. T.   A theoretical and research appraisal of stimulus factors in the TAT. In J. Kagan and G. S. Lesser (Eds.), *Contemporary Issues in Thematic Apperceptive Methods.* Thomas, Springfield, Ill., 1961. Pp. 288-310.

KENNY, D. T. and BIJOU, S. W.   Ambiguity of pictures and extent of personality factors in fantasy responses. *J. Consult. Psychol.*, 1953, **17**, 283-8.

LENNARD, H. L. and BERNSTEIN, A.   *The Anatomy of Psychotherapy.* Columbia University Press, New York, 1960.

LEVIN, H., BALDWIN, A. L., GALLWAY, M., and PAIVIO, A. Audience stress, personality, and speech. *J. Abnorm. Soc. Psychol.*, 1960, **61**, 469-73.

MACLAY, H. and OSGOOD, C. E. Hesitation phenomena in spontaneous English speech. *Word*, 1959, **15**, 19-44.

MAHL, G. F. Disturbances and silences in patient's speech in psychotherapy. *J. Abnorm. Soc. Psychol.*, 1956, **53**, 1-15.

MAHL, G. F. Measures of two expressive aspects of patient's speech in two psychotherapeutic interviews. In L. A. Gottshalk (Ed.), *Comparative Psycholinguistic Analysis of Two Psychotherapeutic Interviews.* International University Press, New York, 1961.

MAHL, G. F. and SCHULZE, G. Psychological research in the extralinguistic area. In T. A. Sebeok (Ed.), *Approaches to Semiotics.* Mouton, The Hague, 1964. Pp. 51-124.

MALMO, R. B. Studies of anxiety: Some clinical origins of the activation concept. In C. D. Spielberger (Ed.), *Anxiety and Behavior.* Academic Press, New York, 1966. Pp. 158-78.

MATARAZZO, J. D., WIENS, A. N., and SASLOW, G. Studies in interview speech behavior. In L. Krasner and L. P. Ullman (Eds.), *Research in Behavior Modification: New Developments and Clinical Implications.* Holt, Rinehart & Winston, New York, 1965. Pp. 179-210.

MURSTEIN, B. I. *Theory and Research in Projective Techniques: Emphasizing the TAT.* Wiley, New York, 1963.

MURSTEIN, B. I. A normative study of TAT ambiguity. *J. Projec. Tech. Personality Assess.*, 1964, **28**, 210-18.

MURSTEIN, B. I. Sex differences in TAT ambiguity, hostility, and projection. *J. Genet. Psychol.*, 1966, **108**, 71-80.

PITTENGER, R. E. Linguistic analysis of tone of voice in communication of affect. *Psychiat. Res. Repts.*, 1958, **8**, 41-54.

POPE, B. and SIEGMAN, A. W. The effect of therapist verbal activity level and specificity on patient productivity and speech disturbance in the initial interview. *J. Consult. Psychol.*, 1962, **26**, 489.

POPE, B. and SIEGMAN, A. W. Interviewer specificity and topical focus in relation to interviewee productivity. *J. Verbal Learn. Verbal Behav.*, 1965, **4**, 188-92.

RIESMAN, D. *Abundance for What?* Doubleday, Garden City, N.Y., 1964.

SIEGMAN, A. W. and POPE, B. An empirical scale for the measurement of therapist specificity in the initial interview. *Psychol. Repts.*, 1962, **11**, 515-20.

SIEGMAN, A. W. and POPE, B. Effects of question specificity and anxiety-arousing messages on verbal fluency in the initial interview. *J. Personality Soc. Psychol.*, 1965, **4**, 188-92. (a)

SIEGMAN, A. W. and POPE, B. Personality variables associated with productivity and verbal fluency in the initial interview. *Proc. 73rd Conv. APA*, 1965, pp. 273-4. (b)

SIEGMAN, A. W. and POPE, B. Stimulus factors in the TAT: Effects of ambiguity on verbal fluency, productivity, and GSR. In *Comptes Rendus* (Proceedings of VI International Congress on the Rorschach and Projective Methods). Societe Francaise du Rorschach et des Methodes Projectives, Paris; 1965. Pp. 223-8. (c)

SIEGMAN, A. W. and POPE, B. Ambiguity and verbal fluency in the TAT. *J. Consult. Psychol.*, 1966, **30**, 239-45. (a)

SIEGMAN, A. W. and Pope, B. The effect of interviewer ambiguity-specificity and topical focus on interviewee vocabulary diversity. *Language and Speech*, 1966, **9**, 242-9. (b)

SIEGMAN, A. W. and POPE, B. The effect of interviewer specificity and topical focus on the predictability of interviewee's response. *Proc. 74th A. Conv. APA*, 1966, 195-6. (c)

SIEGMAN, A. W., POPE, B., and BLASS, T. The effects of interviewer status and duration of interviewer messages on interviewee productivity. *Proc. 77th A. Conv. APA*, 1969, 541-2.

SPENCE, J. T. and SPENCE, K. The effects of anxiety on behavior. In C. D. Spielberger (Ed.), *Anxiety and Behavior*. Academic Press, New York, 1966.
SULLIVAN, H. S. *The Psychiatric Interview*. Norton, New York, 1954.

Chapter 4

Relationship and Verbal Behavior in the Initial Interview[1]

Benjamin Pope and Aron Wolfe Siegman

THIS CHAPTER deals with the findings of three investigations designed as experimental analogues of the initial interview. In these studies the initial interview is regarded as a communication system (Lennard and Bernstein, 1960) consisting of two components, designated "informational exchange" and "relationship." Research findings pertaining to interviewer variables relevant to "informational exchange" (i.e., ambiguity and anxiety-arousal effect of interviewer's communication) are discussed elsewhere in this book (Chapter 3). Here, the focus is on the effects of certain aspects of relationship on the interviewee's verbal behavior.

The usage of the term "relationship" is varied, and often ambiguous. The probability of adequately sampling its different definitions in three experimental studies is very low indeed. In reporting the present studies it is, therefore, important to specify, as accurately as possible, the relationship variables used.

In general, it would seem that the identity of the variable that one might choose as a relationship dimension is determined, in part, by the sort of clinical or research endeavor in which one is engaged. If the view of the initial interview as a communication system has any heuristic value, it should compel us to search for relationship variables that are associated with communication in small groups and, more particularly, dyadic solutions. Working with small groups, Newcomb (1956) found the mutual *attractiveness* of members of a group for each other to be a significant relationship-maintaining force. Indeed, he spoke of the "motivational-affective aspects of attraction . . ." as

[1]Supported in part by NIMH, Research Grant MHO 4287-07, and in part by Vocational Rehabilitation Administration Research Grant VRA-1728.

dynamic influences within a relationship, reinforcing communication. To Newcomb (1956), reciprocal attraction is rewarding to the parties concerned. For example, if A is attracted to B, A is rewarded if B reciprocates this attraction. Moreoever, such a situation of mutual reinforcement is likely to promote communication between A and B.

INTERVIEWEE ATTRACTION TO INTERVIEWER

In the first of the three relationship studies included in the present chapter, it was anticipated that there would be a positive correlation between interviewee attraction to interviewer and both productivity and verbal fluency. The measure of attraction was Libo's Picture Impression Test (Libo, 1956), a projective technique resembling the TAT, for evoking thematic expressions of feeling toward the therapist and the therapy process. These are scored on the basis of a scheme that purports to measure "the strength (attractiveness) of the patient-therapist relationship by capitalizing on the oft-noted sensitivity of projective techniques to the social situation in which they are administered" (Libo, 1957, p. 36). With patient-therapist attraction defined and measured in this way, Libo found a significant relationship between the strength of patient attraction toward the therapist in an outpatient clinic after the initial interview and his subsequent return for treatment.

The data for the present study were collected during the course of conducting an investigation based on an experimental analogue of the initial interview (Pope and Siegman, 1965; Siegman and Pope, 1965). Fifty junior and senior nursing students, all female with ages ranging from 20 to 22, participated as interviewees in the experimental interview. Each S was given the Libo Picture Impression Test, pre- and postinterview. In this way, both a base level of attraction to the interviewer and the postinterview increase or decrease of attraction over the base level were obtained for each S.

The pre- to postinterview change in attraction score was assumed to be a consequence of the interview experience. In order to determine the association between relationship and verbal communication, correlations between attraction score change and the dependent variables utilized in this study were obtained.

Although these variables are defined in detail elsewhere in this book (Siegman and Pope, 1968), convenience requires brief reference to them at this point.

Productivity: The measure of productivity is a simple word count of the interviewee's utterances.

Indices of Verbal Fluency: The Mahl Ah and Non-Ah (Mahl, 1959), ratios were used precisely as defined and scored by Mahl. The *Ah* ratio for a S was determined by dividing the number of expressions of "Ah" and allied hesitation phenomena, by the total number of words uttered. The *Non-Ah* ratio was similarly calculated; it included such categories of flustered speech as sentence corrections, sentence incompletions, repetitions, stutters, stammers, intruding incoherent sounds, tongue slips, and the omission of words or parts of words. Both Ah hesitations and Non-Ah speech disturbances were scored from verbatim transcripts, while simultaneously listening to the tape recordings of the interviews.

To obtain a measure of interscorer reliability, three interviews were scored independently by one of the authors and a research assistant, with a resulting percentage of agreement (Dollard and Auld, 1959, pp. 18-19) of 89 for Ah hesitations and 74 for Non-Ah speech disturbances. After the reliability determination, all remaining interviews were scored by the research assistant.

In addition, three temporal measures were used, i.e., silent pauses, Reaction Time, and Articulation Rate. To obtain measures of these variables the tapes of the interviews were played back and the required time readings were made with a stop watch. The Reaction Time score was a mean of the duration (in seconds) of intervals between interviewer's remarks and the interviewee's responses. Two seconds was the minimum criterion for a silent pause. The durations of all silent pauses for a S were summed and then divided by her total response time to obtain a Silence Quotient. The Articulation Rate of each S was the number of words she uttered per second of speaking time, i.e., total response time minus silent pauses. Interscorer reliability (r) for reaction time, total time of response, and silent pauses, the basic data from which all temporal indices are derived, are respectively .97, .99, and .96.

In previous studies (Siegman and Pope, 1965; Siegman and Pope, 1968), frequent Ahs, long durations of silent pauses, and slow Articulation Rates were found to be associated with uncertainty; frequent Non-Ahs (speech disturbances), and fast Articulation Rates, with anxiety.

The anticipated positive relationship between attraction score increase and productivity did not occur $(r = .054)$. However, a significant negative correlation between attraction score increase and Ah did emerge $(r = -.28; p < .05)$. Thus subjects with large increases in attraction scores have low Ah ratios; i.e., low indices of hesitation. In a previous factor analysis of the dependent variables, both Reaction Time and Silence Quotient occurred together in a single factor. A substantial negative correlation between attraction score increase and this factor ($r = -.38$; $p < .01$), (scored by summating Reaction Time and Silence Quotient) indicates that interviewees with large increments in attraction score manifest few pauses in speech during the interview. Thus the expected correlation between interviewee attraction to interviewer and interviewee fluency in the sense of low hesitation was obtained.

Other interpersonal variables applicable both to interviewer and interviewee have been investigated in a series of studies dealing with the interview relationship. Thus Lorr (1965) constructed an inventory designed to identify the main dimensions of clients' perceptions of their therapists. The 65 variables of this inventory were intercorrelated and factor analyzed with the following five correlated factors resulting: understanding, accepting, authoritarian, critical-hostile, and independence-encouraging. More parsimonious is a basic, two-dimensional system that occurs repeatedly in four studies or groups of studies summarized by Foa (1961). In one of these dealing with individuals in small groups (Carter, 1954), two of the three factors that emerged recurred in the remaining investigations discussed by Foa. These were called "achievement" (the behaviors of the individual related to his efforts to stand out from others and individually achieve personal goals) and "sociability" (the behaviors of the individual related to satisfying social relationships with others). In a second study, Borgatta, Cottrell, and Mann (1958) analyzed the ranked scores of members of small groups of graduate students on 16 personality traits and 24 behavior categories, and obtained two major factors, which they called "individual assertiveness" and "sociability." In a group of studies conducted by Schaefer (1959) dealing with the social and emotional behavior of mothers toward their children, there were again two major dimensions. These were contained within a circumplex model, and were designated "control-autonomy" and "love-hostility." And finally, there is the circular ordering of interpersonal behaviors around the two basic dimensions of "dominance-submission" and "hostility-affection" by Freedman and his associates (1951). Thus the group of studies reviewed by Foa (1961) all have one affect dimension, variously referred to as "love-hostility" or "sociability," and another called "control-autonomy," "dominance-submission," or "achievement."

In a factor analysis of interviewee postinterview ratings of the interviewer, carried out by Pope and Siegman (1967), two factors analogous to those referred to above were found. These were called "warmth" and "competence" or "status."

TABLE I.

Rotated Factor Matrix (Orthogonal) of Interviewees' Postinterview Ratings of Their Interviewer

Variables	I	II	h^2
Intelligent—Unintelligent	-.18	.47	.25
Warm—Cold	-.72	.11	.53
Strong—Weak	-.01	.43	.19
Sympathetic—Unsympathetic	-.61	-.13	.39
Accepting—Rejecting	-.52	.32	.37
Active—Passive	-.22	.16	.73
Understanding—Lacks Understanding	-.73	.09	.54
Pleasant—Unpleasant	-.61	.22	.42
Tense—Relaxed	.14	-.39	.17
Slow—Fast	.04	-.18	.03
Comfortable—Uncomfortable	.03	.64	.41
Competent—Incompetent	-.40	.62	.54
Confident—Lacks Confidence	-.01	.53	.28
a^2	2.33	1.88	4.21
% Total Variance	10.0	21.5	31.5

Note—Factor analysis by the Principal Axis method with Varimax rotation.

The positive pole of the first factor describes an interviewer perceived as warm, sympathetic, understanding, and pleasant; the positive pole of the second, an interviewer perceived as intelligent, strong, comfortable, competent, and confident. The relationship dimension of warmth has been selected as the major independent variable in the second study that follows immediately; and that of competence or status, in the last.

INTERVIEWER WARMTH

Although there is a widely-shared belief that interviewer warmth promotes interviewee communication, there are few experimental tests of this belief. In one (Heller, Davis, and Myers, 1966), the results were negative, and in another (Reece and Whitman, 1962), positive. It should be noted, however, that the latter study dealt with verbal conditioning rather than verbal communication within the interview. Nevertheless, it was anticipated that the present investigation would demonstrate that interviewer warmth facilitates verbal communication by increasing verbal output, activating speech in other ways, reducing hesitation, speech disturbance, and resistiveness.

In addition to the dependent variables used in the first of the present group of three studies, three new scales (designated Non-Resistiveness, Resistiveness, and Superficiality) were used for the first time in the present study. When these scales were devised, the work of other authors who have investigated resistiveness was reviewed (Ashby *et al.*, 1957; Colby, 1961; Gillespie, 1953; Haigh, 1949; Isaacs and Haggard, 1966; Madison, 1961; Speisman, 1959). Some aspects of their work are incorporated in the three scales. *Non-Resistiveness* is attributed to all clauses in which the interviewee introspects about herself evaluatively, speaks freely about deviations from normal behavior, about her own feelings, or in all of these ways about some other significant person. *Resistive* clauses include those in which communication about one's problems are minimized, denied, qualified, weakened, excessively justified, or blocked, and others in which there is a change from a relevant to an irrelevant topic or in which the interviewee is critical of the interviewer. Among *superficial* clauses are those that are objective, trivial, or factual, rather than psychological in orientation.

While the major objective in the present study was the investigation of interviewer warmth, there was an additional attempt to replicate and extend previous results pertaining to interviewer specificity (Pope and Siegman, 1962; Pope and Siegman, 1965; Siegman and Pope, 1965). This aspect of the investigations is discussed in another part of this volume (Siegman and Pope, 1969).

Hypothesis. Warm interviews are associated with higher productivity, less resistiveness, less hesitation and greater fluency than cold interviews.

METHOD

Subjects. Thirty-two junior and senior nursing students, all female with ages ranging from 20 to 22, participated as interviewees. They were volunteers who were paid for their participation.

Warm-cold manipulation. The warm-cold manipulation was achieved by arousing contrasting warm and cold expectancies regarding interviewer behavior before the two interviews in which each S participated, and varying the interviewer's actual behavior to accord with the aroused expectancies. Each S had one warm and one cold interview. Before the warm interview, she was told by the experimenter that she would be interviewed by a "warm and accepting" person; before the cold interview, she was led to expect a "cold and distant" person. Although the words spoken by the interviewers were precisely prescribed, they were both trained to speak in contrasting expressive manners for warm and cold interviews. During a warm interview the interviewer smiled, nodded her head (taking care not to reinforce any particular class of content), and spoke warmly. During a cold interview she spoke unsmilingly; she did not nod her head; and she kept her voice drab and cold. In both conditions the interviewer sat behind a desk and took care not to gesture with her arms and hands, since such forms of expression would be difficult to fit into the warm-cold manipulation.

Experimental design. The main effects under study are the warm-cold dimension, and high vs. low specificity (Siegman and Pope, 1968). The interviewers were two female clinical psychology interns in their mid-twenties.

TABLE II.

Experimental Interviews in Warm-Cold Study

Interview A1

1. Tell me something, anything you wish, about your father.
2. Now tell me something, anything, about your brother, X.
3. Tell me with which parent you got along better.
4. (Use one, as appropriate)
   ____ Has your father been very strict with you?
   ____ Did your father do many things with you?
   I'd like now to talk with you about your school history, O.K.? *(Pause)*
5. Tell me something, anything, about your school before college.
6. Now, something about your first two years in college.
7. Which school, elementary, junior high, high, did you prefer?
8. Which of these schools had the best library facilities?

Interview B1

1. Tell me something, anything you wish, about your mother.
2. Now tell me something, anything, about your sister, X.
3. Please tell me with which parent you were closest.
4. (Use one, as appropriate)
   ____ Has your mother been very strict with you?
   ____ Did your mother do many things with you?
   I'd like now to talk with you about your school history, O.K. *(Pause)*
5. Tell me something, anything, about the elementary school you attended.
6. Now tell me something about the School of Nursing.
7. Did you have many extracurricular interests before college?
8. Did your pre-college schools have good gym facilities?

To counterbalance specificity sequence, there were two interview series designated A1-B1 and A2-B2. The first followed a low specificity-high specificity sequence for each topic; the second, a high specificity-low specificity sequence. In all other respects both series were identical. The duration variable in the interviewer's remarks (Matarazzo *et al.*, 1963) was controlled by making all remarks eight or nine words long.

The design is counterbalanced for warm-cold sequence, specificity sequence, and interviewer sequence. Each subject was his own control with reference to the interviewer variables under study; their sequence effects, however, had to be evaluated between subgroups. The data were submitted to an analysis of variance for repeated measurements on the same subjects (Winer, 1962).

Interview procedure. All interviews were tape recorded. The equipment consisted of two microphones in floor stands placed in front of the interviewer and the interviewee, and connected with a Revox stereo tape recorder in an adjoining room. After the warm-cold induction called for by the experimental design, the interviewee was taken into the interview room by one of the *E*s. She returned to the *E*'s office after the end of the interview. There, in a brief session she completed a postinterview rating scale recording her attitudes toward and perceptions of the interviewer and responded to an adaptation[2] of Pictures II and III of the Libo Picture Impressions Test.

Scoring of dependent variables. Non-resistiveness, Resistiveness, and Superficiality indices are actually percentages of the total number of clauses scored according to Dollard and Auld (1959). For each category, a percentage score was calculated with the number of clauses in the category as the numerator and the total number of clauses as the denominator. Each clause was assigned to one category only. After an initial training period the two investigators were able to distribute the clauses among the three categories with adequate interscorer reliability, achieving a percentage of agreement of 87.7 percent, based on three interviews including 106 clauses.

The scoring of the remaining dependent variables, i.e., productivity, Ah hesitation, Non-Ah speech disturbances, Reaction Time, Articulation Rate, and silent pauses, has been described above in the section dealing with the attraction study. Scoring reliability data for these variables have also been given.

---

[2]Pictures II and III of the female series were redrawn to substitute a female interviewer for the male interviewer in the original set.

RESULTS

The warm-cold manipulation. The effectiveness of the warm-cold manipulation is noted in postinterview ratings made by interviewees on 10 semantic-differential type bipolar scales (t tests ps all $< .01$). They perceived the interviewers in the warm condition as significantly warmer, more accepting, more understanding, pleasanter, more responsive, friendlier, and more interested than those in the cold condition. They liked the warm interviewers better, felt that they were liked better by them, and were considerably happier at the prospect of the interviewers becoming their therapists.

The adaptation of the Libo Picture Impressions Test was scored for interviewee attraction to interviewer. Scoring agreement between the senior author and a research assistant[3] for positive and negative attraction scores was at the level of 82.33 percent based on 60 stories. In an analysis of variance for repeated measures (Winer, 1962) with reference to the Libo attraction scores, the main effect of warm-cold was in the expected direction (i.e., greater interviewee attraction to warm, rather than cold, interviewers), but attained only a significance

TABLE III.

Mean Scores for Warm and Cold Interviews

	Mean Words per Response	Resistiveness Mean % per Response	Superficiality Mean % per Response	Mean Ah Ratio per Response	Mean Non-Ah Ratio per Response	Mean Reac. T. (Secs.) per Response
Warm	85.60	22.25	8.12	1.57	1.52	2.21
Cold	59.20	21.44	8.90	1.61	1.69	2.55
p	$< .005$	N.S.	N.S.	N.S.	N.S.	N.S.

level of $p < .10$. While the attraction scores provide weaker proof of the success of the warm-cold manipulation than the postinterview ratings, the congruence between the two adds emphasis to the evidence provided separately by each.

Effects of the warm-cold manipulation. The results of a series of analyses of variance for repeated measures on the same subjects are summarized in the following two tables.

The significant main effect of the warm-cold variable on pro-

---

[3]We appreciate the scoring and computational assistance of Mrs. Susana Cossio and Miss Roslyn Segal.

ductivity (Table III), (F-ratio=13.74; df=1/29; $p < .005$; ε^4=.55), can be understood only when its interaction with warm-cold sequence is considered (Table IV). The prediction that warm interviews would be associated with greater productivity than cold interviews has, indeed, been borne out, but only when the first, rather than the second, in the sequence of two interviews was warm. In fact, the warm interview, when first, evoked significantly more productivity than the warm interview, when second. Apparently the inhibiting effect of the cold interview, when first, persisted into the second interview. The other interaction demonstrates an additive effect between warmth and low specificity in promoting productivity (Table IV). Thus the warm-low specificity interview segments were

TABLE IV.

Interactions Between Warm-Cold and Other Variables

	Productivity [a]						Non-Ah [b]		
	Warm First	Cold First	p^c	Low Sp.	High Sp.	p^c	Low Sp.	High Sp.	p^c
Warm	102.28	68.93	< .005	124.46	46.74	< .005	1.83	1.21	< .005
Cold	62.94	58.58	N.S.	85.18	36.36	< .005	1.54	1.85	N.S.
p^c	< .005	N.S.		.005	N.S.		N.S.	< .005	

[a] *Number of words per response in designated interview or interview segments.*
[b] *Mean Non-Ah percentage per response in designated interview segment.*
[c] *Significance level on basis of Scheffe's Test for Multiple Comparisons (Edwards, 1960, 154-6).*

the longest, while cold-high specificity segments, the shortest.

    The interaction effect on the Non-Ah ratio (Table IV) permits only a tenuous interpretation. Since Non-Ah has been associated with anxiety, it was expected to be higher when the interviewer was cold rather than warm. This result did, indeed, occur under high specificity conditions. The reason for its failure to occur under conditions of low specificity is not, at the moment, apparent.

    In brief, the hypothesis of this study has been confirmed with

[4]Epsilon is an unbiased estimate of the correlation ratio, eta and may be computed by the formula.

$$\varepsilon = \sqrt{\frac{(F\text{-}1)\ df1}{(F)\ df1 + df2}}$$

where: $df1$ = degrees of freedom associated with the numerator of the F ratio; $df2$ = degrees of freedom associated with the denominator of the F ratio. In terms of its magnitude, ε may be interpreted in much the same way as the product moment, r. Unlike r, ε does not present a linear relationship (Cohen, 1964).

reference to productivity and the Non-Ah ratio, an index of verbal fluency.

Intercorrelations of dependent variables. The intercorrelations in Table V are based on low specificity segments only, since response length in these segments is greater than in high specificity segments and, therefore, more productive of reliable speech indices.

Out of thirty-six intercorrelations, eight were significant at the .05 level or better. With few exceptions the intercorrelations are consistent

TABLE V.

**Intercorrelations of Dependent Variables
(Low Specificity Scores) Warm-Cold Study**

	(1) No. Words	(2) Non-Res.	(3) Res.	(4) Superf.	(5) Ah.	(6) Non-Ah	(7) Reac. T.	(8) Sil. Quot.	(9) Art. Rate
1. No Words		-.177	.189	-.035	.034	.361°	-.141	.216	.409°°
2. Non-Res.			-.435°°	-.393°	-.096	-.401°	-.242	-.307	-.103
3. Res.				-.656°°	.183	.357°	.341	.048	.056
4. Superf.					-.109	-.023	-.155	.208	.032
5. Ah						.104	-.059	.289	-.343
6. Non-Ah							.293	.381°	-.007
7. Reac. T.								.304	-.157
8. Sil. Quot.									.001
9. Artic. Rate									

$°p<.05$, $r = .349$; $°°p<.02$, $r = .409$.

with those obtained in previous studies (Pope and Siegman, 1966; Siegman and Pope, 1965). One of these exceptions was a significantly negative correlation between productivity and Silence Quotient, previously obtained (Pope and Siegman, 1966) but not replicated in the present study. Another exception was a significantly positive correlation between Non-Ah and Silence Quotient in the present, but not in the earlier data.

DISCUSSION

The impact of interviewer warmth is noted in a gross index of interviewee responsiveness—productivity—and in the greater fluency of interviewee speech (low Non-Ah Ratios). The latter finding obtains only under conditions of high specificity. Thus interviewer warmth appears to be a basic condition for a high level of interviewee verbalization. However, the critical importance of first impressions is an equally important finding. When the first interview was cold, rather than warm, it spread its inhibiting effect into the second interview, largely nullifying the effect of the interviewer's warmth. That interviewer's coldness was experienced by the interviewee as stressful was noted in its tendency to increase the rate of interviewee speech disturbance.

INTERVIEWER STATUS

The second basic dimension of relationship that concerns us in the present group of studies is that of interviewer status in the sense of rank and experience. As in the case of interviewer warmth, experimental findings are in short supply. But there is a widely-shared body of opinion that people are more willing to communicate with an interviewer whom they perceive as a competent expert, rather than an unskilled novice. Thus Maccoby and Maccoby (1954) emphasize role as an important element in a relationship situation and status as an important dimension of role. They remark: "In general we know that people are more anxious to communicate to those above them in the hierarchy than to those below them. . . . While upper-class respondents feel they have little to gain by expressing their opinions to an interviewer, lower-class respondents are pleased to be consulted. The *content* of the communication, of course, will be affected by the status relationships: The person of lower status will be motivated to present himself in a favorable light to someone who might be in a position to influence his future" (p. 462).

From the preceding quotation it is apparent that there is some hazard in attributing too much generality to the dimension of status as a facilitator of interviewee communication. The interviewee may, indeed, be more willing to cooperate with a high status, rather than a low status person. But he may, at the same time, be more guarded, more concerned with making a good impression. If the content of that which he is willing to communicate is likely to be affected by the status of the interviewer, it is to be expected that the relevance to the interviewee of the context in which the status differential occurs will be an important factor. Thus a person living in a slum area in the inner city, being interviewed by a graduate student from a school of social work, will be both reinforced and inhibited in different content areas than a graduate student interviewed by a senior member of the faculty. This distinction would probably obtain even if both interviewers played no part in the power structure within which the interviewee finds himself.

Because these contingencies limiting the general effect of interviewer status are still largely speculative, they were not included in the major predictive hypothesis of the present study.

Hypothesis 1. High status interviewers elicit greater interviewee productivity, fluency, and less resistiveness than low status interviewers.

Duration of interviewer utterance has been included as a second independent variable in the present study. This variable has been investigated in a number of studies dealing with interviewer and interviewee *synchrony*, i.e., the covariation of interviewee and interviewer verbal behavior along specified dimensions (Webb, this volume). According to the synchrony model, the interviewee increases or decreases the level of a definite aspect of his speech in direct relation to analogous increases or decreases on the part of the interviewer. Synchrony relations of this kind have been found for duration of utterance (Matarazzo, Weitman, Saslow, and Wiens, 1963), loudness (Black, 1959), Articulation Rate (Webb, 1969), precision of articulation (Tolhurst, 1955), latency of response (Matarazzo and Wiens, 1967), and duration of silences (Jaffe, 1966). Of the preceding variables, duration of interviewee utterances has been the one selected here for evaluation with reference to the synchrony effect. In the present study there is an investigation of duration of interviewer remarks as an independent variable and in interaction with interviewer status. The synchrony model permits a prediction for the main effect of duration of interviewer utterances.

Hypothesis 2. Long interviewer remarks rather than short ones will be associated with greater interviewee productivity.

One explanation offered for synchrony behavior is that it is a form of modeling (Matarazzo and Wiens, 1967). If so, one should expect a greater synchrony effect when the model is of high rather than low status (Flanders, 1968). In the terms of the present study, one should, therefore, expect an interaction effect of interviewer duration and status on productivity.

Hypothesis 3. The synchrony relationship between interviewer duration and interviewee productivity[5] will be more pronounced in high rather than low status interviews.

METHOD

Subjects. As in the case of the warm-cold study, the Ss were 32 junior and senior nursing students, all female with ages ranging from 20 to 22. They were volunteers who were paid for their participation.

---

[5]Although Matarazzo, Weitman, Saslow, and Wiens (1963) use duration of interviewee response as the dependent variable, and the present authors use number of words as the index of productivity, duration of response and number of words in the response are highly correlated.

Status manipulation. Again in the present study, contrasting expectations were aroused in the Ss before the two interviews in which they participated. The following were the two inductions given by the E before each of the interviews: "Your interviewer today will be Dr. B. As you know, Dr. B. is an *experienced* psychologist and is known to his colleagues as an expert interviewer." "Your interviewer today will be Mr. B. Mr. B. is enrolled in a training program for interviewers. He is new in this work, but has consented to help us in this study."

At this point, a basic difference in procedure with the warm-cold study had to be introduced. Because the age of one of the interviewers would have placed the credibility of the inexperienced condition for him under some strain, and since visual cues would have confounded the status manipulation in a multitude of ways, a screen was placed between the interviewee and the interviewer. The words spoken by the interviewer were, of course, precisely the same across both conditions.

TABLE VI.

Status Study Experimental Design

Subjects°	First Interview		Second Interview	
	Interviewer	Status	Interviewer	Status
1-8	X	Experienced	Y	Inexperienced
9-16	Y	Experienced	X	Inexperienced
17-24	X	Inexperienced	Y	Experienced
25-32	Y	Inexperienced	X	Experienced

°*With each group, i.e., 1-8, 9-16 etc., one-half of the subjects followed an interview item duration sequence of short-long-long-short; and the other half, a sequence of long-short-short-long.*

The main effects under study were interviewer status and duration of interviewer remarks. The two interviewers were the senior author of this paper and a younger colleague on the staff of the Division of Clinical Psychology of the Psychiatric Institute, University of Maryland.

To counterbalance duration sequence, there were two interview series designated A1-B1 and A2-B2. In the A1-B1 series, the questions in each interview followed a short-long-long-short sequence; and the other, a long-short-short-long sequence. In all other respects, both series were identical. The specificity variable was controlled by keeping all interviewer questions at a low specificity level.

TABLE VII.

Experimental Interview in Status Study

Interview A1

1. Tell me something, anything you wish, about your father.
2. I'm also interested in learning something about you and other members of your family. Now tell me something, anything you wish, about your brother (sister) A and how you get along.

Interviewer's transitional remark: I'd like now to talk with you about your past school history (3 seconds pause).

3. Now, I'd like you to think back on your school years before college. Tell me something, anything you wish, about your elementary school and how you got along there.
4. Now tell me something about the School of Nursing here.

Interview B1

1. Tell me something, anything you wish, about your mother.
2. Now, I'd like to talk over with you something about you and your relationship with other members of your family. Tell me something about sister (brother) B and how you got along.

Transitional remark: I'd like to talk with you about the school which you attended before college (3 seconds pause).

3. Tell me something, anything you wish, about your high school and how you got along there.
4. Tell me, please, about your first two college years.

The design is counterbalanced for status sequence, duration sequence, and interviewer sequence. Each S was his own control with reference to the interviewer variables under study; their sequence effects, however, had to be evaluated between subgroups. Again the data were submitted to an analysis of variance for repeated measurements on the same Ss (Winer, 1962).

Interview procedure and scoring of dependent variables. These were essentially the same as in the warm-cold study.

RESULTS

Effects of the status manipulation. The effects of the status manipulation are summarized in Tables VIII and IX. Only two main effects for status are significant at the .05 level and better, those for Productivity and for Reaction Time. A third main effect, for Silence Quotient, achieved borderline significance. None of the interactions between

TABLE VIII.

Subjects' Mean Scores per Response on Verbal Indices in Response to High and Low Status Interviewers

Verbal Indices	High Status Interviewer	Low Status Interviewer
Productivity	195.22	155.80°°
Silence Quotient	.1150	.0977+
Reaction Time	1.87	2.16°
Articulation Rate	2.87	2.89
Ah Ratio	.0385	.0381
Speech Disturbance Ratio	.0393	.0428
Resistiveness	.2753	.2592
Superficiality	.2007	.1959

$+p<.10;$ $°p<.05;$ $°°p<.01.$

status and status sequence was significant. For Productivity and for Reaction Time the mean differences were in the predicted direction; for Silence Quotient there was an apparent reversal. Note, however, that there is a significant status sequence main effect for Resistiveness. When the high status, rather than the low status interview is the first of the two, there is a higher level of Resistiveness.

If the analysis of the status results is carried out separately for the two topics, the overall findings appear to be due to the significant differences between high and low status interviewers in the area of school experience, but not in family relations. On the other hand, the low status interviews evoked a higher Speech Disturbance ratio than the high status interviews, but only in the content area of family relations.

TABLE IX.

Mean Scores in Response to High and Low Status Interviewers as a Function of Topical Area

Verbal Indices	Family Relations			School Experiences		
	High Status	Low Status	F^a	High Status	Low Status	F^a
Productivity	151.27	133.39	2.41	239.17	178.22	5.84°
Silence Quotient	.120	.125	.10	.110	.069	5.22+
Reaction Time	1.84	1.91	.18	1.89	2.42	5.81°
Articulation Rate	2.88	2.95	.19	2.85	2.83	.24
Ah Ratio	.0403	.0415	.08	.0367	.0348	.36
SD Ratio	.0373	.0456	5.21°	.0414	.0402	.17

$^a df = 1/31;$ $+p<.10;$ $°p<.05.$

In brief, Hypothesis 1 is impressively supported for interviewee productivity. The findings for verbal fluency are apparently inconsistent, and the results for Resistiveness are ambiguous; i. e., there is a status sequence effect, but no status effect.

EFFECTS OF INTERVIEWER DURATION

There are only two borderline main effects of the duration variable (Table X), one for Productivity and one for the Speech Disturbance ratio. In addition, there are four significant interaction effects for duration and duration sequence, on Silence Quotient, Reaction Time, Articulation Rate, and Superficiality.

TABLE X.

**Subjects' Mean Scores per Response on Verbal Indices
in Response to Short and Long Interviewer Remarks**

Verbal Indices	Interviewer Remarks	
	Short	Long
Productivity	166.43	184.59°
Reaction Time	2.07	1.95
Silence Quotient	.112	.104
Articulation Rate	2.87	2.88
Ah Ratio	.0388	.0375
SD Ratio	.0433	.0389°

°$p<.10$.

There is a greater interviewee productivity for longer, rather than shorter interviewer remarks, but a higher interviewee Speech Disturbance ratio for shorter, rather than longer, interviewer remarks. The predicted positive correlation between duration of interviewer remarks and interviewee productivity in Hypothesis 2 is sustained, but only at a borderline level.

The interaction effects for duration and duration sequence all follow a similar pattern. Short duration interviewer remarks evoke higher Silence Quotients, but only when they come first in the interview. A reversal of duration sequence effects a reversal of Silence Quotient findings. Thus long duration interviewer remarks also evoke higher Silence Quotients, but again, only when they come first. Clearly, these are general interview sequence findings and not duration findings. It would appear that interview remarks that come at the beginning of the interview are likely to evoke higher Silence Quotients than those that occur later in the interview, regardless of whether they are of long or short duration. Similarly, early interview remarks evoke slower Articulation Rates, long Reaction Times, but less Superficiality than later remarks. In brief, the interviewee is more hesitant and inhibited at the beginning of the interview than he is at a later point, but apparently less superficial.

DISCUSSION

Although the findings with reference to the interviewer duration variable are only of borderline significance, there is some support for the synchronous association of duration of interviewer remarks and interviewee productivity. Perhaps the borderline significance may be attributed to the weak manipulation of the duration variable, i.e., there were only two short duration and two long duration interviewer remarks in each interview. The high Speech Disturbance ratio in response to short, rather than long, interviewer remarks would suggest that interviewer verbal activity has a reinforcing consequence for the interviewee. Certainly, Lennard and Bernstein (1960) found evidence for such a consequence both in the interviewee's preferences for and greater responsiveness to high, rather than low, active interviewer roles. Moreover, Matarazzo (1965) postulates that an increase in interviewer duration is an instance of greater interviewer activity, assumed to be expressive of enhanced interest in and positive feeling for the interviewee. Thus long interviewer durations would be reinforcing for the interviewee; short would be punishing and evocative of tension, i.e., high Speech Disturbance ratios.

The modeling hypotheses for explaining synchrony, suggested by Matarazzo and Wiens (1967) in a recent article, is not supported by the evidence of the present study. For example, high status interviews do not manifest greater synchrony than low status interviews, i.e. Hypothesis 3 was not sustained. On the other hand, the present results are more parsimoniously explained by Matarazzo's earlier reinforcement hypothesis (1965).

The finding that high interviewer status is associated with high interviewee productivity is consistent with the impressions of Maccoby and Maccoby (1954) and with Hypothesis 1. The lower Reaction Time and the more extended silent pauses associated with high status appear contradictory at first glance. However, it is possible that the greater authority of the high status interviewer compels a more immediate response from the interviewee, but one that is given with the type of caution that accompanies an attempt to present oneself in a favorable light, as suggested by Maccoby and Maccoby, i.e., with a short Reaction Time and a high Silence Quotient.

What can be said of the differential effect of status within the two topical areas? How does one explain the fact that the school experience topic accounts for most of the significant status findings? One hypothesis that suggests itself is that the effect of status is not as general as that of warmth. Interviewer warmth is a relationship variable that sustains communication in a broad range of interview conditions. On the other hand, the effect of status is contingent on the character of the status relationship and the topic under discussion. This possibility was alluded to by Maccoby and Maccoby (1954) when they remarked that "the content of the communication will be affected by the status relationship." It is possible that status, in the sense of senior faculty position, would have greater relevance to an undergraduate student's discussion of school experience rather than family relations.

However, this type of contingency does not entirely nullify the more general effect of status or experience. Thus the higher Speech Disturbance ratio in low status, rather than high status interview segments dealing with family relationships, may well reflect some conflict or resentment on the part of the Ss about discussing personal matters with an inexperienced novice.

References

ASHBY, J. D., FORD, D. H., GUERNY, B. G., and GUERNY, L. S.   Effects on clients of reflective and leading type of psychotherapy. *Psychol. Monog., Gen. Appl.*, 1957, **71**, (453, Whole No. 24).

BLACK, J. W.   Loudness of speaking. 1. *The Effect of Heard Stimuli on Spoken Responses.* Joint Project No. 2, Contract Nonr N7-411 T.O. I, Project No. NM00I053, U. S. Naval School of Aviation Medicine and Research, Pensacola, Florida and Kenyon College, Gambier, Ohio, 1949.

BORGATTA, E. F., COTTRILL, L. S., Jr., and MANN, J. M.   The spectrum of individual interaction characteristics: An interdimensional analysis. *Psychol. Rep.*, 1958, **4**, 279-319.

CARTER, L. F.   Evaluating the performance of individuals as members of small groups. *Personn. Psychol.*, 1954, **7**, 477-84.

COHEN, J.   Some statistical issues in psychological research. In B.B. Wolman (Ed.), *Handbk. Clin. Psychol.*, McGraw-Hill, 1965, 95-121.

COLBY, K. M.   On the greater amplifying power of causal-correlation over interrogative inputs on free association in an experimental psychoanalytical situation. *J. Nerv. and Men. Dis.*, 1961, **133**, 233-9.

DOLLARD, J. and AULD, F.   *Scoring Human Motives: A Manual.* Yale University Press, New Haven, 1959.

FIEDLER, F. E.   A comparison of therapeutic relationships in psychoanalytic, non-directive and Adlerian therapy. *J. Consult. Psychol.*, 1950, **14**, 426-45.

FIEDLER, F. E.   A method of objective quantification of certain countertransference attitudes. *J. Clin. Psychol.*, VII, 1951, 101-07.

FIEDLER, F. E.   Quantitative studies on the role of therapists' feelings toward their patients. In O. H. Mowrer (Ed.), *Psychotherapy Theory and Research.* Ronald Press, New York, 1953. Pp. 296-315.

FLANDERS, J. P.   A review of research on imitative behavior. *Psychol. Bull.*, 1968, **69**, 316-37.

FOA, U.   Convergences in the analysis of the structure of interpersonal behavior. *Psychol. Rev.*, 1961, **5**, 341-53.

FREEDMAN, M., LEARY, T., OSSORIO, A., and COFFEY, H.   The interpersonal dimensions of personality. *J. Personality*, 1951, **20**, 143-62.

GILLESPIE, J. E., Jr.   Verbal signs of resistance in client-centered therapy. In W. U. Snyder (Ed.), *Group Report of a Program of Research in Psychotherapy.* Pennsylvania State University, 1953. Pp. 105-19.

GOLDSTEIN, A. P.   *Therapist-Patient Expectancies in Psychotherapy.* Macmillan, New York, 1962.

HAIGH, G.   Defensive behavior in client-centered therapy. *J. Consult. Psychol.*, 1949, **13**, 181-9.

HELLER, K., DAVIS, J. D., and MYERS, R. A.   The effects of interviewer style in a standardized interview. *J. Consult. Psychol.*, 1966, **30**, 501-08.

ISAACS, K. S. and HAGGARD, E. A.   Some methods used in the study of affect in psychotherapy. In L.A. Gottschalk and A.H. Auerbach (Eds.), *Methods of Research in Psychotherapy.* Appleton-Century-Crofts, New York, 1966. Pp. 226-39.

JAFFE, J.   Computer analysis of verbal behavior in psychiatric interviews. In D. Rioch (Ed.), *Disorders in Communication: Proceedings of the Association for Research in Nervous and Mental Diseases*, Vol. 42. Williams & Wilkins, Baltimore, 1966

JONES, E. E. and THIBAUT, J. W.   Interaction goals as bases of inference on interpersonal perceptions. In R. Taguiri and L. Petrullo (Eds.), *Person Perception and Interpersonal Behavior.* Stanford University Press, Stanford, 1958. Pp. 151-78.

KUMAR, U.   Client and counselor responses to prior counselor expectancies and to an initial interview. Unpublished doctoral dissertation, Ohio State University, 1965.

LENNARD, H. L. and BERNSTEIN, A.   *The Anatomy of Psychotherapy.* Columbia University Press, New York, 1960.

LIBO, L. M. *Manual for the Picture Impression Test.* University of Maryland School of Medicine, Baltimore, 1956.

LIBO, L. M. The projective expression of patient-therapist attraction. *J. Clin. Psychol.,* 1957, **13**, 33-6.

LORR, M. Client perceptions of therapist. *J. Consult. Psychol.,* **29**, 1965, 146-9.

MACCOBY, E. E. and MACCOBY, N. The interview: A tool of social science. In G. Lindzey (Ed.), *Handbook of Social Psychology.* Addison Wesley, Reading, Mass., 1954. Pp. 449-87.

MACLEOD, R. B. The phenomenological approach to social psychology. In R. Taguiri and L. Petrullo (Eds.), *Person Perception and Interpersonal Behavior.* Stanford University Press, 1958, Pp. 33-53.

MADISON, P. *Freud's Concept of Repression and Defense, It's Theoretical and Observational Language.* University of Minnesota Press, Minneapolis, 1961.

MAHL, G. F. Disturbances and silences in patient's speech in psychotherapy. *J. Abnorm. and Soc. Psychol.,* 1965, **53**, 1-15.

MAHL, G. F. Exploring emotional states by content analysis. In I. Pool (Ed.), *Trends in Content Analysis.* University of Illinois Press, Urbana, 1959. Pp. 83-130.

MATARAZZO, J. D., WEITMAN, M., SASLOW, G., and WIENS, A. N. Interviewer influence on duration of interviewee speech. *J. Verbal Learn. Verbal Behav.,* 1963, **1**, 451-8.

MATARAZZO, J. D. Psychotherapeutic process. *Ann. Rev. Psychol.,* 1965, **16**, 181-224.

MATARAZZO, J. D. and WIENS, A. N. Interviewer influence on duration of interviewee silence. *J. Exper. Res. Personality,* 1967, **2**, 56-69.

NEWCOMB, T. M. The prediction of interpersonal attraction. *Amer. Psychol.,* 1956, **11**, 575-86.

POPE, B. and SIEGMAN, A. W. The effect of therapist verbal activity level and specificity on patient productivity and speech disturbance in the initial interview. *J. Consult. Psychol.,* 1962, **26**, 489.

POPE, B. and SIEGMAN, A. W. Interviewer specificity and topical focus in relation to interviewee productivity. *J. Verbal Learn. Verbal Behav.,* 1965, **4**, 188-92.

POPE, B. and SIEGMAN, A. W. The verbal interaction in the initial interview. Unpublished manuscript, University of Maryland, 1967.

REECE, M. M. and WHITMAN, R. N. Expressive movements, warmth, and verbal reinforcement. *J. Abnorm. Soc. Psychol.,* 1962, **64**, 234-6.

SARBIN, T. R. Role theory. In G. Lindzey (Ed.), *Handbook of Social Psychology.* Addison Wesley, Reading, Mass, 1954. Pp. 223-58.

SCHAEFFER, E. S. A circumplex model for maternal behavior. *J. Abnorm. Soc. Psychol.,* 1959, **59**, 226-35.

SIEGMAN, A. W. and POPE, B. Effects of question specificity and anxiety producing messages on verbal fluency in the initial interview. *J. Personality Soc. Psychol.,* 1965, **2**, 522-30.

SIEGMAN, A. W. and POPE, B. The effects of ambiguity and anxiety on interviewee verbal behavior. This volume, pp. 29-68.

SNYDER, W. U. *The Psychotherapy Relationship.* Macmillan, New York, 1961.

SPEISMAN, J. C. Depth of interpretation and verbal resistance in psychotherapy. *J. Consult. Psychol.,* 1959, **25**, 93-9.

TAGUIRI, R. Social preference and its perception. In R. Taguiri and L. Petrullo (Eds.), *Person Perception and Interpersonal Behavior.* Stanford University Press, 1958. Pp. 316-36.

TOLHURST, G. C. *Some Effects of Changing Time Patterns and Articulation upon Intelligibility and Word Perception.* Contract N6 ONW-22525, Project No. NR 145-993. MMRI Project NM 001 104 500 40. U. S. Naval School of Aviation Medicine, Naval Air Station, Pensacola, Florida, and Ohio State University Research Foundation, Columbus, Ohio, January, 1955.

WEBB, J. T. Interviewer and interviewee synchrony: An investigation of two speech rate measures. This volume, pp. 115-134.

WINER, B. J. *Statistical Principles in Experimental Design.* McGraw-Hill, New York, 1962.

Part II

Temporal Variables
in
Speech

Chapter 5

Temporal Patterns of Dialogue

Basic Research and Reconsiderations [1]

Stanley Feldstein

AN ANALOGY, drawn from crypotology, may serve to put the following research into some perspective and to convey some notion of the excitement that this research, and language research generally, affords the investigator. The analogy concerns cryptography in which the message that is to be disguised is called the "plaintext." The process of disguising the plaintext is called "encoding" or "enciphering," the distinction being related to the status of the plaintext unit replaced. Ciphers operate upon single letters of the plaintext; codes replace units larger than letters, such as syllables, words, phrases, etc. The disguised message is called the "codetext" or "ciphertext," and the process of reconstructing the plaintext by a person who has the appropriate key is called "decoding" or "deciphering." However, the process used to reconstruct the plaintext by a person who does not have the appropriate key is called "cryptanalysis."

It seems not too farfetched to view the study of spoken inter-personal communication as cryptologic. The speaker might be considered the encoder, and his verbal statements the codetext. The person to whom this codetext is directed, i.e., the intended listener, could be considered the decoder because he presumably has the appropriate keys. Unintended listeners, on the other hand, who are presumed not to have the keys, are in the position of cryptanalysts. The psycholinguist, *qua* psycholinguist, is most often in the position of an unintended listener; his job is codebreaking.

[1]The author is deeply indebted to Dr. Bernard Baumrin for his unstinting aid in formulating the recursive model described herein. Grateful acknowledgment is also extended to Dr. Louis Gerstman for his critical reading of a prepublication draft. The research described herein was supported, in part, by NIMH Research Grant No. MH 04571 to The William Alanson White Institute.

91

It is not suggested here that the codetext generated by a speaker is totally incomprehensible, upon first hearing, to the unintended listener or, for that matter, that it is totally comprehensible to the intended listener. It seems unlikely that the plaintext reconstructed by the intended listener is anything more than a closer approximation of the original plaintext than is that reconstructed by the unintended listener (and not always that). What is suggested is that a spoken message is a quite complex phenomenon by virtue, in part at least, of having been encoded at a variety of levels. Few of these levels possess characteristics having consensually validated denotations and/ or connotations. In this sense, they are codes that remain to be broken.

One more important point: the breaking of a code not only enables the cryptanalyst to reconstruct the plaintext, but also frequently enables him to reconstruct the device that generated the codetext. It is the latter operation in which many psycholinguists are particularly interested.

The code or level of interpersonal communication that my past and present colleagues and I have investigated is the temporal organization of the words and word groups used by the participants. Our primary efforts have been directed toward the development of a cogent description of the characteristics of this temporal organization. The characteristics referred to are the vocal sounds and silences of the interacting speakers. The semantic meanings of the sounds are not of concern at this level of analysis, and the only silences considered are those capable of detection by the human ear. That is not to say that the semantic and syntactic features of a conversation are unrelated to its sound-silence patterns, but simply that the relationships, in terms of information conveyed, are not one-to-one.

This chapter will briefly describe an instrument designed to sample automatically the temporal patterns of dialogue and present a descriptive classification of the patterns. It will then review a number of basic studies which examined the stability of the temporal characteristics with respect to people and time, and their modifiability as a function of certain situational and psychological variables. Finally, some problems raised by the descriptive classification will be discussed and a new model briefly explored.

The history of interaction chronography in psychology is little more than three decades old. It was Chapple (1939, 1940), an anthropologist, who first urged that the timing of interpersonal behavior provided an important methodological approach to the reliable assessment of personality. He devised the Interaction Chronograph (Chapple, 1949) to sample the interpersonal time domain. Subsequently, he and a number of other investigators, using the Chronograph and other instruments (Verzeano and Finesinger, 1949; Hargreaves and Starkweather, 1959) made initial probes into the behavior of this domain in interviews with the mentally ill (Chapple, Chapple, Wood, Miklowitz, Kline, and Saunders, 1960; Matarazzo and Saslow, 1961), employment interviews (Chapple and Donald, 1946; Anderson, 1960; Matarazzo, Wiens, and Saslow, 1965), individual and group psychotherapy interviews (Lundy, 1955; Timmons, Rickard, and Taylor, 1960; Matarazzo, Wiens, and Saslow, 1965), and in relation to certain personality variables (Chapple, Chapple, and Rapp, 1954; Cervin, 1957; Matarazzo, Matarazzo, Saslow, and Phillips, 1958). Some effort was also made to assess its relation to semantic content (Kanfer, Phillips, Matarazzo, and Saslow, 1960). Only a minimal attempt, however, was made to explore the time patterns of free, unconstrained conversation (cf. Matarazzo, Saslow, and Matarazzo, 1956, pp. 356-7).

The excursion my colleague, Dr. Joseph Jaffe, and I made into interaction chronography grew out of general concern with psychopathology, our belief that a significant developmental component of psychopathology is disturbed interpersonal communication and our belief that *how* something is said is as important to effective communication as *what* is said. Our prior research had focussed upon such characteristics of language use as vocabulary diversity (Jaffe, 1958; Fink, Jaffe, and Kahn, 1960; Feldstein and Jaffe, 1962a; Feldstein and Jaffe, 1962b), speech disturbances and filled pauses (Feldstein, 1962; Feldstein and Jaffe, 1962a; Feldstein and Jaffe, 1963; Feldstein, Brenner, and Jaffe, 1963; Brenner, Feldstein, and Jaffe, 1965), and speech predictability (Feldstein and Jaffe, 1963; Weinstein, Feldstein, and Jaffe, 1965; Feldstein, Rogalski, and Jaffe, 1966). It was but another step to examining the unfilled pauses, or silences, and the vocalizations, or sounds, of speech.

Although our interest originated with psychopathological communication, it was decided to investigate the time patterns of "normal" communication in order to establish some sort of evaluative baseline. Moreover, we intended to look at relatively free conversational interactions, i.e., conversations that were not constrained by any obvious role or instructional differences between the participants, such as exist, for example, in interview situations. The expectation was that this approach would allow for the formulation of general rules of conversational time patterns. Special types of conversation, such as the interview or monologue, might then be described in terms of specific modifications of the general rules.

THE INSTRUMENT

Initial efforts went into devising an automated system of detecting and recording the sound-silence patterns of dialogue in computer-readable form. Two major reasons prompted this effort. On the one hand, a monumental amount of data processing was anticipated. Thus the use of a computer seemed inescapable and the collection of computer-readable data obviated the possibility of human transcription errors. On the other hand, the Interaction Chronograph was unsatisfactory because it required that a human observer decide when each of the participants was talking or silent. Thus the behavior recorded by the Chronograph confounded the effects of the semantic content of the conversation, the gestures of the participants, and the judgment and reaction time of the observer.

The engineering skill of a former colleague, Dr. Louis Cassotta, translated our requirements into an analogue-to-digital conversion system called the "Automatic Vocal Transaction Analyzer," or AVTA (Cassotta, Feldstein, and Jaffe, 1964; Cassotta, Jaffe, Feldstein, and Moses, 1964). In point of fact, AVTA includes two special components, only one of which will be discussed here.[2]

This component, designed to "listen" to live or audiotaped conversation and to detect and record the presence and absence of speech for each of the participants, is called, for convenience, the "Presence-Absence Component," or PAC. Originally designed to feed information to a cardpunch, PAC now "talks" directly to a small computer[3] which, in turn, provides a printed statistical summary of prespecified temporal characteristics and punches the dyadic sequence of sounds and silences plus the summary on paper tape.

It is important to note that PAC "listens" periodically. That is, it "inquires" about the state of the relay associated with each speaker at predetermined intervals which can range from 100 msec. to 1000 msec. We have always used a 300 msec. interval or, alternatively, a 200 times per minute inquiry rate for reasons that had to do originally with the limitations of the keypunch.

It should also be mentioned that the problem PAC was built to cope with was not simply that of generating a time pattern sequence of the speech of two people. Such a problem only requires two ordinary voice-activated relays with appropriate filtering. The real

---

[2]The component not discussed here is one called the "Vocal Intensity Component" (VIC) which detects and records in computer-readable form the vocal intensity, or loudness, of each participant's voice at regular time intervals of optional length, such as 300 msec.

[3]The computer used is a PDP8/S manufactured by Digital Equipment Corporation.

difficulty lay in achieving adequate voice separation of two speakers who, while talking into separate microphones, are sitting in a face-to-face position at a comfortable distance from each other. The solution utilized a network which electronically cancels the spill of each speaker's voice into the other speaker's channel. It enabled us not only to use vis-à-vis conversations in a naturalistic setting, but also to obtain an accurate account of simultaneous speech.

TEMPORAL PARAMETERS

An explicit effort was made to extract from the dyadic sequence of sounds and silences precisely definable indices that were descriptive rather than attributive. The indices, or parameters, are called "vocalizations," "pauses," "switching pauses," "simultaneous speech," "speaker switches," "utterances," and "floor time." An effort was also made to define all the parameters but simultaneous speech and speaker switches solely in terms of their boundary conditions. Together, these parameters form what we have called a "descriptive classification."

1. A *vocalization* is a segment of continuous sound, i.e., speech, by one speaker that is bounded on each end by either silence or a vocalization of the other speaker.

2. A *pause* is an interval of silence bounded on either end by a vocalization of the same speaker.

3. A *switching pause* is an interval of silence bounded on one end by a vocalization of one speaker and on the other end by a vocalization of the other speaker.

4. Finally, temporally concurrent vocalizations of the speakers are categorized as *simultaneous speech*.

An "utterance" can now be defined as a sequence, or string, of the pauses and vocalizations of one speaker that is bounded on either end by switching pauses or, if there are no switching pauses, by the vocalizations of the other speaker. The parameter rather awkwardly called "floor time" refers to a speaker "having the floor." Each speaker is considered to have the floor until the other speaker takes it. In other words, a single "floor time" is equal to an utterance plus the switching pause that follows it. The number of "floor times" a speaker accrues during the course of a conversation is equal to the number of speaker switches in the conversation, i.e., the number of changes from one speaker to the other.

Immediately following the termination of a dialogue, the AVTA system prints and punches frequencies, average durations, and proportionality constants of all but the utterance parameter. For the present discussion, the definition and implication of a proportionality constant can be ignored.[4] Prior to processing a dialogue, the AVTA

TABLE I.

Sample Output of AVTA System Summarizing a Fifteen-Minute Conversation in Terms of the Temporal Parameters of the Descriptive Classification

Study Name QT6			
Dyad No. 271	Sub Dyad No. 1	Condition 066	Occasion 007

Participant 024   **Participant 023**

Parameter: Pauses

Frequency = 0079   Frequency = 0096
Summed Durations = 0140   Summed Durations = 0188
Average Duration = +1.77215   Average Duration = +1.95833
Proportionality Constant = +0.43571   Proportionality Constant = +0.48936

Parameter: Switching Pauses

Frequency = 0035   Frequency = 0025
Summed Durations = 0108   Summed Durations = 0058
Average Duration = +3.08571   Average Duration = +2.32000
Proportionality Constant = +0.67593   Proportionality Constant = +0.56897

Parameter: Vocalizations

Frequency = 0165   Frequency = 0169
Summed Durations = 1119   Summed Durations = 1455
Average Duration = +6.78182   Average Duration = +8.60947
Proportionality Constant = +0.85255   Proportionality Constant = +0.88385

Parameter: "Floor Time"

Frequency = 0064   Frequency = 0064
Summed Durations = 1258   Summed Durations = 1726
Average Duration = +19.6562   Average Duration = +26.9688
Proportionality Constant = +0.94913   Proportionality Constant = +0.96292

Parameter: Simultaneous Speech

Participants 024 and 023

Frequency = 0054
Summed Durations = 0069
Average Duration = +1.27778
Proportionality Constant = +0.21739

---

[4] A proportionality constant is simply a transformation of the mean duration $[(M-1)/M]$ which characterizes a particular distribution shape, i.e., a negative exponential.

system can be told to divide the dialogue into segments of equal duration. It will then summarize each segment separately after termination of the dialogue (Table I).

These, then, are the parameters of our descriptive classification. They are objective; their definitions are unencumbered by preconceptions about the intentions of the speakers and their measurement excludes observer reaction time. Moreover, their delineation by PAC is highly reliable, i.e., the processing by PAC of the same dialogues on different occasions yields strikingly high reliabilities regardless of the complexity of the dialogues.

At first blush, this descriptive classification seems to offer a structure which provides an unbiased and rather simple description of the actual temporal behavior of dyadic verbal interactions. That in fact it fails to do so is a result of certain constraints built into the hardware and software of the AVTA system and of certain definitional ambiguities. This criticism may be somewhat unfair in that it hinges partially on the use of the word "actual." The system was not designed to examine the actual time patterns, if by "actual" is meant "true." It was mentioned earlier that the only silences considered to be of interest are those capable of detection by the human ear. It is this constraint, introduced into the processing controls of the system, which renders the output of the system a description of the *perceived* temporal patterns of dialogue. As such, however, the description is eminently defensible and furnishes a set of characteristics that are beginning to appear quite useful.

The definitional ambiguities represent a different order of difficulty. In part, they reflect the inherent electronic constraints of the AVTA system. More importantly, they highlight the lack of sufficiently general rules for the categorization of seemingly anomalous configurations or for the unambiguous assignment of all the categories to speakers. As is often the case, it is the consideration of just such problems and their implications that is so provocative and frequently so fruitful. They will be considered further after a discussion of the categories as they now stand. The problem raised need not, at this point, impede an examination of the categories as potentially meaningful psychological variables. The questions initially relevant here concern the reliabilities of the categories and the relations among them. Two experiments were conducted to investigate these questions.

EXPERIMENTAL STUDIES

INDIVIDUALS IN INTERVIEWS

The first experiment was a study of individual differences with respect to four of the parameters of the classification (Cassotta, Feldstein, and Jaffe, 1968). The primary intent was to explore the individual consistency of the parameters, their stability over time, and their modifiability. Because of this focus on the vocal behavior of individuals, the study used an interview format as its conversational paradigm. The subjects were 50 white female students from an urban college whose ages ranged from 17 to 23 years and averaged 19.3 years. They were interviewed on two occasions, each occasion separated by approximately two weeks. On the first occasion, a 16-minute interview was conducted with each subject by one interviewer. On the second occasion, three successive 16-minute interviews were conducted, the first by the interviewer of the first occasion and the remaining two by another interviewer. The interview of occasion one and the first two interviews of occasion two were of the question-and-answer type and dealt with factual biographical information. The last, or fourth, interview was a stress interview.[5] That is, an effort was made in the last interview to ascertain what areas of discussion appeared to arouse anxiety by asking a series of open-ended questions. The subject was then questioned in detail about these areas, with the interviewer displaying reactions calculated to increase the subject's stress. The stress interview was utilized to evaluate the modifiability of the parameters.

All the interviews were tape recorded and the tapes were processed by the AVTA system. It became obvious upon inspection of the data that there were too few occurrences of simultaneous speech to permit an evaluation of its reliability. The analyses, therefore, were concerned only with pauses, switching pauses, and vocalizations. It is important to note that here and in the following study the switching pauses were assigned to the speaker by whom they were terminated. This assignment decision was based upon the assumption that the switching pause represents a reaction, or response time. The results reported are of the analysis of proportionality

---

[5]The interpretation of the interview as stressful is inferential and a more parsimonious interpretation may be possible [e.g., in terms of the differing degrees of ambiguity of the question sets used in the fourth interview as compared with each of the other interviews (Siegman and Pope, 1965)]. The important point is that, by independent assessment, the fourth interview represented a different interview condition.

constants of the parameters rather than of their average durations.[6]

Intercorrelations among the parameters (using only the subjects' data) yielded average coefficients of .40 for the comparison of pauses and switching pauses, —.47 for pauses and vocalizations, and —.36 for switching pauses and vocalizations. While the parameters were obviously not orthogonal in this study, each was considered to carry enough unique variance to remain a separate parameter.

The reliabilities of the parameters were estimated by computing correlation coefficients of the subjects' data among the six possible pairs of the four interviews. The average of the six correlations for each parameter was .68 for pauses, .61 for switching pauses, and .62 for vocalizations. All the coefficients are significant. There were, moreover, no significant differences among the coefficients of the interview pairs. These results indicate that the parameters reliably differentiated individuals and remained stable over time, across interviewers, and even from non-stress to stress conditions. Comparison of the non-stress and stress interviews revealed that, on the average, significantly longer pauses and switching pauses were emitted during the stress interview. Thus pauses and switching pauses appear to be not only stable but modifiable parameters, at least under the impact of stress.

Similar comparisons of the interviewers' data yielded average coefficients of .29 for pauses, .49 for switching pauses, and a nonsignificant .16 for vocalizations. These results suggest that, with regard to pauses and switching pauses, the interviewers tended to behave in consistently different ways with different subjects. Furthermore, since there were no real differences between the coefficients of those interview pairs which had the same or different interviewers, it appears as if the subjects affected the vocal behavior of the interviewers similarly. These results are pertinent to a consideration of interspeaker influence, a topic that will be discussed later.

The results of this study suggested that the temporal parameters, pauses, switching pauses, and vocalizations are stable individual characteristics. The study did, however, elicit conversations within the structure of an interview. Would conversations unconstrained by an imposed structure and explicit role differences between the participants yield similar results? These issues were pursued in a second experiment (Feldstein, Jaffe, and Cassotta, 1966, 1967) which utilized task-oriented, but otherwise free conversational interactions.

---

[6]Since the proportionality constant is a simple transformation of the mean (see footnote 4), it is highly unlikely that correlations of the transformed scores would be markedly different from those of the mean durations.

CONVERSATIONS BETWEEN PEERS

The subjects of the study were 32 white male and 32 white female students, again from an urban college. The average age of the group was 20.6 years, with a sigma of 3.6 years. The experimental design required the participation of each subject in three 40-minute dialogues, each separated by about a three-week interval. Each subject conversed with a member of his own sex on one occasion, a different member of his own sex on a second occasion, and a member of the opposite sex on a third occasion. The task of the participants of each dyad was to attempt to resolve their differences on a questionnaire concerned with the attitudes of white Americans toward Negroes (Collins, 1964). In addition, the 40-minute dialogues were divided into two conditions; namely, during the first or second 20 minutes an opaque screen was placed between the participants in order to eliminate visual communication.

Assessment of the relations among the average durations of the four parameters are presented in Table II. Note that in this study, the

TABLE II.

Product Moment Correlation Coefficients for Comparisons Among Vocalizations (V), Pauses (P), Switching Pauses (SP) and Simultaneous Speech (SS) Averaged Over Occasions and Conditions

	P	SP	SS
V	-.05	-.07	.18
P		.54	-.07
SP			-.05

Note—The N for the individual comparisons was 62.

average correlations between vocalizations and each of the two silence parameters are approximately zero, whereas that between the two types of silence increased by comparison with their correlation in the interview study. Note also that simultaneous speech is statistically independent of the other parameters.

Comparisons of the average durations of pauses, switching pauses, vocalizations, and simultaneous speech of the two 20-minute conditions over occasions yielded average correlation coefficients of .67, .68, .66, and .53, respectively. Note that the individual consistency estimates of the first three parameters are as high as those obtained in the initial study. Moreover, the stability of the parameters remained high over two conditions that have been shown to differentially affect the durations of the parameters (Feldstein, Jaffe, and Cassotta, 1967), indicating again that the parameters are both stable and modifiable.

Thus far, the results of the two studies suggested that the temporal style of an individual's conversational behavior remained consistent so long as he interacted with the same conversational partner. But what if he changed his partner? To answer this question comparisons among the three occasions were made and yielded average stability estimates of .29 for pauses, .30 for switching pauses, .47 for vocalizations, and .27 for simultaneous speech. The stability of the parameters from occasion to occasion was considerably lower than that between conditions, but still significant. Within the context of the experiment, this lowered stability makes sense only if it is seen as resulting from the impact of a different temporal style. The implication here is that an individual's conversational style varies as a function of the style of the person with whom he interacts. There is, in fact, from this and the initial study, evidence of appreciable interspeaker influence. It should be recognized, however, that concern about the parameters as indices of interspeaker influence goes beyond the issue of stability to approach the more interesting question of whether the parameters vary in ways that appear psychologically meaningful.

INTERSPEAKER INFLUENCE

A comparison of the subjects' data in the initial study with those of the interviewers yielded average correlation coefficients of .39 for pauses, .42 for switching pauses, and .32 for vocalizations, all of which are statistically significant. Apparently, the participants in the interviews tended to match each other's average parameter durations. That the correlations are low probably reflects the fact that one of the participants in all the interviews was the same person, namely, the interviewer. In the second study, in which the dyads are all different within each occasion, the average correlations (over occasions) between the average durations of pauses, switching pauses, and vocalizations of dyad participants were .59, .70, and a non-significant -.04, respectively. Obviously, a similar comparison for the average durations of simultaneous speech would be meaningless since both participants in a dyad have the same average duration. The average duration of vocalizations does not appear to be subject, in conversational interactions, to the same degree of modification as are those of pauses and switching pauses. That the duration of vocalizations was as modifiable as those of pauses and switching pauses

in the interview study may reflect the different interactional rules of
an interview and/or the fact that all the subjects spoke to the same
interviewer. Nevertheless, a comparison of the average utterance
durations, which include pauses and vocalizations, of the dyad
participants yielded significant intraclass correlations of .43, .60, and
.44 for the three occasions (Feldstein, 1968), revealing again a
considerable degree of what might be called pattern matching, or
congruence. Indeed, it may be useful to call these correlation
coefficients which compare the behavior of the participants in a
conversation, coefficients of "congruence." It may also be useful to
emphasize that the coefficients of congruence being discussed are
obtained by correlating the average parameter values of one
participant in a dyad with the average parameter values of the other
participant over many dyads. To put it another way, consider one of
the participants in a dyad the speaker and the other participant the
partner. A coefficient of congruence is computed by correlating the
average parameter values of all the speakers with those of all the
partners.[7] This kind of comparison should be distinguished from a
comparison of the temporal patterns of a speaker and partner *within*
a conversation. The latter comparison is much more concerned with
what might be considered the moment-to-moment tracking of each
participant by the other. Thus, for example, were a correlation of the
utterance durations used by two participants during the course of a
conversation found to be significant, it would indicate that the
sequential pattern of the utterance durations of each participant was
matched by that of the other. As a matter of fact, an approximation to
this comparison was used with eight of the dialogues from the second
study (Feldstein, 1968). The length of an utterance was defined by its
number of words rather than by its temporal duration. None of the
eight correlation coefficients even approached significance. This
finding may be a function of the utterance definition, or it may be
that utterance-by-utterance tracking does not occur in relatively
unstructured dialogues. On the other hand, Ray and Webb (1966),
using a similar lexical index, failed to find the occurrence of such
tracking in the question-and-answer press conferences of the late
President Kennedy.

   As another aspect of interspeaker influence, one might examine
the consistency of the effects that the temporal style of one speaker
has upon the temporal styles of all other speakers with whom he

---

[7]Inasmuch as all speakers can be considered partners and vice versa in dyads in
which the participants are not explicitly differentiated (as, e.g., by role), an intraclass
correlation (Haggard, 1958) must be used for comparisons.

interacts. In the second study, each subject conversed with three other subjects or, in the jargon introduced earlier, each speaker conversed with three different partners. The consistency of the speakers' influence on their partners was evaluated by intercorrelating the temporal characteristics of the partners. The average coefficients of these comparisons were .39 for pauses, .37 for switching pauses, and .11 for vocalizations. The first two are low but significant, suggesting that to a discernible degree, at least in terms of silence patterns, a speaker exerts a similar influence upon different conversational partners.

Together, then, the two studies suggest that the temporal patterning of an individual's conversational behavior is a stable characteristic of that individual and, in addition, is capable of modifying and being modified by the temporal patterning of other individuals with whom he interacts.

OTHER QUERIES, OTHER STUDIES

It would seem that the results of these experiments lay a firm foundation for the study of dialogic time patterns as representative of the participants' characteristic modes of interpersonal behavior. A series of questions may clarify this notion. It might be asked, for example, whether it is possible to specify the time it takes for conversationalists to develop congruent temporal behavior. Does this time vary systematically from dyad to dyad and, if so, as a function of what? Can it be demonstrated that the temporal patterns of two conversationalists grow more congruent as they engage in more and more dialogues or, to put it another way, do their patterns tend to converge[8] over dialogues?

The magnitude of the coefficients of congruence obtained in the second study does suggest that the participants in a conversation to some degree mutually modify their temporal behavior in the direction of achieving similarity. Does the extent of this modification vary with individuals? What are the consequences of invariance in this regard? Is such invariance reflective of a more general inflexibility in the face of environmental demands? Similar questions may be asked about the significance of the degree to which individuals exhibit *consistent* temporal behavior, while recognizing that consistency and congruence are not entirely independent phenomena. Is, for example,

---

[8]The use of the term "convergence" rather than "congruence" is arbitrary. My preference is to use "congruence" to describe the degree of interspeaker influence that occurs in a single dialogue, and "convergence" to describe the degree of interspeaker influence that develops over a series of dialogues by the same participants.

the extent to which an individual displays consistent temporal patterns of interaction related to the extent of his consistency in other behavioral domains?

A number of dissertations have investigated the generalizability of certain aspects of temporal behavior. It may be recalled that one finding of the second study was that the absence of visual-gestural communication significantly altered, in complex ways, conversational time patterns. One dissertation (Rogalski, 1968) found a significant, although weak, relationship between the pattern of this altered temporal behavior and cognitive style, i.e., an individual's style of processing environmental input. Another dissertation (Marcus, 1970) found that the extent to which the temporal patterns of interacting speakers converge depends upon the interaction of their cognitive styles.

There are still other interesting questions now under investigation. Is degree of congruence and/or convergence related to the extent to which the participants perceive each other as similar? Or is it related to their actual similarity, as measured by a profile of tests? Or is it related to the similarity of their value systems? Or, finally, is it related to the extent to which they are mutually attracted to each other?

PROBLEMS OF THE DESCRIPTIVE CLASSIFICATION

As stated earlier, all but two of the parameters, or categories, of the classification were defined solely in terms of their boundary conditions. It soon became apparent, however, that such definitions were not always adequate. Among the gritty actualities of real data, there occasionally occur ambiguous temporal configurations, configurations which cannot be categorized solely on the basis of their boundary conditions. Consider, for example, the following case in which an interval of silence is bounded by simultaneous speech which terminates synchronously prior to the silence and begins synchronously subsequent to the silence as in Figure 1. How is the silence to be categorized?

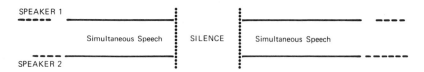

Fig 1. Diagrammatic representation of a silence bounded by two segments of simultaneous speech.

As two switching pauses? As two pauses? Inasmuch as utterances are determined by switching pauses, the decision made in this case affects three of the classification categories.

Apart from the problem of categorization is the problem of assigning switching pauses to a speaker. The definition of an utterance leaves the switching pause unassigned. In the studies reviewed, the switching pauses were arbitrarily assigned to the speaker of the subsequent utterance on the unsupported notion that a switching pause was the response time of the subsequent speaker. It is likely that the electronic constraints of PAC and the inquiry rate utilized are at least partially responsible for generating ambiguous configurations. Nevertheless, such instances, together with the assignment difficulty, uncover the not immediately obvious fact that, within the context of the descriptive classification, the boundary condition of a switching pause is a necessary but not sufficient definition. Put another way, the dependence of a switching pause extends beyond its boundary events. If the parameter "floor time" is now introduced, as it was when the delineation of utterances and switching pauses required too many arbitrary decisions, it becomes possible to resolve most ambiguities. Moreover, the parameter assigns switching pauses to the preceding speaker, on the assumption that a speaker "has the floor" until the other speaker takes it from him.[9] What it does not do is reduce the dependency of a switching pause to its boundary events.

This difficulty of non-arbitrarily categorizing all temporal configurations is a consequence, it would seem, of the lack of an explicit theory that would provide for a coherent integration of the classification categories. It is this kind of integration that is implied in the use of the categories to describe the temporal "pattern" or "organization" of dialogue. Another important consequence is the lack of predictive power. Parenthetically, it might also be suggested that a model frequently serves as the type of challenge that stimulates productive contention.

Although a mathematical model of dyadic temporal interaction has been proposed,[10] it utilizes not the categories of the classification model but the sequence of momentary dyadic states generated by the

---

[9]It might be pointed out that, although its analysis is not dealt with at length in the reported studies, speaker switching could be regarded as the single behavior that most aptly characterizes a dialogue. This view is inherent in a paper by Jaffe, Feldstein, and Cassotta (1967b) and in a recent monograph (Jaffe and Feldstein, 1970), although they have not considered the behavior to be capable, by itself, of determining parameter assignment.

[10]The model was suggested by Jaffe and Norman (1964) and is described succinctly in a more recent report (Jaffe, Feldstein, and Cassotta, 1967a) and at length in the monograph referred to in footnote 9.

instrument, PAC, as its elements. I should like to propose here, and but briefly outline its beginning steps, a recursive model which concerns itself with the categories of the descriptive classification.

A RECURSIVE MODEL: INITIAL STEPS

What are the basic elements which such a model might require? As was said toward the beginning of this discussion, of concern are the sounds and silences of human speech and the time in which and at which they occur.[11] These elements are introduced by the initial expressions of the model. The first expression,

[1] $x_1, x_2, \ldots, x_n$

represents the names of a set of individuals and the second of a set of vocalizations (V) made by individuals,

[2] $Vx_1, Vx_2, \ldots, Vx_n$

The temporal sequence of such vocalizations is indicated by the subscripts of the 'V's in conjunction with the subscripts of the 'x's, as in the expression,

[3] $V_1x_1, V_2x_1, \ldots, V_nx_1$

If silence is considered the *absence* of vocalization, such absence can be specified by negation. Finally,

[4a] 't' names any time, infinitesimal or not (i.e., an interval) (specified as either by use of the notations defined in [4b], [4c], and [4d] as subscripts).

[4b] 't_p', where 'p' is equal to specific infinitesimal times (i.e., clock times).

[4c] 't_e', where 'e' is equal to a non-specific infinitesimal time (e.g., the time constant of PAC).

[4d] 't_i', 't_j', and 't_k', where 'i', 'j', and 'k' stand for temporal intervals of any duration with the constraint that $e < i < j < k$.

[4e] 't_m', where 'm' equals any member of the set e through k, i.e., any time no matter what its duration.

The recursive model of the elements is completed by premises [5] and [6]. The first,

[5] $(x) (V) (\exists t) [Vxt \lor \overline{V}xt]$

assumes as true for all individuals and all vocalizations that at any given instant of time, or for any given interval of time (or both), an individual either vocalizes or does not vocalize, but not both. Put another way, it is not possible for individuals to both vocalize and

---

[11]The representation of the model will utilize the conventions of elementary quantification theory (Quine, 1959).

not vocalize at the same time. The second premise,

[6] (V) (p) $-(\exists x)$ $[V_1 x_1 t_p \cdot (V_2 x_1 t_p \vee V_2 x_1 t_{(p+m)})]$

is that the occurrences of any one individual's vocalizations are temporally unidirectional.

The sign ' $\rightarrow$ ' is used to indicate both temporal contiguity and direction. Vocalizations and non-vocalizations can now be further characterized.[12] Thus the statements

[7a] (V) $(\exists x_1)$ $[Vx_1 \rightarrow Vx_1 = Vx_1]$

and

[7b] $(\overline{V})$ $(\exists x_1)$ $[\overline{V}x_1 \rightarrow \overline{V}x_1 = \overline{V}x_1]$

are illustrations of the idempotency principle and say, in effect, that contiguous vocalizations by the same individual are the same as (or equivalent to) one vocalization, and similarly for non-vocalizations. Furthermore,

[8] $t_i + t_i = t_{(i+i)}$

states that the durations of two elements are additive. It follows that while it is not possible, by virtue of [7a], to have contiguous vocalizations of one individual, whatever their duration, i.e.,

[9] (V) $-(\exists x_1)$ $[V_1 x_1 \rightarrow V_2 x_1]$,

it is possible to have vocalizations of varying durations that are separated by a non-vocalization,

[10] $Vx_1 t_i \rightarrow \overline{V}x_1 t_j \rightarrow Vx_1 t_k \neq 0$,

and, in such cases, the durations of the vocalizations and non-vocalizations can be summed.

Pauses (P) may now be defined as a non-vocalization that intervenes between the vocalizations of one individual:

[11] (V) (P) (t) $[(\exists x_1)$ $(V_1 x_1 t_i \rightarrow \overline{V}x_1 t_i \rightarrow V_2 x_1 t_i) \equiv$
$(\exists x_1)$ $(V_1 x_1 t_i \rightarrow Px_1 t_i \rightarrow V_2 x_1 t_i)]$.

The expression states simply that within the context of vocalizations, 'V', a non-vocalization, $\overline{V}$, is considered a pause, 'P'.

What has been said thus far applies to the speech of a single individual. The verbal interaction of two speakers can be approached by initially describing a speaker switch,[13]

[12] $(\exists x_1)$ $(\exists x_2)$ $(\wedge p)$ $[Vx_1 t_{(p-i)} \rightarrow \overline{V}x t_{(p\pm e)} \rightarrow Vx_2 t_{(p+i)}]$,

i.e., for any two individuals, there is the specific infinitesimal time, p (e.g., 12 o'clock), such that the end of one individual's vocalization at time p is followed, after a silence of a non-specific infinitesimal duration, by the beginning of the other individual's vocalization.

' $\overline{V}t_{(p\pm e)}$ ' is not to be thought of as a discernible silence; the subscript 'e' could take zero as a value, or have a minus value in

---

[12]The sign ' $\rightarrow$ ' is not to be interpreted as representing strict implication.

[13]Hereafter, universal quantification is omitted.

certain cases. In the case in which '$\overline{V}xt_{(p\pm e)}$' does become a discernible silence, it is defined as a switching pause as in statements [13a] and [13b]:

$$[13a] \quad (\exists x_1) \, (\exists x_2) \, (Vx_1t_i \longrightarrow \overline{V}xt_i \longrightarrow Vx_2t_i) \equiv$$
$$(\exists x_1) \, (\exists x_2) \, (Vx_1t_i \longrightarrow SPx_1x_2t_i \longrightarrow Vx_2t_i)$$

and

$$[13b] \quad (\exists x_1) \, (\exists x_2) \, (Vx_2t_i \longrightarrow \overline{V}xt_i \longrightarrow Vx_1t_i) \equiv$$
$$(\exists x_1) \, (\exists x_2) \, (Vx_2t_i \longrightarrow SPx_2x_1t_i \longrightarrow Vx_1t_i)$$

Observe that, by virtue of the assumption of temporal unidirectionality, a switching pause is assigned to the previous speaker. The relational three-place predicates, 'SPx_1x_2t' and SPx_2x_1t', translate as "speaker 1's switching pause to speaker 2 for time t" and, similarly, "speaker 2's switching pause to speaker 1 for time t." In effect, what the definitions imply is that a switching pause is simply a pause of the preceding speaker until it is terminated by the other speaker. What immediately follows from the definitions is a clarification of the categorizing of switching pauses. The configuration diagrammed in Figure 1, for example, presents no categorization problem for the model. If

$$[14] \quad (\exists x_1) \, (\exists x_2) \, (\wedge p) \, [Vx_1t_{(p+i)} \cdot Vx_2t_{(p+i)}]$$

defines simultaneous speech, the configuration may be described by the statement,

$$[15] \quad (\exists x_1) \, (\exists x_2) \, (\wedge p) \, [(Vx_1t_{(p-j)} \cdot Vx_2t_{(p-j)}) \longrightarrow (\overline{V}x_1t_{(p-i)} \cdot$$
$$\overline{V}x_2t_{(p-i)}) \longrightarrow (Vx_1t_{(p+j)} \cdot Vx_2t_{(p+j)})]$$

Namely, there are two individuals, "1" and "2" and a specific infinitesimal time p (a clock time), such that the two individuals speak simultaneously for time p-j, are both silent for time p-i (where i < j), and again speak simultaneously for time p+j. While it is possible to define the '$\overline{V}x_1t_{(p-i)}$' and '$\overline{V}x_2t_{(p-i)}$' of statement [15] as '$SPx_1x_2t_{(p-i)}$' and '$SPx_2x_1t_{(p-i)}$' by virtue of statements [12], [13a], and [13b], they can more straightforwardly, i.e., by virtue of only [11], be defined as '$Px_1t_{(p-i)}$' and '$Px_2t_{(p-i)}$' thusly:

$$[16a] \quad (\exists x_1) \, (\wedge p) \, [Vx_1t_{(p-j)} \longrightarrow Px_1t_{(p-i)} \longrightarrow Vx_1t_{(p+j)}]$$

and

$$[16b] \quad (\exists x_2) \, (\wedge p) \, [Vx_2t_{(p-j)} \longrightarrow Px_2t_{(p-i)} \longrightarrow Vx_2t_{(p+j)}].$$

Another consequence of the model's definition of a switching pause is at least one clear distinction between the time patterns of unstructured conversations and interviews. Remember that, in the second study, the relation between pauses and switching pauses, with the latter assigned to the subsequent speaker, yielded an average coefficient of .54. If, instead, switching pauses are correlated with the pauses of the previous speaker, the coefficient increases to .65. On the other hand, if the switching pauses of the interview study are reassigned according to the definition of the model, the average coefficient of the correlation between the interviewees' pauses and switching pauses decreases from .40 to .24. Although the difference between .54 and .40 is not significant, the difference between .65 and .24 is significant at about the .025 level. If it can be agreed upon other grounds that an interview and an unstructured conversation are different types of dialogue, then the model, by virtue of its assignment of switching pauses, accounts for at least one aspect of this distinction. One prediction suggested by the model's definition of switching pauses is that, in unstructured dialogues, an appreciable number of the total frequency of simultaneous speech will occur at the termination of the switching pause. This prediction has yet to be tested.

SUMMARY AND FUTURE DIRECTIONS

The development of a methodological approach to the study of dialogue has been reviewed. It is an approach which presumes that the temporal patterning of a verbal exchange represents a source of important information about the communication and communicators. Moreover, it is an approach which offers a set of behaviorally defined parameters for the description of such temporal patterning. Finally, it is an approach which has achieved a fully automated system for the processing of dialogues and has, thereby, resolved the usual difficulty in verbal behavior research of accumulating sufficient data upon which to base conclusions.

There was a twofold purpose in presenting this approach. The first was to demonstrate: (a) that the average durations of the sounds and silences of each participant in a dialogue may be considered characteristic of that participant and, at the same time, a function of his interaction with the other participant; and (b) that the temporal patterning of an individual's speech is capable of reflecting the influence, not only of the pattern of another speaker, but also of changes in the psychological context of a dialogue. The second was to describe some of the ambiguities and limitations inherent in a purely empirical parameterization of such sounds and silences, to propose a recursive model for redefining the parameters, and to note a few of the consequences of using the model.

It would seem that further investigations of dialogic time patterns can move in at least several directions. An obvious direction—the one which originally motivated this research—is an exploration of the interaction patterns of individuals considered mentally ill.

Another direction has to do with examining the use of the temporal parameters as personality variables. It seems clear, simply from the results of the studies reviewed here, that the temporal organization of dialogue offers a set of potentially rich descriptors for behaviorally characterizing individuals and the patterns of their interpersonal relationships. Still another direction would involve studying the role of dialogic time patterns in the communication of affect. There are both experimental (Fairbanks and Hoaglin, 1941; Feldstein, 1964) and experiential reasons for believing that the role is a significant one.

A perhaps more basic level of inquiry would be concerned with explicating the interdependence of the temporal and lexical codes of a verbal exchange. Such an inquiry might, for instance, examine the hypothesis that dialogic time patterns are related to semantic content such that there are some patterns and content that frequently co-occur and others that rarely co-occur.[14] At the same time, the inquiry might profitably explore the relations between the temporal and syntactic structures of dialogue. An initial effort in this direction investigated the relative potency of syntactic boundaries (points of linguistically permissible phrase ending) and of silences as cues to speaker switching (Gerstman, Feldstein, and Jaffe, 1967).

The importance of the proposed recursive model is that it provides the basis for a theory of the conversational time patterns of two-person and multi-person groups. If only for heuristic reasons and for the structure it offers, such a theory should be useful in conceptualizing and integrating the research directions mentioned above. Beyond that, it may ultimately be capable of serving as a point of articulation between theories of linguistic competence and performance.

---

[14]An illustration may clarify the point of this hypothesis. Whatever efficacy is attributed to the psychiatric and/or psychotherapeutic interview is associated with its semantic content (i.e., with what the patient and doctor discussed), while the relevance of its demonstrably characteristic temporal configuration has received only passing recognition. Interestingly, the most (although not the only) recognition is implied by the psychoanalytic position, which requires of the therapist that "his predominant reaction is one of silent listening" (Menninger, 1958, p. 86). The rationale underlying this position is that the extended silences of the therapist allow the patient to talk about topics considered therapeutically useful. The important point here is that the semantic content of the dialogue is assumed to be at least somewhat dependent upon its temporal structure.

References

ANDERSON, C. W. The relation between speaking times and decision in the employment interview. *J. Appl. Psychol.*, 1960, **44**, 267-8.

BRENNER, M. S., FELDSTEIN, S., and JAFFE, J. The contribution of statistical uncertainty and test anxiety to speech disruption. *J. Verbal Learn. Verbal Behav.*, 1965, **4**, 300-5.

CASSOTTA, L., FELDSTEIN, S., and JAFFE, J. AVTA: A device for automatic vocal transaction analysis. *J. Exp. Anal. Behav.*, 1964, **7**, 99-104.

CASSOTTA, L., FELDSTEIN, S., and JAFFE, J. Stability, influence, and congruence in dyadic vocal interaction. Paper read at Eastern Psychological Association, Boston, April 1967.

CASSOTTA, L., FELDSTEIN, S., and JAFFE, J. The stability and modifiability of individual vocal characteristics in stress and nonstress interviews. *Res. Bull. No. 2.* The William Alanson White Institute, New York, 1968.

CASSOTTA, L., JAFFE, J., FELDSTEIN, S., and MOSES, R. Operating manual: Automatic Vocal Transaction Analyzer. *Res. Bull. No. 1.* The William Alanson White Institute, New York, 1964.

CERVIN, V. Relationship of ascendant-submissive behavior in dyadic groups of human subjects to their emotional responsiveness. *J. Abnorm. Soc. Psychol.*, 1957, **54**, 241-9.

CHAPPLE, E. D. Quantitative analysis of the interaction of individuals. *Proceed. Natl. Acad. Sci.*, 1939, **25**, 58-67.

CHAPPLE, E. D. "Personality" differences as described by invariant properties of individuals in interaction. *Proceed. Nat. Acad. Sci.*, 1940, **26**, 10-16.

CHAPPLE, E. D., CHAPPLE, M. F., and RAPP, J. A. Behavioral definitions of personality and temperament characteristics. *Human Orgn.*, 1954, **13**, 34-9.

CHAPPLE, E. D., CHAPPLE, M. F., WOOD, L. A., MIKLOWITZ, A., KLINE, N. S., and SAUNDERS, J. C. Interaction Chronograph method for analysis of differences between schizophrenics and controls. *Arch. Gen. Psychiat.*, 1960, **3**, 160-7.

CHAPPLE, E. D., and DONALD, G., JR. A method for evaluating supervisory personnel. *Harvard Bus. Rev.*, 1946, **24**, 197-214.

COLLINS, M. E. Dissimulation factors in attitude measurement: A factor-analytic study of attitudes of white Americans toward the American Negro. Paper read at the Social Psychology Seminar, Columbia University, 1964.

FAIRBANKS G., and HOAGLIN, W. L. An experimental study of the durational characteristics of the voice during the expression of emotion. *Speech Monog.*, 1941, **8**, 85-90.

FELDSTEIN, S. The relationship of interpersonal involvement and affectiveness of content to the verbal communication of schizophrenic patients. *J. Abnorm. Soc. Psychol.*, 1962, **64**, 29-45.

FELDSTEIN, S. Vocal patterning of emotional expression. In J. H. Masserman (Ed.), *Science and Psychoanalysis*, Vol. VII. Grune & Stratton, 1964. Pp. 193-208.

FELDSTEIN, S. Interspeaker influence in conversational interaction. *Psychol. Rep.*, 1968, **22**, 826-8.

FELDSTEIN, S., BRENNER, M. S., and JAFFE, J. The effect of subject sex, verbal interaction, and topical focus on speech disruption. *Language and Speech*, 1963, **6**, 229-39.

FELDSTEIN, S., and JAFFE, J. A note about speech disturbances and vocabulary diversity. *J. Commun.*, 1962, **12**, 166-70. (a)

FELDSTEIN, S., and JAFFE, J. The relationship of speech disruption to the experience of anger. *J. Consult. Psychol.*, 1962, **26**, 505-9. (b)

FELDSTEIN, S., and JAFFE, J. Vocabulary diversity of schizophrenics and normals. *J. Speech Hear. Res.*, 1962, **5**, 76-8. (c)

FELDSTEIN, S., and JAFFE, J. Language predictability as a function of psychotherapeutic interaction. *J. Consult. Psychol.*, 1963, **27**, 123-6. (a)

FELDSTEIN, S., and JAFFE, J.   Schizophrenic speech fluency: A partial replication and an hypothesis. *Psychol. Repts.*, 1963, **13**, 775-80. (b)

FELDSTEIN, S., JAFFE, J., and CASSOTTA, L.   Mathematically predicted time patterns of dialogue. Paper read at Eastern Psychological Association, New York, April 1966.

FELDSTEIN, S., JAFFE, J., and CASSOTTA, L.   The effect of mutual visual access upon conversational time patterns. *Amer. Psychol.*, 1967, **23**, 594. (Abstract)

FELDSTEIN, S., ROGALSKI, C., and JAFFE, J.   Predictability and disruption of spontaneous speech. *Language and Speech*, 1966, **9**, 137-52.

FINK, M., JAFFE, J., and KAHN, R. L.   Drug induced changes in interview patterns: Linguistic and neurophysiologic indices. In G. J. Sarwer-Foner (Ed.), *The Dynamics of Psychiatric Drug Therapy*. Thomas, Springfield, Ill., 1960. Pp. 29-44.

GERSTMAN, L. J., FELDSTEIN, S., and JAFFE, J.   Syntactical versus temporal cues for speaker switching in natural dialogue. Paper read at Acoustical Society of America, Florida, November, 1967.

HAGGARD E. A.   *Intraclass Correlation and the Analysis of Variance*. Drydon, New York, 1958.

HARGREAVES, W. A., and STARKWEATHER, J. A.   Collection of temporal data with the Duration Tabulator. *J. Exper. Anal. of Behav.*, 1959, **2**, 179-83.

JAFFE, J.   Language of the dyad: A method of interaction analysis in psychiatric interviews. *Psychiat.*, 1958, **21**, 249-58.

JAFFE, J. and FELDSTEIN, S.   *Rhythms of dialogue*. Academic Press, New York, 1970.

JAFFE, J., FELDSTEIN, S., and CASSOTTA, L.   A stochastic model of speaker switching in natural dialogue. In K. Salzinger and S. Salzinger (Eds.), *Research in Verbal Behavior and Some Neurophysiological Implications*. Academic Press, New York, 1967. Pp. 281-94. (b)

JAFFE, J., FELDSTEIN, S., and CASSOTTA, L.   Markovian models of dialogic time patterns. *Nature*, 1967, **216**, 93-4. (a)

JAFFE, J. and NORMAN D. A.   A simulation of the time patterns of dialogue. (Scientific Report No. CS-4) Center for Cognitive Studies, Harvard University, Cambridge, Mass., 1964.

KANFER, F. H., PHILLIPS, J. S., MATARAZZO, J. D., and SASLOW, G.   Experimental modification of interview content in standardized interviews. *J. Consult. Psychol.*, 1960, **24**, 528-36.

LUNDY, B. W.   Temporal factors of interaction in psychotherapy. Unpublished doctoral dissertation, University of Chicago, 1955.

MARCUS, E. S.   The relationship of psychological differentiation to the congruence of temporal patterns of speech. Unpublished doctoral dissertation, New York University, 1970.

MATARAZZO, R. G., MATARAZZO, J. D., SASLOW, G., and PHILLIPS, J. S.   Psychological test and organismic correlates of interview interaction behavior. *J. Abnorm. Soc. Psychol.*, 1958, **56**, 329-38.

MATARAZZO, J. D., and SASLOW, G.   Differences in interview interaction behavior among normal and deviant groups. In I. A. Berg and B. M. Bass (Eds.), *Conformity and Deviation*. Harper, New York, 1961. Pp. 286-327.

MATARAZZO, J. D., SASLOW, G., and MATARAZZO, R. G.   The Interaction Chronograph as an instrument for objective measurement of interaction patterns during interviews. *J. Psychol*, 1956, **41**, 347-67.

MATARAZZO, J. D., WIENS, A. N., and SASLOW, G.   Studies in interview speech behavior. In L. Krasner and L. P. Ullmann (Eds.), *Research in Behavior Modification: New Developments and Their Clinical Implications*. Holt, Rinehart & Winston, New York, 1965.

MENNINGER, K.   *Theory of Psychoanalytic Technique*. Basic Books, New York, 1958.

QUINE, W. V. O.   *Methods of Logic*. Holt, Rinehart & Winston, New York, 1959.

RAY, M. L., and WEBB, E. J.   Speech duration effects in the Kennedy news conferences. *Sci.*, 1966, **153**, 899-901.

ROGALSKI, C. J.   Individual differences in verbal behavior. Unpublished doctoral dissertation, New York University, 1968.

SIEGMAN A. W. and POPE, B. Effects of question specificity and anxiety-producing messages on verbal fluency in the initial interview. *J. Personal. Soc. Psychol.*, 1965, **2**, 522-30.

TIMMONS, E. O., RICKARD, H. C., and TAYLOR, R. E. Reliability of content-free, group verbal behavior. *Psychol. Rec.*, 1960, **10**, 297-305.

VERZEANO, M., and FINESINGER, J. E. An automatic analyzer for the study of speech in interaction and in free association. *Sci.*, 1949, **2845**, 45-6.

WEINSTEIN, R., FELDSTEIN, S., and JAFFE, J. The interaction of vocal context and lexical predictability. *Language and Speech*, 1965, **8**, 56-66.

Chapter 6

Interview Synchrony

An Investigation of Two Speech Rate Measures in an Automated Standardized Interview

James T. Webb

SYNCHRONY between interviewer *(E)* and interviewee *(S)* has been noted in numerous and diverse experimental situations. In this context "synchrony" refers to a behavioral phenomenon in which as the *E* varies his interview activity level, the *S* varies his own interview behaviors (i.e., activity level) in a matching manner. Whereas Matarazzo and others have reported synchrony between the behavior of *E* and *S* for such speech behaviors as duration (Matarazzo, Wiens, Saslow, Dunham, and Voas, 1964), and latency (Matarazzo and Wiens, 1967), this contribution will report findings of a synchrony relation between the speech rates of the *E* and the *S*. The reliability of these synchrony phenomena has prompted Matarazzo (1965) to put forth a "synchrony model." This model will be discussed in an attempt to expand it, and some questions concerning its revision will be raised.

The present study is based on an automated interview. Since the methodology used is relatively novel, this report will have both a methodological and substantive focus. The latter focus is concerned with the "synchrony model"; the former with the application of the automated interview in the present and in other relevant studies.

BACKGROUND

Matarazzo postulated that "any greater activity by the interviewer (e.g., head nodding, saying "mm-hmm," increasing his own speech durations) is interpreted by the interviewee as indicating that the

115

interviewer is more interested in, or more empathic toward, the interviewee, or that he otherwise values the interviewee more" (Matarazzo, 1965, p. 208). Accordingly, the S increases or decreases his speech behavior in direct relation to increases or decreases in the E's speech behavior. Such synchrony relations have been demonstrated for duration of utterance (Matarazzo, 1962), loudness (Black, 1949), precision of articulation (Tolhurst, 1955), conversational latency (Matarazzo and Wiens, 1967), and silence length (Jaffe, 1967). Speech rates, however, have received little attention in this regard.

Speech rates have been studied in naturalistic settings and in non-interview situations. Two distinctive measures of speech rate have been described, but functional similarities and differences have not been clearly delineated. Contamination of the two measures has generated ambiguity. An experimental analysis in which both rate measures were independently manipulated during an interview situation seemed needed, with stringent controls for interviewer variables of content, of postural and facial cues, and of other non-content speech variables.

Furthermore, speech rates are compound measures, having syllable (or word) frequency as the numerator and time duration as the denominator. Since duration (Matarazzo, Weitman, Saslow, and Wiens, 1963) and syllable length (Webb, 1967b) have been found to be significant interview parameters, the possibility existed that speech rates interact with speech duration and/or syllable length. Systematic control of durations and syllable lengths of statements within manipulations of the E's speech rates are required to assess this possibility.

RELATED STUDIES

Several investigators, (Clevenger and Clark, 1963; Goldman-Eisler, 1956; Martin, 1955) have pointed out that speech consists of a series of discrete utterances (phonations) separated by hesitation pauses. They have proposed two measures: *Rate I* (absolute rate), which is the number of syllables divided by phonation time, and *Rate II*, which is the number of syllables per unit of time during the period of speech occurring between two utterances made by the other person (Table I). Rate II includes both phonation and pause times and is based on a unit of behavior different from Rate I. The speech unit of Rate II is labeled an action and may be composed of many utterances.

Goldman-Eisler (1956) and Martin (1955) found Rate I and II to be quantitatively and functionally different, although the degree of independence varied with other aspects of the S's and the E's

TABLE I.

Rates and Units of Speech Behavior

utterance =	number of syllables in an unbroken speech act.
action =	sum of syllables in the utterances that compose an action.
t =	time used in producing an utterance.
P.T. =	pause times which separate and thus define utterances.
Rate I =	number of syllables of utterance / t
Rate II = $\sum$	number of syllables of utterances / $\sum t + \sum$ P.T.

interview behavior. Ruesch and Prestwood (1949) and Webb (1967b) found S's Rates I and/or II to be directly influenced by (i.e., synchronous with) E's Rates I and/or II. Results were equivocal, however, for the E's Rates I and II were confounded with other E variables such as gestures, facial expressions, interview style, and variation in the duration of actions and utterances. Further, the S's behavior may have influenced the E's rates.

Lightfoot (1949) and Lightfoot and Black (1949) achieved better control of these variables. Although non-interview situations were used and small behavior samples (5-syllable phrases) were studied, a significant positive relation was found between the speech rates of the E and the S. Both the E's Rate I (Lightfoot, 1949) and Rate II (Lightfoot and Black, 1949) were shown to affect the S's rates. Neither study specified, however, whether the S's Rate I or Rate II was measured.

STATEMENT OF PROBLEM

The investigation of the differential influences of the E's speech Rates I and II on the S's Rates I and II, with regard to possible "synchrony" effects, necessitated stringent control of the E's behavior. It required the elimination of facial cues, head nods, other postural cues, and "directive" or "interpretive" statements. Likewise, control was needed of the E's inflection, loudness, number of pauses per statement, and proportion of pause times to statement duration, while speech rates were systematically manipulated. Finally, it was necessary to develop an interview situation where S's speech patterns could not feed back to influence E's speech behavior.

To achieve such control of *E*'s behavior in an interview while simultaneously maintaining the *S*'s freedom of response, the interviewer was "automated"; his statements were prerecorded on audio tape and he was physically removed from the interviews. Since the tapes were carefully prepared beforehand under circumstances free of social strain, adequate attention could be paid to manipulating the independent variables without extraneous *S* cues (e.g., the *S*'s behavior or attitudes) intervening. By using a common tape, exact stimulus replication (Maccoby and Maccoby, 1954) across the Ss was achieved. Moreover it was possible to remove confounding stimuli such as facial expression, head nods, and postural cues. Contact, inflection, accent, loudness, pause duration, number of pauses per statement, proportion of pause time to statement duration, and the *E*'s speech rates were held constant across the Ss.

In the present automated and standard interview, variations in the *E*'s statement syllable length, pause durations, and statement durations were achieved within manipulations of the *E*'s speech rates, thus allowing for analyses of interaction effects. The analyses of interaction effects were of particular importance in the present study since speech rates are compound measures derived from speech durations and syllable lengths.

AUTOMATING THE INTERVIEW

The task of constructing an automated interview which would appear natural and yet embody the necessary controls poses certain difficulties. On the basis of "live" pilot study interviews (Webb, 1967b), and interview narratives reported by Chapple (1953) and Snyder (1947), non-directive comments were derived of such a general nature as to be relatively independent of specific *S* responses. It was possible to construct such comments by relating them all to a non-specific topic, the world situation.[1] A sample of the *E* statements used in the present study is presented in Table II. To anticipate conversations where a basic statement might not be appropriate, a series of "emergency statements" was constructed. If deemed by *E* to be more relevant to the *S*'s previous response, an emergency statement was selected and introjected into the interview. Both the form and the content of *E*'s statements adhered to Matarazzo's (1962) rules for Chapple's (1939, 1940) Standardized Interview.

---

[1]Interviews for all Ss were conducted during the 20 day period of December 12, 1966 through January 5, 1967, a period when no acute world crises were being reported by news media.

TABLE II.

A Sample of the Experimenter's Prerecorded Statements

(in order of presentation)

Number of Syllables per Statement°		Statement
45	1.	"I wonder if you could tell me / as many different things as you can that seem important to you / about the present world situation / or our international policy."
45	2.	"This seems to you / to be a fairly important aspect of the present world situation / I wonder if perhaps you might be able to tell me / a little bit more about it."
45	3.	"Would you like to carry that on a little bit further / and round it out a bit? / Perhaps you could tell me something about some of the other things / that you know or have heard about it."
45	4.	"Um-hmm, I wonder if / perhaps you might be able to tell me / some of the things you've heard other folks saying recently / about their point of view of this sort of situation."
Condition 1 45	5.	"I'm not exactly sure / if I understand exactly what you mean. / I wonder if you might be able to tell me a bit more / about the sort of thing you had in mind."
30	6.	"Could you continue on some more about this / or some other aspects / that are of particular interest to you?"
30	7.	"These are quite interesting things you have told me; / could you tell me about / some other aspects of the world situation?"
30	8.	"It's often so complex, uh, / but I wonder if you could give / me an example or two of the type of thing you mean."
30	9.	"This then seems to be a fairly important aspect. / Perhaps / you might be able to say a little bit more about it."
45	10.	"I'm not exactly sure / if I understand exactly what you mean. / I wonder if you might be able to tell me a little bit more / about the sort of thing you had in mind."

Number of Syllables per Statement		Emergency Statements
38	1.	"Um-hmm, please don't feel that you have to talk all the time. / Sometimes one needs a little time to think and organize, / so you just tell me / as you think of things."
Conditions 1 and 2 38	2.	"Um-hmm, well, / perhaps you could / elaborate on some aspect of the world situation that you're interested in or / have heard folks talking about."
38	3.	"Um-hmm, well / could you / elaborate on some of the things you said earlier or / on some other aspect of the world situation, either would be fine."

°*Diagonals (/) indicate location of pauses in each statement.*

Investigators using such a Standardized Interview technique have demonstrated significant reliability for S with different Es (Dinoff, Morris, and Hannon, 1963) and significant stability of the S's interactions with the same E (Saslow and Matarazzo, 1959). Verbal content, within limits, has little influence on non-content speech variables (Matarazzo, Weitman, and Saslow, 1963). The S's flexibility in responding is maintained. Experienced clinician-observers, if not informed that a Standardized Interview is in progress, are unable to differentiate these interviews from naturalistic initial interviews (Dinoff, 1967; Matarazzo, 1962). Such success with Standardized Interviews provided encouragement for automation of such a technique.

PROCEDURE

The 14 Ss were told that the E, speaking from an adjoining room, was sampling student attitudes on the world situation. The physical separation of the E and the S was explained as an attempt not to bias the S's responses through facial expressions. Postinterview questioning indicated that the S, in this arrangement, could only rarely discern that the E's questions and comments were prerecorded.

Each S received the four experimental conditions described below. Originally, 20 E statements were to be used in each condition. But pilot interviews indicated E's statements to evoke more S response than anticipated with interviews lasting up to three hours. To control potential fatigue effects, only 10 E statements per condition were used with the present 14 Ss. It is felt that the S population used in the present study put the realism of the automated interview to a severe test. All Ss had an I.Q. of at least 110 as measured by the Vocabulary subscale of the Wechsler Adult Intelligence Scale. They were undergraduate psychology students between the ages of 18 and 25 with no known history of emotional disturbance. The majority of the Ss had participated in other psychology experiments and four Ss were currently enrolled in an advanced undergraduate research course. Consequently, the S population was both bright and "experiment-wise."

Each S was presented the same four conditions of prerecorded E speech rates, with the presentation order counterbalanced across Ss. A condition was terminated after 10 E statements followed by S's subsequent response. Within each condition the variances of the E's speech rates were held constant within a narrow, prespecified range, and the variances across conditions were not significantly different (Webb, 1967a). Each condition presented a different combination of the two rate measures wherein each rate measure was *relatively* high or low in relation to the other rate measure. The four conditions were:

(a) Condition 1: High Rate I with short pauses (i.e., High Rate II);
(b) Condition 2: High Rate I with long pauses (i.e., Low Rate II);
(c) Condition 3: Low Rate I with short pauses (i.e., High Rate II);
(d) Condition 4: Low Rate I with long pauses (i.e., Low Rate II).

TABLE III.

A Priori Criteria of E's Rates, Durations, and Syllable Lengths of Statements for Each Condition

	Condition 1		Condition 2		Condition 3		Condition 4	
	I	II°	I	II	I	II	I	II
Rates (s.p.m.)°°	400	360	400	240	270	240	270	160
Syllable Length	45	45	45	45	45	45	45	45
Duration	6.7	7.5	6.7	11.3	10.0	11.3	10.0	16.9
Total Pause Length°°°		0.8		4.6		1.3		6.9
Number of Pauses per Statement		3		3		3		3
Percent Pause Time of Total Action Time		10.7		40.7		11.5		40.8
Syllable Length	30	30	30	30	30	30	30	30
Duration	4.5	5.0	4.5	7.5	6.7	7.5	6.7	11.3
Total Pause Length		0.5		3.0		0.8		4.6
Number of Pauses per Statement		2		2		2		2
Percent Pause Time of Total Action Time		10.0		40.0		10.7		40.7
Syllable Length					20	20	20	20
Duration					4.5	5.0	4.5	7.5
Total Pause Length						0.5		3.0
Number of Pauses per Statement						1		1
Percent Pause Time of Total Action Time						10.0		40.0
Emergency Statements								
Syllable Length	38	38	38	38	30	30	30	30
Duration	5.7	6.3	5.7	9.5	6.7	7.5	6.7	11.3
Total Pause Length		0.6		3.8		0.8		4.6
Number of Pauses per Statement		3		3		2		2
Percent Pause Time of Total Action Time		10.0		40.0		10.7		40.7

°*Roman numerals I and II designate Rates I and II.*

°°*Syllables per minute (s.p.m.) is obtained by dividing syllable length by duration and multiplying the dividend by 60 seconds.*

°°°*Applies only to Rate II and is expressed in seconds.*

As is seen in Table III, duration and statement syllable length were also varied in each condition according to *a priori* criteria such that subsequent analyses could compare duration and syllable length effects independently of rate conditions.

E statement topics for Conditions 1 and 3 were constructed first. Through successive approximations E was able to successfully meet the *a priori* criteria for these conditions (Webb, 1967a). Conditions 2 and 4 were constructed respectively from the tapes of Conditions 1 and 2 by lengthening the pauses which already existed at syntactically logical points (Lightfoot and Black, 1949). Lengthening was accomplished by splicing in measured pieces of "blank" tape which had matching levels of background noise so as to make the splices imperceptible. "Emergency" tapes containing three E statements each were constructed in similar fashion so that one emergency tape matched the criteria for each condition tape.

Each S was interviewed individually. His microphone led to a voice-operated relay through a preamplifier. The voice-operated relay allowed sensitivity adjustment of the holding interval (i.e., the amplitude needed to activate the relay) and adjustment of the holding interval (i.e., the interval that the relay remained energized after the last sound which exceeded the preset sensitivity level). The holding interval was preset at .15 seconds.

The S's voice-operated relay was connected to a three-second time-delay relay (*i.e.*, a relay having a "drop-out" delay of three seconds). Thus, once the S began speaking, the delay relay remained in the "actuated" state so long as the S did not pause for more than 3.15 seconds. When the S paused longer, the delay relay closed activating relay circuitry, thus causing the E's tape-recorded response to be played. When the E's response ended, the tape recorder stopped and the circuitry reset. The three-second drop-out time was chosen since Goldman-Eisler (1961) found 99 percent of speech pauses to be less than two seconds and no pauses, except speaker switching pauses, to be greater than three seconds. In fact, analysis of the 14 interviews of the present study showed the E's average latency to be 4.25 seconds with a standard deviation of mean latency across interviews of .75 seconds. The one-second difference between the predesignated three-second latency and the actual four-second latency stemmed from the tape "leader" which separated the E statements. This circuitry is described more fully elsewhere (Webb, 1967a). Use of a three-second latency differed from the usual Standardized Interview rule which requires the E to respond in less than one second. This difference was felt to be legitimate, however, since recent Standardized Interview research (Matarazzo and Wiens,

1967) has shown the critical factor to be constancy of latency, rather than latency of a particular length.

The S's comments were constantly monitored by the E. When the upcoming preprogrammed responses on the "main" tape deck appeared inappropriate, the E activated the "emergency" tape deck. This was done during the three-second timer period by a switch on a panel board in front of the E. Following the emergency response, the E switched back to the main tape deck and the interview condition continued until 10 E statements had been played. In the present study, an average of one emergency statement was used for every 18.1 "main" statements.

All interviews were tape recorded and were transcribed verbatim, including such speech errors as repetitions, false starts, etc., and such vague sounds as "eh" and "ah." Speech rates were measured in syllables per minute, since syllables are more appropriate than words for measuring the length of utterances (Cotton, 1936; Goldman-Eisler, 1954, 1956). A Webster's dictionary was used as the criterion on syllable composition except in those cases where the vague sounds of "eh" and "ah" were present. These sounds, though not constituting words, were counted as syllables, since French, Carter, and Koenig (1930) found that 20 percent of conversational utterances consisted of half-completed words and non-word interjections such as "eh" and "ah." Contractions (e.g., "didn't") were counted as separate words.

Scoring of speech and pause times was done following the interview.[2] The tape recordings of the interviews were played at half-speed through the voice-operated relay connected to an Esterline-Angus Operations Recorder. During playback, the hold and sensitivity adjustments on the voice-operated relay were held at a constant position. When the S or the E spoke, the pen was activated. The distances between pen-recorded marks on the operations recorder were measured. Although this phase of the data reduction had the advantage of demanding little sophisticated equipment, the man-hours involved make it prohibitive for large-scale research. More sophisticated and accurate systems which automatically score speech and pause times have been developed by Hargreaves and Stark-weather (1963), by Cassotta, Jaffe, Feldstein, and Moses (1964) and by Wiens, Matarazzo, and Saslow (1965).

---

[2]In the present study, hesitation in speech of 0.2 seconds or longer were counted as pauses. Other pause definitions are 0.2 sec. (Boomer, 1965), 0.25 sec. (Goldman-Eisler, 1958), 0.5 sec. (Verzeano and Finesinger, 1949), 0.75 sec. (Simkins, 1963), and 1.0 sec. (Hargreaves and Starkweather, 1959).

RESULTS

For all statistical analyses the .05 level of probability for two-tailed tests was taken as the acceptable level of statistical significance. Since the experimental procedure allowed each S to be his own control, repeated measures statistics were used wherever possible.

Subject's mean Rate I (absolute rate) differed significantly across conditions ($F=20.89$, $df=3,39$, $p < .001$).[3] A Newman-Keuls test (Winer, 1962) showed the S's Rate I to be higher (faster) in Conditions 1 and 2 than in Conditions 3 and 4. Differences between Conditions 1 and 2 or between Conditions 3 and 4 were non-significant.

It should be noted that in Conditions 1 and 2, the E's Rate I was the same, for these conditions differed only in the length of the E's pauses (and thus in Rate II). Likewise, for Conditions 3 and 4, the E's behavior differed only in pause lengths. Thus, it was concluded that the E's Rate I (absolute rate) directly influences the S's Rate I, but that varying the E's pauses did not influence the S's Rate I.

Subject's Rate II likewise differed significantly across conditions ($F=3.74$, $df=3,39$, $p < .025$). A Newman-Keuls test showed the S's Rate II to be significantly higher in Condition 1 than in Condition 3. But changes in the E's pause durations had no discernible systematic influence on the S's Rate II, for Conditions 2 and 4 did not differ from each other nor from Conditions 1 and 3. It is likely that S's Rate II differences in Conditions 1 and 3 are reflections of S's Rate I differences reported above.

To determine if the differences in the S's Rate II across conditions reflected actual changes in the S's pause times, S's pause durations were compared across conditions. No significant differences were found ($F=.75$, $df=3,39$, n.s.). Differences in the S's Rate II were actually reflecting the E influences on the S's Rate I, rather than any influence on the S's pause durations. Thus inclusion of pauses in measuring S speech rates appears to reduce the sensitivity, for variance contributed by S pausing cannot at present be systematically accounted for.

Rates I and II are compound measures; syllable length is the numerator and speech duration is the denominator. Thus the E's syllable length and duration were examined for influence on the S's Rates I and II. Neither the E's syllable length nor the E's duration directly influenced the S's Rates I and II. But a significant interaction occurred between the E's Rate I and the E's syllable length in

---

[3]Tables of these and subsequent statistical analyses are contained in Webb (1967a).

influencing the S's Rates I and II (F=5.12 and 6.12, respectively, df= 1.13, p < .05). The interaction suggests that synchrony effects are heightened when larger sements of E's speech are presented to the S. The possibility exists that the E's duration also interacts with the E's rates, but this interaction could not be examined in the present design.

DISCUSSION

As was suggested by earlier studies, the present data indicated Rates I and II to be sensitive dependent variables, particularly Rate I. As an independent variable, Rate I was clearly shown to be a salient and powerful parameter in influencing the S's speech behavior. Consequently, Lightfoot's (1949) finding that the E's Rate I influenced the S's Rate I of repeating a five-syllable phrase may be generalized to longer segments of conversational behavior. The present findings likewise demonstrated synchrony between the behavior of the E and the S with regard to Rate I, though not with regard to pauses.

THE SYNCHRONY MODEL

Matarazzo's (1965) synchrony model not only labels a behavioral phenomenon found in many specific aspects of dyads, but also makes a first attempt at describing the underlying mechanism of these behavioral synchrony phenomena. As mentioned earlier, this model posits that any greater activity by the interviewer is perceived by the interviewee as indicating greater interest or empathy by the interviewer and results in increased S behavior. As presented, this model suggests a reinforcement paradigm, and it would appear that Matarazzo is explaining a naturalistic occurrence in reinforcement terms. But examination of the various interviewer activities and situations which result in behavioral synchrony suggests some difficulties for such a reinforcement model as Matarazzo portrays.

Although used to label the model, the term "synchrony" has not as yet been carefully defined. In the present context, synchrony is said to exist when intensity, frequency, or durational characteristics of one's behavior rhythmically agree with similar characteristics of ambient stimuli, whether personal or impersonal in origin. In the present paper, only verbal synchrony will be discussed, although some intriguing experiments suggest similar phenomena occur in postural dimensions of interaction (Condon and Ogston, 1967; Ekman and Friesen, 1967; Kendon, 1968), and even that "self-synchrony" occurs between one's body motions and the cadence of one's speech (Condon and Ogston, 1967).

In interpersonal synchrony, the S varies his speech behavior in direct relation to increases or decreases in the E's speech behavior. In standardized experimental situations, such synchrony has been demonstrated for duration of utterance (Matarazzo, 1962), and of conversational latency (Matarazzo and Wiens, 1967), and for intensity or loudness of speech (Black, 1949). In naturalistic situations, utterance duration synchrony has been replicated (Matarazzo and Wiens, 1967) and synchrony has been found for silence durations (Jaffe, 1964). Further, duration synchrony is independent of visual or postural cues, for the phenomenon occurs even when E is not in the same room as S (Matarazzo, Wiens, Saslow, Dunham and Voas, 1964).

These occurrences may be adequately accounted for by a social reinforcement paradigm, for certainly it is clear that non-content speech behaviors are susceptible to reinforcement (Bachrach, Candland, and Gibson, 1961; Simkins, 1963). But the phenomenon of speech-rate synchrony (Lightfoot, 1949; Webb, 1967a, 1967b) is not consonant with such a reinforcement model. Kanfer has shown that increased speech rates are induced by experimental anxiety (1958a, 1958b) and by emotional conversational topics (1959). Other studies (Ruesch and Prestwood, 1949; Tolhurst, 1955) have demonstrated that listeners find fast speaking rates unpleasant, with one study (Ruesch and Prestwood, 1949) also demonstrating that, in spite of the perceived unpleasantness, the anxiety associated with fast speech rates caused increased anxiety in previously neutral and non-participating listeners. Thus, since high speech rates are apparently major cues of anxiety, they are quite unlikely to be positively rewarding or to convey increased warmth.

A further difficulty for Matarazzo's reinforcement paradigm arises from the temporal characteristics of synchrony phenomena. If reinforcement were operative, learning and extinction curves should occur, and the behavior changes reinforced should be relatively stable. But Black (1949), Lightfoot (1949), Ruesch and Prestwood (1949), and Webb (1967a, 1967b) have powerfully demonstrated changes in various S behaviors to be virtually immediate in relation to maintaining synchrony with ambient stimuli.

Matarazzo and Wiens (1967) have more recently expressed the notion that behavioral synchrony might be related to Bandura's (1965) "modeling" framework. But Bandura's modeling phenomenon implies conscious volition and conscious attending to relevant modeling cues. To date, synchrony behavior investigations show little evidence that synchrony phenomena are either conscious or volitional.

(More investigation is certainly needed concerning possible conscious and/or volitional factors in this area.) Bandura's model, as now stated, does not appear sufficient to encompass the synchrony phenomenon.

An extension of Bandura's model is possible, though, which might make it more encompassing. As one consciously mimics the behavior of a model, it is quite possible that he is also learning a habit of modeling so that many aspects of his subsequent behaviors are unconsciously modeled. In this way, modeling behavior, itself, might come to be a secondary reinforcer, since most of the S's previous experiences with modeling have been rewarded.

Alternate, and more inclusive, is the activation-level model of Fiske and Maddi (1961), which emphasizes activation-level interaction between S and his environment. This model posits that organisms have characteristic activity levels, but increases or decreases in ambient stimuli result in temporarily increased or decreased activation and somatic arousal of the organisms strictly as a function of stimuli impact. Support for this notion is found in such studies as that by John (1967) of the phenomenon of photic driving of EEG patterns and by Zimny and Weidenfeller (1963), in which S's GSR changes corresponded closely with changes in tempo of heard music.

With this model one can explain not only interpersonal synchrony, but also synchrony between one's behavior and the rhythm or cadence of ambient stimuli. Since Licklider and Miller (1951) demonstrated that the "auditory system obviously analyzes along the spatial dimensions (of) . . . intensity, frequency, and time. . . ." (p. 1059), it is reasonable to examine for synchrony between S's behavior and non-personal ambient stimuli along intensity, frequency, and time dimensions (e.g., cadence or rate). Such synchrony apparently exists, and causes further difficulty for Matarazzo's model as presently conceived.

Heckel, Wiggins, and Salzberg (1963) found that when two musical selections, one fast tempo and one slow tempo, were played at audible but not interfering levels, patients in four psychotherapy groups under fast tempo showed a consistent average increase of 22 percent ($p < .001$) in speech rate (Rate II) as compared with conditions of no music or slow music. Brister (1968) replicated the study of Heckel *et al.* (1963) under more controlled conditions, and found similar significant synchrony of the S's speech rate (Rate II) with audible background music of fast and slow tempo.

Visual, but non-behavioral, verbal cues likewise instigate synchrony. Bender and Brister (1968) administered two forms of a sentence completion test in which half of the stimulus items in each form were "short" and half were "long," but which were equated for informational value. A highly significant positive relation was obtained between the number of stimulus words and the number of words in the S's associated responses.

At this point, an activation-level approach to synchrony appears more tenable than a reinforcement model or a "modeling" framework and implies basic, perceptual-physiological mechanism underlying behavioral synchrony. The extent of explanatory applicability of such a model for synchrony phenomena needs more investigation, and certain aspects of the synchrony phenomenon itself remain unclear.

What are the limits of the synchrony phenomenon and what happens when the limits are surpassed? Perhaps the stimulus deprivation studies are relevant by indicating a lower limit of tolerance for synchrony with ambient stimuli, for Ss begin to create their own stimuli after only relatively brief periods of stimulus deprivation.

And what is the interaction of synchrony with perceived role relations? That is, who gets synchronous with whom, or do both of a dyad become synchronous with each other? Are "dominant" or "independent" persons less susceptible to the synchrony phenomenon than "submissive" or "dependent" persons? Matarazzo's (1965) studies would suggest that the Ss tend to synchronize their behavior with the E whom they perceive as having the dominant role.

In addition to role aspects, indications exist which suggest an interaction of personality and synchrony behavior. For example, in an otherwise Standardized Interview, when the E introduced 15-second experimental silences, schizophrenic Ss increased their verbal actions, whereas normal and neurotic Ss decreased their actions in synchrony with E (Matarazzo, 1962).

THE AUTOMATED INTERVIEW

The results of the present study clearly demonstrated an automated interview to be feasible. Effective and sensitive control of the E's content and non-content speech is evidently achieved. Further, the control and systematic manipulation of the E's speech which are obtained through this methodology are sensitively reflected in the S's speech behavior. The automated interview is a highly reliable procedure characterized by exact stimulus replication both across Ss and across investigators. This methodology could be a powerful tool for discovering, in comparative studies, sources of unwanted E influence. Adair and Epstein (1968), using a slightly more rudimentary methodology, have demonstrated the power of such an approach in studying mediation cues of experimenter bias.

Ss' Standardized Interview behaviors, with a few exceptions (Dinoff, Morris, and Hannon, 1963; Hannon, 1963; Morris, 1963; Patterson, 1963), have not been used as dependent variables. But as Dinoff (1967) has noted, this technique has great potential for providing dependent variables for assessing a variety of clinical procedures such as psychotherapy, chemotherapy, hypnosis, operant techniques, stimulus deprivation, and stimulus bombardment. Because of the high reliability of S's behavior in such an interview, rigorous baseline measures are readily obtained. The automation of the E's role in the Standardized Interview should certainly enrich the uses of this technique in evoking dependent variables and allow extended control of extraneous variables.

Extensions of the present methodology are presently feasible. The prerecorded audio-taped E responses are being replaced by using pre-video-taped interviewer responses (Dinoff, et al., 1969). By storing a small library of video-taped E responses, a researcher with simultaneous access to two or more video-tape decks should be able to conduct a reasonably smooth interview. Thus facial and postural cues of the E and the S might be studied as independent variables and in interaction with content and non-content speech.

Investigation of an automated diagnostic intake interview is also feasible. Finesinger (1948) presented a series of interviewer activity levels which he felt to be of value in eliciting diagnostic information. Such activity levels could be readily investigated in automated, video-taped interviews.

A critical consideration, particularly when constructing an automated diagnostic or other clinical interview, is the continuous decision-making whether the upcoming prerecorded statement is relevant to S's conversation, or whether an alternate statement should be used. In the present study such decisions were made "live" by the E. But future experiments might well use computers to make such decisions and provide formal guidelines allowing more congruent simulation of clinical decisions.

Such attempts to interview Ss by means of a computer are presently under way (Bellman, Friend, and Kurland, 1966; Starkweather, 1967; Starkweather, Kamp, and Monto, 1967; Veldman, 1967) whereby the computer mimics and operationalizes interviewer decisions. Large gains may be expected from this approach. As Starkweather et al., (1967) point out, the benefits begin even with the actual construction of the computer program. Assumptions are forced into the open; "implicit ideas must be made explicit and contingencies must be foreseen which, in the course of normal work, are seldom thought about in advance" (p. 15).

A major limitation on computer interviewing at this time, however, is the problem of S's communications with the computer. At present, computers can comprehend and respond to only a very limited spoken vocabulary (Uhr and Vossler, 1961). However, some authors (Hillix, 1963; Uhr and Vossler, 1961) are optimistic about coping successfully with this difficulty. The problem of computers speaking back appears less awesome, as indicated by Estes *et al.*, (1964) who have successfully developed a limited program in which the computer synthesizes subword speech segments so that pitch and temporal characteristics of the computer-produced speech (from library segments) may be independently specified. But, as of now, computer interviewing virtually demands that the S and the computer communicate by typing their responses to each other (Bellman *et al.*, 1966; Starkweather, 1967; Starkweather *et al.*, 1967). This interface, of course, limits the communication to content stimuli.

Although, at present, computer interviewing is only a parallel development to the present automated interview, it is highly likely that the two approaches will be combined in the near future. Particularly does it appear that computer interviewing techniques and results will be relevant to the problems of ongoing decision-making of statement relevance.

References

ADAIR, J. G. and EPSTEIN, J. S.   Verbal cues in the mediation of experimenter bias. *Psychol. Rept.*, 1968, **22**, 1045-53.

BACHRACH, A. J., CANDLAND, D. K., and GIBSON, J. T.   Group reinforcement of individual response: Experiments in verbal behavior. In I. A. Berg and B. M. Bass (Eds.), *Conformity and Deviation*. Harper Bros., New York, 1961. Pp. 258-85.

BANDURA, A.   Behavioral modification through modeling procedures. In L. Krasner and L. P. Ullman (Eds.), *Research in Behavior Modification*. Holt, Rinehart & Winston, New York, 1965.

BELLMAN, R., FRIEND, M. B., and KURLAND, L.   Simulation of the initial psychiatric interview. *Behav. Sci.*, 1966, **11**, 389-99.

BENDER, L. and BRISTER, D. M.   Sex, synchrony and sentence completion. Unpublished manuscript, University of Alabama, 1968.

Black, J. W.   *Loudness of Speaking. I. The Effect of Heard Stimuli on Spoken Responses.* Joint Project No. 2, Contract N7Nonr-411 T.O.I., Project No. NM 001 053. U.S. Naval School of Aviation Medicine and Research, Pensacola, Florida and Kenyon College, Gambier, Ohio, 1949.

BOOMER, D. S.   Hesitation and grammatical encoding. *Language and Speech*, 1965, **8**, 148-58.

BRISTER, D. M.   The effect of music on verbal rate in an interview situation. Unpublished manuscript, University of Alabama, 1968.

CASSOTTA, L., JAFFE, J., FELDSTEIN, S., and MOSES, R.   *Operating Manual: An Automatic Vocal Transaction Analyzer.* William Alanson White Institute, New York, 1964.

CHAPPLE, E. D.   Quantitative analysis of the interaction of individuals. *Proc. Natl. Acad. Sci.*, 1939, **25**, 58-67.

CHAPPLE, E. D.   "Personality" differences as described by invariant properties of individuals in interaction. *Proc. Natl. Acad. Sci.*, 1940, **26**, 10-16.

CHAPPLE, E. D.   The standard experimental (stress) interview as used in Interaction Chronograph investigations. *Hum. Org.*, 1953, **12**, 23-32.

CLEVENGER, T. JR. and CLARK, M. L.   Coincidental variation as a source of confusion in the experimental study of rate. *Language and Speech*, 1963, **6**, 144-50.

CONDON, W. S. and OGSTON, W. D.   A segmentation of behavior. *J. Psychiat. Res.*, 1967, **5**, 221-35.

COTTON, J.   Syllabic rate: A new concept in the study of speech rate variation. *Speech Monographs*, 1936, **3**, 112-17.

DINOFF, M.   Standardized interview norms of elementary school children. In M. Dinoff (Chm.), Application of a standardized interview technique. Symposium presented at the Southeastern Psychological Association, Atlanta, April, 1967.

DINOFF, M., MORRIS, J. R., and HANNON, J. E.   The stability of schizophrenic speech in a standardized interview. *J. Clin. Psychol.*, 1963, **19**, 279-82.

DINOFF, M., CLARK, C. G., REITMAN, L. M., and SMITH, R. E.   The feasibility of video-tape interviewing. *Psychol. Rep.*, 1969, **25**, 239-42.

EKMAN, P. and FRIESEN, W. V.   Origin, usage and coding: The basis for five categories of nonverbal behavior. Paper presented at Symposium on Communication Theory and Linguistic Models. Center for Social Research, Torqcuato Di Tella Institute, Buenos Aires, Argentina, October, 1967.

ESTES, S. E., KERBY, H. R., MACEY, H. D., and WALKER, R. M.   Speech synthesis from stored data. *IBM J. Res. and Develop.*, 1964, **8**, 2-12.

FINESINGER, J. E.   Psychiatric interviewing. *Amer. J. Psychiat.*, 1948, **105**, 187-95.

FISKE, D. W. and MADDI, S. R.   A conceptual framework. In D. W. Fiske and S. R. Maddi (Eds.), *Functions of Varied Experience*. Dorsey Press, Homewood, Ill., 1961, 11-56.

FRENCH, N. R., CARTER, C. W., and KOENIG, W.   The words and sounds of telephone conversation. *Bell System Tech. J.*, 1930, **9**, 290-324.

GOLDMAN-EISLER, F.   On the variability of the speed of talking and its relation to the length of utterances in conversations. *Brit. J. Psychol.*, 1954, **45**, 94-107.

GOLDMAN-EISLER, F.   The determinants of the rate of speech output and their mutual relations. *J. Psychosom. Res.*, 1956, **1**, 137-43.

GOLDMAN-EISLER, F.   Speech production and the predictability of words in context. *Quart. J. Exper. Psychol.*, 1958, **10**, 96-106.

GOLDMAN-EISLER, F.   A comparative study of two hesitation phenomena. *Language and Speech*, 1961, **4**, 18-26.

HANNON, J. E.   Changes in standardized interview behavior in a normal and a schizophrenic group as a function of brief exteroceptive stimulus deprivation. Unpublished doctoral dissertation, University of Alabama, 1963.

HARGREAVES, W. A. and STARKWEATHER, J. A.   Collection of temporal data with the duration tabulator. *J. Exp. Analy. Behav.*, 1959, **2**, 179-83.

HARGREAVES, W. A. and STARKWEATHER, J. A.   Recognition of speaker identity. *Language and Speech*, 1963, **6**, 63-7.

HECKEL R. V., WIGGINS S. L., and SALZBERG, H. C.   The effect of musical tempo in varying operant speech levels in group psychotherapy. *J. Clin. Psychol.*, 1963, **19**, 129.

HILLIX, W. A.   Use of two non-acoustic measures in computer recognition of spoken digits. *J. Acoust. Soc. Amer.*, 1963, **35**, 1978-84.

JAFFE, J.   Computer analysis of verbal behavior in psychiatric interviews. In D. Rioch (Ed.), *Disorders in Communication: Proceedings of the Association for Research in Nervous and Mental Diseases*, Vol. 42. Williams & Wilkins, Baltimore, 1964.

JOHN, E. R.   *Mechanisms of Memory*. Academic Press, New York, 1967.

KANFER, F. H.   Effect of a warning signal preceding a noxious stimulus or verbal rate and heart rate. *J. Exp. Psychol.*, 1958a, **55**, 73-80.

KANFER, F. H.   Supplementary report: Stability of a verbal rate change in experimental anxiety. *J. Exp. Psychol.*, 1958b, **56**, 182.

KANFER, F. H.   Verbal rate, content and adjustment ratings in experimentally structured interviews. *J. Abnorm. Soc. Psychol.*, 1959, **58**, 305-11.

KENDON, A.   Body motion in the social performance. Paper presented at the Research Conference on Interview Behavior. The Psychiatric Institute, University of Maryland, Baltimore, April 22, 1968.

LICKLIDER, J. C. R. and MILLER, G. A.   The perception of speech. In S. S. Stevens (Ed.), *Handbook of Experimental Psychology*. Wiley, New York, 1951.

LIGHTFOOT, C.   *Rate of Speaking. I. Relation Between Original and Repeated Phrases.* Joint Project NR 782 004, Report No. 1, Kenyon College and Naval School of Aviation Medicine and Research, Pensacola, Florida, 1949.

LIGHTFOOT, C. and BLACK, J. W.   *Rate of Speaking, Responses to Heard Stimuli. II. Repetitions of Phrases Containing Logical and Illogical Pauses.* Joint Project NR 782 004, Report No. 1, Kenyon College and Naval School of Aviation Medicine and Research, Pensacola, Florida, 1949.

MACCOBY, E. E. and MACCOBY, N.   The interview: A tool of social science. In G. Lindzey, (Ed.), *Handb. Soc. Psychol.* Addison-Wesley, Reading, Massachusetts, 1954, 449-87. 449-87.

MARTIN, E. W.   The study of speech in interpersonal relationships: Techniques for analyzing rate relationships in a counseling situation. Unpublished M.A. thesis, University of Alabama, 1955.

MATARAZZO, J. D.   Prescribed behavior therapy: Suggestions from interview research. In A. J. Bachrach (Ed.), *Experimental Foundations of Clinical Psychology*. Basic Books, New York, 1962.

MATARAZZO, J. D.   The interview. In B. B. Wolman (Ed.), *Handbook of Clinical Psychology*. McGraw-Hill, New York, 1965. Pp. 403-48.

MATARAZZO, J. D., WEITMAN, M., and SASLOW, G.   Interview content and interviewee speech durations. *J. Clin. Psychol.*, 1963, **19**, 463-72.

MATARAZZO J. D., WEITMAN, M., SASLOW, G., and WIENS, A. N.   Interviewer influence on durations of interviewee speech. *J. Verbal Learn. Verbal Behav.*, 1963, **1**, 451-8.

MATARAZZO, J. D. and WIENS, A. N.   Interviewer influence on duration of interviewee silence. *J. Exp. Res. Personal.*, 1967, **2**, 56-69.

MATARAZZO, J. D., WIENS A. N., SASLOW, G., DUNHAM, R. M., and VOAS, R. B.   Speech durations of astronaut and ground communicator. *Sci.*, 1964, **143**, 148-50.

MORRIS, J. R.   The effects of problem-solving success and social reinforcement on the behavior of chronic schizophrenics. Unpublished doctoral dissertation, University of Alabama, 1963.

PATTERSON, W. E., JR.   Effect of hypnotic suggestion on schizophrenic speech patterns. Unpublished doctoral dissertation, University of Alabama, 1963.

RUESCH, J. and PRESTWOOD, A. R.   Anxiety: Its initiation, communication and interpersonal management. *Arch. Neurol. Psychiat.*, 1949, **62**, 527-50.

SASLOW, G. and MATARAZZO, J. D.   A technique for studying changes in interview behavior. In E. A. Rubenstein and M. B. Parloff (Eds.), *Research in Psychotherapy.* American Psychological Association, Washington, D.C., 1959. Pp. 125-59.

SIMKINS, L.   Modification of pausing behavior. *J. Verbal Learn. Verbal Behav.*, 1963, **2**, 462-9.

SNYDER, W. U.   *Casebook of Nondirective Counseling.* Houghton-Mifflin, Boston, 1947.

STARKWEATHER, J. A.   Computer assisted learning in medical education. *Can. Med. Ass. J.*, 1967, **97**, 733-8.

STARKWEATHER, J. A., KAMP, M., and MONTO, A.   Psychiatric interview simulation by computer. *Meth. Infor. Med.*, 1967, **6**, 15-23.

TOLHURST, G. C.   *Some Effects of Changing Time Patterns and Articulation upon Intelligibility and Word Perception.* Contract N6 onw-22525, Project No. NR 145-993. NMRI Project NM 001 104 500 40. U.S. Naval School of Aviation Medicine, Naval Air Station, Pensacola, Florida, and Ohio State University Research Foundation, Columbus, Ohio, January, 1955.

UHR, L. and VOSSLER, C.   Recognition of speech by computer program that was written to simulate a model for human visual pattern perception. *J. Acous. Soc. Amer.*, 1961, **33**, 1426.

VELDMAN, D. J.   Computer-based sentence-completion interviews. *J. Consult. Psychol.*, 1967, **14**, 153-7.

VERZEANO, M. and FINESINGER, J. E.   An automatic analyzer for the study of speech in interaction and in free association. *Sci.*, 1949, **110**, 45-6.

WEBB, J. T.   An analysis of two speech rate measures in an automated standardized interview. Unpublished doctoral dissertation, University of Alabama, 1967a.

WEBB, J. T.   Subject speech rates as a function of interviewer behavior. In M. Dinoff (Chm.), Application of a standardized interview technique. Symposium presented at the Southeastern Psychological Association, Atlanta, April, 1967b.

WIENS, A. N., MATARAZZO, J. D., and SASLOW, G.   The interaction recorder: An electronic punched paper tape unit for recording speech behavior during interviews. *J. Clin. Psychol.*, 1965, **21**, 142-5.

WINER, B. J.   *Statistical Principles in Experimental Design.* McGraw-Hill, New York, 1962.

ZIMNY, G. H. and WEIDENFELLER, E. W.   Effects of music upon GSR and heart rate. *Amer. J. Psychol.*, 1963, **76**, 311-14.

Part III

Body Movement
in
Dyadic Communication

Chapter 7

The Body Movement-Speech Rhythm
Relationship as a Cue to Speech Encoding

Allen T. Dittmann

WE HAVE by now a good many data on when people move with respect to the rhythmical stream of speech—certainly more than originally anticipated. The implications of what we have learned have relevance to two areas of investigation which do not seem on the surface to be very closely related: the first is emotional expression and the second is psycholinguistics. Emotional expression has been my research interest for some time, and most of my empirical work on body movements has been done in the context of research on interview behavior. The method of studying these movements has been to count their frequency rather than to try to determine their individual meanings. The work can thus most properly be referred to as research in nervousness or fidgetiness. D.S. Boomer of our laboratory has been the local expert in psycholinguistics. He is one of the handful of psychologists in the field who has learned something about linguistics and, more importantly in the context of this report, about speech and its production. But psycholinguistics has lured many workers away from their accustomed paths and this chapter is mainly concerned with work I have done in that field.

The trouble with counting little nervous movements in interviews is that the people are talking while they are fidgeting, and talking casts a shadow over everything else a person does at the same time. Everybody knows this at some level, so it is not a point worth belaboring. What is not known is how much this shadow affects different activities—fidgeting in this case—and this is what we started out to learn. Maybe these little movements are so bound up with the act of talking that there is no point to trying to use them as measures to get at other things, like changing emotional states. In brief, the answer is that by our methods of measurement there is a statistically

135

significant, but not very close relationship between speech and body movement—not close enough to preclude the study of each independently in interview research. In the course of finding this answer, something new was learned about the relationship: that studying movements in detail could throw some light on the act of speaking, or on how speakers get their ideas into words and listeners get those words back into ideas. This is the psycholinguistic aspect of the work.

MOVEMENT AND SPEECH OUTPUT

Let us begin with a brief review of how the answer summarized above was found, then go on to what has been done since we found it. The aspect of speech we have been working on is its rhythmical characteristic, its prosodic nature. This does not mean the tone of voice, which would be very useful to get at more precisely, but the repetitive alteration of features like stress and endings by which the stream of speech is divided up into neat little packages. One such package, which we feel is the least common denominator of rhythm in talking, is known as the phonemic clause, originally described by Trager and Smith in 1951. We believe that it is important to have such a handle on speech rhythm because of our conceptualization of the twin tasks of encoding by the speaker and decoding by the listener. We reason that rhythm is produced by the speaker as a by-product of his ongoing task of casting his thoughts into speech and that it provides important clues to the listener in his ongoing task of understanding— perhaps even hearing—what the speaker has said. I shall refer only briefly to studies of the listener and speech rhythm in this report, and focus on what has been found out about the speaker.

The body movement and the speech studies in our laboratory went their separate ways for some time, because while it was suspected that there might be some relationships between the two, we had no easy methodological bridges between them. Boomer forced the issue in 1963 by finding that certain speech characteristics derived from Mahl's work were correlated with body movement frequencies in interview passages chosen (Dittmann, 1962) to represent different feeling states or moods. This sent us down statistical and experimental paths (Boomer and Dittmann, 1964) to determine the nature of the relationship and led us to conclude that speech and body movement were not correlated except when there was parallel variation in feeling state. But there was doubt about this conclusion because of the common knowledge that people move when they speak.

It seemed, then, that we were involved in a paradox. On the one hand, there was experimental evidence that speech and movement are not related in the absence of differences in feeling state. On the other hand, we knew that speech is accompanied by movements, a fact which every layman recognizes and some professionals have studied. Laymen have made up sayings about it in the course of making passing, usually ethnocentric remarks, such as that Neapolitans can be made mute by tying their hands behind their backs. The professionals who have tried studying these phenomena are Renneker (1963), Ekman (1965, 1968), Condon and Ogston (1966, 1967), Freedman and Hoffman (1967), and now Kendon of this conference, in order of their appearance. The seeming paradox to be faced, our experimental evidence versus common sense and professional opinion, had this in common with most other paradoxes: the two propositions were based on different ways of looking at the same material. In this experiment, and in Boomer's work which led us to do the experiment, the units of analysis were quite long, one and one-half minutes in the original study, and three minutes in the experiment. Units as long as these mask the detailed interplay among factors within the units. The figures we were putting into our analyses were total occurrences of movements and of words or other speech characteristics for the entire duration of each unit. The very length of the units made us miss the ebb and flow of movements which seem to accompany speech.

HESITATIONS AND SPEECH RHYTHM

A very different approach was provided by Boomer's (1965) study of the relationship between a much smaller unit and hesitation forms in speech, the first study relating to speech encoding in our laboratory. Here the unit of analysis was the phonemic clause, and the basic data for the study took the form of the order of events within that unit. In the passage below are four phonemic clauses, one per line, which include all of the characteristics necessary to illustrate the unit. The subject, a college student, is talking about his high school newspaper days and, in the course of this passage, he has divided his speech

> and ah (pause) we would print
> (pause) ah (pause) by the offset process
> (pause) which isn't with a press
> it's a (pause) photographic process

into four neat little packages. Pauses are non-phonations of 200 ms
or more, measured on an oscillographic record of the speech. We
chose 200 ms on rational grounds, dictated by the results of an
earlier experiment (Boomer and Dittmann, 1962). There we found
by standard psychophysical methods that the threshold for discriminating hesitation pauses, that is, pauses separating forms within
a phonemic clause, was about 200 ms. Juncture pauses, non-phonations
between clauses, have much higher thresholds and the 200 ms
definition of pause will, of course, also include them. There are
hesitation pauses in all but the third clause in the passage above, and
juncture pauses between the first and second and between the second
and third. It is important to note, incidentally, that marking pauses
by listening to the tape will miss many hesitation pauses close to
threshold and many more juncture pauses of comparable length, according to our results.

We call a "fluent clause" one which has no non-fluencies within
it. Juncture pauses are not counted as non-fluencies, so the third clause
in our example is the only fluent one. Hesitation pauses, the ones other
than juncture pauses, both filled and unfilled, are considered non-
fluencies. A filled pause is usually an "ah," and it may be accompanied
by additional non-phonation, as they are in our first two clauses
above. Other non-fluencies are false starts, retraces and the like, but
hesitation pauses are by far the most frequent.

Boomer found that if you look at hesitations from the vantage
point of the phonemic clause, you see that they tend to bunch up
toward the beginnings of the clauses. The most frequent location for a
pause, in fact, is after the first word, as it is in the first clause in this
example. In Figure 1 their distribution is plotted against a chance
curve. This latter is simply the proportion of possible places between
words in phonemic clauses where a pause might occur. It is a
decreasing function, because every clause in the sample has at least
two words (one-word clauses, an infrequent occurrence, were excluded) and thus two possible places for a pause, while only longer
clauses had later word boundary positions. The modal clause in this
sample, incidentally, had five words. The difference between these
curves is quite large—the Chi Square is well over 300. It is made up
mostly of that obvious peak at the second position, which contributes
three quarters of the total Chi Square.

MOVEMENT AND SPEECH RHYTHM

Boomer's study, then, showed that speakers hesitate toward the
beginnings of the little packages in which they divide up their
speech. Later, we will return to what this has to do with speech en-

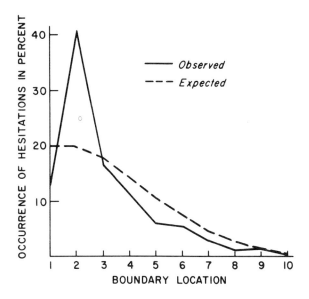

FIG. 1. Comparison of percentages of hesitations occurring at successive boundary locations with those expected by chance. (After Boomer, 1965.)

coding, but only after an explanation of how Llewellyn and I (1969) used this study as a model for investigating movements during speech. The speech sample Boomer used came from the sixteen subjects in the experiment done earlier to prove that speech and movement were unrelated. The method of tabulating the data from different sources in that experiment was to enter everything on a master typescript of the speech. Movies were made of the sessions with our subjects, and the first part of every session was a base-line condition in which the subject gave a three-minute monologue about hobbies, sports, or anything else that interested him. We looked at these movies and entered the discrete body movements onto the typescript at the words where they occurred. The speech sample was also segmented into phonemic clauses during the data analysis phase of the experiment—it was this segmentation which Boomer used later in his study of hesitations.

A look at the clauses with the movements entered indicated a trend toward bunching reminiscent of that for hesitations, a trend at least worth looking at further. There seemed to be a difference in the bunching, though: movements were not concentrated simply at the beginnings of clauses, but rather at the beginnings of fluent speech, be this when the speaker gets started on a clause or when he gets started after some non-fluency within the clause. Our same four clauses with the movements entered show these relationships. Notice that in the

```
And ah (pause) we would print
Foot      Head      Foot
          Hand

(pause) ah (pause) by the offset process
                   Head
                   Hand

(pause) which isn't with a press
                Head

It's a (pause) photographic process
              Head              Head
              Hand              Foot
```

third clause, the one fluent example, there is a head movement at the first word. In the second clause there are head and hand movements on the first word after the hesitation. These were called "Start Positions." We also included the pauses themselves under this rubric—there are movements at Start Positions, then, in all four of these clauses. Non-Start Positions provided comparative data. There are two Non-Start Positions in the first clause, at "would" and at "print," and there is a movement on one of these. It is clear from this illustration that we could count Start Positions and Non-Start Positions for each subject, then tabulate the number of movements at each and do some statistical analysis. The results were quite clear-cut: while about 40 percent of the possible positions were Start Positions, 54 percent of the movements occurred there.

Two more studies were done following up on these results: first, because it was felt that more precise instrumentation was called for to eliminate possible bias in the data gathering and second, because we wanted to know if these trends would hold up within individuals over a number of sessions spanning several weeks. Our instrumentation also enabled us to obtain considerably longer speech samples per subject and thus to extend the generality of the results. We conducted two fifteen-minute conversational interviews with each of a dozen subjects for the first follow-up, and a dozen such sessions covering eight weeks with each of two subjects for the second. The instrumentation left little chance for our wishes or hopes to influence the recording of speech rhythms and movement; movements were sensed by accelerometers and written out by event markers on a strip chart alongside an oscillogram of the concurrent speech. The results of the follow-up were in the same direction as in the original study and a bit more pronounced: the proportion of Start Positions in the speech should have led us to expect 41 percent of the movements to be Start movements; we obtained 59 percent. The Chi Square was over 1200—but then our total N was over 8700 movements and Chi Square is notoriously related to N. To find out how much difference all this made, we converted the movement data to rates and did analyses of variance. The effect of location within clause was highly significant, of course, but for both the original study and the first follow-up it accounted for only about seven percent of the movement variance. Individual differences among subjects was the largest single source of variance—larger than all of the sundry error terms combined. The range shows how wide these differences were: one subject recorded only 40 movements on our apparatus, while another moved 1934 times! But no matter how few or how many movements a subject produced, the location of the movements was the same for every subject: significantly more frequent at Start Positions than might be expected from the structure of their speech. The same was true of the longer period of time within subjects represented in the second follow-up study.

These relationships may be seen in Figure 2 in the same terms of the earlier graph of Boomer's findings. This and the next one are based on a random sample of only 200 clauses, so the curves are not as smooth as the ones from Boomer's study—he used almost four times as many clauses. Here we see how the 117 fluent clauses look, that is, more than expected at the Start Positions, juncture pause, and first word, and fewer or about the same at the subsequent ones. The 83 non-fluent clauses are shown in Figure 3. Again the same patterns obtain, but the only significant difference for this small sample is at the first word following the non-fluency.

SPEECH ENCODING AND DECODING

All of the research discussed so far may be summarized by stating, as I did at the beginning, that there is a "significant" but not very close relationship between speech rhythm and body movement. Both hesitations in speech and body movements tend to appear early in phonemic clauses and, in addition, movements tend to follow hesitations wherever they may appear in clauses. Now, what about encoding? Boomer's study of hesitations arose from a happy serendipity while he was looking for some unit larger than the word to use in analyzing conversational speech. The word is very neat and handy in written language, but often seems not to exist when you listen to people talk. Boomer had a new typescript made of some

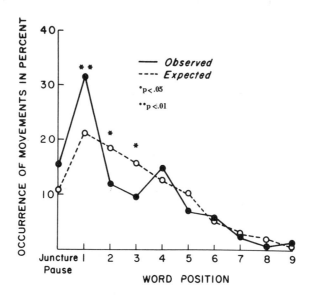

Fɪɢ. 2. Percentages of movements in fluent phonemic clauses at successive word positions compared with those expected by chance. (After Dittmann and Llewellyn, 1969.)

speech which had already been segmented into phonemic clauses. The form of the new typing was the one seen in our first illustrative passage—one clause per line. It was obvious on looking at the first page of this revised typescript that the pauses could be found mainly along the left-hand margin. A number of things seemed suddenly to add up, such as Lounsbury's (1954) hypothesis that hesitation is a sign that the speaker is having encoding problems, either in making a lexical choice or in casting it into the right syntactic form—or both, since the two are intimately tied together. The lexical item, the word with the highest information value in the clause, ordinarily falls at the end, and the function words, the low-information ones which serve as glue to the successive high-information words, precede it. The lexical word is the one which has the strongest stress in the clause, overriding the syllable stress within words. Looking back at the first clause in the four-clause speech sample, we see that it has one unusual word, "print." It was stressed as this student was talking. The other words are common ones, that is, common to many clauses, and serve to cast "print" into the proper syntactic relationship to the next lexical item, "offset process." Incidentally, "offset process" is a good example of how the word is a written phenomenon, not a spoken one. It is one of those adjective-noun pairs which go together as one

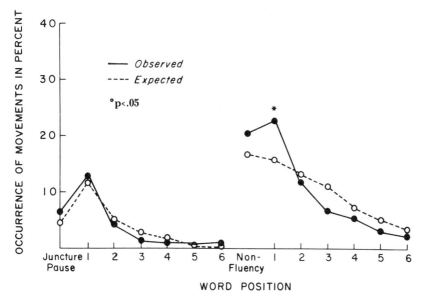

Fɪɢ. 3. Percentages of movements in non-fluent phonemic clauses at successive word positions compared with those expected by chance. (After Dittmann and Llewellyn, 1969.)

thing, or piece of meaning. Some of these are written as one word, like "gearbox" and "flywheel." Others are written separately, like "transmission housing" and "offset process." And still others have to be looked up in the dictionary to find the current convention on whether they are supposed to be *one word* or not.

This is what is meant, then, by a unit larger than the word: a unit which contains both meaning and syntax. Boomer argued that it may well be the fundamental chunk which people use to cast ideas into words. The unit has a certain functional unity to it, too, the most thoroughly investigated evidence for which is Boomer and Laver's (1968) work on tongue slips. These are not only the Freudian slips, but also the many misarticulations where the speaker simply gets his sounds out of order. For the most part they are not noticed by either speaker or listener, both of whom do a sort of continuous editing job as they are conversing. Slips turn out to have a good deal of lawfulness about them, and the main laws are about how the form of the slips fits in with the structure of the phonemic clause. First, the interfering element is almost always the main lexical item in the clause, the stressed word. Second, the phonetic interaction which gives rise to tongue slips usually involves the primary-stressed word and another word in the same clause. In the exceptions—something less than a tenth of all instances—the interaction is between the primary-stressed words of contiguous clauses. This last finding, rare as its examples may be, points out that the phonemic clause is not the only encoding unit. There are undoubtedly larger groupings of clauses or of somethings, otherwise we should only be able to talk very haltingly, if at all. People are constantly planning ahead as they speak and they seem to plan ahead in terms of chunks which include both lexical and syntactic material. The phonemic clause is the smallest chunk which can include both.

Our work on decoding indicates that the same unit is used by listeners as they translate back from speech. In one study (Dittmann and Llewellyn, 1967), it was found that listeners inserted both the familiar "Mm-hmmm," and also more extended comments almost exclusively (about 10:1) between phonemic clauses. The large majority of listener responses occurred at pauses and of these, an even larger proportion (about 20:1) were at juncture pauses as compared with hesitation pauses. In a subsequent study (Dittmann and Llewellyn, 1968) which included another listener response, the head nod, the total response rate at junctures as compared with other locations was about 15:1, while that of head nods alone was surprisingly over 50:1! Thus the listener apparently waits until the end of the clause before acknowledging that he has understood or even that he has been listening to what the speaker has had to say. It should be noted in passing that the phonemic clause has not found its way as a unit of speech into a large body of research, possibly because of doubts on the part of investigators about its reliability. These results should be reassuring on this score: a large number of subjects with no formal linguistic training have shown in these two studies that they are able to identify the unit with considerable accuracy.[1]

A FURTHER ANALYSIS

Let us return now to the significant but not close relationship between these rhythmical units of speech and concurrent movements. The point of getting all these facts about the relationship was to find out how counts of nervous, fidgety movements might be affected. To say that they won't be affected very much is comforting, but the

---

[1]There are differences in response among types of juncture which may terminate a phonemic clause which make it look as if two sizes of unit are involved. The extreme accuracy of response noted above may obtain more in the case of the larger unit—but the point that everyone seems to be able to recognize rhythmical units of speech is still a valid one.

details are of interest in themselves from a psycholinguistic standpoint. Even though the relationship is not close, the production of
movements is not random over time in the stream of speech. Movements are thus not, in communication terms, a constant information
source. Rather, the information value of any movement depends
partly upon the amount of movement which the individual produces over the long run and partly upon what has happened just before
it. In our latest look at the data, we have tried to determine how
much information about movements is wasted in redundancy at
different points in the phonemic clause. To do this, we have studied
the sequential probabilities of the movements as they relate to the
rhythmical structure of the clause. Refer back once again to the four
clauses we have been using as an example for an explanation of
how this is done. In the first clause, the first movement is the foot
movement which, so far as the rhythm of the clause is concerned,
occurs at the time of the first word. From the standpoint of that
movement, the next one occurs—or, in this case, the next ones occur—
at the time of the filled pause following the first word. From the
standpoint of these movements, in turn, the next one is on the word
"would," the material following the non-fluency, and so on. Note
that movements of all body areas are included indiscriminately in
this analysis because, in the earlier study, we found only very small
differences among body areas in the movement-rhythm relationship.
Note, too, that in this sequential analysis only one-step sequences are
considered: given the location of one movement, what is the location
of the next movement following it? Considering three at a time, that
is, seeing where the third movement would fall given the location of
the first two, leads to a much more complicated analysis but one
which could conceivably be done with a larger body of data.
    The terms of the analysis are those of the rhythmical components
of the phonemic clause. Since the rhythm is interrupted by non-
fluencies, these components must be listed separately for fluent and
non-fluent clauses. Fluent clauses have only three components which
are relevant to rhythm: the juncture pause (if any), the main body of
the clause, and the last part of the clause which has to do with the
stressed word and the juncture. About four-fifths of stressed words are
located just before the juncture (Dittmann and Llewellyn, 1969), so the
stress and end of the clause are considered a single component of
rhythm in this analysis. In non-fluent clauses a similar breakdown
yields five rhythmical components: again the juncture pause (if
any), the material preceding the non-fluency, the non-fluency itself,
the material following the non-fluency, and the stress or end. These are
not necessarily mutually exclusive categories in the real world—the

stressed word, for example, is occasionally the only material following the non-fluency—but while coding we must act as if they were. Code numbers were assigned to movements as they were located at these different rhythmical components, 1, 2, and 3, to those of the fluent clauses and 4 through 8, to those of the non-fluent clauses. The number 9 was assigned to the end-of-clause marker, the juncture. A computer was instructed to take the movements in successive overlapping pairs, make several decisions about them and enter them into the necessary tables for further work. Given a first movement at a juncture pause preceding a fluent clause and a second one in the main body of the same clause, for example, the computer made a tally in the appropriate cell of the table. The possible locations for a second movement were the various rhythmical components of the same clause, those of the next following clause and a general category called "later." This last category was included because preliminary work indicated that very few second movements fell beyond the following clause and breaking these down into rhythmical components would produce numbers too small to be stable even with large total Ns.

The material analyzed in this way consisted of the two fifteen-minute interviews from each of twelve college students from the Dittmann and Llewellyn (1969) study, plus the first two interviews of the two longer-term students, some data from which were included in that same report. The material thus comprises seven hours of talking, all in a deliberately relaxed conversational atmosphere. For this analysis, all movements were coded from a total of 8526 phonemic clauses, of which 5547 were fluent and 2979 were non-fluent by our definition. As we might expect from the earlier analysis, there are only half as many movements in fluent clauses as there are in non-fluent ones: .79 movements per fluent as compared with 1.59 movements per non-fluent clause.

The most striking result of the sequential analysis of these movements is the way movements tend to bunch up in non-fluent clauses and to be spread out in fluent ones. Given a first movement in a fluent clause, the next movement following it is about as likely to be in the same clause as in any of the ones succeeding it. Not so in the case of non-fluent clauses. Where the first movement occurs in one of those clauses, the second is about twice as likely to appear within the same clause. The results are shown in Figure 4. We see that movements in fluent clauses are followed by next movements as a decreasing function of the passage of time, a seemingly linear function as graphed, although, of course, the abscissa is not by any means an interval scale of time. Non-fluent clauses, on the other hand, show a

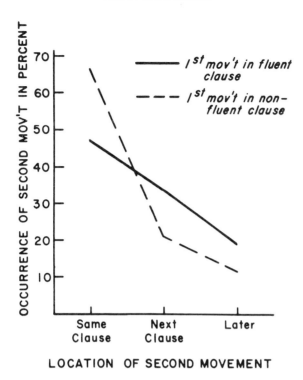

FIG 4. Sequential probabilities of pairs of successive movements beginning in fluent and non-fluent phonemic clauses.

quite different set of relationships between first and second movements, with a large proportion of second movements falling in the
same clause at the expense of both the next clause and all subsequent
locations. In terms of amount of information bound up in the
relationship between speech and movement, there is very little in
fluent clauses and considerably more in non-fluent ones. The proportions of second movements in the different locations in Figure 4
yield figures of 5.3 percent redundancy for fluent clauses, and 21.9
percent for non-fluent ones.

One might argue that these findings are artifacts of the length of
the clauses. Fluent clauses must by definition be shorter, since they
contain none of the time-consuming non-fluencies, especially pauses,
which characterize non-fluent clauses. Thus there would be more time
for second movements to occur within non-fluent clauses. Indeed
there is a significant and sizeable difference in length between the two
types of clause. The average fluent clause takes about 1.2 seconds to

say, while non-fluent clauses average about 2.0 seconds, a difference large enough to lend credence to the artifact hypothesis but not to account fully for the results depicted in Figure 4. If we examine the various rhythmical positions within the clauses, we see that the rapid succession of movements centers around the non-fluency itself. Consider for this purpose only those pairs of movements which are confined to the same clause. If the first movement occurs before the non-fluency, the next movement will follow in 73 percent of cases, either also before the non-fluency or during the non-fluency. Among movement pairs where the first movement coincides with the non-fluency, 54 percent of second movements appear at the same non-fluent part of the clause. These percentages of second movements at the non-fluency must be evaluated in the light of the amount of time taken up by the non-fluency in the clause; it averages 31 percent of the total clause time. Thus movements are concentrated at the non-fluency to a greater extent than should be expected, and it is for this reason that second movements are more likely to be confined to the same clause: where the first movement occurs just before or at the same time as the non-fluency, the next movement is very likely to appear in the same clause—84 and 80 percent of the time, respectively, with redundancies of 50.2 and 41.5 percent.

In those cases where the first movement follows the non-fluency, the pattern of the second movement almost reverts to that of the fluent clause: 60 percent of second movements fall in the same clause (14.5 percent redundancy), as compared with 56 percent of those following first movements in the main body of the fluent clause (10.9 percent redundancy). This small but significant difference indicates that the non-fluency still holds some sway over the movement pattern even after the speaker has got started to finish the rest of the clause.

The little movements which our accelerometers can detect, then, appear to be a constant source of information at some times during speech and not at others, and this depends on what is happening to the speech. Non-fluencies interrupt not only the speech itself, but also the person's characteristic production of movements. In the search for methods of counting fidgety movements, we may conclude that movements which immediately accompany non-fluencies of speech must not be counted as ordinary fidgetiness. Movements which come at other times can be regarded as movements produced by a constant information source, and it is up to some other kind of research to determine what sort of information that source conveys.

THOUGHTS ABOUT THE ENCODING PROCESS

In the meantime, let us do some speculating about speech encoding and what the bunching up of movements around non-fluencies may mean to it. Most non-fluencies are hesitations by our definition: for the average speaker almost 95 percent are either filled or unfilled pauses. Most workers agree that the speaker hesitates at times of decision-making as he is trying to get out into words, that thought on the tip of the tongue. Both lexical and syntactic choices must be made, and the phonemic clause is the smallest package where we can see the marriage of these two types of choice. Remember that the clause contains both the lexical item whose information concerns the topic of conversation and also the various function words whose information is of relationships, of how the lexical items are connected and intended to be understood. The requirements for these choices are quite different; the one oriented outward toward the conversation and "meanings of words;" the other oriented inward toward structure. These tasks have been formulated by Lashley (1951) as quite separate: first, activation of the elements of an action, and second, their temporal organization, using language as his primary example. He concluded "that elements of the sentence are readied or partially activated before the order is imposed upon them in expression (p. 130)." Ordinarily, the two tasks have been performed in that sequence before the overt action, before the speaker utters the sounds of speech, and errors in performance indicate that the organization task, the syntax of speech, functions as an inhibitor to the spilling-out of elements which have been overactivated. Lashley uses slips of the fingers in typing and Spoonerisms in speech to illustrate this process. Later writers, such as Lenneberg (1967, Chap. 4), and Boomer and Laver (1968), have followed his formulation.

It is thus apparent that a good deal of energy is involved in these two tasks, that a delicate balance must be maintained between facilitatory and inhibitory commands to the vocal apparatus. We do not yet know the neurological specifics of these forces, but my belief is that the non-fluency is a sign of their continuous interplay and that the movements which surround the non-fluency are motor manifestations of this balancing act. Also, because of this they are qualitatively different from other movements which make up what we call "fidgetiness." We have seen that individual differences in total movement output are very large, but where these movements occur in the rhythmical pattern of speech is not a function of total number of movements. To be sure, there are significant differences—but again very small ones—in how closely the movements adhere to the speech rhythm. Whether these differences are determined by culture patterns or idiosyncrasies we do not know, but an empirical test of these possibilities is being conducted now by applying the same techniques to speech samples from Sicily. The fact remains, however, that a significant proportion of the movements of everyone studied so far are tied to speech rhythm and thus, inferentially, to the speech encoding process.

If our interest is in fidgetiness as an expression of emotional states, as it originally was and still is, then we should develop some way of eliminating those encoding-related movements from further consideration, for they contribute too much redundancy to the measurement system. This would be easy to do by hand, using the findings presented here as a guide, but such a procedure would be so tedious that no one would be willing to do it for a representative amount of interview material. We fare better in using the findings to alter our system of automation: in future studies of frequencies of body movements, we shall be feeding the outputs of the accelerometers into counters for machine processing. We can capitalize on our knowledge that pauses make up the largest category of non-fluencies by detecting pauses and gating the counters to omit those movements which occur at the same time as the pauses, or just following them. Then we can learn if this extended excursion into psycholinguistics has produced practical as well as theoretical gain.

References

BOOMER, D. S. Speech disturbance and body movement in interviews. *J Nerv. Ment. Dis.*, 1963, **136**, 263-6.

BOOMER, D. S. Hesitation and grammatical encoding. *Language and Speech*, 1965, **8**, 148-58.

BOOMER, D. S. and DITTMANN, A. T. Hesitation pauses and juncture pauses in speech. *Language and Speech*, 1962, **5**, 215-20.

BOOMER, D. S. and DITTMANN, A. T. Speech rate, filled pause, and body movement in interviews. *J. Nerv. Ment. Dis.*, 1964, **139**, 324-7.

BOOMER, D. S. and LAVER, J. D. M. Slips of the tongue. *Br. J. Disord. Commun.*, 1968, **3**, 2-12.

CONDON, W. S. and OGSTON, W. D. Sound film analysis of normal and pathological behavior patterns. *J. Nerv. Ment. Dis*, 1966, **143**, 338-47.

CONDON, W. S. and OGSTON, W. D. A segmentation of behavior. *J. Psychiat. Res.*, 1967, **5**, 221-35.

DITTMANN, A. T. The relationship between body movements and moods in interviews. *J. Consult. Psychol.*, 1962, **26**, 480.

DITTMANN, A. T. and LLEWELLYN, L. G. The phonemic clause as a unit of speech decoding. *J. Personal. Soc. Psychol.*, 1967, **6**, 341-9.

DITTMANN, A. T. and LLEWELLYN, L. G. Relationship between vocalization and head nods as listener responses. *J. Personal Soc. Psychol.*, 1968, **9**, 79-84.

DITTMANN, A. T. and LLEWELLYN, L. G. Body movement and speech rhythm in social conversation. *J. Personal. Soc. Psychol.*, 1969, **11**, 98-106.

EKMAN, P. Communication through nonverbal behavior: A source of information about an interpersonal relationship. In S. Tomkins and C. Izard (Eds.), *Affect, Cognition, and Personality*. Springer, New York, 1965. Pp. 390-442.

EKMAN, P. and FRIESEN, W. V. Nonverbal behavior in psychotherapy research. In J. M. Shlein (Ed.), *Research in Psychotherapy, Volume III*. American Psychological Association, Washington, D.C., 1968. Pp. 179-216.

FREEDMAN, N. and HOFFMAN, S. P. Kinetic behavior in altered clinical states: Approach to objective analysis of motor behavior during clinical interviews. *Perceptual and Motor Skills*, 1967, **24**, 527-39.

LASHLEY, K. S. The problem of serial order in behavior. In L. A. Jeffress (Ed.), *Cerebral Mechanisms in Behavior*. Wiley, New York, 1951. Pp. 112-36.

LENNEBERG, E. H. *Biological Foundations of Language*. Wiley, New York, 1967.

LOUNSBURY, F. G. Transistional probability, linguistic structure, and systems of habit-family hierarchies. In C. E. Osgood and T. A. Sebeok (Eds.), *Psycholinguistics: A Survey of Theory and Research Problems*. Waverly Press, Baltimore, 1954. Pp. 93-101.

RENNEKER, R. Kinesic research and therapeutic processes: Further discussion. In P. H. Knapp (Ed.), *Expression of the Emotions in Man*. International Universities Press, New York, 1963. Pp. 147-60.

TRAGER, G. L. and SMITH, H. L., JR. *An Outline of English Structure. (Studies in Linguistics: Occasional Papers, 3)*. Battenberg Press, Norman, Okla., 1951. (Republished, American Council of Learned Societies, New York, 1965.)

Chapter 8

The Analysis of Movement Behavior During the Clinical Interview[1]

Norbert Freedman

INTRODUCTION

The application of body movement analysis to the objective study of clinical problems is rich in theoretical and clinical possibilities but fraught with methodological hazards. Most clinicians undoubtedly harbor, in the backs of their minds, a quiet awareness that their understanding of a patient and/or therapeutic process is by no means wholly derived from what goes on at the verbal level. One may cite Freud's (1953) observation in the case of Dora in which he notes that when the patient's lips are sealed, she chatters with her finger tips. The systematic research reported to date, though sparse, has presented enough evidence to substantiate the relevance of movement research to the understanding of psychological phenomena (Condon and Ogston, 1966; Ekman and Friesen, 1968; Freedman and Hoffman, 1967; Mahl *et al.*, 1959; Sainsbury, 1958). From a theoretical vantage point, moreover, there is our conviction that movement behavior as a constituent of the communicative effort constitutes a signpost reflecting upon the organization of thought and experience. Such considerations have led to undertaking, as a research objective, the development of an approach to body movements which allows application of this source of data directly to the study of psychopathology in particular, and to the clinical interview in general.

The most casual observation of a patient's behavior reveals that a substantial amount of movement is tied in with the manifest communicative effort. The ideal of the perfectly verbal, motionless man, epitomized by Jules Verne's Phileas Fogg, is probably a rare

[1]This research has been supported by Grant No. 14383 from the United States Public Health Service, National Institute of Mental Health.

153

occurrence. In the total communicative effort, one can note the simultaneous and sequential flow of various processes: vocalization, articulation, postural and kinetic expression. The pioneering work of Birdwhistell (1952) has demonstrated that communication is an "organismic process" in which almost any part of the body can participate. In this context, selecting one aspect of this process from the "whole person" or the whole situation is quite arbitrary. Out of the myriad of possible behavioral events observable on various levels (the linguistic, the paralinguistic, the kinetic, or the parakinetic), invariant constellations can be isolated. Such units then become idiosyncratic for a person or for a context. This view of kinetic behavior has led to the development of the procedures of context analysis advanced by Birdwhistell (1952), Scheflen (1958), and followed by a number of other observers (e.g., Condon and Ogston, 1966).

In full cognizance of the complexity of communicative phenomena and of the desirability to identify "true units" of behavior, we have nonetheless chosen to view movement as an emergent behavior in its own right and have even selected one manifestation, namely, hand movements, as the focus for observations. From these observations, we have sought to isolate nomothetic variables that can be applied to all patients sharing a common clinical manifestation. The data which result from this analysis are clearly abstractions and oversimplifications. Although this path was chosen because it leads more readily to clinical evaluation and quantitative assessment, this was not done on pragmatic grounds alone. Perhaps of more importance, we view the various modes of communicative expression as vehicles of a process of symbolizing and representing more central to our interests. From this vantage point, for example, both speech and movement may have their independent ties to the symbolizing process; their patterning, their relative predominance, one at the expense of the other, their congruence, or consistencies provide data of psychological import.

These studies have focused on the analysis of a patient's hand movements during a clinical interview with the patient sitting in the vis-à-vis position.[2] There are two elements inherent in such an interview situation which allow identification of variables with a presumptive psychological significance. One is directionality. In a

---

[2] It should be noted that this paper is limited to the condition of movements accompanying speech, that is, a context in which a person is expected to talk. Under these conditions, the movements are probably a part of the encoding process. A very different psychological situation is created in a context where the person is expected to listen, e.g. as a member of an audience or the therapist listening to a patient. Such listening movements require a separate conceptualization and are probably a part of the decoding and absorbing process.

clinical interview, a movement emerges in the presence of another person, that is, it arises in a particular spatial, or territorial arrangement. Hand movements may be directed away from the body, reveal lateral in-and-out motions, or they may include body-touching and frank self-stimulation. In these different instances, one can observe different types of focusing on the motor level.

A second element is that of speech relatedness. The interplay of movement and speech has been stressed by Dittmann (1969) who advanced the hypothesis that motor expression may be a regular accompaniment of the rhythmic properties of speech. He has presented important data showing a connection between kinetic expression and hesitation in speech, particularly as these are located at start positions of phonemic clauses. Our emphasis on the speech relatedness of certain movements has been a broader one. We have been struck by the fact that certain classes of hand movements show a congruence with the verbal content. They appear to supplement or even accentuate what is being said; other movements bear no such intrinsic linkage. They appear to exist side by side and seem to function as unconnected part processes. Here, then, is an instance in which the two part processes, movement and speech, may or may not be mutually facilitating and congruent. These are the two parameters which have guided the development of our coding approach: the property of directionality and the property of speech relatedness.

In a previous work (Freedman and Hoffman, 1967), we have introduced the distinction between a class of object-focused and a class of body-focused movements. Object-focused movements usually do not involve body-touching and, moreover, bear an intrinsic relation to what is being said. Body-focused movements, on the other hand, appear unrelated to the spoken word and invariably involve some form of self-stimulation. Distinctions which parallel the present object- body-focused dichotomy have also been made by Krout (1954), Mahl (1966), Rosenfeld (1966), and Sainsbury (1958). Mahl, in particular, has stressed the psychological validity of distinguishing between those movements which appear to be adaptive and "communicative" in an interview situation, that is, those which carry an intent to reach the other from those which signify a preoccupation with private inner or "autistic" events. In the language of Piaget's writings (1955), the distinction can be made between movements signifying an interpersonal *dialogue* from those signifying a *monologue* in the presence of others. It is suggested that these two processes may be observable and traceable through the identification of object- and body-focused activity.

In subsequent work, we have chosen relatively extreme clinical groups as subjects: paranoid patients and depressed patients in their acute and post-acute states. We thus start with observations of patients in more extreme pathological conditions, hoping to derive from them criteria of movement behavior which may also apply to less disturbed patients. Conversely, the identification of motor correlates of the different clinical states may contribute to a broadened behavioral definition of psychopathology and its alteration.

The presentation of the material to follow will be divided into three major sections. A first section outlines our definitions of the object-focused movements. A second section presents our definitions of body-focused movements. In these first two sections, the definition of the categories of analysis will be supplemented by observations of video tape-recorded sessions of patients in initial and subsequent clinical interviews. A third section will attempt to trace variations in object- and body-focused movements within a single interview and relate these to concomitant events during the interview.

The present preliminary report is presented primarily for the purpose of outlining the procedures of analysis and for a provisional conceptualization of the movement categories. A brief outline of some of the procedures of the ongoing study follows.

The study entails consecutive observations of two groups of psychiatric patients (schizophrenic with paranoid symptomatology and non-schizophrenic with depressive symptomatology) observed at various points in their treatment. We have at our disposal, at this time, a total of fifteen coded interviews from ten patients: five schizophrenic patients showing manifest paranoid symptoms at intake and five non-schizophrenic patients showing depressive symptoms at intake. For the five "paranoid" patients, post-acute interviews were also available, taking place approximately eight weeks after the initial recorded "acute" interview. The post-acute session was one in which, according to the clinician's judgment, the patient had shown a significant remission in paranoid symptomatology. Patients were treated with supportive psychotherapy and maintenance phenothiazine treatment which was initiated immediately after the first recorded interview. The post-acute session, then, represents both a "remitted" state and one which may reveal the impact of phenothiazine medication.

Patients are seen by their treating psychiatrist in a soundproof recording room equipped with two television cameras. Since we are interested in the patient rather than in the transaction between him and his therapist, both cameras are trained on the patient, one, a close up *en face* view, the other a whole-body view of the patient. More detailed procedures of our methods for recording and coding interviews were presented in our earlier report (Freedman and Hoffman, 1967).

In analyzing the interview, we focused on ten-minute segments. All frequency and time data to be presented are thus based on ten-minute time samples. The ten-minute segments were selected so as to represent samples of symptom expression, of paranoid grievances, or depressive complaints. We attempted to select the ten-minute segment for the post-acute session to represent the same position within the interview as the first segment. The segments were analyzed by independent coders, i.e., researchers other than the treating psychiatrist. The coding procedure involved the identification of hand/arm movement acts by incidence (with the exception of one coding category based on time scores).

THE ANALYSIS OF OBJECT-FOCUSED MOVEMENTS

Object-focused movements, by definition, are those hand movements which are intimately linked to the formal and/or context aspects of speech. These movements also have a characteristic directionality in that they tend to occur at a distance from the body surface and do not involve body-touching.[3] Why the term "object-focused?" It is evident that not all verbal expression is equally likely to be accompanied by object-focused movements. A patient's hands may be relatively immobile for a considerable span of an interview and then, suddenly, erupt in a series of object-focused activity. Noting conditions associated with the emergence or abatement of such activity may contribute to a broadened definition of object-focused movements.

In one of the few attempts at experimental manipulation of movement behavior, a psychiatrist was asked to interview a paranoid schizophrenic patient under two conditions; in the first condition, covering the first half of the interview, he sought to focus the dialogue on relatively mundane matters such as the patient's ward activities, his appetite, etc., but to avoid issues pertaining to psychopathology. In the second condition, covering the other half of the interview, he attempted to elicit the patient's delusional ideas. When we sub-

---

[3] In one of our first studies of video tape-recorded interviews, we asked judges to rate two aspects of each movement act: its direction and its speech relatedness. Data analysis revealed a very close concordance between movements which failed to touch the body and speech relatedness (95 percent); movements touching the body tended to be judged as unrelated to speech (85 percent), thus laying the basis for the object-focused—body-focused dichotomy. (Freedman and Hoffman, 1967.)

sequently looked at the video tape of this session, without knowing which section was which and even without the benefit of sound, we were struck by the difference in the patient's behavior in the two segments. When talking of his delusional ideas, he looked more alert and interested. He was far more animated—i.e., with a fuller range of facial expressions, more erect posture, gaze directed at the therapist, and many more hand movements. There was no question that he was very much a part of an interaction with the psychiatrist. This little "experiment" was instructive. First, quite apart from the subject of this paper, it seemed to be objective evidence of the restitutive function of the delusion in paranoia. Second, it alerted us to the possibility that speech-related hand movements may serve as objective indices of a patient's focus of attention vis-à-vis other people and himself. Thus, although object-focused movements are perhaps best described as speech-related, their potential significance derives from their participation in a process whereby a patient seeks the attention of his listener, the object. These movements are object-focused in two senses: they are linked to the object of one's verbally expressed experiences, the *objects of representation* (in the case of the patient, his delusion); but they are also linked to the effort to reach the listener, the *object of presence*.

Although all object-focused movements share the common attribute of speech relatedness, there is considerable diversity in the manner in which this relationship is manifested. In our first report, we discriminated among five categories along lines ranging from instances in which the movement appeared to be subservient to the verbal expression, to instances in which the movement progressively assumed a primary expressive function, signifying a greater primacy of motility over speech. More recently, it was found useful to group these five categories on the basis of a major distinction between a speech-primacy movement and a motor-primacy movement. These will be elaborated below.

The defining characteristic of the class of *speech-primacy* movements is their subservience to the spoken word. These hand movements closely parallel the formal and rhythmic properties of speech and are part of a constellation of events in which speech seems to predominate.

One kind of speech-primacy movement which we have identified is the *punctuating* movement. In this movement, the hand traverses a path which is essentially straight and devoid of any molding qualities. These movements may be relatively small, as if they were an overflow from the emphatic aspects of speech, or rather gross. In either event, they tend to occur in bursts, and are in intimate coordination with the rhythmic aspects of speech. Another kind of speech-primacy movement is that which we have labeled (perhaps inappropriately) the *minor qualifier*. This category includes those hand movements in which there is some characteristic form, but where there are no representational properties. Highly conventionalized symbolic movements and the idiosyncratic, stylized accentuation movements constitute the bulk of minor qualifiers. Descriptively, these movements tend to be small, involving often simply a turning of the wrists, well-delineated, but not staccato-like movements; they have a smooth and sinuous quality and tend to be intricate.

Motor-primacy movements may also be closely phased in with the rhythmic properties of speech. Yet their defining characteristic requires that the expression of some "content" message has been delegated to the motor realm. Some partially articulated image, feeling state, or thought is externalized by the movements of the hand. This judgment of relative motor primacy is always made by reference to the spoken word. Motor-primacy movements have their own idiosyncratic shapes, isomorphic to the partially expressed idea.

The class of motor-primacy movements is a broad one, encompassing considerable range in their manifestation and psychological function. Thus we have identified a *representational hand movement* in which either an abstract idea, or an image having clearly definable space and time referents, is given motor expression. These representational movements are frequently literal outlines of a picture image, sometimes a condensation of it. In any event, the representational act often provides considerably more information than is carried by speech alone. The representational movement is of considerable theoretical interest. It deals with the appearance of visual language, the stuff of images and dreams in the context of an ongoing dialogue. Another type of motor-primacy movement is the *concretization* movement. These acts deal with the hand/arm movements which occur during the description of feeling states. Internal experience is being concretized, as it were, through a motor act. Since feelings usually lack precise space and time referents, the movements tend to be vague, and groping in nature. Finally, there are the *major qualifiers* which, in fact, are relatively rare. These movements show the greatest autonomy of movement vis-à-vis speech. Major qualifiers may be observed when movements are apparently disconnected from the verbal dialogue (having a disruptive impact on the viewer). The major qualifiers bear their own mark of disorganization on the motor level alone. They may be gross or awkward forms of the more conventionalized movements, chaotic or unintelligible movements, or undifferentiated and "sloppy" movements.

Thus there is considerable diversity within the broad range of motor-primacy responses, a range from nearly literal reproduction of images to instances of a breakdown of the verbal-motor linkage. What holds the different kinds of motor-primacy acts together is the common feature that partially articulated thought is externalized and relegated to the motor system.

Now to some empirical observations. The incidence of all object-focused movements per category was determined for each ten-minute segment. There are two issues concerning reliability which deserve mention. First, identification of object-focused movement acts. Here agreement is quite high (86 percent between two coders). This high reliability is readily understood if it is remembered that a coder can replay a segment as often as he wishes, and that we are excluding from consideration here, those body-focused movements which do not entail specific acts, but are continuous in nature. Next, there is the issue of category placement. Intercoder agreement for placement in one of the five categories was 70 percent.

In comparing ten-minute segments from the initial interviews of the five paranoid and five depressed patients, there were clear differences between the two groups. The mean number of object-focused movements for paranoid patients was 103.6, for depressed patients, 60.2.[4] One may wonder whether this difference between paranoid and depressed patients simply reflects a difference in total motor activity between the two groups. It is of interest to note that when body-focused activity (expressed in time scores) is considered, there was no difference between paranoid and depressed patients. Paranoid patients had a mean of 196.8 seconds of continuous body-focused activity, depressed patients a mean of 203.4 seconds. The trends, then, suggest that paranoid patients in their initial interview, in a relatively acute state show specifically a higher level of object-focused activity than those of depressed patients.

Next, let us compare initial interviews of the five paranoid patients with subsequent interviews about eight weeks later. For all these patients, the clinicians noted a reduction in paranoid symptomatology after the eight weeks. In terms of total object-focused activity, the mean drops from 103.6 to 82.8 object-focused movements per ten minutes. This decline from initial to the post-acute session was evident, further, for each of the five patients.

More central to our interest are the changes from acute to post-acute interviews defined in terms of kinds of object-focused movements, considering separately speech-primacy movements and

---

[4]No tests of significance are included for these and all subsequent data in view of the preliminary nature of this report and the small number of observations.

motor-primacy movements. These data indicate, first, that there was little change (or at best a slight increase) in the number of speech-primacy movements. There was a mean of 44.8 speech-primacy movements in the acute state and a mean of 53.6 in the post-acute session. Second, when motor-primacy movements are studied, the decrease is dramatic, from 58.8 to 29.2 movements and, again, each of the five patients observed showed this decrease. A decline in the incidence of motor-primacy movements was thus associated with clinical improvement and seemed to be the variable accounting for the overall reduction in object-focused activity. Another way of expressing the foregoing observations is that clinical improvement may be identified to involve both the reduction of motor-primacy movements and a relative increase of speech-primacy movements during the clinical interview.

In sum, during initial interviews, paranoid patients in a relatively acute state showed a greater prevalence of object-focused activity compared to depressed patients. When patients showed an abatement of paranoid grievances during a post-acute interview, the level of speech-primacy movements remained essentially unchanged; motor-primacy movements showed a sharp decline with symptom reduction.

THE ANALYSIS OF BODY-FOCUSED MOVEMENTS

One striking aspect of body-focused activity is an apparent split in the patient's attention. In part, the patient appears to maintain his dialogue with the therapist, yet, at the same time, his hands seem to be engaged elsewhere. Another noteworthy split is suggested in a passage by Ferenczi (1955). There are certain moments in the psychoanalytic situation in which

> Part of the person adopts the role of father or mother in relation to the rest, thereby undoing as it were, the fact of being left deserted. In this play, various parts of the body—hands, fingers, feet, genitals, head, nose, or eyes— become representatives of the whole person, in relation to which all the vicissitudes of the subject's own tragedy are enacted.

Ferenczi here points at an essential feature of the body-focused movement—namely, a split in which the hands become the agents or the subjects acting upon the body as an object.

In an initial report on the analysis of kinetic behavior during the clinical interview, we had not as yet formulated an approach to the examination of body-focused movements. One possible interpretation that suggested itself at that time, was that these movements represent different levels of psychosexual experiences. From the description of these movements, we noted a finite number of aims (scratching, soothing, etc.) and foci (mouth, legs, etc.). However, consistent with the remainder of our coding approach, we have adhered to a more formal analysis of behavior.

The defining characteristic of body-focused movements is that the hands are involved in the stimulation of the body or its adornments. An examination of the range of body-focused activity indicated that these may vary from instances in which self-stimulation is direct, that is, clearly visible and seems to involve the stimulation of the skin surface, to instances in which it is indirect, that is, is disguised and appears only in symbolic form. In this last effort, substitute "thing" objects are enlisted, and interpretatively, self-stimulation appears to be displaced from the body surface onto those "thing" objects. This distinction between direct and symbolic self-stimulation has yielded three categories of body-focused movements:

(1) *Indirect symbolic.* These are movements which involve a "thing" object and which are manipulated by the hand and especially by the fingertips. The extent of stimulation is clearly circumscribed. The mediating object entails articles of clothing, accessories (pen, tie clip, necklace, ring) or items in the immediate physical environment, e.g., armrest. It is of interest that those movements which Mahl (1966) has identified as "anticipatory" movements, that is, those movements which represent a suppressed or repressed thought, have the form of an indirect symbolic activity.

(2) *Direct—hand-to-hand.* These movements involve the continuous stimulation of the hands by each other, of one hand onto the other, or one hand onto itself. They clearly involve skin surface stimulation and, in that sense, must be considered direct body-focused movements. Yet, what is absent is the functional division by which one hand acts as agent upon the rest of the body surface. These movements can be viewed as an interchangeable participation of two equal partners: first one, then the other being acted upon. Descriptively, the quality of hand-to-hand activity appears to be non-gentle, involving squeezing, rubbing, or scratching, and often gives the appearance of fidgetiness.

(3) *Direct—hand-to-body.* These are continuous, repetitive movements which entail the stimulation of the body by the hand. They seem to supply some desired stimulation of the skin surface. There is, of course, a wide range of loci including cheeks, mouth, arms, or legs. The quality of these movements is usually soothing and stroking, involving, for example, the continuous stroking of the lips and neck, and continuous rubbing of the upper arm.

In the observation of samples of body-focused activity, it became evident that in most cases these movements could not be expressed as instances or separate acts; rather, they appeared as continous activity, ranging from 3 to 28 seconds without interruption. Hence, the above categories of body-focused activities are expressed in time scores.

DISCRETE BODY-FOCUSED MOVEMENTS

There are, however, body-focused movements which are discrete and non-continuous. These discrete movements have several features in common: they are all brief, lasting less than three seconds, and they all have a terminal structure. Furthermore, these movements may appear during speech or during pauses and they may be sandwiched between two object-focused movements. Interpretatively, when they follow an affirmative statement, they suggest a momentary withdrawal maneuver. Among these discrete movements, we may again distinguish between those having an indirect focus, such as pulling a skirt hem or straightening a tie, and those having a direct focus, like touching the eye or a stroke of the chin.

The initial interviews of the five paranoid and five depressed patients were compared in terms of the prevalence of the different indices of body-focused activity. It had been expected in general that depressed, compared to paranoid patients, would show a preponderance of body-focused movements.

Let us first consider discrete body-focused acts. There was, as expected, a higher incidence of discrete body-focused acts in the depressed patients compared to patients with manifest paranoid ideas (a mean incidence of 16.0 for depressed and 8.6 for paranoid patients). Moreover, these differences could be attributed exclusively to direct discrete movements, with the frequency of indirect discrete movements being equal for both clinical groups.

Next, we considered the prevalence of continuous body-focused activity per 10-minute segment. As already indicated and contrary to our initial expectations, the time spent in continuous body-focused activity for the two groups of five patients was quite similar. However, examination of the different *kinds* of continuous activity revealed divergent trends. Depressed patients showed substantially more direct continuous body-focused activity, a mean of 150.6 seconds, as compared with 41.2 seconds for paranoid patients. They also spent more time in indirect activity than did paranoid patients, having a mean of 36.6 seconds, compared with an average of 1.2 seconds for paranoid patients. Paranoid patients, on the other hand, showed a preponderance of direct hand-to-hand movements with a mean of 154.4 seconds per 10 minutes compared with a mean of 16.2 seconds for depressed patients. The unexpectedly large amount of hand-to-hand body-focused activity among the paranoid patients is noteworthy, in view of a concomitant high level of motor primacy object-focused movements among these patients. The simultaneous or sequential occurrence of high incidences of such object and body-focused movements in the same interview may constitute a pattern relevant to the definition of a paranoid state.

Unfortunately, we are not in a position to evaluate changes in body-focused movements in terms of changes in clinical states among depressed patients. We did examine shifts in body-focused activity from pre- to post-acute interviews among the five paranoid patients. Several observations are noteworthy. In spite of the previously noted decline in object-focused movements concomitant with symptom reduction, total continuous body-focused movements remained essentially unchanged. Yet there was a trend toward a decline of both direct hand-to-body (from an average of 41.2 to 10.2 seconds) and hand-to-hand movements (from 154.4 to 115.6 seconds) with an increase in indirect-symbolic hand movements (1.2 to 49.0 seconds) with symptomatic improvement.

To summarize thus far, the coding approach that has been outlined distinguishes both object- and body-focused movements, each of which is further analyzed in terms of different levels of organization. Within object-focused movements we distinguished levels of speech-primacy and motor-primacy movements; within body-focused movements we distinguished between indirect-symbolic and direct activity. There are indications in our preliminary observations that movement behavior analyzed in these terms may be associated with different clinical states. Relatively acute paranoid and depressed states can be marked by differences in the focus of the movement activity: a prevalence of motor-primacy object-focused movements in a paranoid state and direct body-focused movements in a depressed state. Changes from an acute to a relatively remitted state can be reflected in a shift within both object- and body-focused movements: a shift toward a relatively higher incidence of speech-primacy object-focused movements, and indirect body-focused movements. Such observations give promise that the coding approach which has been developed may be useful as a dependent variable in the evaluation of treatment.

VARIATIONS OF OBJECT- AND BODY-FOCUSED
MOVEMENTS WITHIN A SINGLE INTERVIEW

So far we have noted the prevalence of object- or body-focused movements either between different individuals or within the same individual between different sessions. Intrasession fluctuations in movement behavior may provide us with objective markers by which different phases of the session, signifying transitory altered states, can be isolated. Moreover, such a study of within-session variations affords an opportunity for an examination of behavioral properties linked to object- and body-focused movements. With these objectives in mind, a more intensive analysis of the interview material from one of our patients with paranoid symptomatology was conducted.

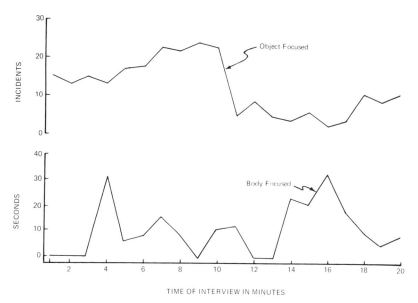

Fɪɢ. 1. Object- and body-focused movements during the first 20 minutes of an initial interview.

The first 20 minutes of the patient's initial interview were analyzed in terms of frequency and duration of object-focused and continuous body-focused movements per 30-second segments. This material is graphically presented in Figure 1. Clearly, object- and body-focused movements showed different phases of saliency in the course of the interview. During the first ten minutes, there is a relative ascendancy in the incidence of object-focused movements which drops sharply at about the ten-minute mark; the level of continuous body-focused movements was relatively low. During the second ten minutes, the level of object-focused movements remains relatively low although toward the end of the session there appears again a slight increase in object-focused activity (lower half of Figure 1). The data are reversed for body-focused movements: continuous body-focused activity during the first ten minutes is relatively low, showing an increase for the second phase of the session (upper half of Figure 1). The above observations are consistent with the findings of a significant negative relationship between the two movement variables during this interview ($r = -.36$).

Using the above tracings of motor activity as an objective guide proved to be a fruitful way of identifying events taking place within the patient and her relationship with her therapist. During the initial period, she spoke rapidly as if under pressure, apparently eager to get her thoughts across to the therapist. She expressed confidence in the therapist and made repeated requests for direct contact ("You know . . ."). Delusional thoughts were not mentioned. She described her relationship with her children and spoke about her achievements at work. Then the therapist confronted the patient with her primary and acute problem, her relationship with her husband. This intervention was almost immediately followed by the drop in object-focused activity noted above. Subsequently, both content and manner of speech changed. Her speech slowed and became more deliberate. She voiced concern about being isolated and unloved by her husband. Yet, these expressions were intermingled with feelings of intense rage about his behavior as well as self-doubt. Then, in response to the therapist's prompting, toward the end of the session, her feelings of hurt and anger crystallized into explicit delusional thoughts. At this point, again, one can note a reemergence of object-focused activity. It seemed that the occasion of the therapist's probably inappropriate intervention initiated a state of intense conflict and mild depression. It also marked a change in her communicative intent toward the therapist, from an eagerness to reach out to a turning upon an injured self. It is of interest that we were unaware of this chain of events, but our attention was drawn to it when we looked at the graph tracing the incidence of movement behavior.

The fluctuations in object- and body-focused movements during this interview presented us with the additional opportunity to examine some of the properties of speech and language in which, of course, these movements are embedded. This issue is relevant to a conceptualization of object- and body-focused movements inasmuch as these movement categories are thought to have a differential relationship to speech. Ideally, such an examination would entail determining the relationship of movement to verbal content, formal aspects of language as well as non-fluencies in speech. These are, in fact, part of the objectives of our current research.

For the above-mentioned session, we can only report relationships between movement behavior, major pauses, and speech volume. For each of the forty 30-second segments, incidents of object-focused movements, duration of body-focused movements, and incidents and duration of major pauses (.5 seconds or more) were determined. The correlations between object-focused movements and major pauses were significant and negative (-.37 for duration, -.31 for incidence of pausing). Thus object-focused movements appear to be linked with more fluent speech. Conversely, the correlation between body-focused movements and incidence of pausing was significant and positive (.33 for duration of pausing, .41 for incidence). Body-focused movements, occurring as we know during the second ten minutes of the interview, appear to be linked with more interrupted and less fluent speech. We did not have an opportunity to check other kinds of hesitation phenomena such as the "Non-Ah" ratio, but it is our impression that the presence of body-focused movements was also accompanied by more incomplete sentences, repetitions, and omissions. Comparing high and low object-focused movement segments suggested a trend, though not statistically significant, toward more frequent volume peaks with high object-focused activity.

The differential association of object- and body-focused movements with pausing is further highlighted as we extend our observations to include also a ten-minute segment from the post-acute session. In this "post-acute" session, while the patient is no longer showing any traces of paranoid ideas, she is clinically in a more depressive state. Comparing the three ten-minute segments (two from the initial and one from the post-acute interview) the following observations were obtained: incidence of object-focused movements declined from 183 to 66 to 24 seconds; time spent in body-focused activity increased from 83 to 157 to 230 seconds; and time spent in major pauses increased from 37 to 77 to 138 seconds per ten-minute segment. Hence, one can observe in these segments a decline in object-focused movements and an increase in continous body-focused movements, as well as in duration of pauses.

Through the study of the more extreme fluctuations that can be observed in a patient with acute psychopathology, certain movement-speech patterns appear to be highlighted. Thus the foregoing interview data suggest that object-focused movements may appear in the context of more fluent, less interrupted speech and perhaps a higher level of speech amplitude; body-focused movements, with slower, more interrupted speech and a trend toward a lower level of speech amplitude. These clusters sustain the notion that the direction of the hand movement (whether it involves body-touching or not) is linked to measurable aspects of speech.

DISCUSSION

Even on the basis of the foregoing sketchy observations, there appears to be support for the notion that the two modes of focusing in movement behavior reflect very different psychological processes. The observations that object-focused movements are more prevalent in paranoid states, body-focused movements in depressive states, are partly self-evident, partly reassuring, and partly provocative. Surely, the occurrence of such movement activity is not limited to paranoid or depressive symptomatology, nor are shifts in such movements confined to changes in clinical states. Some broader behavioral process appears to be at work. We shall attempt some speculative formulations toward this end and return later to the issue of their relevance to psychopathology.

THE OBJECT- BODY-FOCUSED DICHOTOMY AS AN INTENT TO COMMUNICATE

The distinct psychological functions of object- and body-focused movements are suggested not only by their correlation with clinical data, but also by their structures: object-focused movements tend to be single acts, body-focused movements tend to be continuous. They may also bear a differential relationship to speech. As we have seen in one case, there may be less interrupted speech with object-focused movements, more pausing with body-focused movements. Hence, object-focused movements are supplements to speech and constitute an enhanced and fuller effort to communicate with the listener. Body-focused movements may be substitutive maneuvers for what is not verbalized and constitute an effort towards ministration of the body or self.

A general formulation is offered that the object- body-focused dichotomy refers to an intent to communicate, with object-focused movements representing a condition of high intent and body-focused movements signifying a condition of low intent. In general, high compared to low communicative intent refers to the mobilization of the various vehicles of expression (verbal and vocal expression, posture, as well as movement) in the transmission of information to a listener. The movement categories constitute one major element describing such an intent.

This intentionality has two constituents or aspects which we hope to define in future work. There is, first of all, an interpersonal aspect defined by the speaker's intent to reach the listener—the object of presence. Here we would try to define not only movements or words, but the movement's relation to posture and gaze direction as well. There is, further, a cognitive aspect suggested by the writings of Brentano (1874) and, more recently, of Werner and Kaplan (1963), namely, the intent to represent one's experiences symbolically. From this position, we would like to examine the relationship between movement and the adequacy and complexity of symbolic (usually verbal) representations. More specifically, it can then be hypothesized that under conditions of high communicative intent, where object-focused movements predominate, we can observe behavior signifying an approach to the listener and more fully articulated verbal representations. Conversely, under conditions of low communicative intent, where body-focused movements predominate, we can note a withdrawal from the listener and more impoverished and global verbal representations. Implicit in these hypotheses, furthermore, is the notion that the complexity of verbal representation is related to a commitment to an external object.

It is, of course, recognized that the foregoing hypotheses represent a schematization of events; the actual instances of communicative expression rarely polarize in this fashion. Moreover, our coding categories have suggested that there may be different levels of organization in which the communicative intent may manifest itself. Its directional as well as its representational aspects are significantly modified by the different levels within object- and body-focused movements. We shall turn to these next.

COMMUNICATIVE INTENT WITH OBJECT-FOCUSED MOVEMENTS

As a visible sign of communicative intent, the object-focused movement constitutes a commitment to an interchange with another person. Given such a commitment, one can observe different modes of expressing the communicative intent as exemplified by the two levels of object-focused movements, speech- and motor-primacy movements.

The *motor-primacy* movements consist primarily of representational or concretization movements, that is, of movements in which the motor act itself becomes representational. However, the movements appear often only in condensed form and thus have the property of "signs" supplementing the functions of "words" or "symbols." Through his gesture, the patient has achieved a visible expression of his thoughts that can be apprehended both by himself and by his listener. In this sense, the motor-primacy movements constitute a direct and visible contact with the onlooker.

Motor-primacy responses, apart from their transactional significance, have a specific bearing on the symbolizing function. They suggest failure to verbalize, to transform images into word representations (Balkanyi, 1964). Each of these movements expresses a surplus meaning, i.e., something not fully verbalized. This overabundance of imagery must find its immediate and simultaneous expression. The image that comes to mind is that of a traffic jam and the use of a detour avenue for travel (it is distinct from stuttering or stammering where no detour is available and motor blocking occurs). This hypothesis of motor-primacy response as a sign of failure in verbalization was formulated and tested experimentally by Hoffman (1968). As part of his study, Hoffman asked his subjects to describe stimuli of high and low ambiguity (Rorschach and TAT cards). The ambiguous stimuli (Rorschach cards) can be expected to elicit many more images for which no ready-made labels are available and thus put a greater load on the verbalizing process than do non-ambiguous stimuli (TAT cards). The study indeed showed that descriptions of Rorschach cards elicited many more motor-primacy hand movements than did descriptions of TAT cards.

The motor-primacy response assumes a specific clinical significance if its emergence can be traced to an inner state, especially when it is not exclusively contingent upon the communicative situation, such as seating arrangements (face-to-face or back-to-back). There is good evidence that motor-primacy responses do vary with the communicative context (Hoffman, 1968; Mahl, 1966). In our patients, however, the face-to-face seating arrangement was a *constant* factor, yet we observed upsurges and abatements of such movements with changes in their clinical conditions. Ultimately, therefore, the emergence of a motor-primacy act can be traced to an inner state and presumably to a failure in verbalization.

In *speech-primacy* movements, by contrast, speech is the primary vehicle of a message. Movements are part of the effort to reach the listener, but their informational value is subordinated when speech predominates. Whereas the motor-primacy response constituted a direct and visible effort toward contact with a listener, speech-primacy movements, using words as vehicles for contact, may imply a greater psychological distance between the speaker and his listener. However, we can only speculate about the imprint that is left upon the structure of language itself when such movements appear. We suspect that it is specifically among speech-primacy, object-focused movements that language form becomes more differentiated and syntactical structure more complex. We further suspect that these movements may have a self-monitoring and clarifying function similar to that ascribed to vocalization by Klein (1965). Klein emphasized not the expressive but the feedback function of vocalization. Similarly, speech-primacy movements may be instrumental in the sharpening and clarification of thought.

In sum, while all object-focused movements signify a condition of high communicative intent, we can distinguish very different forms of organization expressing this intent. In one form (motor-primacy movements), we note an effort toward direct and visible contact with an object concomitant with failure in verbalization; in the other form (speech-primacy movements), we find a greater sense of boundaries between the speaker and the object and presumably a greater reliance on more complex language forms.

COMMUNICATIVE INTENT WITH
BODY-FOCUSED MOVEMENTS

With the emergence of body-focused activity, the communicative intent lessens. Even when other modes of expression, such as gaze or posture, are geared toward the listener, the movement itself appears to be a sign of withdrawal. The focus of attention is on the self. This preoccupation with the self is vividly illustrated in extreme cases of depression in which persons may have the palpable experience that there is literally "no one out there." It may also be noted in cases of blindness, where self-touching is prevalent. Furthermore, body-touching, as Burlingham (1965) has shown in her film material, declines when blind children become more object- and task-oriented, thus emphasizing the close linkage between body-touching and preoccupation with self.

The absence of an experienced external object associated with continuous body-focused activity is likely to lead to an impoverished level of symbol formation, i.e., the failure to establish referential relationships. For example, in a study reported by Werner and Kaplan (1963), it was shown that more complex language forms, such as specifications of images, are created under conditions in which a person must describe a stimulus as if he were communicating to another person (external speech); conversely, more global and less differentiated language forms are created when a person is asked to describe a comparable stimulus only for himself (inner speech). Whereas we do not yet have any evidence of the complexity of language associated with body-focused activity, we may surmise that these movements conceal a considerable amount of unverbalized experience. It is the duality implicit in a preoccupation with the self which yet remains partially unverbalized, that has led investigators to label these movements as "autistic."[5]

Of course, not all continuous body-focused movements involve a depletion of communicative effort or an impoverishment of symbol formation. We noted earlier that body-focused movements imply a splitting of the speaker's attention. An appropriate model for body-focused movements, therefore, may also be one of conflict between what remains unverbalized and is expressed only in motor form, and what is verbalized.[6] In fact, the different categories of body-focused activity represent different constellations of conflict: conflict signified by withdrawal (direct hand-to-body movements), conflict signified by acute discomfort (fidgetiness of hand-to-hand movements), and a milder form of conflict leading to exploratory and problem-solving behavior (indirect movements). It is suggested that these different forms of body-focused movements imply different levels of anxiety, different modes of relating to the listener, and probably also different levels of verbal articulation.

Of particular interest, from a clinical and theoretical point of view, is the suggestion, already noted, that continuous body-focused movements contain considerable unverbalized experience. This unverbalized activity raises the question of its verbalizability, i.e., of the extent to which the unexpressed may find expression in articulated form. It is suggested that the different categories of continuous body-focused movements entail different forms of resistance to articulation, some inhibiting, others facilitating verbal expression. Let

---

[5]It may be argued that.in a communicative context such "autistic" movements are a part of a non-verbal dialogue and that they may function as signs or signals to an observer-interpreter. Rubenstein (1968) has pointed out that it is inappropriate to attribute the property of intention, which fits the sender-receiver model in linguistics, to unconscious fantasies. This point seems to be equally relevant to the unverbalized fantasies associated with body-focused movements. Identifying these movements as having low communicative intent does not, of course, negate the fact that the movements and the associative fantasies may have an important impact on the line of manifest communication.

[6]Krout was able to induce autistic or body-focused movements experimentally by presenting subjects with conflict situations in which they were blocked from expressing previously verbalized statements (1954).

us illustrate this idea by further examining two of our categories:

(1) In the case of direct, continuous body-focused activity, the movement is the primary carrier of some unverbalized thought or wish. Pausing appears to be pronounced and there is likely to be a gaze aversion as if the person were "out of it." Movements appear to function as direct need gratifiers. One may suspect that these movements lack not only their ideational content (the patient saying, "My mind is a blank") but also inhibit, by virtue of their need-gratifying activity, the production of verbal associations. From the vantage point of psychoanalytic theory, these movements appear to provide an operational definition of primary narcissism. When they occur in the course of a session, especially in response to a therapist's intervention, they may become an objective manifestation of a negative transference.

(2) In contrast to direct body-focused activity, indirect symbolic hand movements appear to facilitate verbal expression. Mahl's (1966) anticipatory movements, which are much like our indirect movements, were shown to be associatively linked to suppressed or repressed thought. When the thoughts were verbalized, the movements dropped out. Such movements seem to contain fantasies not only about the self, but also about the self's relationship to significant others and appear as part of a free floating contemplation. The resistance to articulated speech is relatively low.

In sum, body-focused activity implies a reduction in communicative intent, a withdrawal from the interchange and the possible impoverishment of symbolic activity. Yet this reduction varies with the different categories of body-focused movement, each representing different constellations of conflict between what is and what is not verbalized. The formal organization of the movement categories may have a bearing on the ability to verbalize experiences associated with these movements.

RELEVANCE TO PSYCHOPATHOLOGY

We are now in a position to sketch out the possible relevance of the analysis of movement behavior to psychopathological states.

Continuous body-focused activity, as we have seen, provides a guide for identifying a relative reduction in communicative intent. Depression is one clinical condition which highlights such a reduction in intent. Continuous stroking or soothing movements are indeed a sign of depression. Moreover, the categories of body-focused activity may suggest different themes of depressive experiences: the theme of stroking or soothing, e.g., gentle self-ministration, or the theme of squeezing or scratching, e.g., punitive self-ministration. Perhaps the most striking observation in our data was the sheer amount of continuous body-focused activity. When the time samples of all interviews are considered, the patients spent one-third of their time in such behavior. Even in the absence of normative data from a non-patient control group, this proportion appears high and of significance to psychopathological and/or regressive states. It suggests that continuous body-focused activity provides an observational tool by which to define a range of clinical conditions, having as their common denominator the experience of being "cut off" and a behavior signifying disengagement from contact.

Object-focused movements as we have attempted to show, reflect a condition of high communicative intent. A paranoid state exemplifies this condition, especially when one considers a patient's eagerness to capture the listener's attention, and his preoccupation with an external object, be it hostile or benign. When motor-primacy object-focused movements are dominant, during an acute state, we can infer an overabundance of unverbalized thought demanding expression. When speech-primacy movements predominate, in a remitted state, we can also infer a remission of unverbalized surplus thought. An observed shift from a predominance of motor-primacy to speech-primacy movements, of course, does not exclusively define a change from a paranoid to a non-paranoid state. Such a shift may, more generally, delineate behavioral changes associated with altered symptomatic conditions (e.g., from agitated anxious states to states of greater tranquility).

The cogency of the movement categories to specific psychopathological constellations is probably greater when the categories are considered in patterned form, than when considered in the form of single variables. Thus a pattern more specific to the organization of paranoia may be found in the appearance of object-focused movements followed closely by hand-to-hand movements. Here one can note the ambivalence between reaching out and restraint, suggesting a more basic split in the perception of the object, a split often deemed to be a characteristic of paranoia. An even more profound ambivalence is reflected in the vacillation between motor-primacy movements and continuous self-ministration noted among our more psychotic patients. Such a contradiction in the communicative intent may suggest an observable instance of a thought disorder.

The consistencies and contradictions in the communicative intent, as they become evident in body movements, thus define an important component of the communicative process in general, and of the pathology of communication in particular.

References

BALKANYI, C. On verbalization. *Int. J. Psychoanal.*, 1964, **46**, 64-74.

BIRDWHISTELL, R. *Introduction to Kinesics.* University of Louisville Press, 1952.

BRENTANO, F. *Psychologie vom empirischen Standpunkt*, 1874.

BURLINGHAM, D. Some problems of ego development in blind children. *Psychoanal. Stud. Child.*, 1965, **20**, 194-208.

CONDON, W. S. and OGSTON, M. B. Sound film analysis of normal and pathological behavior patterns. *J. Nerv. Ment. Dis.*, 1966, **143**, 338-47.

DITTMANN, A. T. and LLEWELLYN, L. G. Body movement and speech rhythm in social conversation. *J. Pers. Soc. Psychol.*, 1969, **11**, 98-106.

EKMAN, P. and FRIESEN, W. V. Nonverbal behavior in psychotherapy research. In J. Shlien (Ed.), *Research in Psychotherapy*, American Psychological Association, 1968, Vol. III.

FERENCZI, S. Child analysis in the analysis of adults. In M. Balint (Ed.), *Final Contributions to the Problems and Methods of Psycho-Analysis.* Basic Books, New York, 1955, 126-42.

FREEDMAN, N. and HOFFMAN, S. P. Kinetic behavior in altered clinical states: Approach to objective analysis of motor behavior during clinical interviews. *Percept. Motor Skills*, 1967, **24**, 527-39.

FREUD, S. Fragment of an analysis of a case of hysteria. *The Standard Edition of the Complete Psychological Works of Sigmund Freud*, Vol. VII. Hogarth Press, London, 1953.

HOFFMAN, S. P. An empirical study of representational hand movements. Doctoral dissertation, New York University, 1968.

KLEIN, G. S. On hearing one's own voice. In M. Schur (Ed.), *Drives, Affects and Behavior*, Vol. II, International University Press, New York, 1965.

KROUT, M. H. An experimental attempt to produce unconscious manual symbolic movements. *J. Gen. Psychol.*, 1954, **51**, 94-120.

MAHL, G. F. Expression of the unverbalized in autistic actions: Psychoanalytic observations. Paper prepared for the Third Research in Psychotherapy Conference, Chicago, June 1-4, 1966.

MAHL, G. F. Gestures and body movements in initial interviews. Paper prepared for Third Research in Psychotherapy Conference, Chicago, June 1-4, 1966.

MAHL, G. F. The visual situation of the interview: Its effect on gestures and body movements. Paper prepared for the Third Research in Psychotherapy Conference, Chicago, June 1-4, 1966.

MAHL, G. F., DANET, B., and NORTON, N. Reflection of major personality characteristics in gestures and body movements. Presented at American Psychological Association annual meeting, 1959.

PIAGET, J. *The Language and Thought of the Child.* Noonday Press, New York, 1955.

ROSENFELD, H. M. Instrumental affiliative functions of facial and gestural expressions. *J. Pers. Soc. Psychol.*, 1966, **4**, 65-72.

RUBENSTEIN, B. Discussion of paper by Rosen, V. H. Sign phenomena and their relationship to unconscious meaning. New York Psychoanalytic Society, October 29, 1968.

SAINSBURY, P. Gestural movement during psychiatric interview. *Psychosom. Med.*, 1958, **17**, 458-69.

SCHEFLEN, A. E. Communication: Behavioral programs and their integration in interaction. *Behav. Sci.*, 1958, **13**, 44-53.

WERNER, H. and KAPLAN, B. *Symbol Formation.* Wiley, New York, 1963.

WERNER, H. and KAPLAN, B. Inner versus external speech in normal adults. In *Symbol Formation* (Chapter 17). Wiley, New York, 1963.

Chapter 9

Some Relationships Between Body Motion and Speech

An Analysis of an Example[1]

Adam Kendon

INTRODUCTION

An analysis is reported here of some relationships between the movements and speech in a single individual. The aim will be to describe the character of these movements, how they are organized, and how this organization appears to be fitted to the speech they accompany. Such a descriptive analysis is seen as preliminary to any understanding of the functions of body motion in a speaker, whether from the point of view of its function in communication or its possible role in the process of speech production.

The concern will be with gesticulation, those complex movements of the hands and arm and head that may often be observed in a speaker. It is widely supposed that these movements are closely related to what the speaker is saying and that they serve to dramatize, emphasize, or to illustrate his words. At one time, indeed, training in public speaking included instruction in gesticulation, and quite elaborate schemes were available in which the various gestures were described and their recommended use detailed.[2] Systematic investi-

[1]This work was done while I was a Visiting Assistant Professor at Cornell University. I am grateful to the Department of Psychology for making the necessary film-analysis equipment available to me. Dr. Rose Marie Weber offered advice on points of linguistic analysis and I am very grateful to her and also to Mrs. Rita Weisbrod for helpful discussions and valuable comments on an earlier draft of this paper.

[2]See, for example, Mosher (1916), or Ott (1902).

gation is sparse, however.[3] Apart from such rather general works as those of McDonald Critchley (1939) and Charlotte Wolf (1945), the only really detailed work on gesticulation has been that of Efron (1941). In this work, he not only amassed a great deal of historical material, but he also undertook detailed analyses of the gesticulations of a large number of people. He compared the gesticulatory styles of Jews and Italians in New York City, and showed that the differences he was able to demonstrate were due to learning. Jews and Italians who had become assimilated to American culture showed much less difference in their styles of gesticulation. In addition to this, Efron also provided some analysis of the way in which gesticulation appeared to relate to what a speaker was saying. Thus he described how a speaker may beat time to the rhythm of his speech, marking out the points of emphasis with strokes of the hand or arm; how he may diagram in space the logical relationships between the things he is talking about; or how he may illustrate what he is saying by a series of symbolic gestures. Similar analyses of the relations between gesture and speech have been put forward recently by Ekman and Friesen (1969) and by Freedman and Hoffman (1967).

The assumption of these investigations has been that the primary function of these movements is to facilitate communication between speaker and listener. The analyses of the relations between movement and speech are done in terms of how the movements appear to express the content of what is being said. Other writers have suggested, however, that gesticulation may also be related to the process of speech production. It is seen as a more primitive mode of cognitive representation which will be resorted to when the speaker is unable to formulate his ideas in words (De Laguna, 1927; Werner and Kaplan, 1963). It has also been suggested that the enactment of ideas in movement may facilitate the speech encoding process (Moscovici, 1967). Another recent suggestion is that movements associated with speech are a result of a spill-over into the motor system of tensions that arise when the speech production process is blocked, as it is where choices have to be made in formulating what next is to be said. Dittmann (1968), who has put forward this view, suggests that whatever communicative functions

---

[3]The only systematic body of work undertaken on body motion as it is related to communicational behavior is that of Ray L. Birdwhistell (1952, 1961, 1965, 1966, 1967). Until recently, however, he has been mainly concerned with the communicative functions of body motion as it operates independently or separately from speech. For a thorough survey of the more traditional work in gesture and body motion, see LaBarre (1964). Hayes (1957) provides a comprehensive reference.

these movements may have, have been secondarily acquired.

Most of the work on the relation between body motion and speech has been concerned with how body motion may express aspects of what the speaker is saying or, as in the case of the work of Deutsch (1966) and Loeb (1967), how it may express additional, usually unconscious thoughts and feelings. It would appear, however, that a prior task should be a description of how body motion that accompanies speech is organized, and how it is related to the patterning of speech. Such an analysis would enable a statement to be made about which aspects of speech body motion is related to. Findings from this approach might also have other implications. For instance, if gesticulation is primarily functional for the speaker, we might expect that it would anticipate what he is saying and be found more often at those points in his speech where verbal planning may be presumed to be occurring than where he is running off well-planned phrases. If it is in some sense an addition, or an overflow, we might expect that it would be produced along with the flow of speech, or perhaps even lag behind it somewhat.

The only work so far reported in which an attempt has been made to describe how body motion is organized and patterned in relation to speech is that of Condon and Ogston (1966, 1967). We shall describe their findings in detail in a later section, for it is their method of analysis that will largely be followed here. In this, sound film is used, and this has the advantage, as Condon and Ogston have shown, that a chart may be made of the patterns of movement and this may be precisely matched to a plot of the speech sounds. This plot of the speech sounds may be made independently from the sound track of the film, and the relations between movement and speech may be determined in a way that bypasses those errors of judgment which may be made if the observer must watch movement and listen to the sound simultaneously.

In the analysis reported here, we hope to show how the configurations of movement are organized and how they relate to the sound patterns of the co-occurring speech. The question of what types of movement occur and how these relate to the content of what is being said will also be touched upon, but a full treatment with the methods adopted here must await the accumulation of more data.

MATERIAL

The individual studied in this research, who will be referred to as X, was one of a number of people who were filmed as they drank and talked in the private lounge of a London pub.[4] Many of the participants were regular customers at the pub and they were encouraged to come into the lounge from the bar. The camera and sound recording equipment were set in operation and those in the lounge were stimulated to some discussion which, after an initial rather stilted phase, they engaged in with spontaneity and enthusiasm. About an hour and a half of this discussion was filmed.

The excerpt from this film, which is analyzed here, shows a man of perhaps thirty-five years of age who, to judge from his manner and style of speech, is of upper-middle class background, with a university education. He is sitting on a sofa taking part in a discussion on British national character, in which he is the main speaker. His interlocutor is the film-maker, an American anthropologist. Discussed here is the first minute and a half of a three-minute speech which X makes in response to something his interlocutor has just said.

X's remarks are organized into a kind of argument. As may be seen from the transcript, his speech for the most part is made up of fully formed sentences and it appears to meet the criteria for what Joos (1962) has called "consultative" speech style, a speech style that is used, as it is here, for the exposition of ideas or for conveying information where those involved may be said to be collaborating together on a common problem. Here, as Joos describes it, the listener actively participates, supplying "attention signals" and occasional short comments or questions. This contrasts, for instance, with "formal" speech style where instead of a collaboration between speaker and listener, the speaker expounds and the listener (or, more usually, listeners) passively receives. In the present situation, X is sitting some eight feet away from his interlocutor and, though he addresses his remarks specifically to him, they are fully audible to at least the five or six others who are sitting nearby. Though silent here, these people are full participants in the discussion and, later, several of them join in.

---

[4]The film, known as TRD 009 London Pub Scene, was made in London by Dr. Ray L. Birdwhistell and Mr. Jacques D. Van Vlack. It was produced by Temple University and the Commonwealth of Pennsylvania, with assistance from the Institute for Intercultural Studies. I am grateful to Dr. Birdwhistell for letting me use excerpts from this film, and to Mr. Van Vlack for technical assistance.

The individual whose behavior is to be analyzed, then, is engaged in a specific kind of speech activity (which we shall here call "discourse") within a speech situation[5] of a particular kind. No doubt many of the features of his performance that will be described belong to this type of task and situation. For a proper appreciation of this, of course, comparable descriptions of performances of individuals in other speech situations are needed. None exist at the present time, but it is hoped that we shall be able to present some in future reports.

BODY MOTION AND SPEECH:
THE WORK OF WILLIAM CONDON

In this study, the approach adopted owes most to the methods and findings of Condon and Ogston (1966, 1967). In this work, the aim is to describe the flow of movement as it occurs in a speaker and to show how this movement flow relates to the flow of speech. Condon and his coworker have sought to plot, in the form of a flow chart, all the observable movement in the body of a speaker. This is done by examining sound film with numbered frames by means of a time-motion analyzer, a projector which may be operated by hand. Close and repeated scrutiny of very short stretches of film is thus possible, and the movement patterns may be broken down into their smallest components.[6] The movement of each body part[7] is examined and the points of change in movement are marked out on a time chart, each division of which corresponds to a frame of the film.

When this is done for a stretch of behavior, it is found that the points of change in the movement for separate parts of the body coincide. That is to say, the body parts change and sustain speed and direction of movement together. This does not mean that all the body parts are moving in the same way. Some may not be moving at all. Those that are may have different spatial and directional relationships to one another. Thus the head may turn to the right as the arms are lowered, as the fingers are spread, as the trunk bows forward. Further, some body parts may sustain a given movement over

---

[5]For a useful treatment of the features of speech situations, see Dell Hymes (1967).

[6]Smallest, that is, within the limits set by the film record. Only visible changes in the relative position of body parts can be recorded and this, of course, can only be done to the nearest frame—a twenty-fourth of a second if standard speed sound film is used.

[7]"Body part" is defined in terms of the joints by which it is articulated.

several changes in other body parts. For instance, the subject may lean forward (flex his trunk from the hip joints) while several complex changes may occur in his arms and hands and eyes. What emerges from this is a description of the flow of movement as a series of contrasting waves of movement where, within the larger waves (i.e., those that last longer), smaller waves are contained. These successive configurations of movement constitute what Condon has called the "process units" of behavior. He defines a "process unit" as the "initiation and sustaining of directionality of change of body parts with each other . . . through a given interval of time as contrasted with preceding and succeeding sets of similarly sustained configurations of movements." (Condon and Ogston, 1966, p. 342.)

When such a flow chart of the body movement is matched against a chart showing how the flow of speech sounds changes from frame to frame of the film, it is found that these "configurations of change" occur synchronously with the articulation of the sounds. In other words, the body moves synchronously, and synchronously, too, with the changes in the geometry of the oral-pharyngeal regions that occur with speech. Thus as the subject speaks so he moves, the whole organism behaving as an integrated whole.

This phenomenon can be demonstrated quite easily with a film and a time-motion analyzer in the manner of Condon. Eric Lenneberg (1968) has also demonstrated how if a subject is asked to tap at regular intervals while speaking, his speaking and tapping very quickly come to coincide with the beginnings of the syllables. In the particular experiment Lenneberg described, the subject was asked to "tap at a quick but comfortable speed." After about ten seconds he began to speak into the microphone and he *began* to speak at the moment of the beat of his tap.

Condon's analysis, then, leads us to understand the flow of movement as a flow of configurations of movement in which the parts of the body change and sustain directionality in synchrony. But we also saw that not all body parts will change at the same rate, so that one body part may go through one movement while there are several changes in the movement flow in other body parts. In fact, we can imagine a sort of hierarchy in the organization of movement in which some body parts are more commonly involved in frequent changes than others are. Thus, as we shall see in the speaker studied here, there is a tendency for the wrist and fingers to change more often, followed by the forearm, then the upper arm. The elements of the face (eyes, brows, and mouth), as a rule, change more often than the head. The trunk and lower limbs change relatively rarely. It appears, in fact, that those parts of the body which have to do most directly with transactions with the environment—whether physical or social—show most changes in movement.

Condon has suggested, in an unpublished paper (Condon, 1964), that in a speaking individual the changes in these more slowly changing body parts occur at the boundaries of the larger units in the flow of speech. For instance, he suggests that sweeps of the arm or movements of the head may be sustained over larger linguistic units, such as phrases, while eye shifts, wrist and finger movements occur over smaller segments, such as syllables. The chief purpose of this study is to explore these higher order aspects of the organization of body motion in a speaker to see whether it can be established that body motion and speech are integrated at levels of organization above that of the successive changes associated with each syllable.

METHOD OF ANALYSIS

In analyzing the film, the first step was to make a "map" of the main features of movement. Here, for example, the point at which major shifts in posture occur, or the point where there are clear changes in which body parts are involved in movement would be plotted. When such a "map" of the main features of movement has been made, selected portions are then examined in greater detail. A time-motion analyzer is used to scan the film in small segments, with the aim of picking out those successive groups of frames over which is sustained a single direction of movement in a given body part. In the movement flow chart which is plotted, a separate horizontal line is used for each body part. Each segment on each line represents that stretch of frames over which no change in movement could be detected. The movement that occurs in each segment is labeled, using a set of terms modified from those proposed by the American College of Surgeons for describing joint function (Boyd and Banks, 1965). A simplified extract from such a flow chart is given in Figure 5 (see p. 201).

The speech was transcribed from the soundtrack, and a precise matching of the points of change in the sound with the frames of the film was made using a sound reader and a properly calibrated frame counter. The speech transcription was made with the phonetic notation outlined by Daniel Jones (1956).[8]

---

[8]The film-analysis apparatus included a Bell and Howell BD173, Bell and Howell Filmosound 552, and a Precision Sound Reader Model No. 600.

THE DISCOURSE

As has already been stated, the primary aim here is to describe how the movements observed to occur as X speaks are organized, not from the point of view of their possible significance as gestures —though this perspective has not been disregarded entirely—but as patterns or configurations of movement, and how these are related to the flow of speech, considered as a pattern of sound and rhythm. The approach to the analysis of the speech has, therefore, been phonetic. Since rather little has been done on the phonetics of long stretches of speech or discourse, we have found it convenient to use a terminology of our own invention.[9] We begin with a recognized phonetic unit, the "tone group," but then try to show how these units are grouped together into larger units. The scheme put forward is very provisional. It does, however, appear to be a convenient way of describing the way this particular stretch of speech is organized and, as we shall see, it also "works" in terms of the associated analysis of body motion.

A lexical transcript of X's speech, with some phonological information, is provided on p.186. Intonation has been described with the system of tonetic stress marks developed by Roger Kingdon (1958), and tempo, loudness, and register have been described with Trager's (1958) notation. Silences between speech units are given in twenty-fourths of a second.

The speech has been divided into "tone groups,"[10] which are here called "phrases" or, more accurately, "prosodic phrases." This unit may be defined as the smallest grouping of syllables over which a completed intonation tune occurs. Somewhat different definitions of it have been offered by other writers, but there seems to be wide agreement that it represents a basic unit of speech, the basic move, as it were, of the speaking process (Boomer, 1965; Halliday, 1963; Lieberman, 1967).

---

[9]Though phoneticians have developed the description of the phrase and the sentence to a high level of sophistication, remarkably little attention seems to have been paid to the question of how relations between phrases or sentences are signaled. But see Crystal and Quirk (1964).

[10]Reference to the transcript will show that in three instances phrases have been further subdivided and the resulting parts treated as separate phrases. This has been done in those cases where what is effectively the prehead of a tone unit is set off from the rest of the phrase so distinctly that it apparently constitutes an almost independent piece of speech. Thus phrase 2 is divided from phrase 3 by a pause, although these two really belong together in the same intonation group. Phrase 20 and phrase 22 are also separated from the phrases they are really part of by a marked pause, and also by marked paralinguistic differences.

These phrases combine together in various ways to form higher order groupings and the way these have been constituted for X's speech may be seen in the diagram below. Four groupings of phrases above the level of the phrase have been distinguished, and an outline of the criteria by which these have been arrived at follows.

Transcription of X's Speech: Explanation of Conventions.

(a) *Intonation and Stress.* In Kingdon's tonetic stress-mark system, each stressed syllable is marked. A vertical mark (ı) represents a level tone, a forward sloping mark (´) a rising tone, a backward sloping mark (`) a falling tone. If the mark is placed on the upper line the starting pitch level is high, if it is placed on the lower line the starting pitch level is low. If the mark is doubled (ıı), the syllable receives extra stress. In the present transcription, the most prominent syllable in each phrase (the "center") has been underlined.

(b) *Paralanguage.* Tempo, loudness and register have been noted. The marks which are placed at the beginning and end of the affected segment, are as follows:

	1 degree	2 degrees
Overloud	∧	⋀̂
Oversoft	∨	⋁̂
Fast	>	≫
Slow	<	≪
Pitch level raised	⋏	⋏̂
Pitch level lowered	⋎	⋎̂
Drawl	ᴧ	

(c) Numbers in brackets between speech units give the length of silence in twenty-fourths of a second.

(d) *Abbreviations* pc=phrase cluster, L=Locution, Lg=Locution Group, LC= Locution cluster.

(e) Dotted lines represent speech which could not be deciphered.

The principal unit into which phrases combine is called the "Locution." The locution tends to correspond to a complete sentence. It is separated by a distinct pause from any immediately preceding locution and there is a clear increase in the loudness of the voice when the first phrase of a locution is compared to the last phrase of the one that preceded it. The kinetic tone at the nucleus of the last phrase of the locution tends to be more marked (there is a greater degree of change in pitch) than it is at the nuclei of other phrases within the locution. If there is a "tail" to the locution, the voice is markedly softened and, in all of X's examples, it is lowered.

Within the locution we find that some phrases are sometimes more closely bound together than others are, and it seems useful to distinguish what will here be called the "phrase cluster." Phrases within such clusters are not usually separated by a pause and there is a distinct continuity in the second and subsequent intonation tunes with the first in the cluster. The range of variation in pitch levels within subsequent phrases in a cluster is progressively narrowed and

TRANSCRIPT OF X's SPEECH
From TRD, 1, 2700-39270

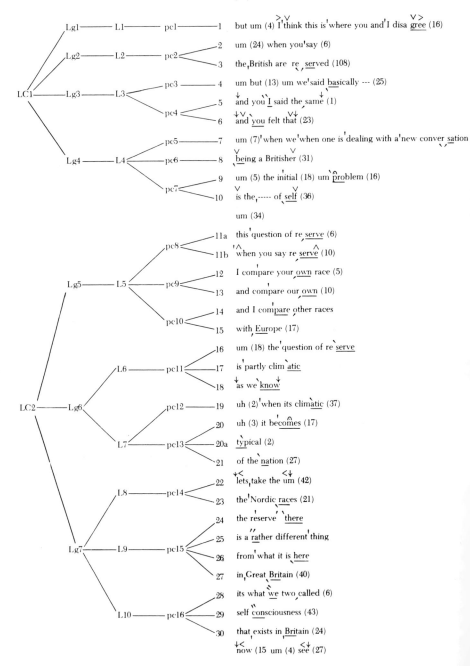

1 but um (4) I think this is where you and I disa gree (16)

2 um (24) when you say (6)

3 the British are re served (108)

4 um but (13) um we said basically --- (25)

5 and you I said the same (1)

6 and you felt that (23)

7 um (7) when we when one is dealing with a new conver sation

8 being a Britisher (31)

9 um (5) the initial (18) um problem (16)

10 is the, ----- of self (36)

um (34)

11a this question of re serve (6)

11b when you say re serve (10)

12 I compare your own race (5)

13 and compare our own (10)

14 and I compare other races

15 with Europe (17)

16 um (18) the question of re serve

17 is partly clim atic

18 as we know

19 uh (2) when its climatic (37)

20 uh (3) it becomes (17)

20a typical (2)

21 of the nation (27)

22 lets take the um (42)

23 the Nordic races (21)

24 the reserve there

25 is a rather different thing

26 from what it is here

27 in Great Britain (40)

28 its what we two called (6)

29 self consciousness (43)

30 that exists in Britain (24)

now (15 um (4) see (27)

TRANSCRIPT OF X's SPEECH
From TRD, 1, 2700-39270 (cont.)

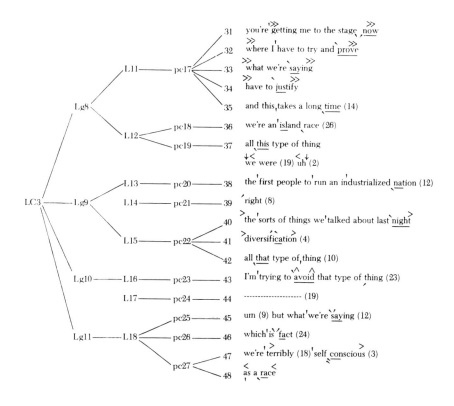

there also tends to be an overall lowering of pitch level with each successive phrase.

Locutions may occur together in "locution groups." These are constituted of adjacent locutions which share certain features in common which distinguish them from locutions in neighboring groups. For instance, in locution group 5 the phrases all take a low rising intonation (Kingdon's Tune IL), whereas in locution group 6, the phrases all take a falling intonation (Kingdon's Tune II). In locution group 7, we find examples of the rise-fall (Kingdon's Tune III) and of emphasis devices not found elsewhere. In locution group 8, there is a distinct increase in tempo and there is also a slight lowering of the voice together with a greater "resonance" (not marked in the transcript).

The locution groups combine into "locution clusters." These are the highest level speech-units below the level of discourse. Each cluster is separated from the next by a marked pause, and "temporizers," repeated or corrected phrases, or sequences of vocal segregates are more likely to occur at the beginning of a cluster than within it. There is a change of "key" in which the voice is "played" and there is also a distinct shift in the subject matter. Locution clusters are the paragraphs of discourse.

The theme of X's remarks is evidently to show that the British are "reserved." His discourse divides clearly into three locution clusters. In the first, where four of the locutions that occur are incomplete, X is evidently attempting to discuss the question of British "reserve" from the point of view of an individual Briton's experience on meeting new people. In the second cluster, which is remarkably fluent, he attempts to deal with British "reserve" in terms of broad distinctions between national characters. At the end of this cluster, in locution 10, he brings out his main assertion, that the British are "self-conscious," not reserved. In the third cluster, which then follows, X acknowledges that he should say more to support his assertion but he, at the same time, declines to do this. He ends this cluster with a reassertion of his main point.

THE ANALYSIS OF THE BODY MOTION

We shall now present data to show that associated with each unit of speech, as this was defined above, there is a configuration of movement that is distinctive or contrasting with the movement configuration associated with the speech unit that preceded it at the same level of analysis. Thus, if we take each phrase in succession,

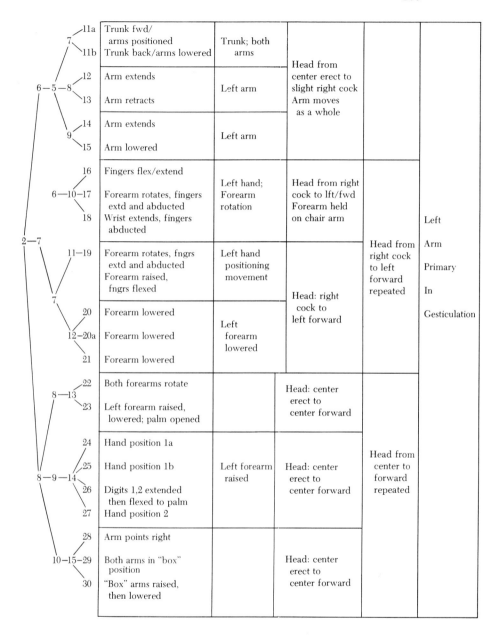

Fɪɢ. 1. Organization of movement patterns in hand, arm and head in association with speech units in locution cluster 2.

we may observe a distinctive position of a body part or a distinctive pattern of movement associated with each one. But then, if we take each locution in succession, we may again find a pattern of movement or a position which is characteristic of the locution as a whole, which sets it off, in movement, from locutions on either side. Thus we find that, just as we may see the units of the flow of speech as having an hierarchic organization—the successive syllables combining into phrases, which themselves combine into locutions, locution groups, and locution clusters—so we may see that the pattern of movement that co-occurs with the speech has an hierarchic organization which appears to match that of the speech units.

In this analysis we are concerned only with movement that accompanies or is associated with speech. This movement is here referred to as "gesticulation," and it characteristically involves the hands and arms. There are also movements of the head, changes in the face, and changes in body posture which occur in close association with speech, and we shall be concerned with these as well. However, X may be observed to engage in a number of other movements which appear to stand apart from the speech-related movements considered here. These include several examples of "autistic" movements and examples too of movements which appear to have a regulatory function—that is, they play a part in the coordination of X's performance with that of his listener, but are not also part of the pattern of action associated with speaking.[11]

We shall now describe how each speech unit at each level of the hierarchy is distinguished in the body motion associated with it. Figure 1 is a chart showing how patterns of movement in hand, arm, and head are organized in association with speech units up to the level of the locution cluster, in this case, locution cluster 2.

1. THE DISCOURSE

This is the highest level unit dealt with here and, in the section we analyze, we only deal with the opening part of it. It is an example of a communication unit at the level of Scheflen's (1964) *position*. Thus we may speak of X in a "discourse position" as opposed to, say, a "listening position." In terms of speech, of course, these two units are markedly distinct. During "listening," we find little speech—mostly attention signals, or occasional short questions, or other kinds of short utterances. During "discourse," speech is more

---

[11]For a rough, but suggestive treatment of different functional "systems" of body motion, see Ekman and Friesen (1969).

nearly continuous, consisting in a series of more or less well-organized utterances.

In terms of body motion there is also a clear distinction, both in the general position of the body and in the movements of the body parts. Sometime prior to the onset of speech, a shift in posture, often substantial, may be observed to occur. The contrast between X's listening posture and his discourse posture is shown in Figure 2.

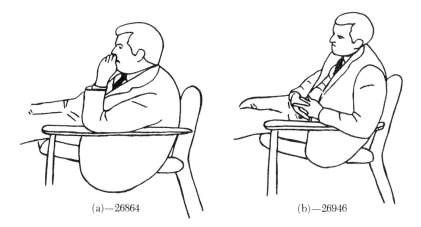

(a)—26864   (b)—26946

Fig. 2. (a) X as he sits and listens to his interlocutor. (b) X's position just after his posture shift, just prior to speaking. Number under each figure identifies the frame from which drawing was made.

The posture shift is begun at 26867[12] nearly nine seconds before the onset of speech. Scheflen (1964) has reported how major changes in body position appear to mark the points of change between one major unit of communicational activity and another. The posture shift that occurs in X, prior to his discourse, would appear to be an example of this phenomenon.

2.   THE LOCUTION CLUSTER

This is the highest level communication (or speech) unit within the discourse and it can be thought of as equivalent to a "paragraph." In terms of speech, it is distinguished by a change in what the speaker is talking about or in how he is treating the topic of discussion, and there is a break in the vocal flow between clusters. Accompanying

---

[12]The numbers refer to the numbers of the frames of the film. Unless otherwise specified, all film references are to Reel 1 of TRD009.

each locution cluster we find that X employs his hands and arms in gesticulation in a distinct fashion, and where X changes from one locution cluster to the next, there is movement in the trunk and legs which does not occur within clusters. Thus there is a forward-backward shift of the trunk beginning at 27144, and another beginning at 27857, and some lateral shift of the trunk with movement of the legs, beginning at 28750. These are the points at which X changes from one locution cluster to the next.

So far as body motion within the cluster is concerned, the most distinctive character in X's performance is in the limbs employed in gesticulation. In cluster 1, he uses primarily his right arm; in cluster 2, he uses his left arm; and in cluster 3, he uses both arms together.

3.   THE LOCUTION GROUP

As will be seen in more detail, there is a distinctive head movement associated with each locution. However, locutions which belong together in the same group, share the same type of head movement. For example, both locution 6 and 7, which belong together in the same group (group 6), start with the head cocked slightly to the right. The head is held still over the first few syllables, it then begins to move left, followed by a forward tilt, so that in each locution in this group the terminal head position is one in which the head is tilted forward and cocked to the left. In contrast, for locutions 8, 9, and 10 (which all belong together in locution group 7), the head starts from an erect position, and is simply tilted forward.

Thus locutions may be combined into locution groups kinesically by the fact that over locutions within the same group, the pattern of head movement is repeated or, as in the case of groups 8 and 9, the patterns distinguishing the component locutions are joined together to form a distinctive overall pattern.

There is one other feature which may function to effect the grouping of locutions kinesically, one that will be described more fully in the next section. We find, at least in some cases, that some element of movement from the end of the previous locution is repeated in association with the initial phrase of the one that follows.

4.   LOCUTIONS

In X's discourse, in each case, the locutions are made kinesically distinct from one another by a different movement or position which is sustained over the whole speech unit. There are also patterns of head movement by which locutions are set off from one another.

Specifically, for X, we find a contrast between the position of the head at the start of locutions and its position at the end of them. At the beginning of each of X's locutions, the head is held either erect and central, or it is held erect and cocked somewhat to the right. As the locution ends, the head is tilted forward or lowered and, in several cases, it is either turned or cocked to the left. Figures 3c and 3d illustrate this contrast and Table I shows that it holds for most of the

TABLE I.

Position of Head at Start and Finish of Locutions

Locution	Start	Finish
1	Right headcock	Head lifted
2	Trunk back, no change in head	No change in head
3	Right headcock	Head center, erect
4	Slight left headcock	Head lowered, center
5	Head center	Slight right headcock
6	Slight right headcock	Left headcock, lowered
7	Slight right headcock	Left headcock, lowered
8	Head center	Head center, lowered
9	Head center	Head center, lowered
10	Head center, raised	Head center, lowered
11	Right headcock	Head rotated, left, lowered
12	Head rotated left, raised	Head rotated, left, lowered
13	Right headcock	Head center, lowered
15+	Head center, raised	Left headcock, lowered
16	Head center, slight lower	Head center, slight lower
17	Right headcock	Left headcock, lower
18	Right headcock°	Head center, lower

+14 omitted because it is uttered during movement of head to start position for 15.
° As he begins phrase 47.

locutions in the present specimen. Of the exceptions, locutions 14 and 16 are parenthetical insertions, locution 4 represents a locution begun again as a correction for locution 3. In this case, it ends with a lowered head. Locution 1 is a "temporizer" or "floor acceptance" signal by which X both indicates the topic of the discourse and, perhaps at the same time, gains time for working out what he is going to say. Evidently the kind of start/finish contrast in head positions that is found will depend upon the kind of locution in question. For the present specimen, the predominant pattern we have described belongs to locutions whose primary function is to move the substance of the discourse forward. Those locutions which function rather as commentary on the discourse or as "footnotes" or "parentheses," or those which, like locution 14, are regulatory, stand apart in the kind of head-movement pattern that they have.[13]

---

[13]It will be noted that locution 5 also does not end with a lowered head, yet it is certainly substantive in its function in the discourse. However, note that it is the only completed locution in the sample which ends with a rising tone.

It is of some interest to look at the relationship in time between the beginning of speech for a particular locution and the associated head movement. As suggested, at the beginning of each locution the head is found in a particular position which contrasts with its position associated with the end of the locution. We find that, in every case, the head begins to move into the "start" position before the onset of speech of any kind and, in most cases, this "start" position is reached either before the onset of speech or just as it begins. Table II gives for each positioning movement the length of time that elapses between the beginning of each movement and the onset of the first phrase of the locution, and also the onset of speech of any kind, including "vocal segregates" and phrases which are subsequently repeated or corrected. It will be seen that where a phrase is preceded by such a pre-phrase vocalization, in six out of the nine cases reported here, this pre-phrase vocalization occurs during the positioning movement, as if X cannot speak coherently until his head is positioned appropriately. Also included in the table are the positioning movements of the arm in those cases where a distinct arm position is assumed at the beginning of the locution. Again, it will be seen that the positioning movement is begun and usually completed before speech begins.

There is a good deal of variation in the time that intervenes between the beginning of the positioning movement and the onset of the phrase. No attempt will be made to investigate this variation here (more examples should be collected before this would be profitable), though perhaps it is worth noting, nevertheless, that for those locutions which are also the first locutions in a cluster, the positioning movement begins earlier in relation to the beginning of the first principal phrase of the locution than it does for any subsequent locution in the cluster.

We now turn to consider how in a specific sequence of locutions, each is distinguished kinesically from the other. This will be done by describing the distinctive kinesic features of each of the locutions in locution cluster 2. Drawings from the film which show some of the contrasts between each locution are given in Figures 3 and 4.

Locution 5. The most predominant pattern of arm movement in this locution is extension and retraction of the whole left arm, with no differential activity in the wrist or fingers. However, over the first two phrases—11a and 11b—there is a forward-backward movement of the trunk, and both arms are, for a short time, brought into gesticulatory play. This trunk shift has already been referred to in

TABLE II.

Elapsed time (in 24th of a second) Between the Beginning and Ending of "Positioning Movement" and Onset of Speech for Locutions

Locution	Type of positioning movement	Time from beginning of movement to beginning of phrase	Time from the end of movement to	
			pre-phrase	first phrase
1	Right headcock	33	0	17
2	Trunk forward and back	17	+	-14
3	Right headcock	37	3	9
4	Forearm positioned	47	11	17
5	Slight left headcock	11	+	11
6	Trunk foward	37	-21°	6¹
7	Movement in left hand	0		0
8	Right headcock	20	-8	0
	Left forearm raised	20	-6	0
	Head rotated center	15		6
9	Forearm raised	11		0
10	Forearm raised	1		-4
	Head rotated to center	9	-9	-5
11	Right headcock	74		56
12	Head lifted	12		6
13	Right headcock	22	-13	24
15°°	Head lifted	13		3
16	Spine straightens	13		5
17	Right headcock	21		0
18	Arms readied for "box"	3	-34	-17

° Negative value means speech began before movement ended.
¹ first phrase is here 11b.
+ Pre-phrase uttered before positioning movement began.
°° Locution 14 omitted because it occurs during the head lift that precedes 15.

discussing boundaries between locution clusters. As will be seen in the discussion of prosodic phrases, the successive components of this trunk shift and then the successive extensions and retractions of the left arm are associated with each of the phrases within this locution (Figs. 3a and 3b).

(a)—27886

(b)—27954

(c)—28086

(d)—28144

FIG. 3. (a) and (b) show position at end of phrase 11a and 12 in Locution 5. (c) and (d) show positions for phrases 16 and 18 for Locution 6. Note position of head, which illustrates the difference between its position at the beginning and at the end of a locution.

Locution 6. At the end of locution 5, the left arm is lowered to the chair arm so that the forearm rests along it. It stays in this position throughout this locution, and gesticulation is confined to movements of the fingers and rotatory movements of the forearm. The pattern of movement in the head has already been described (Figs. 3c and 3d).

Locution 7. Over the opening phrase here, the forearm is kept in the same position as it was in locution 6 and, with fingers extended, the forearm is rotated from the elbow. A pause follows, and during this pause the elbow is flexed so that the forearm is raised to a near vertical position. It is then lowered in three successive steps, each step just preceding the stressed syllable of each of the three phrases of which the rest of this locution is composed. The distinctive kinesic character of this locution, then, is found in the raised forearm which is then lowered (Fig. 4a).

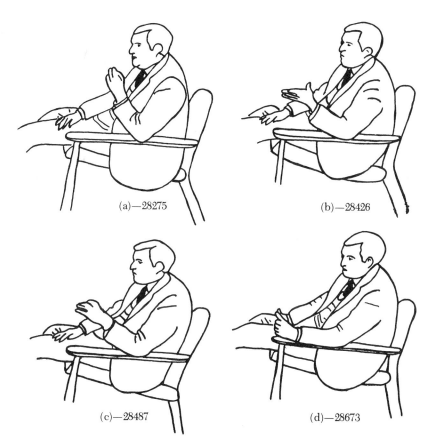

FIG. 4. Contrasting arm positions for Locutions 7, 8, 9, and 10. Number under each figure is the frame from which drawing was made.

There are two comments to be made about the forearm rotation movement over the first phrase. First, this movement is nearly identical with the movement made in association with phrase 17, locution 6, but it is combined here with the start position for the head, whereas in locution 6 it is associated with the terminal position.

Secondly, however, the forearm movement which characterizes locution 7 occurs over just that part of the locution which conveys its main content, that part which is, in lexical terms, its most distinctive part. The associated movement over the opening phrase which is, as it were, "borrowed" from the movement pattern of the previous locution, occurs over a phrase which serves to coordinate locution 7 with locution 6. This phrase though not carrying any part of the main point of the locution is, nevertheless, essential for sense to be made out of the locution group. It would seem that X, in repeating a pattern of movement over this opening phrase which occurred over a phrase in the previous locution, thereby establishes kinesically the link between locutions 6 and 7 at the same time as he is doing this verbally.

Locution 8. This consists of two parts. The first part—where X says, "let's take the um. . ."—which is uttered in somewhat overlow register and in slow tempo, appears largely to function as a signal that X is searching for what next to say. Here, there is no change in the position of the head and the hands are left limp in the lap, except briefly, over "the um," when both right and left forearms rotate to supinate the palms of the hands, followed immediately by a reversal of this movement with both hands being dropped back to the lap again. The second part—"the Nordic races"—is uttered with markedly increased tempo and with register and loudness at normal levels. Here, the elbow is flexed to bring the forearm into a near vertical position with the hand held with the wrist extended, palm facing upwards with fingers extended and adducted (see Fig. 4b). The arm and hand are put into this position just before the onset of vocalization (at 28419). Over "the Nordic" there is a slight extension of the fingers. Over "races," the first syllable of which takes the main stress of the phrase, the forearm is lowered rapidly to the arm of the chair.

Locution 9. This is a series of four phrases spoken very fluently with no pauses in between. It is characterized kinesically by the uplifted forearm and a complex series of hand positions. With the opening of the locution, the elbow is flexed, lifting the forearm to approximately a 45° position. During the locution, there are minor movements of the forearm and, as it closes, in association with the last stressed syllable of the locution, the elbow is extended, lowering the forearm to the arm of the chair once again (Fig. 4c).

It is to be noted that there are certain features of the movements associated with locution 9 that suggest that it is another example of the partial carry-over in movement associated with the previous locution. Thus, as the forearm is lifted at the beginning of locution 9, there is no change in the pose of the hand from the position it was in at the end of locution 8. Furthermore, there is no change in the position of the head from its terminal position in locution 8 until we reach the first stressed syllable of the second phrase in locution 9. Here the head is pushed forward and slightly raised. And, just as in the previously described example we found that the "carried-over" movement configuration occurred in association with the initial phrase of the locution which served to coordinate it with the previous one, the same is true here. The terminal head position of locution 8 is retained only through the initial phrase of locution 9, which is a coordinating phrase.

Locution 10. In this locution, X makes his "main point"; he presents the main assertion that his whole discourse is developed to support. He introduces several vocal devices to mark this locution off as the carrier of a specially important message. Most notable is that the key word, "self-consciousness," is uttered as a separate phrase and there is a very long pause following it before the last phrase of the locution. The second syllable of "self-consciousness" also receives very strong stress. The locution is also marked kinesically in a way that is quite unlike the way the other locutions are marked. Over "it's what we two called," X moves his left arm to point at a girl who is sitting on his right, as if to link her with him in his point of view. During the pause that follows, X touches his nose with the forefinger and thumb of his left hand[14] and then, over "self-consciousness," he brings both hands together so that the tips of the fingers of each hand are touching with palms facing inwards, rather as if he were "boxing in" something. This position is arrived at by the third syllable of "self-consciousness," and it is maintained throughout the ensuing pause and the last phrase of the locution (see Fig. 4d).

We have now seen how each locution differs in the way the gesticulating arm is used: locution 5 has broad in-out arm movements; locution 6 has the arm at rest with gesticulation only in the hand; in locution 7, the forearm is raised, then lowered, the hand held in a kind of fist throughout; in locution 8, the forearm is again

---

[14]This movement is not part of the gesticulatory system, but is an example of an "autistic" movement (Krout 1934) or a "body-focused" movement (Freedman and Hoffman, 1967).

raised and lowered rapidly, but with the hand now in quite a different pose; in locution 9, the forearm is raised again, but this time not to the same degree and it is kept in a particular position throughout the locution while the hand goes through a sequence of positions; finally, in locution 10, there was a special hand position involving both arms.

5.   THE PROSODIC PHRASE

This is the smallest unit of speech to be dealt with. It was defined as the smallest grouping of syllables over which a complete intonation tune occurs. Here, associated with each phrase, there is a distinctive pattern of movement or a distinctive position. This may be seen by reference to Figure 1 where the distinguishing movements or positions for each phrase in locution cluster 2 are given. In many instances, it appears to be best to say that the movement that distinguishes each phrase is a *movement to a position* that is distinctive for the phrase. Where this is so, we find that this position is reached at the center of the phrase, that is, at the point in the phrase where the most prominent syllable occurs (Hockett, 1958). This position may be held, or there may be a comparatively slow change that follows, or the movement that is to lead to the next distinctive position may be begun. The length of the movement before the position is reached and what happens after this probably depend partly upon the position of the center within the phrase and, in part also, upon the degree of prominence given the phrase as a whole, relative to the other phrases in the cluster to which it belongs.

Some of these points may be illustrated by reference to a specific example, in this case, locution 5. Locution 5 is composed of six phrases and the movement associated with it may be analyzed into six components. Each component may be said to be completed when the distinctive position is reached, and this is said to occur where there is a pause or slowing in the movement or where there is a marked change in the direction of the movement.

The components associated with each phrase in locution 5 may be described as follows:
1.   11a—Trunk forward, left and right arm positioned (see Fig. 3a).
2.   11b—Left and right arms lowered, trunk back.
3.   12 —Left arm extended (Fig. 3b).
4.   13 —Left arm retracted, hand raised, fingers retracted.
5.   14 —Left arm extended, lowered to chair arm.
6.   15 —Left hand lowered to chair arm.

The relations between these components and the phrases they accompany may be seen in Figure 5. The movement segments shown in the chart are labeled by letter or number and are referred to in the description that follows. In each case a distinct change is seen, either to the next component or to some "transitional" movement between components, immediately after the central syllable in each phrase.

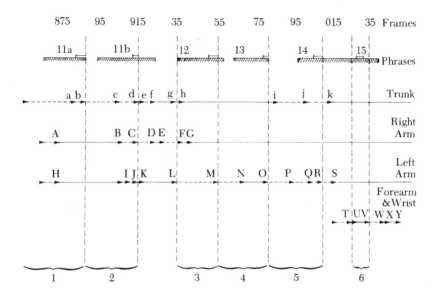

FIG. 5. This is a simplified movement flow-chart for the movement associated with Locution 5. Movements of the trunk, the arms and the left forearm, wrist, and hand have been noted. The arrow heads on each horizontal line mark the points of change in movement. Where the shaft of the arrow is broken, this indicates that the body part in question is moving in the manner indicated. A solid line indicates that the body part is held still. Each segment of movement is labeled by a letter or number. These are referred to in the text where an account of this is given. The phrases are indicated by hatched blocks on the upper line, and the bar above each indicates the extension in time of the "central" syllable in each phrase.

In 11a, the trunk stops leaning forward at the boundary of the center (a) and rotates left during it (b), and begins leaning back immediately afterwards (c). In 11b, the center is reached at the point where the left arm is arrested in its lowering movement (I), which it does not resume until the end of the central syllable (K). It will be noted that there is a change in the movement of the trunk and of the right arm coincident with the boundary of the center and with the boundary of the phrase (e,D,K;g,E). In 12, the extension of the left arm is completed with the completion of the central syllable (m) and, in 13, the retracted left arm is held in position until the end of the center (O,P). In 14, the hand is kept stationary on the chair arm until the end of the center (S), as is also the case in phrase 15.

It will not escape notice that for three of the phrases (12, 13, and 14) in the example discussed, the limb position distinctive for each, which is reached at the center of the phrase, is appropriate to the content of the phrase. Thus, as X says "I compare your own race," he moves his left arm outwards toward his interlocutor (who is an American). Then, he draws his left arm in toward himself and lifts his hand up slightly, moving his fingers inward as he says, "and compare our own." Then, as he says "and compare other races," he extends his arm out again, but this time in a different direction (brought about by the lateral shift of the trunk) and his palm is now rotated to face upwards.

If we examine the other phrases in which a pronoun or other substitute is to be found at the center of the phrase, we find, in each case, that the movement distinctive for that phrase is a movement whose direction is appropriate to the meaning of the prominent word. This may be seen in Table III, where for each phrase with a substitute at its center, the movement of the gesticulating limb that is associated with it is given. Also shown is the time that elapses between the completion of the movement and the central syllable, and the time that elapses between the beginning of the movement and the completion of the central syllable. It is clear that, in most cases, the movement is completed at the point where the central syllable is completed.

The data reported here, which are of a preliminary nature only, appear to confirm observations reported recently by Birdwhistell (1965). He states that "in address or reference the head, a finger, the hand, or a glance may be moved so that an . . . extension of the movement can be interpreted by members of the movement community as moving toward the object or event referred to" (Birdwhistell, 1965, p. 27). Thus, in association with personal pronouns and with "this," "here," and "now," a movement toward the self may be observed. In association with "he," "you," "they," and with "that," "there," and "then," a movement away from the self may be observed. These movements Birdwhistell has called "kinesic pronominal markers." In the small sample examined here, it would appear that only where the item occurs at the center of a phrase does it receive a kinesic marker of the kind described by Birdwhistell. Thus pronouns not occupying this position (for instance, "I" in

TABLE III.

Kinesic Markers for Specific or Non-Generic Pronouns and Other "Substitutes," and Their Relations in Time with the Marked Item

Phrase	Movement	No. of frames before completion of marked item that	
		movement begins	movement ends
5 and you I said the same°	Right hand points to self	17	0
6 and you felt that	Right move away from self	8	0
12 I compare your own race	Left arm extended	13	0
13 and compare our own	Left digits flexed to self	3	0
26 from what it is here	Fingers flexed to palm	12	0°
28 its what we two called	Point (to girl at right) upward sweep	20	0
37 all this type of thing	Hands thrust outwards	15	0
42 All that type of	Hands thrust outwards	5°	0°
44 but what we're saying	Hand moved towards self	3	0

°*Word underlined is the marked item.*

°*From beginning of marked items.*

phrases 1, 12, 14, 32, 43; or "you" in 2, 11b, 31) do not receive a kinesic marker.

Further samples of speech clearly deserve examination for this phenomenon and we should also look further for examples of some of the other kinesic markers Birdwhistell has described—those said to be associated with certain verbs, prepositions, and adverbs. Only "pronominals" (in Birdwhistell's sense; this class of words appears to correspond to Hockett's class of substitutes) have been examined here, since we had an adequate sample of them.

CONTEXT SPECIFIC HAND POSITIONS

Another phenomenon of some interest is suggested by two sets of observations that may now be mentioned. In locution 10, we described the "box" position of the hands that occurred in association with the word "self-consciousness"—the key word in the "main point" of X's discourse. This hand position occurs again in one other place in the fragment, namely, in locution 18 where X is again asserting his "main point," as if X has reserved this "box" position of his hands as a special marker for the locution in which he makes his main point. Another example of a hand position recurring in a specific context has already been described. The position arrived at in phrase 17 (in locution 6) is repeated in phrase 19, the first phrase of locution 7 and the one that specifically refers back to the previous locution. Examples such as these raise the question as to whether, when a speaker is gesticulating, he may be making use of a limited repertoire of hand positions which are used only in certain contexts. We do not now have the necessary data to attempt to specify the nature of these contexts nor whether, if X does indeed have context specific hand positions, other speakers also have similar repertoires of hand positions which they make use of in similar ways.

DISCUSSION

The main conclusions to be drawn from the foregoing analysis will now be summarized. They may be regarded as hypotheses about how speech and movement are related which may guide analyses to be made in the future.

(1) Just as the flow of speech may be regarded as an hierarchically ordered set of units, so we may see the patterns of body motion that are associated with it as organized in a similar fashion, as if each unit of speech has its"equivalent" in body motion.

(2)   Each speech unit is distinguished by a pattern of movement and of body-part involvement in movement. The larger the speech unit, the greater the difference in the form of movement and the body parts involved. For example, the locution groups were distinguished by the limb or limbs involved in gesticulation. Each locution was distinguished by a different pattern of movement within the same limb.

(3)   Prior to each speech unit there is a change in position of one or more body parts. This was termed "speech-preparatory" movement. The larger the speech unit, the more body parts there are that are involved in this movement. For locutions, for instance, only the head and the gesticulating limb are involved. For locution groups, there is a shift in the trunk as well. For very high level units, such as "discourse" or "listening," there is a major change in the speaker's total bodily position.

(4)   Speech-preparatory movement begins sooner in relation to the size of a given speech unit. The larger the speech unit, the earlier and more extensive are the preparatory movements (see Table II).

(5)   Our analyses confirmed Condon and Ogston's finding that changes in the patterning of movement which occurs as the subject is speaking are coordinated with changes in the pattern of sound. We also examined movement from the point of view of how it is related in form to the lexical content of the speech. We found in those instances where the form of the movement could be distinctly matched to a lexical item, as was the case with the pointing movement associated with the class of items known as substitutes, that the movement in question began before the lexical item it was to mark, but was completed the moment the lexical item was completed. It seems that the speech-accompanying movement is produced along with the speech, as if the speech production process is manifested in two forms of activity simultaneously: in the vocal organs and also in bodily movement, particularly in movements of the hands and arms.

This last finding would appear to have implications for the view that gesticulation is a more primitive mode of cognitive representation and that it will be resorted to where the speaker is at a loss for linguistic means to express what he has to say. On this view, gesture is seen as an aid to speech in which the enactment of ideas in movement is thought to facilitate their transformation into words (DeLaguna, 1927; Mead, 1934; Werner and Kaplan, 1963). Occasionally we have observed instances which would support this idea. For example, at the beginning of the first locution: "I think this is where you and I disagree," as X says, "but um," he unclasps his hands which have been resting in his lap. He moves his left hand forward with the fingers momentarily posed in a "point," while he lifts his right hand up and then moves it towards himself. The pattern of movement that co-occurs with the locution is quite different, but here, very briefly, we see what is clearly a personal pronoun marker in the right arm and a "deictic" marker in the left. In the interval during which we may suppose speech planning to have been most active, thus, X marks out in his movement the "this" and the "I" which appear in the utterance that immediately follows.

However, though it seems probable that gesticulation may occur as a substitute for speech and perhaps play a part in the development of full-fledged utterances, it is not apparent that this is the function of the elaborate gesticulation that accompanies speech such as we have described for X. In this, it will be recalled, his speech was fluent and where, as in the case of the kinesic markers, a particular movement could be identified as being associated with a particular word, we saw that the coordination with the speech was precise. This suggests, as already said, that speech and movement that directly accompanies it, at least, are under the guidance of the same controlling mechanism. The accompanying gestures would not, in this case, play a part in the development of the speech. It is of interest to note that Baxter, Winters, and Hammer (1968) reached a similar conclusion when they found that, in an interview, those speakers who used elaborate gesticulation did so when they were talking fluently about a topic with which they were familiar.

There is another possible way in which speech-accompanying movements may play some part in the speech production process, however. In particular, the hierarchic organization of body motion that we have described for X, and the way it appears to match the hierarchic organization that may be stated for his speech units, may be of relevance for this question. Thus it has been argued that speaking, like other complex activities, unfolds in time under the guidance of a hierarchy of instructions, or a plan which is largely worked out in advance (see Lashley, 1951; Miller, Galanter, and Pribram, 1960). Miller and his colleagues point out that when a plan is being carried out, its details must be stored in a specially accessible "working memory" so that they can be immediately available as a reference against which progress in the execution of the plan may be checked. Perhaps the "working memory" for the execution of speaking plans is partly represented in the body positions the speaker assumes. As we have seen, the body part is positioned before the speech unit in question is begun. A particular posture is maintained throughout a high-order speech unit, while successively different arm positions, say, are adopted for the successive components of the unit, the locutions. These body positions and the different movement sequences perhaps can function as a means of storing information about which stage of the plan is in operation.

The other question that should be commented on is that of the possible communicative function of gesticulation. It is widely assumed that this is its primary function, though little has been done to investigate this. We have suggested that in gesticulation there is a complete representation of the speech that it accompanies. If this is so, however, it need not follow that all of this is available for recipients to decode. It seems likely that the communicative contribution of this movement will have more to do with holding the recipient's attention and keeping him forewarned of the sort of things the speaker is likely to say next, than with assisting in the transmission of details concerning what is being said. These points may be briefly elaborated.

In the first place, it has been recognized by writers on the technique of public speaking that the addition of a kinetic accompaniment to speech may, in some circumstances, make the speaker a more vivid and interesting source to attend to. It is clear that if these movements are not integrated with the flow of speech at all levels, they could constitute an important source of distraction. It may also be added that the hierarchical organization these movements appear to have may be seen to provide at least a partial diagram of the relations between the units of the speaker's discourse. There is the possibility that this could be used by the recipients as an aid in integrating successive low-level speech units into higher-order groupings, which any recipient must be able to do if he is to understand what is being said.

Finally, it will be recalled that we were led to draw a distinction between speech-preparatory movement and speech-accompanying movement. In the movement that preceded speech, the head, or limb, or perhaps the whole body is brought to new position from which the movements that specifically accompany the speech are made. This positioning of the head, limb, or body can clearly serve as an advance warning of what is to come and may be part of the system of "floor-apportionment" signals which assist in regulating interchanges between interlocutors. (Kendon, 1967). In addition, we cited some evidence that suggested that the speech-preparatory movement would differ according to the type of speech unit to follow. The larger the speech unit, for example, the more extensive is the respositioning to be observed. Further, it appeared that there might be differences according to the type of speech unit, considered from the point of view of its function in relation to the others in the discourse. This could give the listener advance warning of the sort of thing the speaker was going to say and would allow him to adjust his listener role accordingly.

References

BAXTER, J. C., WINTERS, E. P., and HAMMER, R. E.   Gestural behavior during a brief interview as a function of cognitive variables. *J. Pers. Soc. Psychol.*, 1968, **8**, 303-07.

BIRDWHISTELL, R. L.   *Introduction to Kinesics*. U. S. Department of State Foreign Service Institute, Washington, D.C., 1952. Reprinted (1954) University of Louisville, Ky.

BIRDWHISTELL, R. L.   Paralanguage: 25 years after Sapir. In H. W. Brosin (Ed.), *Lectures in Experimental Psychiatry*. University of Pittsburgh Press, 1961.

BIRDWHISTELL, R. L.   Communication with words. To be published in P. Alexandre (Ed.), *L'Aventure Humaine*, 1964.

BIRDWHISTELL, R. L.   Some body motion elements accompanying spoken American English. In A. G. Smith (Ed.), *Communication and Culture*. Holt, Rinehart & Winston, 1966.

BIRDWHISTELL, R. L.   Chapter III in N. A. McQuown (Ed.), *Natural History of the Interview*, 1967. Forthcoming.

BOOMER, D. S.   Hesitation and grammatical encoding. *Language and Speech*, 1965, **8**, 145-58.

BOYD, H. B. and BANKS, S. W.   *An Outline of the Treatment of Fractures*. American College of Surgeons, 8th ed., Saunders, Philadelphia, 1965.

CONDON, W. S.   Process in communication. Unpublished manuscript, Western Psychiatric Institute and Clinic, Pittsburgh, Pa., July, 1964.

CONDON, W. S. and OGSTON, W. D.   Soundfilm analysis of normal and pathological behavior patterns. *J. Nerv. Mental Dis.*, 1966, **143**, 338-47.

CONDON, W. S. and OGSTON, W. D.   A segmentation of behavior. *J. Psychiat. Res.*, 1967, **5**, 221-35.

CRITCHLEY, McD.   *The Language of Gesture*. Edward Arnold, London, 1939.

CRYSTAL, D. and QUIRK, R.   *Systems of Prosodic and Paralinguistic Features in English*. Janua Linguarum, Series Minor No. 39, Mouton, The Hague, 1964.

DELAGUNA, G. A.   *Speech: Its function and development*. Yale University Press, New Haven, 1927.

DEUTSCH, F.   Some principles of correlating verbal and non-verbal communication. In L. A. Gottschalk and A. R. Auerbach (Eds.), *Methods of Research in Psychotherapy*. Appleton-Century-Crofts, New York, 1966.

DITTMANN, A. T.   Speech and body motion. Paper presented at the Research Conference on Interview Behavior, The Psychiatric Institute, University of Maryland, Baltimore, April 22, 1968.

EFRON, D.   *Gesture and Environment*. King's Crown Press, New York, 1941.

EKMAN, P. and FRIESEN, W. V.   The repertoire of nonverbal behavior: Cateogries, origins, usage, and coding. *Semiotica*, 1969, **1**, 49-98.

FREEDMAN, N. and HOFFMAN, S. P.   Kinetic behavior in altered clinical states: An approach to objective analysis of motor behavior during clinical interviews. *Percept. Motor Skills*, 1967, **24**, 527-39.

HALLIDAY, M. A. K.   The tones of English. *Arch. Linguist.*, 1963, **15**, 1-28.

HAYES, F.   Gestures: A working bibliography. *South Folklore Quart.*, 1957, **21**, 218-317.

HOCKETT, C. F.   *A Course in Modern Linguistics*. Macmillan, New York, 1958.

HYMES, D.   Model of the interaction of language and social setting. *J. Soc. Issues*, 1967, **23**, 8-28.

JONES, D.   *An Outline of English Phonetics*. Heffer, Cambridge, 8th ed., 1956.

JOOS, M.   The five clocks. *Internat. J. Am. Linguist.*, 1962, **28**(2), Part V.

KENDON, A.   Some functions of gaze direction in social interaction. *Acta Psychol.*, 1967, **26**, 22-63.

KINGDON, R.   *The Groundwork of English Intonation*. Longmans Green, London, 1958.

KROUT, M. H.   Autistic gestures, an experimental study in symbolic movement. *Psych. Monog.*, 1935, **208**, 46.

LaBarre, W. Paralinguistics, kinesics, and cultural anthropology. In T. Sebeok, A. S. Hayes, and M. C. Bateson (Eds.), *Approaches to Semiotics.* Mouton, The Hague, 1964.

Lashley, K. The problem of serial order in behavior. In L. A. Jeffress (Ed.), *Cerebral Mechanisms in Behavior.* Wiley, New York, 1951.

Lenneberg, E. The importance of temporal factors in behavior. Discussion of a paper by W. Condon and W. Ogston, presented at the Conference on Speech Perception, Pittsburgh, February, 1968.

Lieberman, P. *Intonation, Perception, and Language.* MIT Press, Cambridge, Mass., 1967.

Loeb, F. The fist. Unpublished manuscript, Western Psychiatric Institute, Pittsburgh, Pa., 1967.

Mead, G. H. *Mind, Self, and Society.* University of Chicago Press, 1934.

Miller, G. A., Galanter, E., and Pribram, K. *Plans and the Structure of Behavior.* Holt, New York, 1960.

Moscovici, S. Communication processes and the properties of language. In L. Berkowitz (Ed.), *Advances in Experimental Social Psychology,* Vol. III. Academic Press, New York, 1967.

Mosher, J. A. *The Essentials of Effective Gesture.* Macmillan, New York, 1916.

Ott, E. A. *How to Gesture.* Hinds & Nobel, New York, Revised ed., 1902.

Scheflen, A. E. The significance of posture in communicational systems. *Psychiat.,* 1964, **27**, 316-21.

Trager, G. L. Paralanguage: A fist approximation. *Sil.,* 1958, **13**, 1-12.

Werner, H. and Kaplan, B. *Symbol Formation.* Wiley, New York, 1963.

Wolfe, C. *The Psychology of Gesture.* London, 1945.

Part IV

Special Problems
in
Interview Research

Chapter 10

People Talking When They Can't Hear Their Voices[1]

George F. Mahl

THE SITUATION of spontaneous speech usually includes two ubiquitous conditions: people hear themselves as they talk and they see their interlocutors. Primarily, this chapter concerns the role of the auditory feedback in the control of spontaneous speech and interaction, and in determining subjective experience. Very secondarily, it also deals with the role of the visual input from the audience.

The significance of feedback in the regulation of behavior has been recognized implicitly or explicitly for a long time. On the physiological level, for example, the early work of Bell (1826), Bernard (1858), and Sherrington and Mott (1895) demonstrated the critical role of proprioceptive feedback in the regulation of voluntary motor activity. The clinical condition of *tabes dorsalis* did the same. Cannon's elucidation of homeostatic mechanisms (1932) often dealt with complex feedback systems.

Viewed retrospectively, it is clear that Freud's psychological models also included feedback systems although they were not articulated as such. This is most apparent in the regulatory role Freud ascribed to *self-observation*. To mention a few major instances, Freud explicitly or implicitly dealt with this process in his hypothesis of Cs as a sense organ that monitors the workings of the psychic apparatus (1900, pp. 615ff.); in his concept of dream censorship (1900); in his hypotheses of the self-observing, self-evaluating, and self-critical functions of the Super-ego (1914, 1923); and in his revived and revised theory of anxiety and defense (1926).

[1]The basic observations reported in this paper were first presented at the 16th International Congress of Psychology, Bonn, 1960. The bulk of this paper was prepared when the author was at the Center for Advanced Study in the Behavioral Sciences, 1963-64. This research was supported by USPHS Grants M-1052 and MH-07317-01.

One could say with some validity that one thing Freud did as he developed his theory was to articulate in more detail feedback processes involved in self-observation and self-regulation and to attribute greater significance to them. The relevance of psychoanalytic theory to feedback concepts and to this paper is clearly implied in Freud's brief statement (1901, p. 101) that "we may hear the stifled voice of the author's self-criticism . . ." in the speech disturbances of everyday life and in contorted writing. In the Discussion, we consider further the relation of this paper and psychoanalytic theory.

Wiener (1948, 1950) pointed out the early application of feedback principles in the use of the governor and the steering machine for the control of the speed of the steam engine and the position of the rudder. He cites Maxwell's paper (1868) on governors as the "first significant paper on feedback mechanisms . . ." (1948, p. 19). One does not have to agree with this judgment to realize that in both the practical use and the theoretical understanding of machine behavior, "feedback" has a long history.

In spite of this history, as well as that indicated for physiology and psychology, it was Norbert Wiener who articulated the feedback concept and with his colleagues (Rosenblueth, Wiener, and Bigelow, 1943) pioneered in showing the relevance of feedback theory to the behavior of machines and of man.

With the appearance of *Cybernetics* and Lee's related discovery of the effects of delayed auditory feedback (1950a, 1950b, 1951), a previously latent, and only sporadically manifested, interest in the role of auditory feedback in speech regulation gained momentum. The speech deficit of the deaf had always provided dramatic evidence that auditory feedback was critical for speech development and regulation. But it is largely due to the research of the past fifteen years that a more exact picture of the feedback regulation of speech has begun to emerge. We will review this research by summarizing the findings of studies in which

    1.   the temporal aspect of auditory feedback has been altered,
    2.   other aspects of auditory feedback have been changed,
    3.   auditory feedback has been abolished or masked.

EFFECTS OF CHANGING THE TIMING
OF AUDITORY FEEDBACK

1. **Delayed auditory feedback (DAF).** (Also called "delayed sidetone.") Black (1954), himself a pioneer investigator in this area, observed that Fletcher's notes contained a brief reference in 1918 to this

problem as it might arise with increasing distance of side-tone transmission over telephone circuits. But Lee's paper (1950a), which was actually a "letter to the editor," is generally regarded as the first report on the effects of DAF. Nine years later Chase, Sutton, and First (1959) listed 101 references in their DAF bibliography; Smith's integrative reviews (1962, 1963) contain additional references. There is obviously a voluminous DAF literature. The reader is urged to consult Lee's original papers and to use the bibliography of Chase *et al.,* and Smith's reviews as guides to this literature, for only the major findings will be cited here.

Lee (1950a, 1950b) discovered that if a person's speech was returned to his ears through earphones at an amplified level and delayed by one-eighth or one-quarter second, the individual stuttered, spoke slower, increased the pitch or volume of his speech, and sometimes stopped speaking. A delay of only one-fifteenth second had little or no effect, which indicated that the time factor was critical. Marked speech disruption only occurs if the delayed feedback *replaces* normal feedback. The use of earphones and amplification of the signal produces this condition, for the former decreases normal airborne feedback and the latter masks bone-conduction feedbacks as well as any airborne feedback still effective through the earphones.

Lee also observed other effects. Some subjects developed "a quavering slow speech" reminiscent of cerebral palsy. Emotional arousal was indicated by reddening of the face. Extension of the DAF condition for more than two minutes caused physical fatigue. Individual differences in all the DAF effects were apparent.

Subsequent research has confirmed and refined Lee's original observations. The work of Fairbanks (1955) and Fairbanks and Guttman (1958) is particularly relevant. They verified the critical significance of the time factor, finding that the general peak disturbance of speech during oral reading occurred with a delay of .2 seconds. They also demonstrated, however, that different types of articulatory disturbances were maximal with slightly different delay intervals. This finding emphasized *the intricacy of the feedback control of speech.*

Chase, Sutton, First, and Zubin (1961) compared the effect of DAF on the impromptu speech of children 4-6 years old and 7-9 years old. DAF caused the children of both age groups to repeat more words and syllables, to prolong more syllables, and to speak slower. The last two effects, however, were significantly greater in the older than in the younger children. Correlated with this age difference, the older children indicated in an Inquiry greater dependence on and sensitivity to auditory feedback than did the younger children. Nearly all the older children recognized their own voices through the earphones in both control and DAF conditions; only half of the younger children did in both conditions! The children were asked how the voice they heard in the DAF condition differed from that of the control condition. Half of the older children showed some awareness of the delay factor, but not a single one of the younger children did!

2. **Accelerated auditory feedback.** It takes time for normal auditory feedback to reach one's cochlea. Peters (1954) cites Stromsta's estimate that normal bone-conducted feedback takes at least .0003 seconds and normal air-conducted feedback at least .001 seconds. Peters then investigated the effect on reading rate of decreasing these normal delay intervals to .00015 seconds by electronic means. This accelerated feedback *increased* the reading rate, whereas delayed feedback decreases it.

EFFECTS OF CHANGING OTHER DIMENSIONS OF AUDITORY FEEDBACK

If the timing of the speaker's auditory feedback is left untouched but feedback is altered in other ways, his speech will still be affected. The speaker will vary the *intensity* of his voice inversely with the intensity of his feedback (Black, 1950a; Lightfoot and Morrill, 1949). The intelligibility of heard speech varies directly with the intensity of it and also depends upon the high-frequency components in it. A speaker will increase the *intelligibility* of his speech if the intensity of his feedback is lowered (Black, 1950a; Black, Tolhurst, and Morrill, 1953) or if the high-frequency component is filtered out of his feedback (Peters, 1955).

In the preceding studies, the feedback was delivered to the speakers' ears through earphones and was altered electronically. Black (1950a, 1950b) also manipulated feedback characteristics by varying the acoustical environment in which subjects spoke. He found that people spoke louder in "dead" than in "live" rooms. Moreover, their voices became progressively louder in the "dead" rooms but softer in the "live" rooms. Wiener (1950, p. 170) mentions a related phenomenon: when people use a "dead" telephone system, in which their own speech is not fed back to their ears through the receiver, they start shouting into the telephone.

In short, speech appears to change in ways that compensate for experimentally produced variations in auditory feedback. *Again, the feedback regulatory system emerges as a very intricate one.*

EFFECTS OF ABOLISHING OR
MASKING AUDITORY FEEDBACK

1. **Speech changes in the deafened.** Congenital or early deafness seriously impairs the development of speech. Of special interest here is the fact that the individual who suffers a hearing loss after he has learned to talk manifests several characteristic changes in his speech: a deterioration of precision of enunciation, a flattening of the intonation patterns, and a loss of control of loudness of his voice (Carhart, 1960). The latter varies with the etiology of the hearing loss. In conduction-deafness, where there is damage primarily to the middle ear and not to the inner ear, the individual speaks very softly. Since his bone-conducted auditory feedback has not been impaired while air-conducted input has, his own voice sounds louder to him than the voices of others. He compensates for this differential "ear experience" by lowering the intensity of his own voice. In perception-deafness (nerve deafness), where there is damage to the inner ear or the auditory neural pathways, the individual speaks very loudly. He compensates for the total loss of auditory feedback. Thus the painful experiment of nature provided in the deafened individual demonstrates that the maintenance of acquired speech patterns depends upon the presence of auditory feedback.

2. **Experimental, temporary hearing loss.** Prolonged exposure to loud noises and tones results in temporary hearing loss of the perception type (Davis *et al.*, 1950, e.g.). Black (1951) studied the effects of such temporary deafness on speech intensity by comparing the voice intensity *following exposure to loud noise* for two hours with that preceding such treatment. He confirmed the production of a temporary hearing loss by appropriate auditory measurements. His subjects spoke louder immediately following the exposure to noise and their voices decreased in intensity as their auditory thresholds recovered.

3. **Masking of auditory feedback.** This may be accomplished by means of loud low-frequency tones and especially broad-band noises which include low-frequency components; that is, by the same

techniques that mask perception of the speech of other people (Miller, 1951). When such tones and noises are administered through earphones to *both* ears, a speaker's auditory feedback may be partially or completely masked. The actual extent of the masking varies with the intensity and frequency composition of the noise, assuming that it is continuous. Such masking interferes with both bone-conducted and airborne feedback. The work of Galambos and Davis (1943) and Galambos (1944), as well as that of Lowy (1945), strongly suggests that this masking is due to neural processes in the cochlea itself.

One well-known effect of masking feedback is an increase in voice intensity. This is the Lombard effect (Lombard, 1910) which forms the basis of one procedure used to identify non-organic deafness. Hanley and Steer (1949) found that as a binaurally administered, "airplane type" masking noise was systematically increased in intensity, speakers increased the loudness of their speech, lengthened syllables, and decreased their word rate. Winchester and Gibbons (1958) obtained similar results for word rate but their data failed to reach statistical significance. Their study, however, was not an exact replication of Hanley and Steer's.

Wood (1950) observed subjectively the speech changes during oral reading by twenty college students when a "high level white noise" completely masked their auditory feedback. He judged that every subject increased his voice intensity and decreased his speech rate with this experimental treatment.

Wood believed that the masking condition also caused changes in the pitch, resonance, and intonation patterns of the voice. We will refer to his description of these effects later in the Discussion.

Four different investigators, apparently quite independently, discovered that the masking of auditory feedback *improves* abnormal speech. Kern (1932), Shane (1955, research done in 1946), and Cherry and co-workers (Cherry, Sayers, and Marland, 1955; Cherry and Sayers, 1956) found that binaural masking produced a striking decrease in stuttering. Cherry and Sayers demonstrated, furthermore, that the effect of a low-frequency masking noise was much greater than the effect of a high-frequency noise (cut-off point was 500 c.p.s.). This finding is important for it indicates that feedback masking is the crucial factor and not the mere use of noise. Only with the low-frequency noise is complete masking achieved. The masking techniques of Kern and Shane utilized low-frequency sounds. Birch (1956; Birch and Lee, 1955) masked the speech of patients with *expressive aphasia* with a low-frequency tone of 256 c.p.s. and found that, "In approximately 75 percent of the patients tested, (verbal) performance was decisively improved."

The speech deterioration of the deafened provides clear evidence that continual auditory feedback plays a significant role in the preservation of developed speech patterns. The effects on speech of experimentally produced temporary hearing loss and of binaural masking underscore the dependence of speech patterns on auditory feedback. Habitual speech changes within seconds or minutes when feedback is masked. An increase in loudness of voice is the most well-documented change. The literature is scant as far as other changes are concerned, but what there is suggests that feedback masking affects a broad spectrum of the dimensions of speech: rate of speech, pitch, vocal quality, and intonation, and those factors involved in the abnormal speech of stuttering and expressive aphasia. As meager as the data are in these respects, they too suggest that the feedback control of speech is an intricate matter. The DAF literature and the manipulation of nontemporal aspects of feedback pointed in the same direction. *It appears that multiple attributes of speech are delicately regulated by corresponding, multiple channels of auditory feedback. And these feedback sub-systems are all integrated in the regulation of the entire speech pattern.* The literature supports the increasingly complex feedback models proposed by Lee (1950b), Fairbanks (1954), and Smith (1962).

The feedback literature also poses a challenge. A sketchy outline of *the aural monitor* has been emerging during the past fifteen years. Most of the information on which the sketch is based has come from studies of delayed auditory feedback, but the temporal is only one aspect of feedback. A great deal of work needs to be done on other aspects of auditory feedback to verify, correct, and extend what is now known or believed. This will not only result in a more detailed picture of the aural monitor and how it works; there is a strong possibility that future work on feedback in speech will be of more general significance, since feedback control is such a prevalent behavioral phenomenon.

PURPOSE OF THE PRESENT STUDY

Originally, this experiment was designed to determine the role of auditory feedback from one's own voice and visual input from interlocutors in the occurrence of common disturbances of spontaneous speech (Mahl, 1955, 1956a, b, 1959a, b). Subsequent reports will present those results and other microscopic speech data. As the experiment was conducted for the original purpose, it became apparent that the masking of auditory feedback had many striking, grossly observable effects, many of which have not been reported in the literature or at least are not generally known. The purpose of this paper is to present a survey of those effects and to consider their potential theoretical significance. The paper is exploratory. It does not test any general hypotheses; that doesn't seem fruitful at present. It does, however, lead to some hypotheses for further research.

The paper is related to the research reviewed above in the following ways:

a. The auditory feedback manipulation is *complete binaural masking.*

b. The effects on *normal, spontaneous,* and *extended speech* of a speaker engaged *in a dialogue* are studied. When this research was conducted, only Wood (1950) had studied the effect of complete binaural masking on normal speech, as far as we know, and his subjects read in a monologue for a maximum of three and a half minutes. With only rare exceptions, the previous feedback studies have utilized the monologue, oral reading of brief phrases, or sentences.

c. The effects of binaural masking on *the more general psychological state* of the speaker are studied, as well as the effects on speech.

METHOD

Overall plan. College students were interviewed under four different conditions: (a) when they sat in the usual face-to-face situation (F); (b) when they faced the interviewer but could not hear themselves because of the administration of a masking noise through earphones they were wearing (F-N); (c) when they were not facing the interviewer and thus could not see him because he sat behind them (B); and (d) when they could neither see the interviewer nor hear themselves talk (B-N). Exploratory work demonstrated the feasibility of these interview conditions. Students and associates and the writer himself spoke under the projected conditions without physical or psychological discomfort after an initial period of adaptation. The writer found he could interview under the projected conditions and gained familiarity with doing so.

To distinguish between initial effects due to the pure novelty of the experimental conditions and the effects due to the essential nature of the conditions, each subject was interviewed three times. All interviews were tape-recorded and transcribed. The clinical and objective study of the tape recordings and interview transcripts, as well as recorded reports by the subjects during an inquiry at the close of each interview, provide the basic data of the study. The subjects took the Minnesota Multiphasic Personality Inventory (MMPI) and were given the Wechsler Adult Intelligence Scale (WAIS) between interviews. Home interviews with the mothers of each subject occurred after he had completed his interviews; they are not relevant to the present paper but are mentioned for the sake of completeness.[2] In the following paragraphs, the Method will be described in more detail.

Subjects. A psychology professor at a small state university, primarily concerned with training public school teachers, recruited the subjects from his second and third year classes. He stated that a psychologist at Yale was seeking both male and female subjects, whose parents lived within an hour's drive of the school, for an experiment involving several interviews, psychological tests including the WAIS, and interviews with their mothers. He stated that the subjects would receive, in return, the experience, a small fee, and the results of the WAIS which he himself would convey to them.

Seventeen students, eight male and nine female, volunteered. Fourteen intended to become school teachers. Their ages ranged from 20 to 27, fourteen being 20 to 22 years old. The group was above average in intelligence and of higher verbal than performance ability, as the following summary of the WAIS scores shows.

Scores	$\overline{X}$	S.D.
Vocabulary Scale	13	1.4
Verbal IQ	117	6.5
Performance IQ	113	8.2
Full Scale IQ	116	4.4

No precise social class indexing was carried out, but nine of the subjects seemed to be of lower-middle class background, seven from upper-middle class households and one from a lower-upper class household. The ethnic home background of the sample was quite heterogeneous, as is indicated by the following tabulation of the nationality or ethnic membership of the subjects' parents:

[2] I am grateful to the following people for their contributions to this project: the subjects, Drs. Richard Waite and William Trinkaus, Naomi Miller, Irene Bickenbach, Judith Tillson, Genoveva Palmieri, Gene Schulze, Sue Cohen, Susan Ehrlich, and Ruth Johnson.

Ethnic Influences in Home of Origin	N
Anglo-Saxon ("American")	4
Italian	5
Jewish	2
Irish-American	1
Greek	1
Czech	1
Hungarian	1
Irish-American and Jewish	1
Polish and Anglo-Saxon	1
	17

All subjects were white and had been born and spent their entire lives in the United States. English was the native language for all subjects. Some had limited familiarity with the original language of their parents where this was other than English. No subject gave any gross signs of speech pathology or "foreign accent."

The Interviews. Each subject went through the following schedule: Interview I, Inquiry, followed immediately by the self-administered, individual form of the MMPI; Interview II, Inquiry, followed immediately by WAIS; Interview III, Inquiry. The home interviews with the mothers occurred within seven weeks after Interview III, except in one case when it took place on the day of Interview II. Interviews I, II, III occurred on different days, being distributed over spans of four to sixteen days, with a modal span of eight days for seven subjects. They took place in a room especially designed for high-fidelity sound recording of interviews.

The personal, psychological interview, modeled after the initial psychiatric interview, was used in the belief that it would afford equally for interviewer and subject the most meaningful and useful situation for sustained repeated interaction.

The following outline sketches the essentials of the three interviews: further comments below describe certain features more fully.

Interview I, (familiarization) about fifty minutes long.
    Introductory phase: five to ten minutes
    Interview proper: thirty minutes
        Continuous topics: interests, family, academic choice
        Conditions, fixed sequence: F, F-N, B-N.
    Inquiry: ten minutes

Interview II, about fifty minutes long.
    Discontinuous topics: fixed sequence
      1. Current activities in school, work, hobbies.
      2. Most significant person in current life:

nature of the person and relationship with subject.
3. Most significant person in past life:
    nature of the person and relationship with subject.
4. MMPI experience
Conditions: sequence varied by subject

F	ten minutes
F-N	ten minutes
B	ten minutes
B-N	ten minutes

    (one topic per condition)
Inquiry: ten minutes

Interview III, about fifty minutes long.
    Topic content and schedule ordinarily the same as in Interview II.
    Conditions: same as in Interview II, except that each subject starts with
    what was his second condition in Interview II.

Interview I, familiarization. This interview opened with the first meeting between the interviewer and the subject. They sat face-to-face and spent approximately the first five minutes discussing the nature of the scheduled procedures, time arrangements, and payment of fees. The essence of what the interviewer told each subject about the nature and purpose of the study was as follows:

In this experiment, I'm interested in people's reactions when they are talking under different conditions. First, when you're talking with me like this, face-to-face, under the usual conditions. Then, when you can't hear yourself talk because of a noise playing through earphones in your ears. The noise will not be painful, but it is loud enough and has such characteristics that you won't be able to hear yourself talk. The next condition is when you're not looking at me. In that case, I just turn your chair around and I sit behind you. The final condition is when we are talking and you can't hear yourself because of the noise while you are sitting with your back to me.

I am doing this study now with well-functioning people like yourself and the other students. Later I may compare the reactions of all you people with hospitalized psychiatric patients.

Another thing I'm interested in is how different kinds of people react to these situations. We are all different and we all have different reactions to things. To help define the difference between yourself and your classmates, I'll also ask you to take the Wechsler intelligence test and a personality test, and I'd like to have an interview done with your mother. In all of these interviews, tests, etc., I'm not interested in how smart you are or whether you have such and such a complex. I'm only interested in seeing how you're different from the others and if your reactions to these conditions are related to these differences between yourself and the others.

Today you can get used to the conditions while we talk and I can get to know a little bit about you. We'll talk sitting like this, then with the noise, and then with the noise while you're facing away from me. In the next two interviews, we'll use all four of the conditions and they'll be in a different order each time. We'll be more systematic then.

The instructions were designed to orient the subjects to *their general reactions* when talking under the different conditions rather than to the specific details of the speech process itself. In his responses to the initial questions asked by the subjects, the interviewer attempted to reinforce this general emphasis and it was further reinforced by the general nature of the Inquiry questions.

Following the introductory phase, the interview proper began with this remark by the Interviewer: "I'd like to begin by finding out something about you—how old you are, what your interests are, how you came to go to teacher's college, about your family, and so on." This comment defines the areas covered in Interview I, proper, which lasted for about thirty minutes. The goal of this interview section was to familiarize the subject with the various conditions under which he would be speaking, with the interviewer in this particular role and he with the subject and with the general situation of a personal interview.

The Inquiry always consisted of an open-ended exploration of the following questions:

1. How did you feel in the different conditions? What was your inner experience like when you spoke with the noise on? When facing away from me? And when these two were combined?
2. What did the noise remind you of?
3. How would you rank the conditions for comfort or discomfort? For ease of talking?
4. When we were talking in the various conditions you might have had some peripheral, fleeting thoughts you didn't have a chance to mention. Do you recall any? Could you tell me about them?
5. Is there anything else you think of that would shed light on how you experienced the different conditions?

Interview II. This included all four conditions of talking and a somewhat restricted schedule of four general topics, one topic being considered in each condition. The topic sequence was the same for all subjects, but the sequence of the conditions was varied systematically from subject to subject. The topics mentioned in the outline above were explored in an open-ended manner.

The sequence of conditions for Interview II was determined in the following manner. A basic sequence of F, F-N, B, and B-N, in that order, was designated. The subjects were listed according to the order in which they were scheduled for their first interview. The first subject started the basic sequence in F condition, the second subject in F-N, the third in B, the fourth in B-N, the fifth in F, etc. This system provided four condition sequences, with four subjects in three sequences and five in the other.

N Subjects	Sequence			
	F	F-N	B	B-N
5	1	2	3	4
4	4	1	2	3
4	3	4	1	2
4	2	3	4	1

Interview III. It also included all four conditions. Now each subject started one step over in the sequence he followed in Interview II. Again, four subjects followed three of the sequences and five the other sequence. The topic schedule was more variable in this interview. Since the maintenance of "natural" and spontaneous interchange was the principal goal, the interviewer played it by ear. While he basically attempted to renew discussion of the topics of Interview II in the same sequence, he did deviate from this approach whenever he felt it resulted in constrained interaction or seemed forced and artificial. In such cases, he pursued something from the preceding portions of this or the first two interviews which the subject seemed interested in discussing further.

THE MASKING NOISE

This consisted of frequencies up to 500 c.p.s. in equal intensities. This particular masking noise was chosen for several reasons. It is very effective in masking all auditory feedback, both bone- and air-conducted. Cherry and Sayers (1956) had demonstrated that the use of this masking noise produced a striking reduction in stuttering. And such a noise is somewhat less noxious than one containing higher frequencies.

The noise, produced electronically and permanently recorded on tape, was administered into the subjects' ears through padded earphones simply by playing the tape on a recorder. The author operated the recorder by means of a foot switch. In the noise conditions, the masking noise was administered at all times except when the interviewer spoke. The subject could hear the interviewer easily when the noise was stopped even though he was wearing earphones. The interviewer, of course, could always hear his own speech and that of the subject.

The subject first donned the earphones after the introductory phase of Interview I. Thereafter, he wore them in all conditions except during the inquiries. The noise playback volume was variable, being set and maintained at that level reported by the subject to produce complete masking of his voice. The average volume was approximately 93 db above the reference level of .0002 dynes/cm^2. The important thing is that, generally speaking, subjects had no awareness whatever of their voices with this procedure. There was a total of six noise conditions for each subject in the three interviews.

STUDY OF THE TAPES AND TRANSCRIPTS

Externally observable effects of interview conditions. The author observed certain effects of the masking procedure during the exploratory work, during the actual interviews of this study, and in listening to all the interview tapes. From these observations, he established a set of categories used in a careful restudy of the recordings and transcripts. The categories, listed in Table I, are of two general classes: one class refers to *speech attributes* per se, such as loudness, pitch, etc.; the other refers to *more general psychological changes* inferred from or manifested in verbal behavior. Nearly all the raw data of this study pertaining to externally observable effects of the masking noise are *judgments* by the author. In some cases, supplementary, more objective data were obtained by procedures that are more appropriately described when these additional data are presented in Results.

Subjective experiences of subjects. The open-ended inquiries were summarized and then coded with a set of categories, some of which generally convey the things frequently reported by the subjects and others of which provide information about the subjects' experience of certain of the phenomena that could be observed externally.

RESULTS

The externally observable effects of the masking noise will be described first. In the course of doing so, the subjective experiences especially relevant to the observable changes will be cited. The final section of Results will consider the subjective experiences as a whole.

EXTERNALLY OBSERVABLE EFFECTS
OF MASKING NOISE

The masking noise condition produced the effects summarized in Table I. As far as could be determined by the gross observational

TABLE I.

Observable Linguistic and Behavioral Changes in
Speech During Masking of Auditory Feedback

Category	Nature of Change	N of the 17 Subjects Showing the Change	Average N Noise Conditions per Subject in which the change was judged to occur. (Highest possible 6)
A. Linguistic			
Loudness	increase	17	5.8
Intonation	flattens	17	5.5
Voice style	changes	17	4.9
Prolongation	increase	17	4.6
Pitch	changes	15	4.5
	(higher	9)	
	(lower	6)	
Vocal Noises	increase	15	3.4
Slurring	increase	12	1.5
Rate	changes	12	1.8
	(decrease	7)	
	(increase	5)	
Phrasing	more distinct	10	1.8
B. Behavioral-Psychological			
Affect Expression	increase	14	2.1
Associative Response	freer	14	2.1
Cognitive Confusion	increase	11	1.2
"Thinking aloud"	increase	5	.5

method employed, these effects were the same in the F-N and B-N
conditions. The following comments elaborate and illustrate the
data of Table I.

LINGUISTIC CHANGES

Loudness. All subjects spoke louder with the masking noise. This
change was usually sustained throughout a given condition, but the
level of loudness was not constant. Occasionally, the voice would
become dramatically loud, and a few subjects momentarily spoke
with subaudible intensity. Voluntary control of voice volume was
apparently minimal in the masking conditions, for subjects persisted
in speaking very loudly even though the interviewer told them they
were doing so and that he would be able to hear them clearly if
they lowered their voices.

Intonation. The subjects characteristically showed some degree of flattening of the intonation pattern of the English sentence. In extreme instances, sentences showed very little variation in pitch or stress.

Voice style. This term refers to a variety of changes. The specification of the exact details of the change is a task for the trained phonologist and linguist; all the writer can do is present here for each subject, terms and images that occurred to him as he listened to the tapes. The following summary itemizes changes judged to have occurred in each subject with the masking noise and the number of noise conditions in which the change occurred. If this number is less than four, the interview will also be given. Generally, the changes noted were characteristic of most or the entire duration of the condition.

Female Subjects

Subject 1. Voice loses whispering quality (6 conditions).

Subject 2. Loss of subdued, voiceless quality (5 conditions) and, in addition, voice is piercing and clear (2 of these conditions).

Subject 3. Voice is more nasal (5 conditions).

Subject 4. Voice is more nasal (4 conditions).

Subject 5. Voice is more nasal, and loses its whispery, wistful, soulful tone (4 conditions). Also, speech sounds less cultured (1 condition of Interview II).

Subject 6. Voice is more nasal and sounds less cultured, causing this listener to think of speech of Molly Goldberg and Jack Benny's telephone operator (4 conditions).

Subject 7. Voice loses whispering quality (1 condition, Interview I) and sounds more nasal (1 condition, Interview III).

Subject 8. Sounds "voiceless" and boyish at times (1 condition, Interview III).

Subject 9. Sounds "voiceless" and hollow at times (1 condition, Interview II).

Male Subjects

Subject 10. Denasalization occurs causing the subject to sound less cultured; like he has a "code in the head" and to remind the listener of the stereotype of the "punch drunk" fighter (6 conditions).

Subject 11. Voice sounds less hoarse or raspy, and speech becomes telegraphic and uncultivated (6 conditions).

Subject 12. Voice sounds less hoarse and "growly"; sounds "mouthier" and speech is less cultured (6 conditions).

Subject 13. Voice is less "picky"; sounds harsher and more aggressive and masculine; dialect is less cultured (6 conditions).

Subject 14. Voice quavers (5 conditions).

Subject 15. Sounds more resonant (5 conditions) and "tougher" (2 conditions—one each in Interview I and II).

Subject 16. Increased nasality (3 conditions: 2 in Interview I, and 1 in Interview II).

Subject 17. Sounds less "froggy" and less strained (2 conditions, Interview I).

A shift towards lower social status dialect, i.e., in phonological features, was the principal determinant of the impression that six subjects sounded "less cultivated" when speaking in the masking conditions. Thus, Subject 13, American-born of Italian immigrant parents, characteristically said the sound / θ / in "think, through, etc." more like "tink, trough" in the masking condition, and the voiced sound / ð / in "that, this" more like "dat, dis." He also showed shifts toward the lower social status phonetic position of the vowel / ô / in words like caught, talk, thought, and saw.

The author *heard* such changes in the speech of Subject 13 as the masking voice conditions were introduced. In this particular instance, an analysis by a linguist, Professor William Labov of Columbia University, who has studied intensively social class dialect on the Eastern seaboard (Labov, 1966), provides invaluable data. Labov carefully analyzed the tape recordings of this subject's speech during the four experimental conditions in all three interviews. Table II summarizes the frequency with which Labov observed the subject using the standard variants, / θ / and / ð / (as in think and that), and the substandard variants, / t / and / d / (as in tink, and dat), in the four conditions. Table II shows that both the masking noise and the interruption of visual contact with the interviewer were associated with a shift towards the lower-class forms. Thus, in the face-to-face condition without the masking noise, only 13 percent of this subject's 'th' variants were of the lower-class forms; but when the masking noise was introduced, 25 percent were of the lower-class forms. There was a similar increase from 24 to 31 percent when the noise was introduced into the "facing-away"

TABLE II.

Frequency (Percentage) of "th" Variants in Speech of Subject 13 in the 4 Conditions

Variants	Facing-No Noise	Facing Away-No Noise	Facing-Noise	Facing Away-Noise
θ,ð (think, that)	86.5	75.9	74.5	68.8
t, d (tink, dat)	13.5	24.1	25.5	31.2
	100.0	100.0	100.0	100.0
N Occurrences	333	261	541	362

condition. Changing from the face-face conditions to the facing-away conditions was also associated with comparable increases in the use of the lower-class forms. The author had not detected *this* effect. Thus it is possible that a more refined analysis of all the tapes would reveal effects of the change in the visual condition of the interview which the author did not observe in his more global assessments.

Occasionally there was increased use of entire word-forms characteristic of less cultivated English speech. Subject 13, for example, uttered the vocative form "see" fourteen times in his first masking condition of Interview I, after he had spoken throughout the preceding non-masking condition without a single instance of this form. This differential use of "see" in the masking-non-masking conditions did not occur in subsequent interviews, where the form appeared at most twice in a given condition. Subject 6, a young woman born in this country of Jewish parents and reared in the Jewish community, showed the Yiddish feature of starting utterances with "so, ____," in contexts where an American English speaker might say "And ____," but when neither conjunctive form is essential to the meaning of the utterance. In all the masking conditions, she used this form 49 times; but in the non-masking conditions the frequency was only 35, (X^2 = 2.33, p = .07 t_1). Thus the frequency of this form increased 40 percent in the masking condition. This subject also responded twice to interviewer queries in one masking condition with the expressive introductions to her replies, "Don't ask me." In the same condition she also said, "So he said to me 'what am I thinking about.' " Such striking idiomatic expressions never occurred in the non-masking conditions. All of these usages were among the cues that reminded the author of "Molly Goldberg's speech."

Prolongation. This was a phenomenon of intermittently increasing the duration of sounds. When it did occur it was usually at the end of phrases or sentences and consisted of protracting the phonation of single syllable words or the endings of longer words, as in the following example from the speech of Subject 13:

> I mean, she . . . ah . . . didn't wanta be alooone. Like if . . . ah . . . my mother and father went out, why she would call them up where they were and say come on hooome. Y'know. I don't like to be left alooone. Little things like that.

The combination of prolongation and flattened intonation often imparted a marked singsong quality to the speech.

Pitch. All but two subjects spoke at a different pitch level in the masking conditions than in the non-masking conditions. Nine subjects raised their general pitch level while six lowered it. Whenever a change in pitch occurred it was consistently in the same direction for a given subject.

Vocal noises. When speaking with the masking noise all but three of the subjects produced guttural sounds. These were "noises" in that they are not English phonemes and did not sound like the usual vocalizations—ah, uh, etc. Some were similar to "croaking" or "choking," strangulation noises. These metaphorical terms might create the impression that the subjects were straining in an effort to talk when they produced the noises. That would be erroneous. They did not seem to be doing so to the interviewer. The noises could occur in the absence of any visible sign of effort and were not disruptive of speech. These noises occurred either during pauses or upon the onset of a word, phrase, or sentence. The following interview excerpts illustrate the positions and linguistic contexts in which they occurred. An "x" indicates the occurrence of a noise approximately the duration of a syllable.

The following subject was unusual in that one of his noises replaced the word "she," illustrated in the first passage, and some of his noises lasted several seconds as in the second passage.

Subject 11

First excerpt

Interviewer: I wonder if you could give a picture of what she's like? (i.e., subject's wife).

Subject: Well, (omits "she") . . . (xxxx) is wonderful, and a very good wife, a very good girl, a good Catholic, uncomplicated. And . . . uh . . . (xxx) she's not overly intelligent, but I mean in the affairs of everyday life she's . . . (xx) well, she's down to earth. And . . . uh . . . well, she's . . . uh . . . uncomplicated.

Second excerpt

And . . . uh . . . I dunno what age they (i.e., mother and father) were when they got married. —(xxxx . . . xxxx . . . xxxx)—. Anyway, we lived in B— for awhile, and I was born in B—, etc.

Slurring. Unusually indistinct articulation occasionally occurred in the masking conditions. Only one subject showed increased slurring in all six masking conditions; he spoke the least distinctly of all the subjects without the masking noise as well. Six subjects slurred only in the third interview and four subjects did it for the first time in the second interview. Only two subjects slurred in the first interview. Thus this was a late-appearing phenomenon, which fact may account for its low incidence in Table I.

Rate. No sharp distinction was made between articulation rate when speaking and overall word-rate per unit time in judging rate of speech. As Table I indicates, some subjects spoke slower and some faster in a small number of the masking conditions. There was no relationship between the incidence of rate changes and slurring.

The following tabulation shows that the male and female subjects differed considerably in this effect of the masking condition.

	Kind of Rate Change		
	Faster	Slower	None
Males	0	6	2
Females	4	1	4

Phrasing. This term refers to the fragmentation of a continuous utterance into a discontinuous series of phrases demarcated by noticeable but brief pauses. The net effect was the impression that the subject was speaking in phrases and not in sentences.

GENERAL BEHAVIORAL-PSYCHOLOGICAL CHANGES

Affect expression. Fourteen subjects manifested greater affect in one or more of the masking-noise conditions than in any of their non-masking conditions. The *types of changes* observed included: variations in laughter, greater general spontaneity of affect expression, increased excitement, anger, and sensuality or erotism.

In the masking conditions, the laughter was more frequent, of longer duration, louder of course, sometimes more paroxysmal and more erotic. Changes in laughter were largely characteristic of the female subjects, being apparent in seven of them but in only one of the men.

In some cases, the change in affect expression was general throughout a condition. Male Subject 13, for example, characteristically sounded assertive and aggressive in the masking conditions, but obsequious and somewhat effeminate in the non-masking conditions. The lower-upper class young woman, Subject 4, characteristically spoke with greater vitality and spontaneity with the noise, causing the listener to be more interested in what she was saying and to find greater enjoyment in hearing her speak than was true when she spoke in the non-masking conditions.

At times, intense affect was expressed in relation to the personal content being discussed by the subject. Female Subject 9, who was usually quite pleasant and easygoing, sounded exceedingly angry and spoke in an extremely loud shouting voice as she recounted having been angered several years earlier by an unreasonable high school teacher. No comparable intensity of affect was observed in the non-masking condition.

An especially interesting increase in content-related affect was shown by female Subject No. 7 as the following interchange took place in one of the masking conditions. Just before this fragment of the interview the patient was speaking about her religious conversion at an Evangelical Bible Camp three years ago ("vocal noises" also indicated by x):

Interviewer: But did you have any kind of an emotional experience?
Subject: Yes I did.
Interviewer: What was that like?
Subject: (Subject characteristically seemed excited when speaking with masking noise. In this passage her excitement increased and her face started to become red.) Well, . . . ah . . . I'm very emotional anyway when it comes to sad things so I can't say this is just a sad experience or a happy experience or an emotional experience. I feel as if the Holy Spirit really touched my heart and made me want to repent. And take Christ as my personal saviour. And . . . ah . . . it brought tears to my eyes. But I don't want to believe that this is just an emotional experience. I . . . because that's not enough.
Interviewer: Uhuh.
Subject: Because if it was, it wouldn't last. So it's something that you (x) take for life. In other words, your eternal life begins right then, instead of beginning when you die. Begins right on earth.
Interviewer: Uhuh. What did it seem like when you had that experience? You felt that the Holy Spirit had touched your heart?
Subject: (With the following utterance, her excitement becomes very intense, face becomes redder, and towards the end of it her upper lip is curled back on one side.) Well, I felt like a very (x) insignificant sinner who had been forgiven by my decision. And I felt very happy. Extremely happy. Although it's no bowl of cherries because (x) most anyone who has any type of . . . ah . . . strict religion, is usually persecuted in some way. And as a Christian, I know I'd be persecuted. In fact, I know I haven't really been persecuted enough, because I haven't stood up for what I should. That's one of the reasons I feel I have back-slidden—because I haven't stood up for what I really believe, in many situations.

(As he listened to this psychotically flavored content and observed her increasing level of agitation, the interviewer thought he should determine her immediate capacity for "testing reality" and coping with her paranoid ideation. He felt somewhat alarmed and was considering bringing the experiment to a close for this subject.)

Interviewer: Uhuh. How do you think the . . . ah . . . how are the Christians persecuted?
Subject: (sounding quite surprised) Pardon me?
Interviewer: You know, you said that you felt that you hadn't been persecuted enough. Can you explain that to me? . . . I'm interested in finding out.

Subject: At first when I had this conversion experience and took Jesus as my saviour—
Interviewer: Yeah.
Subject: (x) A lot of people laughed at me, and
Interviewer: Uhuh.
Subject: And you know . . . not laughed, but at school you're different. You are no longer a worldly person. And . . . ah . . . people noticed it. And now I feel as if I've become very worldly again. I'm not living the type of life I should, and . . . Not that I want people to laugh at me. I don't. And I don't think that's the idea of becoming a Christian, just to be persecuted. I think as a Christian you—
Interviewer: Yeah.
Subject: Spread the message and you show your love. You don't go around being self-righteous. That's not what I mean. But (x) I . . . I . . . I feel as if I . . . (x) . . . I'm not standing up to what I really believe enough.
Interviewer: (Feeling now that a crisis was past, perceiving the subject quieted as she progressively reassessed and negated the paranoid ideation.) Uhuh. That's interesting, I'd like to talk more about that in some of the other interviews.

This young woman became excited in five of the six masking-noise conditions and on two other occasions her excitement reached a high level as she spoke about specific content: once when speaking of her boy friend when she also laughed in a "devilish and libidinal" manner, and again when she uttered a loosely organized, symbolically toned, almost incoherent statement about her teaching aspirations.

This subject's MMPI scores were all within normal limits, but they showed the typical "schizophrenic cluster" on the paranoid, psychasthenic, and schizophrenic scales and these scale scores all feel very close to the upper limit of the normal range. Apparently her definite capacity for heated thought, psychotically-toned both in form and content, springs from her general psychological status at the time of this investigation. In the non-masking conditions she frequently negated paranoid thoughts. Several times, for example, she said of her present life circumstances, "I'm not the victim of circumstances." But in the masking conditions, the underlying psychotic affective and ideational tendencies episodically became more manifest.

At times, the increased affect expression consisted of direct emotional responses to the interviewer. In evaluating the examples about to be presented, the reader should picture the interviewer through the subject's eyes: he's visibly twenty years older, a stranger, and a gray-haired, pipe-smoking "professor" of psychology at a university which overshadowed the subject's college.

Some of the emotional reactions towards the interviewer were openly positive or thinly veiled erotic ones. Thus one of the young women, No. 1, spoke affectionately as she said the following in a masking condition in the third interview:

Subject: (After a long description of her not completely satisfactory relationship with her boyfriend, including episodes of his being inconsiderate, she suddenly laughed.) I'm thinking of you sitting over there (laugh).
Interviewer: What are you thinking?
Subject: I was just watching you smoking. You look so calm and relaxed.
Interviewer: Well, what did you think?
Subject: I was . . . I was thinking you looked so . . . ah . . . well, I guess I should use the word 'understanding' again. You look so understanding sitting there and . . . I just felt like talking. (laugh) I've nothing in mind to say, but you are the type of person that people can talk to.
Interviewer: Thank you.
Subject: You are really. (laughs). I'm not trying to give out compliments but, I mean, it . . . (xx) . . . I think that's a wonderful trait for a person in your field to have because you really need it.
Interviewer: I like to talk with people.
Subject: You can see you do.

Subjects also expressed anger towards the interviewer. Thus a female subject, No. 5, *suddenly and sarcastically* spoke as follows in one of the masking conditions:

Subject: You're quite comical (laughing).
Interviewer: What?
Subject: You're quite comical (laughing).
Interviewer: Why? Why?
Subject: The position you have.
Interviewer: Oh? Why? T . . . tell me about that. How did it seem comical to you?
Subject: (Pause) Well, I don't know (laughing), it's just the idea that you're interfering.
Interviewer: How . . . ?
Subject: (interrupting) Can't you hear me?
Interviewer: Yeah.
Subject: Oh, can you hear me?
Interviewer: Yeah, yeah, sure.
Subject: You're interfering in my train of thought.
Interviewer: How?
Subject: By pressing it, of course (laughing).
Interviewer: (laughs) But you said my position was comical. What did you mean?
Subject: Yes. You're sitting there with a pipe, just like . . . ah . . . I don't know, some English gentleman I suppose (laughing).

Associative response. This term refers to the flow of utterances by the subject during the interviews. "Freer associative response" means that the subject talks more readily, a change which he may manifest in several ways. He may say more in response to the interviewer's comments; he may respond more quickly to the interviewer; and the interviewer may find that it is not as necessary to ask questions and that simple acknowledgments that he is listening are all that are necessary on his side to maintain a continual stream of utterances from the subject. At times this effect of the masking condition was very impressive, for the subjects would continue talking at such length that the interview transcripts would run two or three pages consecutively with only one comment per page by the interviewer, and often none at all.

Quantitative measures reflect more objectively the "freer associative responses" observed in the clinical survey of the interviews. The interview typescripts followed the format of the interview excerpts that have been presented throughout this paper and the page margins were fixed. Upon inspecting this format it will be apparent that a count of the number of words uttered by the subject per page provides an index of the quantitative aspect of what we have called the "associative response." Therefore, we tabulated the words per page under the masking and non-masking conditions for each subject. These tabulations were carried out only for Interviews II and III. The inclusion of Interview I would have introduced a constant bias in the results because the non-masking condition was always the first condition of that interview and at the same time it was always one in which the interviewer was most active. The interviewer's relatively high-activity level in itself would automatically lower the subject's page word count in the non-masking condition of Interview I. The effect of the masking condition was clearly to increase the verbal productivity for the group as a whole ($p < .001$); the average percentage change in average words per page was 24.

One also gained the distinct clinical impression that *a qualitative difference* in the associative response occurred, as well as the quantitative change just reported. The subjects revealed fairly intimate, personal material in these interviews, and often to a greater degree in the masking conditions. The following instance illustrates this apparent phenomenon. During one of the masking conditions, a male subject, when asked to tell the interviewer about his family, told the following in detail. When he was a very young child his father, a factory worker, brought a male friend to his home. Soon this man became a roomer in the household. He and the subject's mother became lovers and would have intercourse upstairs at night, while the father would become drunk downstairs. This home situation persisted for many years and resulted in one illegitimate child, a half-brother of the subject. In the Inquiry, this subject said he preferred the masking condition of this interview because he didn't hear the unpleasant things he was saying.

Eleven subjects, six females and five males, spontaneously (!) referred during the Inquiries to the externally observable changes in associative response. Their comments revealed an awareness by them of both the quantitative and qualitative effects of the masking conditions. Three subjects felt they "rambled" during the masking conditions. Eight subjects stated quite directly, although in various ways, that they felt less inhibited when talking in the masking conditions.

> One subject felt an "urge to confess" and felt less inhibited but, at the same time, "resistant at letting out all these intimate things."
> Another said he had told something he had never told anyone before—i.e. his complex private feelings about the appearance of his acne-marred face.
> Two subjects felt they said "too much," "revealed too much." One sensed an increase in her ability to recall memories of her past life and in the vividness of the memories. Another thought "maybe I admit things I wouldn't ordinarily bear to think" in the noise condition. Still another subject said she had discussed things she ordinarily wouldn't discuss.
> The final subject said that during the masking conditions he felt he had a lot to say and wanted to tell so much that there wasn't enough time.

Cognitive confusion. This category includes relatively minor variations in normal syntax, simple forgetting of what one was talking about, and disorganized sequence of utterances.

The following excerpt from masked speech illustrates some of the *minor, but unusual, syntactical variations*. Subject No. 2 said:

> I took piano and he took accordion. And . . . uh . . . I guess *I took about eight or nine years lessons.*

The following interchange with another subject, No. 10, contains a more complicated syntactical confusion; it involves the underlined "quite often," not the many normal sentence changes. The solid and dotted arrows will be discussed below.

> *Interviewer:* Do you see a lot of her?
>
> *Subject:* Well I have more during the . . . since we've been out from school. Wh . . . when I went to school, I had one . . . I was in one class with her. But other than that I . . . I saw her perhaps for five or ten minutes a day. So the only time we've ever got to go out would be on a Friday or Saturday. So . . . however since the . . . uh . . . school's been let out, I've seen a lot more of her. Wh . . . she . . . uh . . . she and I go to the beach   We went
> to the beach yesterday quite often. I expect to see her tonight. And we're going
>   (lower volume)
> to go to X_____ and maybe I'll see her . . . uh . . . well, Saturday, maybe tomorrow night.

The "quite often" occurs out of context but it was uttered without a break in tempo. Possibly the "quite often" migrated from the end of the preceding statement, as indicated by the solid arrow;

the reconstructed, "She and I go to the beach quite often," is meaningful. But it is also possible that it migrated from some earlier point in time, such as that indicated by the broken arrow. This reconstruction also "makes sense." (The fact that the "quite often" was uttered at a lower volume level suggests another possibility: that it was the subject's intention to inhibit these words. The basis for this speculation will become clear when more definite examples of "thinking aloud" are examined below.)

There were many instances in the masking conditions where *subjects lost their train of thought, forgot what they were talking about,* and simply acknowledged that fact and fell silent. Sometimes the subjects coped with their loss of train of thought by repeating earlier words or phrases. They reported this device enabled them to proceed with only a minimal amount of confusion.

Sometimes the loss of train of thought was obviously due to the sudden intrusion of other trains of thought. Vacillation between different lines of thought often produced a series of utterances confusing to the listener. This happened in the following interchange, at the end of which the subject (No. 11) picks up the original train of thought. The instances of "cognitive confusion" caused by intruding thoughts are underlined and asterisked. Except where indicated the subject is speaking very loudly.

> *Interviewer:* Mhm. What kind of things do you do together?
> *Subject:* Well, before the baby came we just . . . ah . . . went to the movies, played cards . . . ah . . . went swimming, went for rides, and . . . ah just spent our time together at home, xx (vocal noise) and television. And . . . ah . . . now we don't get to go out much. We spend most of our nights at home watching television or . . . she'll help me study for a test, . . . but . . . ah . . . our social life is pretty limited now.
> *Interviewer:* Get along okay together? (i.e., subject and his wife)
> * *Subject:* We get along very good. I mean . . . ah . . . I get along . . . ah . . . we get along fine. I mean . . .⠀⠀⠀⠀⠀(much lower volume)
> ah . . . she's a little . . . ah . . . gets a little tired and cross at times because she has to . . . ah . . . stay in. I mean she doesn't like to go out all the time, but she likes to meet people. She's a very friendly girl. She makes friends with . . . ah . . . everyone she meets. And she gets a little lonely because she's . . . for all of her life she's worked in an office and had a lot of girl friends. And she comes from a big family, so it gets a little lonely at times for her. And I'm not financially . . . or . . . ah . . . ah . . . I don't have enough time to . . . ah . . . go out
> * dancing or go to the . . . movies . . . or spend as much time away from my studies as I would be if I wasn't married. But . . . ah . . . xxx (vocal noise) . . .
> * as far as doing things together . . . ah . . . getting along, that's it, getting along (silent laugh) . . . ah . . . we get along in an uncomplicated way.

In the last passage, the subject spent most of his time talking about his wife's feelings. As he was doing so, however, statements referring to his own sentiments intruded out of context on two different occasions. And as he spoke of how he and his wife got along together, a statement about their doing things together intruded, apparently being the product of the perseveration of the line of thought relevant to the *preceding passage*. The subject himself showed awareness of his cognitive confusion in the last utterance of the excerpt.

Another type of cognitive confusion consisted of an *exceptional degree of fragmentation and syntactical disorganization of utterances*, such as occurred in the following excerpt.

> *Interviewer:* What was it about her (i.e., a former teacher) that you liked?
> *Subject No. 7:* Well, x (vocal noise) at the time I . . . I didn't really know what a good teacher was and what a bad teacher . . . their teaching methods. She seemed to be a fairly good teacher, in . . . in the actual teaching, and yet she was a very nice person. She was a person to be expected . . . respected, and she's a person that . . . ah . . . in a wh . . . she inter . . . within her teaching program . . . ah . . . within teaching us she . . . ah . . . intramingled . . . ah . . . the teaching of democracy and teaching of high principles for us as citizens. Yet it didn't sound corny, it sounded very good, and I think x (vocal noise) that's one reason I like her, because I respected her so much as a person.

The subject remembered this episode in the inquiry at the end of the interview. She felt she needed help putting the words in the right order.

In all, *fourteen subjects reported experiencing "cognitive confusion" at some time during the masking conditions*. Twelve subjects experienced losing their train of thought or forgetting what they wanted to say; nine subjects reported a sense of having difficulty in expressing their thoughts such as finding the right word, keeping their words in the right order, or coherently organizing their thoughts.

"Thinking aloud." In this rare but striking event, subjects said aloud things which they were thinking, but apparently were not aware of and/or did not intend to be audible. One instance occurred in the following interchange, at the asterisked point. The subject, No. 1, is speaking of a recent event: her boy friend did not take her to a veterans' group party after all.

> *Subject:* Well, it's strange. All along I assumed that I was going. He kept saying, "I'm not taking anyone to this." He kept saying, "I . . . I wouldn't take a dog there" (laughs). He said, "I don't like the locality, I don't like the neighborhood." It's a very tough neighborhood. And he . . . he kept saying that he thought it would just end up into be a . . . being a beer brawl. And he said he didn't want me around. But I thought he was kidding all the time. And so up until Friday I thought I was going, even though I wasn't. (laughs) So I talked to him Friday and it became more clear to me what was happening, because he said he was going to give out drinks all night. And . . . ah . . . so I realized that he wasn't just fooling around. In the beginning though I just thought he was just joking. Because we go every place together.

Interviewer: Uhuh.

* *Subject:* And, -?-?-?-? (incomprehensible, lowvolume mutter)

Interviewer: What did you say then?

Subject: What did I say then? Oh, I was just thinking about the party. He was telling me . . .

Interviewer: What . . . what were your thoughts?

Subject: I was thinking about the beer party.

Interviewer: Yeah.

Subject: I was just thinking about the beer party. Because he said that they were nine deep at the bar and he said he couldn't give out the beer fast enough (said laughing).

The incomprehensible, low-volume mutter occurred at a time when the subject was "just thinking." To that extent, she thought out loud.

Early in the first interview, a twenty-seven year old male subject (No. 16), a Jew, said, "And my father's been dead for twenty years," while speaking without the masking noise. The next reference to "father" occurred in the following interchange when the subject was speaking under a masking condition of the same interview.

Interviewer: When was this that you lived in X_____ and Y_____?

Subject: I lived in X_____ when . . . I musta been about one or two years old. Then we moved to Y_____ and . . . ah . . . lived there for two years. And then my father got a position in Z_____ , and . . . ah . . . we moved to Z_____ . And that's where he died.

Interviewer: What kind of work did your father do?

Subject: Well my father, av'sholom, was a rabbi.

Interviewer: What did you say?

Subject: My father, av'sholom, was a rabbi.

Interviewer: Mhm. Ah . . . you sa . . . you said a word there. You said, "My . . .

Subject: Oh. Ah . . . that means . . . ah . . . "may he rest in peace." In . . . in . . . when . . . in . . . Je . . . when you're Jewish, whenever you speak of a dead person, you always say that—which means "may he rest in peace."

The subject had not, however, said "av'sholom" as he spoke earlier of his father, even of his father's death, when he could hear himself. Nor did he ever use this expression again when speaking upon several occasions about his father.

His father, who died when the subject was seven, was "an extremely Orthodox Jew." The subject regarded himself as a Conservative Jew, for he kept a Kosher home and observed the Holidays. In the third interview, the subject was aware of thinking but not saying "av'sholom" as he spoke of his dead, Orthodox aunts. As he thought about the incident of the first interview he realized that he did not use this expression when speaking with someone who was not a Jew, and that upon meeting the interviewer he had preconsciously categorized him as not Jewish. Finally, the verbatim extract shows how the subject's speech became very "flustered" when the interviewer asked about the use of "av'sholom." These facts suggest that this subject always said "av'sholom" when speaking of the dead, but to himself when speaking with a non-Jew, and that he only spoke it aloud with the interviewer because of the influence of the masking condition.

The next-to-last example of cognitive confusion contained an instance of "thinking aloud" that is more complicated than the preceding ones. It is the utterance out-of-context, and at low volume, of the thought fragment, "I get along." The schematization of Figure 1 illustrates what is assumed by the author to have happened after the interviewer asked: "Get along okay together?" The intended statements, those at the top, are unified both syntactically and

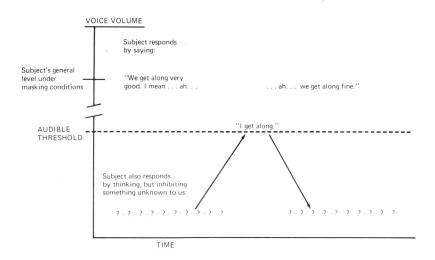

Fɪɢ. 1. Schematization of hypothesized processes to account for subject's thinking aloud, "I get along," which is spoken at a barely audible intensity and out-of-context.

acoustically. The "I get along" is a syntactic and acoustic foreign element. It seems to belong to an inhibited, conflicted line of thought, concurrent with the intended statements. The instigation to utter the inhibited line of thought seems to have become stronger with the passage of time. This produced another conflict, one between uttering the intended statements and those belonging to the inhibited line of thought. The conflicts are manifested in the pausing behavior and the conjoined "I get along." From the subject's standpoint, the conflicts were resolved in favor of his intended statements. For the moment only, however. A rereading of the entire passage excerpted earlier will show that as the subject continues he speaks of how his wife feels. But then there occurs the statement:

> And I'm not financially . . . or . . . ah . . . ah . . . I don't have enough time to . . . ah . . . go out dancing or go to the . . . movies . . . or spend as much time away from my studies as I would if I wasn't married.

which is completely unrelated to what he has been saying, causing the listener to be confused. It seems quite possible that this statement is a result of, and thus further evidence of, the private inhibited line of thought we have inferred to be accompanying the public, intended statements.

CHANGES OVER TIME OF EXTERNALLY OBSERVABLE EFFECTS OF MASKING NOISE

The precise determination of changes over time was not attempted in this study. This could only be done through a great deal of additional scrutiny of the tapes where this determination was the sole purpose. Nevertheless, the writer did form some definite impressions. Those pertaining to the degree to which effects were sustained during individual noise conditions were presented in the discussion of the individual effects. Two further impressions were formed.

Immediacy of speech changes. Speech changes dramatically *the moment* the masking noise is administered. Colleagues and audiences who have heard excerpts of the tapes have been struck by this fact. Immediate increased loudness, flattening of intonation, and changes in "voice style" are especially striking. The second generation Italian-American, male subject (No. 13) who has been mentioned illustrates the immediacy of change very clearly. Before the masking noise was first administered he spoke softly and precisely and sounded effeminate and obsequious. The moment the masking noise was administered he spoke loudly, with flattened intonation, and sounded harsher, more masculine and aggressive. And his lower social status dialect characteristics immediately became noticeable. Before the masking he sounded like an "overly-refined young man"; the moment the masking occurred he sounded like a "tough kid." The masking noise was deliberately turned on and off for brief periods in one of the noise conditions of the third interview to obtain a record that would demonstrate the immediacy of its effects. His two styles of speech changed regularly, *as though they were being switched on and off.*

In all the subjects, the return to normal speech with cessation of the masking noise was just as striking as the masking-induced change. Occasionally, a definite transition period of about thirty seconds could be observed. One got the impression in these instances that the subject was in the process of regaining his auditory feedback, as though his auditory threshold was decreasing over a brief period of time.

Adaptation. The category showing the most noticeable evidence of adaptation over the three interviews was loudness. Subject 17 was even able to talk in Interview III with only a little difference in volume in the masking and non-masking conditions. He had set volume control as a definite goal for himself. While he finally approached it, he didn't completely achieve it.

Generally, however, signs of adaptation were not remarkable nor consistent. By the end of the third interview a few subjects gave a general impression of some adaptation, but most did not; and a few subjects became increasingly affected by the masking conditions. Furthermore, trends over interviews were not always in the same direction in all categories. Some subjects who showed adaptation in loudness, for example, made more vocal noises in the third interview than earlier. The late occurrence of slurring was noted previously.

SUBJECTIVE EXPERIENCES IN MASKING CONDITIONS

The subjective report data were sometimes congruent with the externally observable behavior discussed above, and sometimes they were not. Generally speaking, the subjects' *reported* experience of the masking conditions was negative, more so initially than after the first interview. Some important exceptions will be cited below. Also, the inquiry data will be compared with the impression formed by the interviewer of the subjects' general reactions to the masking conditions.

Fifteen of the seventeen subjects felt it was easier to talk without the masking noise in Interview I. Nine subjects felt this way in the third interview. The major reported aversive qualities of the masking conditions included the noise itself, the physical effort of talking in its presence, the inability to hear oneself, the interference with cognitive processes of "keeping one's train of thought" and verbal articulation, a sense of loss of contact with oneself or the interviewer, and negative affects. It is not surprising that nearly a third of the subjects felt angry during the masking conditions of the first interview. The aversive qualities were especially marked at that time; nearly all of them were reported considerably less frequently after the first interview. Correlated with this change was the report of considerable adaptation to the masking condition by every one of the subjects and an increase from two subjects at the time of the first interview, to eight in the third interview who did not find it more difficult or unpleasant to talk with the masking noise. This is the general outline of the reported subjective experiences in the masking conditions.

This overall picture conflicts in two important ways with the impression produced in the interviewer by the overt verbal, vocal, and general behavior of the subjects. First, the subjects did not appear to be "suffering" as much as is suggested by their reports, even in the first interview. In fact, some of them seemed to enjoy the experience even in Interview I and certainly in the investigation as a whole. The interviewer was more struck with how easily the subjects talked than with initial or episodic disturbances in talking. As a group, the subjects impressed the writer with their involvement in the interview transactions and in the experiment. *Not a single subject postponed, arrived late, or missed an appointment.* Secondly, there is no agreement between the "objective" signs of adaptation and the subjective sense of it on the part of the subjects. While every subject reported considerable adaptation to the noise as a stimulus and to the lack of auditory feedback, few subjects gave objective evidence in their speech behavior of progressively and extensively adapting. In fact, four of the subjects distinctly appeared to be more affected in the second or third interviews than in the first. Yet one of these said it was easier to talk with the noise than without it in Interviews II and III.

Turning now to illustrate and examine in more detail the *negative subjective experiences,* we will begin with the stimulus properties of the noise itself. The noise reminded the subjects of rushing air or water, various mechanical sounds, and of radio or telephone static. When the noise was experienced as a noxious stimulus, as it was for fourteen subjects in Interview I, it was primarily because of its intensity and of its intrusive quality, both of which preempted the subject's attention. The following paraphrased comments illustrate this kind of reaction to the noise in the first interview.

> It was a hostile sound coming in on you. It wasn't welcome. It was distracting to have that noise going around in my ears. It was like this was inside my head. When I start talking my brain doesn't grasp onto the thought and right away the noise becomes the most prominent thing.

Some subjects, six in Interview I and two in Interview II, complained that talking with the masking noise was effortful. Some of their comments were:

> You had to force your thoughts to take place and to express yourself in words rather than just talk naturally. The first time I was worn out after I left. I was too pooped to pop.

Not every subject complained about the fact that he couldn't hear himself, but twelve, eight, and two did so in Interviews I, II, and III respectively.

Difficulty in cognitive organization and syntactic expression was reported nearly as often as the noxious properties of the noise in Interview I and more frequently in Interviews II and III. Subjects often attributed this difficulty both to the intrusive-preemptive quality of the noise and to the feedback deficit, as the following paraphrased reports demonstrate.

> *Subject No. 7:* I felt as if I couldn't express myself in any way possible because I couldn't hear myself. I wasn't sure I was using the right words, verb forms, and sentence structure. And I think I was more inclined to forget what I had just said.

> *Subject 9, Interview I:* In the beginning it really distracted me. I couldn't think of what I was saying. I had a sensation that I wasn't really speaking. I almost felt that I was thinking of this. (i.e., instead of speaking). That was when I coughed and realized I was speaking. I wasn't quite sure of what I was doing. *Interview II:* I didn't find the noise as distracting this time as last time. I still had to fish around a few times for a particular word I wanted. Maybe it's because I can't hear it and I don't know whether I'm saying it right or not. That's why with that word "sick"—I was trying to say "afflicted" and I didn't know whether it was going to come out right so I just didn't say it.

Some subjects reported what we have come to call "*Loss of Contact with Self or Interviewer*" during the masking condition. This experience was most frequently reported in Interview I and when the subject was deprived of both auditory feedback from his own voice and visual contact with the interviewer. The following paraphrased remarks indicate the nature of the experience.

> *Subject 1, Interview I:* It's harder to talk with the noise. But it was easier when you were in front of me than behind me, because at least there was some contact with something—something you could see, something concrete. Whereas when you're behind me it's very abstract. I felt there was no one there to talk to really even though I realized you were behind me.

> *Subject 8, Interview I:* With the noise I felt like I was talking to myself. I talk but I don't seem to have a part in what I'm saying. It's even funnier facing

away from you. It's like talking to no one; it's like nobody's there. *Interview II:* It's a lot harder to talk with the noise on. You don't know how you're saying things; you don't even know what you're saying; you sort of forget things; you don't know if you did or didn't say something. It leaves you with an empty feeling. And the noise seems to push you back. It seems to put you out of reality in a way. It feels like you're talking through clouds or something.

Subject 10, Interview I: It made me feel like I was sitting in a big room and the room was so big that as I was talking I wasn't getting any rebound off the walls and my ears. I was just talking into emptiness.

Subject 11, Interview I: It took me away from reality. It was like being separated from everything, being in some kind of ether. I mean some never-never land. It was more subjective. I was all alone with the sound. (In B-N condition.)

All of the preceding negative aspects of the masking-noise condition were stated or implied to be causes of general discomfort for the subjects. Except for the physical effort required in talking, these negative aspects were also the causes for the more specific affects of anxiety and tension, and for anger as well. It is worth noting that the reports of anxiety and tension were the only ones of the "negative reactions" that did not decrease from Interview I to Interview III.

The general decrease in frequency of negative references about the masking conditions was associated with reports by every subject of considerable adaptation by the third interview. Even the nine subjects who stated that it was easier to talk without noise than with it in the third interview reported considerable adaptation by that time.

Six subjects specified certain "positive" features of the masking conditions. And at one time or another during the interview series, four subjects preferred talking in the masking condition while five others reported having no preference between the masking and the unmasking condition. For seven of these nine subjects, the masking condition achieved its preferred or neutral status only in Interviews II and III, indicating the importance of experienced adaptation.

A most unusual and informative case was Subject 5, a young woman, who from the first interview preferred the masking conditions—even though she found the noise itself a noxious stimulus in that interview and complained that it interfered with thinking and verbal expression. She insisted that she didn't like to hear her own voice and felt more relaxed and at ease when the masking noise prevented her from doing so. Her singular reaction is consistent with the total picture that emerges from observing her speech style and considering it in the light of her social context and personal history. This young woman persistently tried to speak the dialect of the American stage and theatre. Her normal speech

style reminded the interviewer from the beginning of Bette Davis'—
in caricature. She spoke with exaggerated articulatory movements
and strenuous attempts at acoustic precision. Yet she came from a
lower-middle class Italian-American background. The total impression was one of affectation. This configuration of factors indicates that she was concerned with how she sounded. One determinant
of her speech style was an avowed aspiration to be an actress. Another, fully conscious, determinant was an "obsession for perfection"
in action and speech which she attributed to her mother's perfec-
tionism and to her own sense of worthlessness. Her relevant remarks,
paraphrased and condensed, were:

> *Subject:* My mother required perfection. She always reprimanded me for
> the way I acted or the way I talked. My sister was a year older and she mastered
> things before I did and spoke better. And before I knew it, nothing was
> quite right anymore in the way I walked, the way I talked, or the way I did
> things.
> *Interviewer:* Why don't you want to hear your voice?
> *Subject:* I have an obsession for perfection. I don't like my voice. I don't feel
> it's good. It comes from my mother pestering me all these years about the
> way I speak, about my voice and my diction.

The subject also reported that when she talked with the masking
noise she felt more relaxed generally, *and her mouth seemed to
move more freely* than was true without the noise.

We infer the following from these data. The subject had inter-
nalized her mother's observing and critical functions. When she
spoke under normal conditions she was continually trying to be
"perfect" and was continually listening to her speech to see if it
was "perfect," i.e., as good as her rival older sister's and as good as
her actress ideals. She judged it negatively, but continued trying to
speak perfectly. Tension and effortful speech were some of the
results. The caricature that resulted may also have had a hostile
component directed toward her mother, for even her "perfect"
speech angered her mother. When the subject couldn't hear herself
speak, she was spared both the sense of worthlessness prompted by
what she felt were "imperfect" qualities of her voice and diction and
the strenuous attempt to overcome this low self-esteem. Now she
could relax and articulate more freely.

One might expect this subject, normally so self-conscious about
her speech, to become anxious instead of comfortable when she
couldn't hear herself speak, since she then had no way of knowing
if she sounded "perfect" or not. The reason this did not happen may
be related to her report that talking with the masking noise, while
facing away from the interviewer, "was close to sitting and day-

dreaming." This was another positive aspect of the masking condition for her. Talking in the masking condition was not like talking, it was like being half divorced from reality in fantasy, when she would have no reason to be concerned with how she sounded. Apparently the capacity of the masking condition to decrease contact with reality and herself brought positive relief from such concerns to this subject, not discomfort, even panic, as it did in the instances of negative reactions discussed above.

Subject 14 was also unusual in that he had no preference for masking or non-masking in any of the interviews. He enjoyed hearing the noise, at least in Interview I, because it had a hypnotic quality for him. He compared it pleasantly with static he used to pick up with his short-wave radio as a boy which he used to fantasy was the sound of the surf on some island shore far off in the ocean. He experienced talking in the masking condition in Interview II as a comfortable state akin to fantasy. He said it was "like musing" and that then the interviewer became just part of his "own imagination." Apparently these positive elements were balanced by negative ones, some of which he specified. He felt he skipped syllables occasionally with the noise and "felt a spasm of resistance at letting out all these intimate things" which he attributed to "an urge to confess" in the masking conditions.

Other subjects reported positive experiences similar to those of the preceding two subjects. Subject 1 preferred the masking-noise conditions in Inteview III because she felt as though she were "escaping reality," and she felt "more secure" because she experienced "less fear of criticism" for what she said when she couldn't hear herself. Subject 11 reported greater comfort with the noise in Interviews II and III. He specified in Interview II that with the noise he didn't have to hear unpleasant things he said, by which he meant certain personal details of his life causing him shame and embarrassment which he felt an inner compulsion to tell. His comment in the Inquiry of Interview III, "the sound is an old friend," implies that the same sense of security was produced by the masking condition in that interview also and was a reason for preferring that condition then.

Subject 8 experienced increased visual vividness of, and greater accessibility to memories of her childhood in the noise conditions of Interviews II and III. She seemed to enjoy being thus "pushed back by the noise."

Seven subjects reported an interesting phenomenon at one time or another: the intensity of the noise seemed lower when they talked than when they were silent. We will call this the "attention phenomenon."

Subject 5: You can deafen the noise with your own thoughts.
Subject 8: When the noise was on, you sort of wanted to keep talking so you wouldn't hear the noise. You couldn't hear yourself anyway, but at least you had something to think about when you were talking.

This phenomenon raises a question about the mechanism responsible for the increased verbal output in the masking conditions. In our choice of the category label "freer associative response," we implied that a mechanism of disinhibition was responsible for the increased output. The phenomenon now discussed, especially as formulated by Subject 8, raises the possibility that the increased verbal output may occur because speaking is rewarded by decreasing the aversiveness of the masking condition. The following comparison of the increase in verbal output in the masking conditions for those seven subjects reporting this phenomenon with that for those subjects

	Mean % Increase in Verbal Output in Masking Conditions Of Interviews II and III
Subjects Reporting Attention Phenomenon	17%
Subjects Not Reporting Attention Phenomenon	28%
	$p = .20$ (t_2)

not reporting it bears on this question. These data are inconsistent with the avoidance hypothesis.

DISCUSSION

Many striking changes were observed in the speech and in the more general behavior of our subjects during the masking conditions. The fact that the subjects were as a group quite intelligent and of high verbal skills perhaps makes the changes all the more impressive. We do not claim to have observed all the effects of the experimental condition. This survey only deals systematically with those effects that originally caught our attention as we conducted the interviews and screened the tape recordings. Others approaching the interviews with different perspectives might find additional effects of the experimental manipulations.

In the following discussion we shall consider the reliability and generality of these observations, the probable cause of the changes associated with the masking conditions, the possible role of feedback in "ego-functions," and some miscellaneous ideas and questions suggested by this study.

PARTIAL CONFIRMATION IN THE WORK OF OTHERS

How *reliable* are the observations of the linguistic and psychological changes associated with the administration of the masking noise? This question arises because many of the observations consist of the "subjective" judgments and inferences of a single observer. How *general* are the presumed effects of the masking noise? Are they unique to these subjects, to the interview situation involving this particular interviewer, etc? While we are aware of only a few other studies of completely masked speech, their results and ours appear to be very similar.

Changes in speech.   Several investigators have noted various changes in the speech process. Shane (1955) and Cherry and Sayers (1956) found that stutterers spoke much more fluently when their speech was masked by noise. Birch (1955, 1956) observed a similar change in the disturbed speech of expressive aphasia. These findings are comparable to ours in showing that speech in general is altered by masking. They also bear on our observations of a possible disinhibition process, as will be discussed later.

Most of the specific categories listed in Table I as "linguistic changes" have been observed by others: increased loudness, flattened intonation, and prolongation of syllables have been reported by Wood (1950) and Klein (1965). Wood, Klein, and Shane also observed changes in "voice quality." Also, Wood noted increased pitch; Klein and Shane, slurring; and Shane as well as Holmes and Holzman (1966), changes in rate of speech. The only "linguistic" categories in Table I not reported by others are those of vocal noises and more distinct phrasing, although the latter may very well be a manifestation of "increased editing" observed by Klein in some subjects. These two phenomena were so apparent when they occurred that the lack of confirmation by others is not regarded as a serious matter. Wood noted, as we did, that the most varied speech changes occurred immediately, or nearly so, upon the onset of masking.

Behavioral-psychological changes.   For the purposes of this discussion we will group together the externally observable changes listed under this heading in Table I and the subjective experiences reported by the subjects in the inquiries. Here, too, most of our important basic observations have also been noted by others.

Friedhoff, Alpert, and Kurtzberg (1962) investigated the *expression of affect* in voice intensity when subjects were required to lie repeatedly to the experimenter. The intensity of these subjects' voices did not change upon lying when they could hear themselves. But it did change if the subjects could not hear their own voices because of a masking noise. Upon lying, under this condition, the voices consistently became louder or softer, depending upon the individual concerned. If one regards these vocal changes as manifestations of affects associated with lying, then these findings are comparable to our observation of increased affect expression in the masking conditions of the interviews.

Our *associative response* category referred to both the quantity of talking and a variety of qualitative attributes, such as the degree of spontaneity, of defensiveness, and the readiness to reveal intimate and personal material. We judged from external criteria that the associative response was freer during the masking conditions. Certain of the subjects reported that they experienced this change. Klein (1965) observed similar phenomena when subjects were asked to respond to paintings, Rorschach cards, and stimulus words under normal hearing and masked auditory-feedback conditions. The introduction of a white masking noise increased the quantity of responses, the vividness of imagery, and the number of drive-related contents in the imagery. The subjects experienced their imagery as livelier and more vivid. Holmes and Holzman (1966) asked subjects to tell about a very embarrassing experience using only a nonsense language of their own invention instead of English. Under white noise masking, the subjects spoke in significantly longer utterances and tended to begin speaking sooner than under normal conditions. Thus the associative process became freer in both of these studies.

While no investigator has reported observations exactly like our *thinking aloud* category, as far as we are aware, the fate of English words which the subjects of Holmes and Holzman had to inhibit and translate into nonsense language was that they were frequently "thought aloud" in our terms. That is, more English words crept into the accounts spoken in nonsense language during the white noise than during the normal condition.

Cognitive confusion phenomena, apparently quite similar to those observed in and experienced by our subjects, were also noted by Klein.

Increased affect expression, freer associative responding, "thinking aloud," as well as the preference of some subjects for speaking with the noise when they couldn't hear their (to them) unpleasant voices and the distressing things they were saying, were among the reasons for our hypothesizing (Mahl, 1960) that disinhibition took place in our subjects under the masking conditions. We will discuss this hypothesis in more detail in a moment. We mention it here because the studies by Klein, Holmes, and Holzman, and others bear upon it. The quantitative changes reported in the first two of these studies are consistent with this hypothesis, as are the qualitative changes in the responses of Klein's subjects. So is the difference in English word usage observed by Holmes and Holzman.

Stanton (1968) studied a more familiar form of disinhibition. He asked subjects to utter as many taboo words as possible to standardized listeners under masking and normal conditions. The subjects said many more such words when they could not hear their own voices. The majority of Stanton's subjects expressed a preference for uttering taboo words under the noise condition. But we cannot be sure if this finding is comparable to similar reports by some of our subjects, for Stanton's control subjects who never experienced the noise condition expressed the same preference as did his experimental subjects.

If one assumes that the subjects of Friedhoff, Alpert, and Kurtzberg were attempting to conceal vocal clues of their lying, then the appearance of changes in voice intensity with the introduction of a masking noise is also a case of disinhibition. And so is the increased fluency of stutterers observed by Cherry and Sayers, if one assumes that speech inhibition is the crucial factor involved in stuttering.

In short, there are several results from other studies in addition to the present one that are compatible with the inference that an underlying process of disinhibition occurs when people speak during the masking-noise condition. Why disinhibition might occur will be considered in a moment.

Three other findings remain to be checked against the results of others: the loss of contact with self or interviewer, the attention phenomenon, and adaptation, both observed and experienced, to the masking condition. There have not been reports on the latter two phenomena. Klein's preliminary report suggests that some of his subjects, too, felt a change in sense of self and reality. Thus, he notes that some subjects reported uncertainty about what they were saying and he comments on a "feeling of isolation" that may have been induced partly by the masking noise and partly by the physical isolation of his subjects in a darkened room. On the whole, there is less confirmation of our findings concerning the subjective experiences than of the externally observable changes in linguistic and more general processes. This may be due to the fact that the other investigators have not studied the subjective experiences in great detail. This appears to be the case.

The fact that most of our basic observations have also been reported by others is important on two counts. First, it indicates that these observations were reliable, for in effect ours were *independent* ones. Until several years later, we did not know of any of the studies reviewed except that of Cherry and Sayers and those of Birch. The papers by Wood and Shane were published in obscure places; the others were reported after this study was completed. Second, the basic phenomena listed in Table I appear to have a high degree of generalizability across samples of people and various speaking situations. Most of the linguistic changes, for example, have occurred if the subjects read aloud as they did for Shane and Wood, or if they spoke spontaneously as they did for us and for Klein. Furthermore, both linguistic changes and the rather striking, more general psychological changes have not only been observed in the interview situation used here, but in the various situations used by Holmes and Holzman, Klein, and Stanton, each of which was markedly different from the others. It is quite obvious that some genuine phenomena have been observed in these studies.

CAUSE OF THE PHENOMENA: NOISE INPUT AND/OR FEEDBACK DEFICIT?

This question raises many theoretical alternatives. To begin, the masking condition introduces two distinct elements: the stimulus input of the noise and the deficit in feedback of auditory cues from the subject's own speech. Either element might produce one or more different internal states. (a) The stimulus input, for example, might increase the general level of activation or arousal, or it might specifically stress the subject. Or the noise input might cause the subject to automatically make an erroneous unconscious inference: that the interviewer also heard the noise. After all, in his previous experience, any loud noise that interfered with his hearing also affected others present and required loud speech. (b) The significance of the feedback deficit, for example, might consist simply in the fact of the deficit, of there being something missing that is essential for normal or customary functioning. Or the deficit might be a stressor since it disrupts the organization of the organism on many levels: the relationship to reality and to himself, cognitive organization, normal speech patterns, for example. (c) Various factors, arising either from the noise input or the feedback deficit of auditory feedback, might operate simultaneously. And they might do so either convergently so that every observed effect is multiply caused, or heterogeneously, so that different effects result from different features of the masking condition. In addition, some or all of the effects might be direct results of the factors mentioned or they might be indirect results of attempts to cope with the states engendered by the masking condition. Finally, different causes or mechanisms may be operative in different individuals.

Some of these various conceivable attributes of the masking condition appear capable of explaining certain results. The input-arousal hypothesis, for example, could account for the greater loudness, affect expression, and verbal productivity. The simple deficit hypothesis can also account for these phenomena. Ideally, we should present at this point a detailed examination of the various interpretations, concluding with a statement of those alternatives which seem the most likely, and then await the results of experimental testing of these conclusions. Instead of engaging in that exercise, we will present a provisional "armchair" evaluation of the alternatives that seems quite plausible, leaving the final explication and testing of the various alternatives where they belong—to future controlled empirical analysis.

Considerable *experienced* adaptation to the masking noise occurred over the course of the six exposures to it in the three interviews. Every subject reported experiencing some adaptation. There was also a decrease in the frequency of negative references about the masking condition and in the number of subjects who stated it was more difficult to talk with the noise. Some subjects even developed a preference for the masking condition and some preferred it from the start. The observable phenomena, however, did not show a parallel change. They not only did not systematically decrease, but actually became more prominent in some cases. These observations suggest that neither the novelty nor the stress caused the speech and other behavioral effects. Furthermore, a test of a stress-related hypothesis concerning increased productivity yielded negative results.

When they spoke in the masking conditions, the subjects sounded like individuals who have become deaf after learning to talk. These people sound alike in at least two respects: in loudness and the flattening of intonation. The similarity is so striking that the speech of one would be mistaken for the other. This resemblance strongly suggests that the feedback deficit was a critical factor. But there is no reason why auditory feedback would function only in the regulation of loudness and intonation. It seems quite possible that the feedback deficit was also responsible for other linguistic changes: the prolongation, pitch changes, the vocal noises, slurring, rate changes, and exaggerated phrasing. These are all aspects of the speech skill which the delayed auditory feedback literature (Chase, Sutton, and First, 1959; Lee, 1950a, b) has shown to be dependent upon normal feedback.

Viewed from the standpoint of either learning theory or psychoanalytic psychology, the remaining observable results—the cognitive confusions, the changes in voice quality, increased affect expression, freer associative response, and "thinking aloud"—could also be due to a deficit in auditory feedback. One must merely assume that the control of these aspects of behavior—one's vocal style, the degree and quality of affect expression while talking, spontaneity and freedom in verbalizing, and cognitive organization —is a negative feedback system. According to this assumption, any *deviations* in the auditory feedback from the vocal style, etc., which the individual characteristically "sets" for himself, constitute signals which activate modulations and defenses that inhibit the audible deviations or the underlying processes instigating such deviations. In learning theory terms, such deviations in the auditory feedback would function as Hullian response-produced cues ($r \rightarrow s$) to which inhibitory responses and/or their drives were conditioned. In psychoanalytic theory, such deviations would function as self-produced stimuli perceived by the self-observing and self-evaluating superego functions which, in turn, instigate ego regulation and defense.

HYPOTHESIS: DISINHIBITION DUE TO DEFICIT IN AUDITORY FEEDBACK

The results and the reasoning in the preceding paragraphs suggest that disinhibition due to the deficit in auditory feedback was a central result of the masking-noise condition. Here we will summarize the evidence and arguments in favor of this hypothesis.

In the present study, the behavior during the masking-noise conditions included such phenomena as:
1. increased loudness,
2. less cultured speech
3. more ethnocentric speech,
4. increased laughter,
5. freer expression of positive and negative affect and thought,

which sometimes concerned the interviewer,

6. increased amount of talking, reaching monologue proportions at times,
7. revelation of very intimate personal information,
8. the voicing of thoughts meant to be silent,
9. the misplacement of thought fragments in the flow of speech.

This all adds up to "strange" behavior under any conditions, especially on the part of college students interacting with a stranger and a "college professor" at that. The assumption of a process of disinhibition makes this strange behavior understandable. As we noted above, the results of other independent investigators are compatible with this assumption.

Several considerations suggest that this disinhibition is due to the deficit in auditory feedback and not to the noise input per se. (a) The failure to actually adapt to the masking condition in spite of the subjective experience of adaptation to the *noise* and the similarity of the subjects' speech to that of the deaf are highly suggestive in this regard. (b) The immediacy of the behavior change and the exquisite "off-on" nature of the relationship between the changes and the use of the masking noise seem more compatible with the deficit hypothesis than with the input hypothesis. (c) As we have shown, it is theoretically conceivable that the disinhibition could be due to the deficit in auditory feedback. (d) Many of the subjects' reports support this interpretation, for the relief from anxiety and self-criticism based on auditory feedback appeared to be the major reason why some subjects preferred to talk under the masking condition. The fact that some subjects were distressed by the noise condition is not evidence against the feedback deficit hypothesis. Indeed, such a deficit appears to be frightening for some people for the very reason that it appears to be preferred by others, i.e., its disruption of the customary drive-defense balance. In addition, the disturbance in customary modes of thought and speech and in the sense of self and reality could be indirect noxious results of a sensory deficit for some people.

Thus the hypothesis provides a relatively coherent explanation of the observable phenomena and many of the major experiential reports by the subjects. This hypothesis is consistent with conclusions about the role of sensory feedback derived from studies of distorted auditory feedback and the extensive studies of sensory deprivation. Indeed, our general behavioral categories are reminiscent of findings of the latter, as Klein (1965) has also pointed out. But the hypothesis clearly needs empirical testing.

Stanton (1968) has made the first attempt at such empirical testing, in the study cited earlier. His design included a normal no-noise condition, and two noise conditions. In one of the latter, a white noise of complete feedback masking intensity was used; in the other, the noise was loud, but not quite loud enough to cause feedback masking. His subjects did not utter more tabooed words in the latter noise condition than in the no-noise condition. But they did utter more tabooed words in the masking-noise condition than in either the control-noise condition or the control no-noise condition. Thus Stanton's results not only demonstrated disinhibition when subjects could not hear themselves, but also showed that a loud noise per se was not sufficient to produce this disinhibition. Further studies of this type are needed to determine which of the full range of behaviors observed by ourselves and others are functions of a feedback deficit and which might be caused by noise alone.[3]

THE POSSIBLY GENERAL ROLE OF
SENSORY FEEDBACK IN EGO FUNCTIONING

It is now well-known that sensory feedback from the organism plays a crucial role in complex skills (e.g., Smith, 1962). Speech is simply a particularly interesting and important case in point. The results of this study, and those of Holmes and Holzman, Klein, and Stanton suggest that other ego functions may also be part of complex feedback systems. This discussion has emphasized the possibility that defense and other forms of inhibitory control are aspects of negative feedback systems. Klein's (1965) discussion emphasizes the role of auditory feedback in secondary process thinking.

One naturally wonders, next, if the role of actual *sensory* feedback is not more extensive in ego functioning than is realized. There are two aspects to this question, both of which suggest problems for future research. On the one hand, one can ask: "What is the range of sensory feedback signals involved in any particular ego function?" Consider the process of defense against aggression, for example. Is it possible that proprioceptor feedback from the skeletal musculature, somesthetic feedback from the autonomic musculature (the "heat" of anger and the felt pounding of the heart, or their absence, for

---

[3]Janis (1959, p. 214) proposed that the use of a masking noise might result in ". . . verbalization [that] would more closely approximate his own silent thoughts than if he could hear himself talk." On this basis, Janis and Terwilliger (1962) obtained subjects' associations to fearful communications under masking-noise conditions, but they did not test the underlying premise.

example), visual feedback from one's overt actions, auditory feedback from one's voice, as well as the feedback of one's thoughts, all play a crucial role in defense against aggression? Is it possible that deviations in such *feedback signals* from those body sense perceptions one has come to tolerate are critical for the instigation and maintenance of defense? Is the essence of defense the minimization of such deviations from one's customarily tolerable feedback sense perceptions?

On the other hand, one can ask: "What is the range of ego functions in which sensory feedback from the organism's activities plays a significant role?" Some of our observations suggest that other complex ego functions, in addition to the processes of defense and organized thought, may be just as dependent upon feedback as are sensory-motor skills. Feeling "empty" when deprived of auditory feedback, as some subjects did, suggests that sensory feedback is critical for one's *basic sense of being.* An inability to maintain the presentation of oneself as the realization of a fantasied cultivated actress with the loss of auditory feedback, as well as the return of less cultured and more ethnocentric speech in several young adults striving for upward social mobility and greater acculturation, suggest that one's *sense of identity* may depend upon organismic feedback. Perhaps the *basic mechanism of achieving identifications* is a negative feedback process in which the individual is continually monitoring the most assorted sensory feedback from himself and is continually minimizing all deviations in this feedback from that totality of sense impressions arising from his memories and fantasies of the person with whom he is identifying. By such a process one could transform himself into a replica of the identification object. This would merely be a complex, generalized form of the process by which a hearing child presumably comes to speak as his parents do. *Self-observation, self-evaluation, and self-regulation* appear to be major ego functions having general significance. But what is the basic material that is observed, and what is the observing, evaluating, and regulating agent? The observations from studies of masked speech suggest that the basic material may consist, to a significant degree, of concrete sensory feedback and that the observing, evaluating, and regulating agent is the brain and its sensory-perceptual and memory systems. Thus studies of the role of feedback in complex ego functions may bring together Freud's conceptions of personality functioning set forth in Chapter 7 of *The Interpretation of Dreams* (1900) and *The Ego and the Id* (1923) and modern neurophysiology, to the mutual advantage of both approaches.

These conceptions presume that extremely complex and intricate feedback processes operate in behavior. This seems quite possible in view of the intricate, multifaceted feedback regulation of speech revealed by the studies which were reviewed in the introductory section of this paper.

MISCELLANY

A few other aspects and implications of the study merit some brief comments.

1. *The effect of the masking condition varied with the individual.* Klein found the same to be true in his study. This implies that people vary in the degree to which auditory feedback is involved in the regulation of their behavior. This, in turn, raises a number of questions for further investigation. Some of them are: What accounts for these individual differences? Are they a function of personality differences? Does this individual variation reflect variation in the degree of "internalization" of behavioral controls? What other cues or mechanisms can replace those involved in auditory feedback?

2. We have noted but not discussed the fact that *some aspects of language were essentially unaffected by the feedback deficit.* This seems very interesting in view of the other marked effects it has. It would appear that some aspects of speech in adults are independent of auditory feedback. Some of them, such as the phonetic-articulatory, may be primarily dependent upon kinesthetic feedback. Perhaps there are other aspects of language which can be, and have been—over and over again—performed silently, and thus become independent of auditory feedback. All through life a person "thinks" in the grammatical forms of his language. Such patterns can become independent of auditory feedback, in contrast to the strictly vocal, audible aspects of language. This consideration has two obvious research implications: one developmental, the other cross-cultural. Would the masking noise have greater effects on the "basic" linguistic patterns with younger subjects simply because of the parallel decreased frequency of silent practice? Would feedback deficit have greater effects on the basic linguistic patterns as the different modes of silent practice varied? In children unable to read and write, for example, or in illiterate cultures?

3. Subjects reported that when they talked the noise did not sound as loud as when they were not talking. This could be an "attention phenomenon." The subjects' reports supply striking confirmation of certain aspects of Freud's theory of consciousness and

attention as stated in Chapter 7, *The Interpretation of Dreams,*
and elsewhere. David Rapaport (1960, pp. 227ff) provided a brilliant,
and the most useful, synthesis of this theory and a historical perspective of Freud's thinking about it. Of the fourteen propositions
(pp. 228-9) Rapaport derived from Freud's formulations, the following are especially relevant here:

1. The subjective conscious experience is determined by the distribution
   of a limited quantity of mental energy termed attention cathexis.
3. Attention cathexis is part of the energy of the system Cs-Pcs (in present-
   day terminology, the ego) which is termed hypercathexis.
4. Excitations within the mental apparatus (internal) or on the receptor
   organs (external) attract attention cathexes proportionately to their
   intensity.
5. Attention cathexis, if so attracted and if exceeding a certain amount
   (threshold), gives rise to the conscious experience of the excitation.
6. Simultaneous or contiguous excitations compete for the limited
   quantity of attention cathexis.
9. Defenses and *other processes* utilizing great amounts of hypercathexes
   diminish the quantity of attention cathexis available.
   (Italics ours. In psychoanalytic theory, "other processes" would include
   the ego functions of speech and secondary process-thinking such as our
   subjects were engaging in during the interviews.)

When our subjects talked in the masking conditions they were doing
two things which, according to Freud's theory of consciousness,
should have caused the masking noise to decrease in loudness.
First, they were producing receptor-excitation (proprioceptive) and
"internal" excitation (ideational content of verbal images) that com-
peted for attention cathexis with the auditory excitations from the
masking noise (Propositions 1, 4, 5, 6). Secondly, when talking, the
subjects were utilizing "ego energy," hypercathexes (Propositions
1, 3, 9). Not only is Freud's theory of consciousness supported by
the raw data, it thereby provides one explanation of them.

Aside from the relation to psychoanalytic theory, the subjects'
reports of the basic phenomenon has some interesting implications. Generalizing from their reports, one would have this proposition: there is an inverse relationship between talking and the perceived intensity of receptor stimulation. Talking decreases it and
not talking increases it. This implies something potentially important
about human interaction: that when a person talks he is less aware
of cues emanating from his interlocutor than when he is silent.
The generalization also implies something about intrapsychic functioning: that when a person talks he is less aware of stimulation
arising from within himself than when he is silent.

Common clinical observations and everyday experiences seem
to be consistent with these ideas. The "compulsive talker," for exam-

ple, is inaccessible to the ordinary external influences in interaction and appears clinically to talk in order to defend himself against inner sensations of anxiety. The latter is a form of resistance (defense) well-known to the psychoanalyst. Under the guise of free associating par excellence, a patient may actually be successfully avoiding experiencing his anxieties. The increased self-awareness that often comes with silence may be due, in part, to the mechanism underlying the attention phenomenon. It is obvious that this phenomenon suggests a wide range of problems for further investigation. Is the interpretation of the subjects' experiences as an attention phenomenon valid? What actually are the intrapsychic consequences of simply talking or not talking, disregarding content? What are the interactional consequences? Do non-verbal interactional cues, for example, have greater influence during brief pauses—when one is the listener, not the talker?

4. The vocal noises generally occurred during pauses and at the onset of sentences and phrases. While some of them were described as resembling "straining" sounds, it should be emphasized that the subjects did not show visible signs of making greater physical effort at these particular times. Nor were the sounds part of a speech-block pattern. The sounds, in their speech contexts, gave one the impression they resulted either from resting, aimless activity of the speech musculature during pauses, or from motor preparation for articulation at the onset of sentences or phrases. Obviously, slow muscular contractions or tensions in the speech apparatus produced them. Perhaps the same tensions are occurring regularly during normal speech, but at subaudible intensities.

The findings of this study and their interpretation result in a view of *the internal states of talking people* **that is somewhat different than one suspects from their normal overt speech.** Subaudible muscular tensions in the speech apparatus; silent speech, often unrelated to or in conflict with audible utterances and even unknown to the speaker; reined dispositions to use seemingly discarded idiolects and dialects; stronger affects and impulses than are manifested overtly; promptings to talk at length and to say more personal things; perpetual self-observation and self-regulation; the continual maintenance of a sense of self and of reality—all these must form part of the current of behavior flowing silently beneath the rippling surface of the stream of overt speech.

SUMMARY

Seventeen college students, male and female, participated in three individual personal interviews which were tape-recorded. During the interviews the subjects spoke under four different conditions: (a) in the usual face-to-face situation; (b) when they couldn't hear their own voices because of a masking noise administered through earphones; (c) when they couldn't see the interviewer who was sitting behind them, but could hear themselves; and (d) when they could neither see the interviewer nor hear themselves talk. Each interview concluded with an open-ended inquiry. The tape recordings and typescripts were primarily studied by the systematic, clinical-observational method; some supplementary quantitative procedures were used.

This report focuses on the effect of the masking-noise conditions. During these conditions, all subjects spoke in a much louder voice, with flattened intonation and, at times, lengthened syllables—all of which gave their speech a "sing-song" nature. All subjects also showed changes of various kinds in their "voice quality." Some of these changes were of a general phonological nature, such as increased nasality, while others included social class dialect shifts of a "regressive" nature. Changes in pitch, meaningless vocal noises, slurring of articulation, changes in rate of speaking, and more distinctive phrasing also occurred in the masking conditions, in decreasing frequency.

More general behavioral changes also occurred, including: increased affect expression; freer associative response, indicated quantitatively by increased verbal productivity and qualitatively by increased spontaneity and the communication of highly personal information; increased cognitive confusion; and "thinking aloud." The latter, rare but striking, phenomenon consisted of the unintended and unconscious utterance of content often just above the audible threshold. In one instance, a subject disclaimed even the "thoughts" involved.

All subjects reported experiencing considerable adaptation to the masking conditions, but there was no consistent external evidence of it. Control of loudness of the voice showed the greatest adaptation.

Most subjects, especially in the first interview, preferred to talk without the noise. A small number, however, preferred talking with the noise and the non-noise preference decreased as the interviews progressed. The major aversive qualities of the masking conditions included: the noise itself, the physical effort of talking in its presence, the voice feedback deficit, interference with cognition and articulation, a sense of loss of contact with oneself and the interviewer, and negative affects. Many subjects reported that the noise sounded less intense when they talked than when they didn't. The generally negative portrayal of the subjects' experience contradicts the external impression of the subjects' behavior during the interviews. No subject failed to complete the experiment and all appointments were kept.

"Positive" reports about the masking condition included statements that the noise induced relaxation, a state akin to daydreaming, relief from reality and self-criticism.

It is important to note that the basic linguistic patterns persisted in the masking conditions: the subjects could still "speak English."

An evaluation of various mechanisms that might have mediated the effects of the masking conditions leads to the conclusion that the feedback deficit was crucial and that normal auditory feedback plays an important role in the regulation of many *vocal* dimensions of language behavior, in the control of the vocal expression of affects and thoughts, and in the maintenance of a sense of self and of reality. Various additional implications of the findings were discussed.

Postscript. For a vigorous study and further discussion of the disinhibition hypothesis, the reader is referred to a recent study published when these pages were already set in type: Holzman, P. and Rousey, C. Monitoring, activation, and disinhibition: Effects of white noise masking on spoken thought. *J. Abnorm. Psychol.*, 1970, **75**, 227-41.

References

BELL, C. On the nervous circle which connects the voluntary muscles with the brain. Phil. Trans.; 1826, (2) 163-75. In C. Bell, *The Nervous System of the Human Body.* (3rd ed.) Henry Renshaw, London, 1844, 193-203.

BERNARD, C. Leçons sur la Physiologie et la Pathologie du Système Nerveux. Balliere, Paris, 1858, 1, 246-66.

BIRCH, H. G. Experimental investigations in expressive aphasia. *N.Y. S. J. Med.*, 1956, **56**, 3849-52.

BIRCH, H. G. and LEE, J. L. Cortical inhibition in expressive aphasia. *Arch. Neurol. Physchiat.*, 1955, **74**, 514-17.

BLACK, J. W. Some effects of auditory stimuli upon voice. *J. Aviat. Med.* (Now *J. Aerospace Med.*) 1950a, **21**, 251-5, 277.

BLACK, J. W. The effect of room characteristics upon vocal intensity and rate. *J. Acoust. Soc. Amer.*, 1950b, **22**, 174-6.

BLACK, J. W. The effect of noise induced temporary deafness upon vocal intensity. *Speech Monographs*, 1951, **18**, 74-7.

BLACK, J. W. Systematic research in experiential phonetics: 2. Signal reception: Intelligibility and side-tone. *J. Speech Hear. Dis.*, 1954, **19**, 140-6.

BLACK, J. W., TOLHURST, G. C., and MORRILL, S. N. Application of multiple-choice speech intelligibility tests in the evaluations and use of voice communication equipment. Pensacola: Joint Project Ohio State Univ. Res. Found. & U.S. Naval School of Av. Med., 1953. Joint Project Report No. 19, Bureau of Medicine and Surgery Research Project No. NM 001-064.01.19 (cited by Peters, 1955).

CANNON, W. B. *The Wisdom of the Body.* Norton, New York, 1932.

CARHART, R. Conservation of speech. In H. Davis and S. R. Silverman, (Eds.), *Hearing and Deafness.* (Rev. ed.), Holt, Rinehart & Winston, New York, 1960. Pp. 387-402.

CHASE, R. A., SUTTON, S., and FIRST, D. Bibliography: Delayed auditory feedback. *J. Speech Hear. Res.*, 1959, **2**, 193-200.

CHASE, R. A., SUTTON, S., FIRST, D., and ZUBIN, J. A developmental study of changes in behavior under delayed auditory feedback. *J. Genetic Psychol.*, 1961, **99**, 101-12.

CHERRY, C., SAYERS, B. M., and MARLAND, P. M. Experiments on the complete suppression of stammering. *Nature*, 1955, **176**, 874-5.

CHERRY, C. and SAYERS, B. M. Experiments upon the total inhibition of stammering by external control, and some clinical results. *J. Psychosom. Res.*, 1956, **1**, 233-46.

DAVIS, H., MORGAN, C. T., HAWKINS, J. E., GALAMBOS, R., and SMITH, F. W. Temporary deafness following exposure to loud tones and noise. *Acta Oto-laryngolica Supplementum, LXXXVIII*, 1950, 56 pp.

FAIRBANKS, G. Selective vocal effects of delayed auditory feedback. *J. Speech Hear. Dis.*, 1955, **20**, 333-46.

FAIRBANKS, G. and GUTTMAN, N. Effects of delayed auditory feedback upon articulation. *J. Speech Hear. Res.*, 1958, **1**, 12-22.

FREUD, S. The interpretation of dreams. 1900. In J. Strachey (Ed.), *The Standard Edition of the Complete Psychological Works of Sigmund Freud.* Hogarth Press, London, Vols. 4 and 5, 1953.

FREUD, S. The psychopathology of everyday life. 1901. In J. Strachey (Ed.), *The Standard Edition of the Complete Psychological Works of Sigmund Freud.* Hogarth Press, London, Vol. 6, 1960.

FREUD, S. On Narcissism: An introduction. 1914. In J. Strachey (Ed.), *The Standard Edition of the Complete Psychological Works of Sigmund Freud.* Hogarth Press, London, Vol. 14, 67-105. 1957.

FREUD, S. The Ego and the Id. 1923. In J. Strachey (Ed.), *The Standard Edition of the Complete Psychological Works of Sigmund Freud.* Hogarth Press, London, Vol. 19, 3-69. 1961.

FREUD, S. Inhibitions, symptoms, and anxiety. 1926. In J. Strachey (Ed.), *The Standard Edition of the Complete Psychological Works of Sigmund Freud.* Hogarth Press, London, Vol. 20, 77-179, 1959.

FRIEDHOFF, A. J., ALPERT, M., and KURTZBERG, R. L. An effect of emotion on voice. *Nature*, 1962, **193**, 357-8.

GALAMBOS, R. and DAVIS, H. The response of single auditory nerve fibers to acoustic stimulation. *J. Neurophysiol.*, 1943, **6**, 39-58.

GALAMBOS, R. and DAVIS, H. The response of single auditory nerve fibers to acoustic stimulation. *J. Neurophysiol.*, 1944, **7**, 287-303.

HANLEY, T. D. and STEER, M. D. Effect of level of distracting noise upon speaking rate, duration, and intensity. *J. Speech Hear. Dis.*, 1949, **14**, 363-8.

HOLMES, C. and HOLZMAN, P. Effect of white noise on disinhibition of verbal expression. *Percept. Motor Skills.* 1966, **23**, 1039-42.

JANIS, I. L. Motivational factors in the resolution of decisional conflicts. In M. R. Jones (Ed.), *Nebraska Symposium on Motivation.* Vol. 7. University of Nebraska Press, Lincoln, 1959. Pp. 199-223.

JANIS, I. L. and TERWILLIGER, R. F. An experimental study of psychological resistances to fear arousing communications. *J. Abnorm. Soc. Psychol.*, 1962, **65**, 403-10.

KERN, A. Der einflusz des hörens auf das stottern. *Arch. Psychiat und Nervenkrankheiten*, 1932, **97**, 429-49.

KLEIN, G. S. On hearing one's own voice. In M. Schur (Ed.), *Drives, Affects, Behavior.* Vol. 2. International University Press, New York, 1965. Pp. 87-117.

LABOV, W. *The Social Stratification of English in New York City.* Center for Applied Linguistics, Washington, D.C., 1966.

LEE, B. S. Some effects of side-tone delay. *J. Acoust. Soc. Amer.*, 1950a, **22**, 639-40.

LEE, B. S. Effects of delayed speech feedback. *J. Acoust. Soc. Amer.*, 1950b, **22**, 823-6.

LEE, B. S. Artificial stutter. *J. Speech Hear. Dis.*, 1951, **16**, 53-5.

LOMBARD, E. Contribution a la semeilogie de la surdité; un nouveau signe pour en dévoiler la simulation. *Bull. Acad. de Méd.*, Paris, 1910, S. 3, **64**, 127-30. (Reported by M. Weiss.)

LOWY, K. Some experimental evidence for peripheral auditory masking. *J. Acoust. Soc. Amer.*, 1945, **16**, 197-202.

LIGHTFOOT, C. and MORRILL, S. N. Loudness of speaking: The effect of the intensity of side-tone upon the intensity of the speaker. Jt. Proj. no. N.M. 001 053. Kenyon College and U.S. Naval School Aviation Medicine Rept. No. 4, 1949.

MAHL, G. F. The use of 'ah' in spontaneous speech. Paper read at Annual Meeting, Eastern Psychological Assoc., 1955.

MAHL, G. F. Normal disturbances in spontaneous speech: General quantitative aspects. *Amer. Psychol.*, 1956a, **11**, 390.

MAHL, G. F. Disturbances and silences in the patient's speech in psychotherapy. *J. Abnorm. Soc. Psychol.*, 1956b, **53**, 1-15.

MAHL, G. F. Measuring the patient's anxiety during interviews from expressive aspects of his speech. *Trans. N. Y. Acad. Sci.*, 1959a, **21**, 249-57.

MAHL, G. F. Exploring emotional states by content analysis. In I. Pool (Ed.), *Trends in Content Analysis.* University of Illinois Press, Urbana, 1959b. Pp. 89-130.

MAHL, G. F. Sensory factors in the control of expressive behavior. 16th Int. Congress of Psychology, Bonn, 1960.

MILLER, G. A. *Language and Communication.* McGraw-Hill, New York, 1951.

PETERS, R. W. The effect of changes in side-tone delay and level upon rate of oral reading of normal speakers. *J. Speech Hear. Dis.*, 1954, **19**, 483-90.

PETERS, R. W. The effect of filtering of side-tone upon speaker intelligibility. *J. Speech Hear. Dis.*, 1955, **20**, 371-5.

RAPAPORT, D. On the psychoanalytic theory of motivation. In M. R. Jones (Ed.), *Nebraska Symposium on Motivation.* Vol. 8. University of Nebraska Press, Lincoln, 1960. Pp. 173-287.

ROSENBLUETH, A., WIENER, N., and BIGELOW, S. Behavior, purpose, and teleology. *Phil. of Sci.*, 1943, **10,** 18-24.

SHANE, M. S. Effect on stuttering of alteration in auditory feedback. In W. M. Johnson (Ed.), *Stuttering in Children and Adults.* University of Minnesota Press, Minneapolis, 1955. Pp. 286-97.

SHERRINGTON, C. S. and MOTT, F. W. Experiments upon the influence of sensory nerves upon movement and nutrition of the limbs. *Proc. Roy. Soc.*, 1895, **57,** 481-8.

SMITH, K. U. *Delayed Sensory Feedback and Behavior.* Saunders, Philadelphia, London, 1962.

SMITH, K. U., ANSELL, S., and SMITH, W. M. Sensory feedback analysis in medical research. I Delayed sensory feedback in behavior and neural function. *Am. J. Physical Med.*, 1963, **42,** 228-62.

STANTON, M. D. Social disinhibition under high-intensity wide-band noise. Doctoral dissertation, University of Maryland, 1968.

WINCHESTER, R. A. and GIBBONS, E. W. The effect of auditory masking upon oral reading rate. *J. Speech Hear. Dis.*, 1958, **23,** 250-2.

WIENER, N. *The Human Use of Human Beings.* Houghton Mifflin, New York, 1950.

WIENER, N. *Cybernetics.* Wiley, New York, 1948.

WOOD, K. S. A preliminary study of speech deterioration under complete binaural masking. *Western Speech*, 1950, **14,** 38-40.

Chapter 11

Personal Adaptation as Reflected in Verbal Behavior[1]

Harriet Aronson and Walter Weintraub

A NUMBER of systems have been developed based upon variables that are pertinent to the description and analysis of verbal behavior (e.g., Dollard and Mowrer, 1947; Gottschalk *et al.*, 1957; Hogan, 1952). This chapter will describe such a system and will summarize the findings of empirical studies which deal with its use, its areas of effectiveness, and which provide normative data that could be helpful in comparative investigations.

The scoring system, devised by the authors to measure adjustive patterns by means of verbal behavior, is based upon the following assumptions and reasoning:

Mental processes are channeled by the manner in which individual thoughts are phrased. People who learn different language patterns would not only think and communicate but also, as a result of this channeling, behave differently.

Certain concepts, if expressed, will accentuate conflict in interpersonal exchanges. Since ideas become more—or less—acceptable to others in accordance with the manner of their expression, an individual would learn to form thoughts and their verbal counterparts within an accepted framework. He would, essentially, develop an adjustive habit pattern of expression. Congruent behavior would, from our theory, follow quite naturally.

Depending upon the content which might bring acceptance or rejection by principal listeners and upon the intellectual maturity of the individual at the time a speech habit is formed, different defensive or adjustive maneuvers would be more readily chosen by different

[1]This investigation was supported, in part, by Public Health Service Award K3-MH-19393, and Grant MH-07434, from the National Institutes of Health, USPHS.

individuals. The imprint of defensive style upon speech may be particularly explicit during periods of psychological stress. But, it is assumed that the relationship between patterns of defense and speech has achieved sufficient stability by the adult years to be present in a broad range of situations, regardless of the specific quantity of stress.

Analytic theory describes a number of mental maneuvers by which ideas are circumvented or, at least, made more socially acceptable. Other maneuvers have been described in the literature as having become apparent to therapists as they worked. The authors have focused upon these maneuvers and the forms in which they may be expressed verbally.

It is also assumed, from psychoanalytic theory, that all people are at all times using adjustive devices. It is more reasonable to describe the kinds of adjustment being utilized than the general degree of defensiveness. According to this view, serious psychopathology is characterized not by too much or too little defensiveness, but rather by the presence of a pattern of alternative behaviors lacking the flexibility and/or subtlety to permit adequate functioning in important areas of life.

It was our intent, as we developed our instrument, to objectively define or delineate a wide range of verbal mechanisms. Since intra-person and interjudge reliability were of paramount importance, criteria were devised only for maneuvers found sufficiently often to allow statistical analysis. Bizarre forms, by definition used infrequently, were not included. In fact, since the pilot work for this method was done with normal speech material, all the categories arrived upon are in general use by "normal" speakers (Weintraub and Aronson, 1962).

The authors have delineated verbal styles associated with several pathological behavioral patterns. For example, we studied patients who had impulsive outbursts (Weintraub and Aronson, 1964), patients whose symptoms included delusional material (Weintraub and Aronson, 1965), depressed patients (Weintraub and Aronson, 1967; Aronson and Weintraub, 1967a), and patients whose symptoms included compulsively ritualistic behavior (unpublished).

In each case, the strategy has been as follows: we chose pathological groups that followed specific patterns of defensive adaptation which were measurable by our scoring categories. The verbal scores of those pathological groups were then obtained and compared with scores obtained under the same instructions from a normal group. We related the differences found to those patterns theoretically expected in order to determine whether we had, in fact, been able to discern a meaningful difference through our verbal measures. Sufficient correspondence was obtained to retain all but one of our original measures. The categories presented below relate to those measures which have been retained for further study.

When a group of 14 males was tested and retested after two weeks, the reliability of categories, measured by Spearman Rank-Order correlation, ranged from .50 to .88. Complete interjudge agreement on scoring, again on 14 subjects, ranged from 70 to 94 percent. This latter is a conservative estimate which considered as a scoreable unit only that material which either of two judges scored, and ignored the many portions of material which the judges independently agreed not to score (Weintraub and Aronson, 1962). A sex difference was found, for normal subjects, on two of the scoring categories (Aronson and Weintraub, 1967b) and all comparisons were reanalyzed to adjust for sex. No significant differences between pathological and normal groups were lost upon application of this adjustment.

Others who utilized our measures include Eichler (1966), who studied imprisoned sociopaths, and Ackerman (1967), who compared "normal" third with fifth grade children and our normal adults. Both of the above authors followed the same method. They compared a specific group of speakers with another particular group and interpreted the differences obtained in light of theoretically or empirically delineated personality differences.

It has been found rather consistently that groups of people who exhibit deviant or immature behavior differ on one or another of our scoring categories, usually in the direction of making greater use of a stratagem, when compared to a relatively symptom-free or more mature group. It is the interpretation of these differences that will be examined here. Are these undifferentiated quantitative differences, or do verbal category profiles occur which vary from one group to another? In the former case, verbal scores would simply register varying degrees of pathology, ie., levels of undifferentiated defensiveness or anxiety. In the latter case, they would reflect such qualitative factors as attitudes, styles of defense or adaptation, or even motivational dynamics.

Have we shown that our scores reflect particular attitudes or styles or, on the contrary, are we only demonstrating that patients are different from non-patients? Do we go unreasonably beyond our data to interpret our findings as reflecting actual personality? It is to such questions that this study will address itself.

If these measures are simply undifferentiated indicators of anxiety or defensiveness, the various patient groups would be expected to distribute themselves in one of two ways. We will consider those two alternatives as our null-hypotheses:

1.   First, take the possibility that our measures are characterized by a low level of random variability. Then, if we are measuring only the degree of pathology, the groups should show similar profiles along our categories when plotted geometrically. Those groups in which the patients are "sicker" should have more extreme scores. Those groups with less general pathology should reflect this "health" with less extreme verbal scores.

2.   On the other hand, our measures may include considerable variability due to unrelated factors, such as the effect upon the speaker of his awareness of his role as a patient. In such a case, the groups' category scores would differ in an irregular manner. Such differences should not be consistent enough to allow discrimination between groups of equal patient status or role.

We will consider the above null-hypotheses worthy of rejection if the behavioral groups show non-parallel profiles, the individual categories of which are significantly differentiable.

METHOD

Subjects. The subjects for our investigation were the groups of patients and non-patients that have been collected and studied individually in the past, i.e., the groups which were categorized as being "normal," over-eating, depressed, delusional, impulsive, or ritualistic in their behavior. Each of the above groups was composed of from 15 to 45 individuals whose behavior, but not necessarily whose diagnosis, came within the criteria for inclusion in that group. While the subjects do not overlap, the criteria are not mutually exclusive. That is, a person can easily be both depressed and delusional, etc. However, each subject was chosen for inclusion in only one group for the studies reported here.

Each of the psychiatric groups has already been found to be different in three or more categories from a "normal" group. To test the second null-hypothesis, only the four psychiatric patient groups will be compared. Should patients be found to differ from non-patient groups, little would be established. If, however, groups which share the characteristics of being patients, having psychiatric pathology, etc., could be differentiated, a better argument could be made to reject the second null-hypothesis.

Procedure. Immediately after introducing himself to S, E requested that S talk for ten minutes on any subject or subjects he or she desired. S was further informed that he or she would not be interrupted during the ten-minute period and that E would not answer questions until that period was over. S was told that E would signify the time when ten minutes were past. After indicating that S could begin, E simply tape-recorded whatever was said. E made no verbal responses during the ten-minute taping and listened passively, i.e., he refrained from nodding, leaning forward, or giving other non-verbal signs of special interest.

Scoring. The following categories were scored. The rules given here are descriptive short versions. To conserve space, no reference is made to previous work which suggested various aspects of the categories. Scoring manuals including more detail can be obtained from the authors (Aronson and Weintraub, 1961).

Number of words—The score for this category is calculated by simply counting all audible words. The category was chosen in the belief that both hypo- and hyper-productivity reflected adjustive maneuvers.

Silence—All periods beyond five seconds in length in which no words were uttered are added. The final score is the sum of all silence, minus the first five seconds of each silence. The category was chosen as demonstrating, in its extreme, a "block" reaction to stress.

Rate of speech—The total number of words is divided by the number of "non-silent" minutes, calculated to the nearest fifteen seconds. The rationale for this category is self-evident. Preliminary work has shown that this score need not correlate with the "Silence" score (Weintraub and Aronson, 1962).

Non-personal reference—A "personal" clause is one whose grammatical subject refers to a person or persons conceivably known to the speaker. All clauses not scored "personal" are considered "non-personal." The final score is a proportion of the two totals. This category was chosen as reflecting a tendency for the speaker to choose neutral subject matter or to make close material more remote. For example, "I had a hard time keeping my temper" is scored as "personal" while "One finds it hard to keep one's temper" is scored as "Non-personal." We believe that this scoring taps, without differentiating among them, avoidance, isolation, and displacement.

Negation—All negatives, e.g., "not," "no," "never," etc., are scored. We believe this category reflects a tendency to negate and deny. Analysts generally consider negation as the more superficial defense of the two. In actual practice, it is often difficult to differentiate negation from denial. The latter can be phrased in a manner which is not scored under this system.

Qualification—Three principal maneuvers are scored: (1) Uncertainty, e.g., "I *suppose* he is all right." (2) Modifiers which detract force without adding information, e.g., "It's *more or less* a nice day." (3) The suggestion that a word or phrase is used loosely, e.g., "I did *what you might call* a loop-de-loop." The scoring for this category was chosen to reflect what psychoanalysts consider "undoing before the fact."

Retraction—A "retractor" is a word, phrase, or clause which takes back what has been thought or stated. The statement, "I believe in freedom of the press. Still, there are some books which must be kept from the public" is an example of retracting. Also, words such as "although," "but," "on the other hand," "except," etc., are so frequently used to refute other material that they are scored automatically. The maneuver focused upon here is similar to what analysts call "undoing."

Explaining—This category is scored when the speaker uses a word, phrase, or clause which (1) states a causal relationship, e.g., "because," "due to," "as a result of," etc., (2) gives a reason for an action, thought, or attitude, e.g., "The purpose of the trip is to . . ." or (3) contains a participial phrase which provides justification, e.g., "Having been there, I can speak with authority." We believe this category is a measure of the use of rationalization.

Direct reference—Here, specific references made concerning the experimenter, the experimental method, and/or the physical surroundings are scored. While in most categories items are scored for each individual use, here consecutive scoreable material is regarded as a single unit and no further score is given until the speaker makes an intervening statement on some other subject. We believe this category taps something comparable to filling in during a "block." It may relate in function to naming an object in the room for an association in a word association test. At times the category measures a direct call for help. More subtly, it may also indicate an attempt to manipulate the examiner. We believe that this category covers a variety of maneuvers, none of which is used often enough by "normals" to be scored separately. "Normals" appear to understand and "play the game" without much recourse to this maneuver. We have come to interpret large scores on this category as indicating lack of "ego strength."

Feelings—All clauses are scored in which the speaker describes himself as experiencing or having experienced: attraction-aversion, like-dislike, satisfaction-dissatisfaction, pleasure-displeasure, hope, fear, enjoyment, shock, etc. We have no analytic name for this maneuver. It appeared, clinically, that some people avoid facts by concentrating on emotion while others reverse this process. The category was included in the hope that either extreme would be reflected.

Evaluation—The expression of value judgment is scored in the following areas: goodness-badness (e.g., "He's an excellent student."), useful-useless, right-wrong, propriety-impropriety, and pleasant-unpleasant. This category was added as an indicator of the defensive use of opinions and preoccupation with what is proper and right. A high score may reflect a strong or precociously developed superego.

In order to adjust for the number of words spoken, each of the last seven categories listed above is reported in terms of frequency per hundred spoken words. Since preliminary studies found that they do not achieve intraindividual reliability under conditions of fewer words being spoken (Weintraub and Aronson, 1962), Negation and Explanation are scored only for those Ss who spoke at least 600 (Neg.) or 800 (Exp.) words during the test period.

RESULTS

Hypothesis 1. Figure 1 demonstrates the absence of parallel structure of our group profiles. Note that we have utilized the median scores rather than the means of our various groups. Skewed scores are common to the kinds of measurement studied here. The skewness is frequently sufficient to result in significant heterogeneity of variance. The findings are given with intervals to suggest those points at which differences from "normal" speakers have been determined in past studies. Since some of that work was done parametrically and some non-parametrically and since the Ns and variances were not equal, there exist instances where a smaller difference resulted in a significant difference while a larger difference did not establish significance. The upper and lower limit lines on Figure 1 are, therefore, schematic representations chosen to approximate rather than specify t scores of plus and minus two sigmas from the "normal" mean.

It is obvious that each of the different groups is in a most extreme position at least once and that there is divergence as well as similarity between patternings. In fact, on four of our measures, patient groups are sufficiently dissimilar to occupy both the highest and the lowest extreme positions when compared to non-patient groups. Also, the over-eating women, who are functioning without psychiatric intervention and are, behaviorally, the least "sick" non-normal group, obtained several scores as extreme or more extreme than those of groups largely composed of patients sufficiently disturbed to be hospitalized.

We have, by inspection, eliminated our first null-hypothesis. While individual categories may reflect the differential use of various

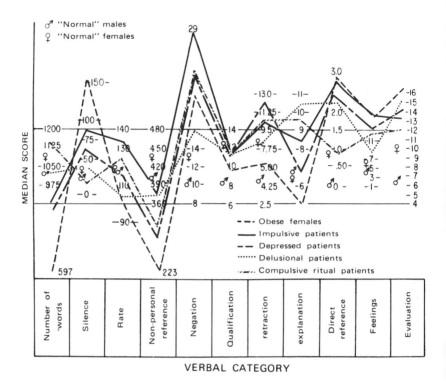

Fɪɢ. 1. Median verbal behavior scores of normal control and patient groups.

maneuvers, the groups do not fall into parallel patterns reflecting the degree of pathology between groups.

Hypothesis 2. The four patient groups, Depressed, Delusional, Impulsive, and Compulsively Ritualistic, were then compared on each of the scales by means of the Kruskal-Wallis non-parametric test of analysis of variance. This comparison determines whether the observed divergences are regularly related to group status or can be attributed only to unexplained variability. The results of that analysis are shown in Table I. It demonstrates that on all but two of the measures there is considerable difference between experimental groups, eight of which are significant and one of which approaches significance ($p < .06$).

One of the two measures which does not differentiate between groups is Qualification, which also did not differentiate between our

TABLE I.

Median Verbal Behavior Scores of Impulsive, Delusional, Depressed
and Compulsively Ritualistic Patients

| Category | Patient Group | | | | Kruskal-Wallis H | p |
	Imp. N=15	Del. N=16	Depr. N=45	C. R. N=17		
Number of words	906.0	1016.5	597.0	1136.0	10.5	< .02
Silence	84	34.5	157	17	10.6	< .02
Rate	133.1	104.4	99.0	124.1	11.4	< .01
Non-personal reference	372.0	373.0	223.2	326.1	12.1	< .01
Negation°	29.4	16.0	19.6	22.4	8.7	< .05
Qualification	11.0	11.2	9.4	11.1	1.2	NS
Retraction	9.9	8.0	6.6	10.5	9.5	< .05
Explanation°°	8.4	10.4	5.0	9.6	11.7	< .01
Direct reference	2.7	2.2	2.8	.8	7.6	< .06
Feelings	16.8	7.7	16.6	12.5	12.4	< .01
Evaluation	13.3	15.2	16.4	12.0	2.3	NS

°Ns reduced by requirement of 600 word minimum word count to: 11, 12, 22,
and 15, respectively.
°°Ns reduced by requirement of 800 word minimum word count to: 9, 11, 20,
and 15, respectively.

"normal" speakers and individual patient groups. The other non-significant variable, Evaluation, apparently does not differentiate one patient group from another while it does differentiate several of the patient groups from "normals." Direct Reference remains borderline in differentiating groups. Here, while the other pathological groups' medians were well above normal, the ritualistic group remained within the range of our two "normal" groups. This difference would be significant at the .06 level.

We have, by statistical argument, reason to reject the second null-hypothesis. The patient groups are tangibly different from one another. Note that while it may be true that, for one or another category, only one group's extreme scoring results in a significant difference, no single group is consistent in being critically extreme across all the categories.

DISCUSSION

This report has concerned itself with the interpretation of scores obtained with one method of analyzing verbal behavior. Previously, findings utilizing this method were discussed in terms of correspondence with personality theory. Here, the argument has drawn more upon logic and less upon the specific meaning of any particular differentiation. We have demonstrated that groups whose members shared the characteristics of being patients and displaying aberrant symptoms but who differed in the form of aberration also differed from one another in manner of speech; and, that this dissimilarity was not only a matter of degree but also of kind. With this demonstration we have provided a strong argument that our verbal scores measure something beyond the fact of patient status or the presence of pathology. We believe that the results of our past studies within the individual groups indicate at least the possibility that the "something beyond" may be designated by such terms as adjustive style, character, or personality.

In previous studies, we traced parallels between scores on our verbal categories and both the dynamics and adaptive mechanisms which have been attributed to each symptomatic group on the basis of psychoanalytic theory. For example, we speculated that by differing from normals in their use of Feelings, Negators, Direct References, Evaluators, and Retractors, our Impulsive Group reflected the dynamic picture of: intolerable feelings of anxiety (Feelings high) $\longrightarrow$ denial of both uncomfortable feelings and the consequences of alleviative behavior (Negation high) $\longrightarrow$ manipulation of the human environment to reduce tension (Direct reference high) $\longrightarrow$ guilt over the impulsive act (Evaluation high) $\longrightarrow$ attempt to undo the impulsive deed (Retraction high). A dynamic formulation was conceptualized for each of the groups studied separately.

Each patient group studied has differed from a comparative group of normals in at least three categories. In fact, several of the patient groups made either extreme or infrequent use of the same defensive maneuvers. It is statistically reasonable to find more than one group with the same scores quantitatively different from normal. It is also theoretically feasible for various maneuvers to be shared by several patient groups. Despite the overlap, there are differences between patient groups which are critical and deserve comment.

Consider the situation of an individual who has been diagnosed as a patient. It is realized that he may differ from normals in his use of defensive maneuvers. But here we are no longer concerned with comparing the patient to normal controls in order to describe his range of defenses. We wish instead to compare this one patient to other patients to find if his verbal habits characterize his symptomatic state. How might we predict this patient's choice of pathological behavior from his verbal scores? How might we differentiate his scores from those of other patients with other symptomatic disturbances? Figure 2, which restates the verbal patterns of the experimental groups, may be of aid here.

Verbal Category / Symptom Group	No Words	Silence	Rate	Non-personal Reference	Negation	Qualification	Retraction	Explanation	Direct Reference	Feelings	Evaluation
Obesity (Female)						—	↑				—
Depression	↓	↑	↓	↓		—	↓	↓			—
Impulsivity			↑		↑	—					—
Compulsive Ritual	↑					—			↓		—
Delusional					↓	—		↑		↓	—

FIG. 2. High and low verbal behavior differentiators for determining symptomatic group.

Figure 2 designates those categories in which one patient group can be differentiated from the others by either an especially higher or an especially lower score. It ignores those significant differences from normal speech which were scored at about the same amplitude by several symptomatic groups. It highlights those categories in which patient groups differ from one another, whether by much greater divergence from—or by much closer resemblance to—normal speech patterns.

Note that Depressive patients are differentiable by the rate (lowest Rate) and quantity (lowest No. Words, Silence) of their speech[2], by their tendency to speak about subjects closely related to their feelings (lowest Non-personal Reference), and by the infrequent use of the more intellectualized defenses (lowest Retraction, lowest Explanation). The obese females gave speech samples which resemble the speech of the Depressed patients closely in pattern but not degree. However, their scores differ sharply in one category from those of Depressives. Just as these women frequently attempt to undo

[2]Agitated depressives differ from other depressives in the direction of their scores. They demonstrate a noticeably high rate and high quantity of speech. The pattern of prominent defenses remains constant. However, the direction of the peak is reversed.

the effects of their eating binges, they are also unusual in the frequency of their attempts to take back what they have just said (highest Retraction).

Impulsive patients also choose several of the same maneuvers as Depressed patients, as would be predicted by analytic theory. However, they differ, both from the Depressed and other patient groups, by their extraordinarily frequent use of a maneuver we believe to be related to denial (highest Negation). Apparently, the Delusional patient does not so frequently deny what he knows (Negation low relative to other patients). However, instead of reacting to what he knows (lowest Feelings), the Delusional patient is much more inclined to put that knowledge into a framework to which he can accommodate (highest Explanation).

The Compulsive patient stands out for talking a good deal (highest No. Words). Yet, with all the talk, and again unlike other patients, he generally ignores the specific situation in which he finds himself (low Direct Reference).

Our past discussions emphasized the dynamic aspects of interpreting verbal scores. The above remarks attempt to describe patients in terms of their most salient or most striking features as seen in their verbal behavior. These descriptions appear reasonable in terms of the symptomatic behavior present. While analytic theory was an essential ingredient of our more detailed interpretation, it can be seen from the above that it is possible to deal with information obtained from verbal behavior with relatively little reliance upon any particular personality theory.

Some mention should be made of the two scoring categories which do not differentiate between patient groups. What can be said about their meaning and/or usefulness within an array of categories? Qualification, that is, delimiting or modifying the extent of a statement, was not found to differentiate any of the individual patient groups from "normals." Here, as seen, it also does not differentiate between patient groups. We have retained the category and are still interested in its meaning in light of the finding by Ackerman that the category allowed third and fifth graders to be differentiated both from "normals" and from one another. There, the younger children used very little qualifying, the older children used somewhat more, and "normals" still more. Eichler also found Qualification to be a significant discriminator. His sociopaths were found to score more than "normals." A category which places children at one extreme and prisoners at the other, with "normals" and patients lying between, is not easy to understand in terms of defensive or adjustive mechanisms, per se. It may reflect a hesitancy produced as a reaction to the social situation in which speech is collected and, thereby, indicate more about the interaction than about the speaker.

A recent paper by Hermann (1968) would corroborate this interpretation. She found upon studying video-clips of interviews of the negotiators during stressful and non-stressful periods of a labor dispute, that qualifiers, negators, and a somewhat different way of scoring non-personal references were correlated with—and differentiated the same speakers between—stress and non-stress interviews.

Evaluation is generally scored more by patients than "normals," occasionally to a significant degree. It was also scored more by our "normal" females than our "normal" males. It does not, as we have seen here, differentiate between patient groups. This may be due to a lack of homogeneity in the measure which would produce a high degree of variability. It may become necessary to redefine the scoring in order to obtain a more unidimensional measure. Direct reference, which was found to be borderline as a between patient-group discriminator, also suffers from the fact that it may measure several kinds of maneuvers without differentiating between them.

For a method to be useful it should be known to be reliable, sensitive, and meaningful. We have found the method to have reasonable degrees of interjudge and test-retest reliability. It has been found to differentiate younger from older children, males from females, and women who over-eat but appear to function relatively well, from other females who are not notable for such a lack of restraint. With such less extreme groups, the ability of a measure to differentiate suggests that it may have an adequate degree of sensitivity. The fact that significance has been found using very small numbers also suggests that the categories we have chosen are sensitive to differences.

A number of studies with patient groups have shown that the method has some meaningfulness as a discriminator of pathological behavior. This report has summarized much of the evidence about the meaningfulness of the verbal scores and resulting profiles.

In calibrating the measures we have described, our goal has been to distinguish between groups which differ in their general behavior. Additionally, we have hoped that our measures would be sufficiently sensitive to permit assessment of change in internal states within speakers, such as might be produced by various pharmacological agents, by psychotherapy, and by changes in the external situation, e.g., stress vs. non-stress, relating to friends vs. non-friends, etc. Aside from the work by Hermann, mentioned above, and a study of our own (Aronson and Weintraub, 1967) on productivity shifts with recovery from depression, very little such use has yet been made of our instrument. We are directing future plans to that area of endeavor and hope that others will make use of this method for such investigation.

References

ACKERMAN, H. Speech patterns of third and fifth grade children. Doctoral dissertation, University of Maryland, College Park, 1966.

ARONSON, H. and WEINTRAUB, W. *A Scoring Manual for Verbal Behavior Analysis.* The Psychiatric Institute, Baltimore, 1961.

ARONSON, H. and WEINTRAUB, W. Verbal productivity as a measure of change in affective status. *Psychol. Repts.,* 1967, **20**, 483-7. (a)

ARONSON, H. and WEINTRAUB, W. Sex differences in verbal behavior related to adjustive mechanisms. *Psychol. Repts.,* 1967, **21**, 965-71. (b)

DOLLARD, J. and MOWRER, O. H. A method of measuring tension in written documents. *J. Abnorm. Soc. Psychol.,* 1947, **42**, 3-32.

EICHLER, M. The application of verbal behavior analysis to the study of psychological defense mechanisms: Speech patterns associated with sociopathic behavior. *J. Nerv. Ment. Dis.,* 1966, **141**, 658-63.

GOTTSCHALK, L. A., GLESER, G. C., and HAMBRIDGE, G., JR. Verbal behavior analysis: Some content and form variables in speech relevant to personality adjustment. *AMA Arch. Neurol. Psychiat.,* 1957, **17**, 300-11.

HERMANN, M. G. Verbal behavior of negotiators in periods of high and low stress. Paper read at the Eastern Psychological Association, Washington, April 18-20, 1968.

HOGAN, R. A. A measure of client defensiveness. In W. Wolff and J. A. Precker, (Eds.), *Success in Psychotherapy.* Grune & Stratton, New York, 1952. Pp. 112-42.

WEINTRAUB, W. and ARONSON, H. The application of verbal behavior analysis to the study of psychological defense mechanisms: Methodology and preliminary report. *J. Nerv. Ment. Dis.,* 1962, **134**, 169-81.

WEINTRAUB, W. and ARONSON, H. The application of verbal behavior analysis to the study of psychological defense mechanisms: II. Speech pattern associated with impulsive behavior. *J. Nerv. Ment. Dis.,* 1964, **139**, 75-82.

WEINTRAUB, W. and ARONSON, H. The application of verbal behavior analysis to the study of psychological defense mechanisms: III. Speech pattern associated with delusional behavior. *J. Nerv. Ment. Dis.,* 1965, **141**, 172-9.

WEINTRAUB, W. and ARONSON, H. The application of verbal behavior analysis to the study of psychological defense mechanisms: IV. Speech pattern associated with depressive behavior. *J. Nerv. Ment. Dis.,* 1967, **144**, 22-8.

WEINTRAUB, W. and ARONSON, H. The application of verbal behavior analysis to the study of psychological defense mechanisms. *Arch. Gen. Psychiat.,* 1969, **21**, 739-44.

Part V

Theoretical Considerations

Chapter 12

Toward Including Listening in a
Model of The Interview[1]

Herbert S. Gross

THE DEPTH of Freud's understanding of people is reflected in the novel idea that a prolonged encounter between two people, wherein one is primarily a speaker and the other primarily a listener, could be useful. There has been much effort on the part of clinicians and researchers directed at understanding such asymmetrical encounters that use natural language as a vehicle for information exchange. Some of the discontinuity between the clinical and research literature is, in part, unavoidable, but the interchange between the two could be enhanced if both would focus on the listening skills of interviewers.

Listening is a behavior that seems vulnerable to de-emphasis. The invisibility of the process creates a special problem, for listening must be inferred from overt response behavior. If one thinks about listening in terms of an *ideal* behavior, there rushes into awareness all the unanswered questions that we have about both psychological processes and language use. If, however, we think of the interaction between *actual speakers* and *actual listeners*, who might be found to possess varying degrees of skill, we can begin to think of models of linguistic performance (Schwarcz, 1967).

In an asymmetrical interview, the task of the interviewee is to speak and the primary task of the interviewer is to listen. Each has a secondary task as well. The interviewer makes listening-contingent remarks; the interviewee is expected to listen to the interviewer. The interviewee's subsequent speech is considered contingent on the interviewer's interventions. It is assumed that both parties are equally skilled in the use of language and that speaking and listening are

[1] I would like to acknowledge a debt to those trainees in psychotherapy whose problem-sharing contributed much to this paper.

considered to involve some of the same underlying processes. Such assumptions have been stated by neurophysiologists (Lashley, 1951), linguists (Hockett, 1961), and psycholinguists (Flavell, 1961; Martin and Roberts, 1966; Rosenberg and Cohen, 1966). The alternative point of view, that speaking and listening might be discrete behaviors, has intuitive support. We all know individuals who are eloquent speakers but are inept listeners and others who are skilled listeners but quite inarticulate. Moreover, what of the belief that a skilled listener can "listen between the lines?"

Together with Raymond Johnson, a study was made on the speaking and listening skills of subjects in an instrumental communication task (Johnson and Gross, 1968). An instrumental communication task is one in which the speaker generates natural language descriptive of a specific stimulus. The listener attempts to identify the stimulus solely on the basis of the descriptive text. Such instrumental communication tasks provide an extra-textual measure of communicative effectiveness, namely, the accuracy with which the message enables a listener to select an object from a set of similar objects (Lantz and Stefflre, 1964). Verbal descriptions of forty Munsell color chips were elicited and tape-recorded from four subjects who were graduate students of art. Later, these same subjects tried to identify the chips on the basis of the descriptions. Every subject served as speaker and listener for every other subject, including himself. We set out to test the hypothesis that effective communication could be attributed to a single undimensional skill. The latter was not the case, for two and possibly three dimensions were found. The most important dimension corresponded to listening skill.[2]

It was not the case that all subjects were able to use their own descriptions as or more effectively than others. Subjects who were skilled listeners seemed able to extract more information from a description than did the speaker. The least effective listener overall was listened to by the three others with more success than he had listening to his own text.

If the conclusion that speaking and listening are discrete psycholinguistic skills could be extended to the asymmetrical interview, models of interviewing that would not take listening skills into account, would be incomplete. Such models would not provide a basis for the hypothesis that successful interviews are contingent, in part, on the listening skill of interviewers.

---

[2]The second dimension corresponded to the subject's skill in speaking to both himself and others, and the third represented a measure of response similarity among subjects.

A PRELIMINARY MODEL

The successful clinical interview is one in which the interviewee has benefited from the information exchange, by acquiring some degree of "insight." The belief here is that the criterial attribute of what is usually meant by "insight" is represented by, or reflected in, increments in the skill with which the interviewee describes his experience. The task of the interviewee is to generate descriptive data in natural language and to be curious about the fit between his verbal report and its referent, the actual experience. The task of the interviewer is to listen to the data in such a way that its flow is maximally useful to the interviewee, by engaging the interviewee's curiosity about the sufficiency (accuracy, detail, and parsimony) of his report. The interviewee and interviewer dyad monitors the text of the interviewee with implicit psycholinguistic criteria of adequacy. When they note departures from a shared baseline expectation they redirect their attention to the "relatively inadequate text," and the curiosity of the dyad is satisfied when the account returns to baseline. The revisions of the text that accrue represent the increments in descriptive skill which, in turn, serves to motivate the progressive sharing of data.

The generation of language descriptive of experience by an interviewee in both clinical and research settings is conceptualized as a hot-cognitive task (Abelson, 1963) in which both affective and cognitive information is joined. The interviewee is unable to generate a competent text descriptive of given experience to the extent that his affective-cognitive style contains distorting "wants." In the vernacular, he tells-it-how-he-wants-it-to-seem rather than how-it-is, or experiential hang-ups are reflected in hung-up texts. It is expected that during a sequence of therapeutic interviews he will learn to make more effective use of either affective or cognitive information, e.g., an obsessional learns to make use of affective data, or a hysteric learns to attend cognitive information. This is accomplished by the attention directed to the report of his experiences in natural language.

The psycholinguistic task of the interviewer is similarly conceptualized as a hot-cognitive process, and his responses to the interviewee are useful to the extent that he becomes versed in the style with which the interviewee reports his experience. Interviewer responses are directed at challenging the sufficiency of the text generated by the interviewee. In this regard, the interviewer comments constitute a hypothesis offered to the interviewee. He is in effect saying, "I note that such and such seems inappropriate to its context" or "I note that such and such could be or is included in the text because of . . . ." The interviewer can expect his comments to be accepted or rejected depending on his ability to gauge some state of the interviewee. Interviewee receptivity has been conceptualized in the clinical literature as an interviewee attribute, a leading edge of emerging awareness. It has also been considered an attribute of the interviewer. Most agree, however, that the acquisition of "insight" by an interviewee is a result of the interaction and cannot be ascribed primarily to either participant.

> An analyst encountering a new patient is in a position surprisingly similar to that of a linguist who encounters a community which speaks an unfamiliar language. To get his bearings he explores how much language they have in common, listens to him and by locating the contexts in which initially incomprehensible utterances occur and referring back in his own mind to other languages he knows, he gradually learns his patient's language, and makes himself familiar with his imagery and style of thought and feeling (Rycroft, 1967).

The model of the clinical interview must to some extent be learned by every clinical trainee and is recapitulated in some measure by every therapeutic dyad as sequences of interviews proceed. The training experiences of clinicians and some events of psychotherapy have common characteristics that point to the necessity of including listening skills in a model of the interview.

Some, if not most, clinical trainees are, at first, reluctant to become actively participant interviewers. Their role uncertainty is resolved by adopting the caricature of the silent non-participant and they derive support from the overly simple belief that interview success can be defined in terms of interviewee productivity. His reluctance to participate is explained by the model as due to the challenging nature of effective participation. He doubts his ability to become adequately versed in the style of the interviewee and expects the interviewee to reject his comments. In repeated comments, Sullivan enjoins the interviewer to participate, for his aim is to be useful even at the expense of risking interviewee resentment. It is only by overcoming such a reluctance to participate on the part of the interviewers that therapeutic dyads truly consolidate. The interviewer gradually becomes comfortable enough to freely listen and respond to interviewee text and the interviewee becomes accustomed to having a listener.

THE INSTRUMENTAL CORE OF
CLINICAL INTERVIEW TRANSACTIONS

The problem of the relationship of the descriptive text generated by the interviewee, to its referent, the actual experience being described, must also be negotiated by every clinician and is to some extent recapitulated by each psychotherapeutic dyad. The model proposed above conceptualizes the task of the dyad (and this is also primarily the task of the interviewer) to be a scanning of the text generated by the interviewee with an eye out for departures from a baseline sufficiency of text construction. There is a parallel process, engaged in primarily by the interviewer, usually called "empathy." A general discussion of empathy is inappropriate here, but neither can some consideration of empathic process be omitted from a serious model of interviewer listening. The interviewer empathically processes what he supposes the actual experience of the interviewee to have been. The interviewer's empathic attention seems directed at the referent of the text generated by the interviewee. From the restricted point of view of a psycholinguistic model of listening, I would suggest that the interviewer empathically assesses the *codability* of the experience (Roger Brown, 1965). In this sense, the empathic process has an instrumental function; it gives the interviewer the sense that he knows what the interviewee is describing. It is only the most consolidated of therapeutic dyads, namely, the psychoanalytic dyad, and the most fragmented of dyads, the interview with the so-called schizophrenic, that come to seriously question the illusion that the interviewer effectively knows empathically what the interviewee has experienced.

In order that he be able to empathically assess the codability of an experience, an interviewer must be familiar with the actual experiences within a linguistic community and the capacity of the language to code average experiences. Experiences vary in codability and some language systems provide sets of words with more discriminating power than do others.[3] Some experiences can be effectively described in cool-cognitive language, whereas others require a more abundant use of affect-laden words. The gap between the sufficiency of the descriptive text and the actual experience is permitted to widen by the interviewer to the extent that he judges the actual experience difficult to encode. If the interviewer does not

---

[3]Although this has been most clearly demonstrated across cultures, (e.g., Roger Brown, 1965) it is a commonplace of clinical experience that within-culture experiences also vary in codability.

ascribe the gap to the general codability of the experience, he directs the interviewee to revise the text. Again, although the above judgments are made primarily by the interviewer, they are in principle mutual judgments. It is only the most consolidated of dyads that fully explores the dilemma posed by the inability to mutually assign the discrepancy between the text and the actual experience to a deficiency of the language, or interviewee encoding or of interviewer decoding. This dilemma is especially difficult to resolve as the dyad approaches a neurotic kernel. As the point is approached, the interviewee becomes convinced that the gap perceived by the interviewer is caused by inept listening. As his perceptions of ineptitude accrue, the interviewee brings the neurotic kernel into the consulting room in a phenomenon called the "Transference Neurosis." The feature of the transference neurosis pertinent here is that the analytic dyad can only resolve the four-sided entanglement, comprised of interviewee, interviewer, language capacity, and dimensions of the neurotic kernel, by shifting the communicative transaction to an instrumental task; by actually experiencing the distortion together. Until the clinician (and, indeed, each psychotherapeutic dyad) has come to experience the full range of doubt and mistrust that can characterize such imbroglios, he (they) is (are) unaware of the full extent of the participant role and the instrumental basis of the interview transaction is unrealized.

It not uncommonly happens that an interviewee's report of his circumstance is such that an interviewer cannot relate to a set of experiences with which he is familiar even though the culture and language of both are congruent. The interviewer experiences an elusive, uncanny state that characterized the communicative transaction with the so-called schizophrenic. It is a rather interesting fact that within the language of a so-called schizophrenic one can recognize his culture of origin. In these cases, the experiences of the interviewee are both different from the interviewer and uncodable. The less able the interviewer is to anchor himself in the patient's report, the more likely he is to hospitalize the patient; for hospitalization permits the experience of the patient to be discerned through the eyes of both. From such experiences, the clinician also comes to appreciate the instrumental basis of therapeutic communication, for it is by such maneuvering that he becomes anchored in the information exchange with the so-called schizophrenic.

THE EXPERIMENTAL INTERVIEW

For different reasons, interview research is at a crossroads analogous to the beginning trainee whose task is to become an efficient participant; both emphasize interviewee speech productivity and de-emphasize, or curb, the participation of the interviewer. Just as the clinician learns by means of participant observation that therapeutic communication has an instrumental base, so can the research interview be more useful if its communicative transaction is anchored. It is suggested here that the experimental interview could profit from concerning itself with instrumental communication. The interview dyad could have a non-verbal problem whose solution would require their exchanging information in natural language. The success with which the dyad solves the non-verbal problem would constitute a measure of the effectiveness of their use of language. With some experimenter ingenuity, the transaction would simulate features of the clinical interview. The task could require more talk from one participant and it could call for affect-laden language. The task could obligate the listener to make actual use of the speaker language, such that enhancing speaker effectiveness is a listener goal. From such interaction, we would be in a position to assess the skill with which people actually use language and the social psychological determinants of effective interaction. The dyad would sense that it is in a genuine exchange of information wherein the meaning of the language to the other makes a difference. The participant subjects in such experiments serve as informants from a linguistic community and the task of the researcher is to discover the extrinsic and intrinsic correlates of skill. Such correlates would be of value to clinicians, e.g., in evaluating teaching methods, and to psycholinguists as a source of hypotheses.

The research interviews, reported elsewhere in this volume, are typical of those that have been used with success for a number of years. In general, such research interviews have a surface similarity to interviews in a variety of settings, e.g., industry, opinion research, vocational training, in addition to clinical interviews. This author believes that the characteristic common to all interview settings is the exchange of information using *descriptive* natural language and further suggests that interview research could be directed at more fundamental features of the natural language information exchange.

Interview research has focused on the speech of the interviewee and has elaborated some interesting models of speech production (Feldstein and Jaffee). Pope and Siegman and Heller have done much to elaborate the social psychological determinants of speech production. Speech is a visible behavior and words-per-minute, or talk-time are variables that seem "behavioristically pure." However, there is some dissatisfaction with speech productivity as a primary criterion of interview success, for the question of the minute-to-minute engagement of the dyad with respect to "meaning" is evaded. The effect on productivity of such biases that have been studied by Pope and Siegman and Heller is clear only across subjects within a condition. The asymmetry of the clinical interview has an unavoidable artificiality when compared to non-interview settings. When the interviewer is truly participant in "reciprocally contingent interaction" (Heller), the artificiality is reduced. If, however, the interviewer is preprogrammed to respond with a bias directed at achieving "experimental control," the artificiality is compounded. It is not certain that a preprogrammed interviewer bias for a prolonged period, such as 5-15 minutes, is equivalent to a sudden blundering into the perception of warmth, or coldness, or disagreement. The body movement studies such as have been reported in this volume point to more rapid turnover times in interviewee set and we could infer that an interviewer comment would affect the interviewee differently from "moment to moment" within a fifteen-minute period. Dyadic interaction is characterized by a co-contingent hot-cognitive attention to the meaning of the speech (the referent of the description), and, as such, an explicit consideration of the meaning of descriptive speech to the dyad seems feasible in task-oriented communication.

Current knowledge is such that the meaning of texts of limited size can be only crudely assessed without extra-textual information. Content-analysis techniques tell us of the meaning of a typescript to the raters. Much of the information is sacrificed in the transition from speech to typescript and in the achievement of inter-rater reliability. Moreover, the meaning of the text to the raters cannot be assumed to be the meaning of the text to the speaker. Content-free measures such as type-token ratios, Yule's K coefficient, indices derived from information theory, and frequency listings of rare words, either vary with the size of text or of the clause unit. Both the size of the text and the size of the sentence unit are arbitrary. When compared to the information extracted by a freely listening member of a linguistic community, such techniques seem most unsatisfactory. The current techniques of inferring meaning could be considerably refined if the natural language exchange was yoked to a specific problem-solving task. For example, it is possible to speculate on the one hand, that some redundancy is necessary or, on the other, that some diversity of speech is optimal. From the actual interaction styles of particular dyads one could observe the balance struck on continua of diversity-redundancy and correlate such balances with non-linguistic measures of the actual effectiveness of the communication. The early studies of Jaffee and Feldstein demonstrated patterns of interactive tracking in an evolving dyad. An instrumental communication paradigm might make it feasible to extend such observations to some preliminary consideration of meaning.

The clinician spends much of his work day listening to the speech of members of his linguistic community. Speaking and listening are behaviors whose emotional and cognitive determinants are "over-learned" and these skills could be put to a more adequate test. There is little to be gained by waiting for ideal models of language use and there is much that can be done to develop performance models of language use derived from actual speakers and listeners in interaction.

References

ABELSON, R. P. Computer simulation of "hot" cognition. In S. S. Tomkins and S. Messick (Eds.), *Computer Simulation of Personality*. Wiley, New York, 1963. Pp. 277-98.

BROWN, R. *Social Psychology*. Free Press, New York, 1965. Pp. 332.

FLAVELL, J. H. The Ontogenetic Development of Verbal Communication Skills. Final progress report, NIMH Grant M-2268, 1961.

HELLER, K. Interview structure and interviewer style in initial interviews. In this volume.

HOCKETT, C. F. Grammar for the hearer. In R. Jakobson, (Ed.), *Structure of Language and its Mathematical Aspects*. American Mathematical Society, 1961, p. 220. Providence, R.I.

JAFFE, J. Computer analyses of verbal behavior in psychiatric interviews. In D. M. Rioch and E. A. Weinstein (Eds.), *Disorders of Communication*, Vol. 42, Chap. XXVII. Williams & Wilkins, Baltimore, Md., 1964.

JAFFE, J., CASSOTTA, L., and FELDSTEIN, S. Markovian models of time patterns of speech. *Sci.*, 1964, **144**, 884-6.

JOHNSON, R. L. and GROSS, H. S. Some factors in effective communication. *Language and Speech*. Vol. 11, Oct.-Dec. 1968, **4**, 259-63.

LANTZ, D. and STEFFLRE, V. Language and cognition revisited. *J. Abn. Soc. Psychol.*, 1964, **69**, 472.

LASHLEY, K. S. The problem of serial order in behavior. In L. A. Jeffress (Ed.), *Cerebral Mechanisms in Behavior*. Wiley, New York, 1951. P. 112.

MARTIN, E. and ROBERTS, K. H. Grammatical factors in sentence retention. *J. Verb. Learn. Verb. Behav.*, 1966, **5**, 211.

POPE, B. and SIEGMAN, A. Relationship and verbal behavior in the initial interview. In this volume.

ROSENBERG, S. and COHEN, B. D. Referential processes of speakers and listeners. *Psychol. Rev.*, 1966, **73**, 208.

RYCROFT, C. (Ed.) *Psychoanalysis Observed*. Coward-McCann, New York, 1967. P. 19.

SCHWARCZ, R. M. Steps toward a model of linguistic performance: A preliminary sketch. *Mechanical Translation and Computational Linguistics*. Vol. 10, 3 & 4, Sept., Dec., 1967. Pp. 39-52.

Chapter 13

Resource Exchange

Toward A Structural Theory of Interpersonal Communication[1]

Uriel G. Foa and Edna B. Foa

INTRODUCTION

The study of interpersonal communication may focus on meaning as well as on formal properties such as productivity and fluency. This chapter is concerned with a classification of meaning and its relationship to social structure, child development, pathology, and treatment.

Consider some messages, such as, "It is now five o'clock," "I love you," or "I feel so guilty." They are all forms of communication, but obviously quite different ones. The first and second messages deal with different resources: information and love respectively. Both the second and third messages are concerned with love, but this resource is handled differently: in the second communication, love is given to other, whereas in the third one, it is taken away from self. Simple and intuitive considerations like these suggest that a classification of social resources and of the behaviors used for dealing with them provide a way for categorizing the variety of interpersonal communication.

The notion of resource exchange stems from the work of the economists who have long been concerned with the exchange of particular resources, mainly, money, goods, and services. Several attempts were made to broaden the notion of exchange to cover and interpret all social behavior within a unified framework. Outstanding among these are the studies of Blau (1967), Homans (1961), and of

[1]This work was supported, in part, by Grant GS-2094 from the National Science Foundation. The comments and suggestions of Richard Longabaugh and Aron W. Siegman are most gratefully acknowledged. Thanks are also expressed to Jim L. Turner for his several contributions and to Kjell Tornblom for assistance.

Thibaut and Kelley (1959), which have become classics on this topic. These studies have shown how useful it is to look at social behavior in terms of exchange. At the same time, they have brought to the fore the need for classifying the resources involved (i.e., what is exchanged) and the behaviors by which these resources are dealt with (i.e., the modes of exchange). These classifications are necessary for the development of hypotheses about the interrelationship of means and modes toward a theory of interpersonal communication.

An important step in this direction has been taken by Longabaugh (1963). Although his classification of modes (1963 and 1967) and means (1964) is intuitive rather than systematic, he and his associates obtained interesting differential findings in comparing exchange communication of normals and schizophrenics in hospital wards, and of mother and child in various family situations (Eldred, Bell, Longabaugh, and Sherman, 1964; Eldred, Bell, Sherman, and Longabaugh, 1964; Longabaugh, 1963; Longabaugh, Eldred, Bell, and Sherman, 1966). In view of these results, it seems worthwhile to pursue the exploration of the area.

This report begins with a classification of both resources and exchange behaviors, based on their specific characteristics. Resources as well as behaviors are ordered according to their similarity on the dimensions which define them. In this manner, two circular orders are obtained: one for resources and another for behaviors. An hypothesis about the relationship between these two orders brings to a close the structural analysis. In the second part of the chapter, these structural notions are applied to integrate concepts and to generate new hypotheses pertaining to interpersonal communication. Thus power and need are defined respectively in terms of accumulation and deficit of resources through exchange behaviors, and motivation is viewed as an effort toward restoring a deficient resource to an optimal level. This immediately provides us with an ordered classification for powers, needs, and motives according to their specific resource, as well as with hypotheses about the relationships among the various kinds of powers, needs, and motives. The assumption that resources, and accordingly needs and motives, are gradually differentiated, leads to an analysis of the conditions and sequence of the cognitive development required for resource exchange. Resource differentiation in the child is modeled on institutional specialization of resources in society at large; therefore, both seem to follow the same order. This order shows up again in comparing the resources which are specific to each of the major schools of psychotherapy so that they may be viewed as different social institutions attempting, each one in its own way, to reduce deviance in the cognitive structure of the patient. Some comparison data on the cognitive organization of love and status exchanges in mental patients and normals provides, indeed, evidence of such deviance. Finally, in discussing resource exchange in the interview situations, the notions developed here are related to some other studies of this volume.

SECTION ONE:
THE STRUCTURE OF RESOURCE EXCHANGE

A CLASSIFICATION OF RESOURCES

A resource is anything which can be communicated or transmitted in a social situation: a material object, money, an activity performed on the body of a person (cutting his hair, giving an injection) or on things belonging to him (cleaning his clothes), an item of information, an expression of love or warmth, of respect, esteem, or appreciation.

It is suggested that resources can be classified into the following classes: love (affect, warmth); status (prestige, esteem); information (including the processing of preexisting information, but excluding information which can be classed as love or status); services (activities on the body of a person or his belongings); material goods; and money. Sex does not appear to constitute a separate class of resources, as it may be included in either love or service, depending on the circumstances.

These six classes of resources can be ordered on two dimensions: a dimension of *particularism* (Parsons, 1951, pp. 62-3), going from the most particularist to the most impersonal or universal, and a dimension of *concreteness*, going from concrete to symbolic. Particularism indicates the extent to which the specific individual, with whom the resource is to be exchanged, constitutes a condition for actual occurrence of the exchange. This dimension was earlier suggested by Longabaugh (1966) and is similar to Blau's intrinsic-extrinsic notion (1967, pp. 15-16, 95). Love (affect, warmth) is probably the most particularistic resource and money the most impersonal one. The particular person with whom love is exchanged makes a great deal of difference, whereas a change of clerks in the cashier's office, where a bill is paid or a salary received, would scarcely be noticed. Between these extremes, services are more particularistic than goods, and status (prestige, respect) is more particularistic than information. On the second dimension, services and goods appear to be concrete while status and information are symbolic; love and money occupy an intermediate position as they share both concrete and symbolic aspects. A classification of resources along these two dimensions suggests an order among them, which is given in Table I.

TABLE I.

Classification of Resources by Particularism and Concreteness

Particularism	Concreteness	
	More	Less
More	Love	
	Services	Status
	Goods	Information
Less	Money	

This order is circular so that each resource has two neighbors. Love, for example, is a neighbor of services and status; money is a neighbor of goods and information; and information is closest to status and money. This order may have some relevance to the problem of substituting one resource for another. It may be suggested, for example, that a substitution will be more likely to occur or will be more successful when the substitute resource is a neighbor of the original one, than when it is farther removed from it in the order. Giving status where love is expected may be more acceptable, for example, than giving money or goods. Some other applications of this order will be discussed later.

Traditionally, the exchange of money, goods, and services has been within the province of the economist. Status, love, and information have been the concern of other social scientists. This dichotomy has created problems in analyzing situations where both economic and non-economic resources are involved. Bringing both kinds of resources into the same theoretical framework may throw light on situations such as when a person prefers a job having a lot of prestige and paying less money to one where he could get a higher salary but less prestige. The problem of the American blacks may also be better understood in this framework. In modern culture, impersonal resources have come to be regarded as particularly important, possibly because they can be transferred without consideration of their original source. Thus money, information, and goods are suggested as means to achieve a solution for the Negro problem, while the resource of which blacks have been deprived most, status, is rarely mentioned. It is significant in this respect that, as soon as they have some money, Negroes frequently rush to exchange it for conspicuous consumption goods like flashy cars, clothes, etc., exchangeable, in turn, with status. The apparent inconsistency of some black groups, who demand integrated facilities where there is separation and separate ones where there is integration, becomes clear when the status implication of these behaviors is considered: refusal of social contact, through shared facilities or otherwise, means taking away status from the rejected ones. Thus the real issue is who is taking away status from whom, rather than integration versus separation. Likewise, the actions of the more activistic black groups appear designed to achieve status more than anything else. The use of violence for achieving self-respect or status has been noted by Fanon (1963, p. 73). Violence toward an out-group has the double effect of taking away love and status and possibly other resources as well, while the perpetrator obtains status from his in-group and becomes a hero. Thus disparate means like violence, conspicuous consumption, and rejecting or demanding integration may constitute different paths to the most needed resource, status. Perhaps a direct giving of status would provide more satisfaction by a shorter route.

Considering means of exchange as an organized whole seems to explain patterns of behavior which cannot be easily understood when each one of the resources involved is treated separately, or when communication is classified solely by formal criteria, at the exclusion of substantive ones.

MODES OF EXCHANGE

In previous work (Foa, 1966), we have suggested two modes of exchange: giving and taking away. It is somewhat unfortunate that in this work these modes were called "content of behavior," while the term "mode" was used for indicating the two resources discussed, love and status. Giving is defined as a behavior which *increases* the amount of particular resource of the person to whom it is given. Taking away is a behavior which *decreases* the amount of the specific resource available to the person from whom it is taken. Non-giving is lack of behavior, zero frequency of either giving or taking away. It is, however, true that when there is high expectation to receive a resource, non-giving may have a meaning quite close to taking away and would be called "withholding." The notion of giving love, status, information, money, services, and goods is self-explanatory. The meaning of the other mode, taking away, can be clarified by examples for various resources. Showing hostility or hate are instances of taking away love; showing disesteem or disrespect are examples of taking away status. Deceiving or misleading are instances of taking away information. Taking away money or goods would be an example of stealing. With regard to services, it is proposed that a damaging act on the person or property of the person should be classed as taking away of a service (e.g., beating, burning the house).

For each communicative act there is an actor doing the behavior and there is an object or recipient of this behavior. There are always at least two recipients in social communication: another individual and the actor himself. The self as recipient has not been explicitly included in most previous formulations of social exchange. Its inclusion appears, however, necessary to obtain a more complete picture of the exchange process. Each behavior can be considered at two (or more) levels: actual level, what is being *actually* given or taken away; and the ideal or aspiration level, what the actor *offers* to give or *seeks* to take away. The definition of four classes of exchange behavior (giving to and taking away from self and other) raises the problem of the relationship among them, which is relevant to the understanding of communicative behavior.

Three questions can be asked here:

1. If one gives a resource to other, or takes it away from him, what does this do to the amount of the same resource left for himself?

2. If one gives to himself, or to other, does this exclude a simultaneous taking away of this resource from the same object?

3. Do all resources share the same rules? If rules are specific to each class of resources will rules of neighboring resources, in the order, be more similar than those of more distant ones?

For each resource four classes of exchange behaviors have been proposed, resulting from the combinations of two modes (giving and taking away) and two objects (self and other):

1. Giving to other;
2. Giving to self;
3. Taking away from self;
4. Taking away from other.

Each behavior shares the same mode with a second behavior and the same object with a third one. Neither mode nor object is shared with the remaining behavior. For example, giving to self and giving to other share the same mode, giving. Giving to self and taking away from self share the same object, self. Giving to self and taking away from other are different in both mode and object. Two behaviors which share either mode or object are expected to be empirically related more than two behaviors having neither facet in common. Since each behavior has two neighbor behaviors and one removed, it follows that the four exchange behaviors can be ordered circularly. With regard to love and status, this circular order has been repeatedly obtained (see, for example, Foa, 1966). The same order may or may not hold for other resources.

The circular order requires that behaviors differing in both object and mode will correlate less than behaviors differing in either object or mode. Thus the circular order specifies the *relative* size, but says nothing about the *absolute* size of the relationships between pairs of behaviors sharing the same mode or object. Previous data (Foa, 1966) suggest, however, that the size of the relationship between these pairs of behaviors is higher for love than for status. Other resources may be similarly ordered.

GIVING TO SELF AND TO OTHER

Consider the relationship between the behaviors of giving to self and giving to other, as well as between taking away from self and taking away from other. Three gross possibilities may occur:

1. Positive relationship: giving to other implies also giving to self.
2. Independence: giving to other neither implies nor excludes giving to self.
3. Negative relationship: giving to other excludes giving to self.

It is proposed that the actual occurrence of any one of these possible relationships depends on the resource being exchanged. For love, a substantial positive relationship has been reported between giving to other and giving to self in normal married couples (Foa, 1966). In the same study, the relationship with regard to status is still positive, but systematically lower than for love.

Sharing information with another person does not appear to reduce the amount of it remaining in possession of the giver. It can, however, be argued that sharing may reduce the *value* of the information if the situation is competitive (e.g., industrial or military secrets). On the other hand, transmission of information may also result in some increase of information available to self, as, for instance, when repressed information is brought to the surface during a psychotherapeutic session. On the whole, information may exhibit independence or a slight (positive or negative) relationship.

The negative relationship seems to be strongest with regard to money and goods. Here, giving to other precludes giving to self. Services may show a moderate negative relationship: performing a service for another person appears likely to reduce the opportunity of simultaneously serving oneself.

The considerations just made suggest that the relationship between giving to other and giving to self changes gradually for the various means of exchange following their order in the two dimensions of particularism and concreteness (see Table I), so that the relationship is apparently related to the position of the resources in such an order: love has the most positive relationship; status is less positive; information, independent; money and goods most negative. Service is again less negative. It is thus possible that the proposed order of resource may help discover shared properties of neighboring resources other than those two which provided the base for arranging the resources into a pattern. The relationship between giving and taking away, discussed in the next session, appears indeed to be similarly ordered.

GIVING TO AND TAKING FROM THE SAME OBJECT

We turn now to behaviors differing in mode: giving to and taking away from other; giving to and taking away from self. One may wonder whether it is really necessary to discuss this relationship. Are not these terms antithetic, so that giving excludes taking away and vice versa? This may be true of money, but not necessarily of all other means of exchange. In love, for example, a situation of mixed feelings, of giving and taking away, is denoted by the term "ambivalence." One can, at the same time, love and hate another person or himself. According to some previous data (Foa, 1966) there is, in love, a considerable amount of ambivalence even among normal individuals and especially so toward the self: the correlation between giving and taking away, although negative, is far from reaching —1.00, as should be the case for a complete absence of ambivalence. The same source of data shows that ambivalence is lower for status than for love but, here too, the situation is far from mutual exclusiveness. Ambivalence in status is well exemplified by expressions like "to pay respect grudgingly." Still less ambivalence may be expected in information; yet some error, or misleading or ambiguous item may be included in a given transmission of information. Likewise, mainly erroneous information may contain some correct items. Sometimes one tells "half the truth." Money suggests absence of ambivalence; giving money appears to exclude taking it away. Even counterfeit money is just not given, but neither is it taken away. The fact that what was exchanged for worthless money is taken away is not relevant here. Ranking of means of exchange by decreasing degree of ambivalence has followed, so far, the order of resources given in Table I. If the order is also valid for the remaining resources, ambivalence will now increase as we are again approaching the most ambivalent resource, love, from the left side of the circle. For goods, the extent to which giving and taking occur jointly may be slightly higher than for money: defective goods may actually cause damage.

The "ambivalence" of services may be higher than for goods. It happens that some damage is done in the performance of a service: the barber may cut the skin of the client, the physician may cause some damage to the body of the patient in the course of treatment, the mover damage the furniture, and the housewife burn the roast. These considerations suggest the joint occurrence of giving and taking away will follow the circular order of resources shown in Table I, being highest for love and lowest for money. These two means of exchange are at opposite ends also with regard to the previously discussed relationship between self and other as objects.

PRODUCTION AND EXCHANGE OF RESOURCES

The preceding analysis of the relationship among exchange behaviors proposes that different resources do not obey the same rules. The change from one resource to another appears, however, to be gradual and to follow the order of the resources. At one extreme there is money, where giving to self excludes giving to other and taking away excludes giving. For money, therefore, each transaction can be described by a single value: if A gives five dollars to B, A has five dollars less and B five dollars more. As any accountant knows, the amount credited to an account should be the same as the amount debited to another account. At the other extreme there is love; our accountant would probably tend his resignation if requested to keep books on love exchanges. Here, giving to the other often increases the amount left for self and giving does not necessarily rule out a certain amount of taking away. The other resources fall between these extremes of love and money according to their position in the order of resources.

If by giving love to other one increases the amount left for self, then this resource is apparently produced through exchange.

Production through exchange is less pronounced for status and even less so for information. For resources at the other extreme of the order, namely money and goods, production and exchange appear to be quite distinct. The lack of mutual exclusiveness between giving and taking away, which seems to characterize love and, to a lesser extent, its neighboring resources, suggests that the production of these resources is accompanied by a certain degree of destruction or waste. Interestingly enough, the production of other resources appears also to generate hostile feelings, as shown, for example, by the work of Bales (1951) on task groups. It is possible, therefore, that the concomitance of giving and taking away characterizes production rather than exchange. Ambivalence in love would then result from the overlapping of production and exchange in this resource.

Parsons (1951, p. 124) had already noted that money has properties not shared by other phenomena in the societal system. It should be noted, however, that the same types of behavior occur for money as for other resources. It is only the relationship among these behaviors that varies for different resources, becoming perfect for money. Focusing on this difference between money and other resources rather than on the common behaviors has caused some difficulties in extending the notion of exchange to other forms of interpersonal communication. The fact that one can give without reducing the amount in his possession has been considered contradictory to the very notion of exchange (Cartwright and Zander, 1968, p. 223).

After this structural analysis of resources and behaviors, we turn to consider its relevance to other communication concepts, starting from the notions of power and need, the possession and deficit of resources in an individual.

SECTION TWO:
THEORETICAL IMPLICATIONS
AND APPLICATIONS

POWER AND NEED

Power has been defined as the ability to influence the behavior of others (Blau, 1967, p. 117) or the amount of reward and punishment one can administer to others (Thibaut and Kelley, 1959, p. 101). Behavior is changed through the administration of reward and punishment, which can be interpreted, respectively, as giving and taking away of a resource. This close relation between power and resources has been repeatedly noted by earlier investigators, as pointed out by Cartwright and Zander (1968, Chapter 17). In some cases, a specific power has been defined as possession of a specific resource, like expert power or possession of information (French and Raven, 1968). Power is defined here as the amount of a given resource that is available to an individual for eventual giving. According to this definition, power is specific to a given means of exchange, so that a person may have power in a certain situation and not in another one depending on the resource in use. With certain limitations, some of which are noted later, means are interchangeable, so that a person having great power in a particular resource may also acquire power in other means through exchange (Benoit, 1966). This may be the reason why power tends to be perceived as global rather than specific.

One could argue that the power of an individual will increase in proportion to the amount of a given resource he receives. This may be true of the more concrete resources like money and goods, but with regard to the more symbolic ones, there is need for some qualification. Receiving an amount of resource well above the expectation level may result in the phenomenon of satiation (Gewirtz and Baer, 1958). Expectation, in turn, depends on previous experience in the receiving of a given resource. If expectation is low, satiation will occur after a small amount of resource has been given. In such a case, rapid increase in power through accumulation of a resource may not be quite feasible. The finding (Eldred, Bell, Sherman, and Longabaugh, 1964) that schizophrenics appear unsuccessful in obtaining resources from other persons even after making allowances for their resource bankruptcy is significant in this respect. A person possessing little power seems to be less able to increase it, not only because he has little to offer in exchange, but also because he is less able to receive exchange for the little he has to give. Inability to receive also causes, paradoxically, a limitation in the power of the other person. This may explain the feeling of helplessness sometimes experienced in interacting with an emotionally disturbed individual. As Cartwright and Zander (1968, pp. 216-17) have pointed out, power cannot be exercised unless there is a corresponding need or motive base on the part of the potential receiver of the resource. A person can have great potential power and little actual power when there is scarce demand for the resource he possesses in abundance. The potential-actual distinction also applies to needs. Potential need is defined as shortage of a resource. Actual need is the deficit between the amount of resource received as compared with the expected one. The results of Eldred *et al.*, just noted, suggests that the schizophrenic has great potential need and little actual need. In the same way as for power, the classification and ordering of resources provides an ordered categorization of needs: to each resource corresponds a specific need. Furthermore, the needs of proximal resources may be more related than those of distal ones. Some of the needs and motivations appearing in the literature can be identified as specific to a given resource. Approval (Crowne and Marlowe, 1964), for example, appears related to love; achievement (McClelland, Atkinson, Clark, and Lowell, 1953) refers to status; curiosity or exploration (Harlow, 1953) may reflect need for information.

A communication situation where one side has great power and the other participant a strong need cannot be easily explained in terms of exchange with the other, since the latter has so little to give. Yet such situations are quite common and indeed typical in communication between a grown-up and a child: the grown-up gives more than he receives, so that his resources decrease in interaction with children. Apparently balance is restored by what the grown-up gives to himself, in status and love, by following the norm appropriate to the situation. The mother of a satisfied child perceives herself as a good mother, i.e., gives to herself love and status. In independence training, the parent gives to the child and requires in "exchange" that the child should give to himself; e.g., the child is praised for washing his hands. This exchange occurs also in the psychotherapeutic situation which is discussed later. In both cases the balance is apparently made up by self-giving of the more powerful partner. Giving to himself may enable an individual to continue a communicative situation which is, in reality or in appearance, to his own disadvantage in interpersonal terms. Inclusion of self as recipient offers, therefore, a possible solution to the problem of egoism (Gouldner, 1966, p. 141). It follows that social exchange is not, for most resources, a zero-sum game (Thibaut and Kelley, 1959, p. 24): what an individual receives is usually more than what the other gives to him, since it includes also what the individual gives to himself. As the poet said, "I have what I have given."

RESOURCES AND COGNITIVE GROWTH

Resources are transmitted from parents to child, so that children will tend to be deficient in resources scarce to their parents. This statement is self-evident with regard to material things, money and goods, but, paradoxically, it may apply with even more cogency to less tangible resources like love, status, and information. There is, indeed, evidence indicating that for the latter resources, deficit in early age impairs ability for exchange later on. With regard to information, an exhaustive review of findings in animals and humans is given by Hunt, who concludes: "It is fairly clear from the evidence surveyed in these chapters that impoverishment of experience during the early months can slow up the development of intelligence" (Hunt, 1961, p. 346). Studying the effects of early deprivation of contacts with mother and/or peers presumably involving love and status, Harlow and Harlow (1962) found that deprived baby monkeys had later difficulty in mating, in establishing dominance relations (status), and were unable to give love to their offsprings. As these findings suggest, the ability to function efficiently and autonomously in exchanging resources as an adult member of society may, therefore, depend on receiving adequate resources in early age. This statement rests on two hypotheses which should be examined separately. The first hypothesis proposes that efficient communicative behavior requires a certain degree of cognitive differentiation, similar for both the sender and the receiver of the communication. The second hypothesis suggests that such a cognitive differentiation develops in childhood through adequate differential stimuli from the social environment. When stimuli are scarce or inappropriate the child's cognitive structure will deviate from that of other individuals, thus hindering his communication with them.

COGNITIVE MATCHING IN COMMUNICATION

Overt behavior (raising the right hand, smiling, uttering certain words) is without meaning unless it is recognized as an instance of a given conceptual class, such as giving love to the other. It is well-known that the same behavior may have a different meaning in various cultures: a pat on the back means giving love in Western culture and taking away status in the Far Eastern one. Thus cognitive organization may be regarded as a device for encoding outgoing messages and for decoding forthcoming ones. A received message acquires meaning by being matched against the appropriate cognitive class. It is of interest to note that matching-response models have been suggested to account for perception of external stimuli in general (MacKay, 1963; Miller, Galanter, and Pribram, 1960; quoted by Rodgers and Ziegler, 1967). In social communication, however, the stimulus emitted by the sender originates in his cognitive organization so that, ultimately, the matching is between the cognitive structures of the participants in the communication. Mismatching will occur: (1)

when the sender and the receiver use different cognitive classes or meanings for the same overt behavior, as in the case of an American patting a Far Easterner on the back; and (2) when the structures of the sender and the receiver are dissimilar in degree of differentiation among cognitive classes. It has been found, for example, that differentiation between love and status is higher in modern Western culture than in the traditional society of the Middle East (Foa, 1964). The following real life episode will illustrate how this cognitive difference may affect communication. An Arab student is working with some American students on a class project. Some of the proposals made by the Arab student are criticized by one of the Americans. The two students had planned to go to the movies together after the class, but the Arab student says he is busy and will not be able to go. For the American, differentiation between status and love is fairly clear-cut. Criticisim of the Arab's proposal meant a mild denial of status but did not have any affective implication. This differentiation is rather weak in the cognitive organization of the Arab, so that for him, denial of status means denial of love. "He does not like me," translates the Arab student, and then: "Why should I give him affect by going to the movies with him?" The Arab and American students had difficulties in communicating because of differences in their respective cognitive structures, reflecting, in turn, cultural diversity (Foa, 1967).

These culturally determined degrees of differentiation are transmitted to the child by his parents and other adults with whom he communicates. If these adults deviate from the prevailing culture, the child is likely to pick up these deviations, although absence of deviation in the communicator does not necessarily assure that the child will not deviate.

LEARNING TO DIFFERENTIATE

The child may learn the appropriate degree of differentiation by imitating the differentiating behaviors of the adult (Bandura and Walters, 1963) and by differential rewards and punishments contingent upon his behavior (Bijou and Baer, 1961). Parents will, for example, punish the child for taking away behaviors and will reward him for giving behaviors. In this manner, they provide models of giving (reward) and taking away (punishment) behaviors while, at the same time, exposing the child to differential reinforcements of the same behaviors when emitted by him. The two learning models, imitation and reinforcement, may lead to opposite predictions about change in the child's behavior. Consider, for example, a child who has been punished for beating his younger brother (taking away services). The imitation model predicts an increase in taking away behavior of the child, who will imitate the aggressive punitive parent. The reinforcement model, on the other hand, predicts a decrease of the punished behavior. A solution to this dilemma may be provided by the findings of Sears, Maccoby, and Levin (1957, Chapter 7). Their results suggest that if the child takes away a service (e.g., beating) and he's punished by his parents by taking away the *same* resource from him (physical punishment), the imitation model will prevail and the child will show high frequency of taking away services. If, on the other hand, punishment consists of taking away from the child a *different* resource, such as status ("you are a bad boy") then the reinforcement model will operate with consequent low frequency of the punished behavior. This interpretation of Sears' findings suggests that imitation is more resource-specific than reinforcement. Both mechanisms, however, require that the differentiation to be learned by the child preexists in the adult. If, in the behavior of the parents, giving and taking away are not well-differentiated, it will be difficult for the child to acquire such a differentiation. Likewise, when the behavior of the parents is determined by their own needs rather than by those of the child, differentiation between self and other as objects can be impaired. A child receiving money or goods where love and status would be appropriate, may experience difficulties in differentiating among resources.

It will be apparent, by now, that the proposed classification of resources and communication behaviors is essentially an attempt to spell out some of the differentiations that a child should acquire in order to become a resource-exchanging member of adult society. This classification implies indeed a cognitive organization differentiating between giving and taking, between objects or receivers, and among the various resources. In an earlier discussion of the differentiation between giving and taking, as well as between self and other as objects, it has been proposed that the former precedes the latter in the development sequence of the child (Foa, 1966). Here we shall devote some attention to the sequence of differentiation among resources.

SEQUENCE OF DIFFERENTIATION
AMONG RESOURCES

In early infancy the infant is exposed to an undifferentiated bundle of love and service: the flowing milk, the warmth and softness of his mother's body, and her care for him. The differentiation between love and services becomes possible after the child has acquired some psychomotoric skills sufficient for giving some services to himself, like feeding himself, washing hands, etc. At this time, mother can give him love without services by requesting him to serve himself and, at the same time, encouraging him to do so (Parsons, 1955, pp. 69-77). Thus differentiation between love and services appear closely related to differentiation between self and others as *actors* (Foa, 1966): mother gives love, the child gives services (to himself). A situation in which love and services were, from the onset, provided by different actors was experimentally devised by Harlow (1958): infant monkeys were given two mother surrogates, one soft (love giving) and one hard. Only one of the two mothers lactated; thus in the group where the wire mother provided milk (service), the two resources of love and service were given by different mothers. The monkeys developed affection (giving love) for the soft mother, independently of whether she lactated or not.

Successively to this first differentiation between love and services, goods are differentiated from services and status from love. Consumption goods, like food, are hard to differentiate from service, since they can be used only once. It is only when the child becomes interested in durable goods, such as toys which can be used again and again, that the differentiation between services and goods becomes feasible. The differentiation of status from love requires some acquisition of language because most status-giving behaviors ("gee you did it") are verbal. It appears also to be related to the differentiation between mother and father as social objects (Foa, Triandis, and Katz, 1966): love is given mainly by mother and status by father (Parsons, 1955, p. 45; Zelditch, 1955). In some animals, rituals for establishing status are evolved from love rituals, i.e., behaviors toward mate or elders (Lorenz, 1966, pp. 135-6). Later on, money is differentiated from goods and information from status. Money is a promise of future goods, so that this differentiation requires some ability to delay rewards. Children have been trained to accept tokens (a kind of money) by first having them paired with valuable goods, like M & M candies (Hamblin, Buckhold, Bushell, Ellis, and Feritor, 1969). At first, information is hardly distinguishable from status: parents praise their children for the new information they have acquired. When the child broadens his social world to contact with peers, he has the opportunity to discover criteria for status, such as strength, which are different from information.

This sequence of resource differentiation in the child, progressing by stages from love to money, offers a developmental explanation of the relationship among exchange behaviors. The differentiation between giving and taking and between objects is relatively weak for love and increases as one moves from love to money along the order of resources. The concept of love develops early, at a time when differentiation among behaviors is still weak. Later on, while new resources become differentiated, differentiation among behaviors also increases. Thus, the more distal is a resource from love, i.e., the later it develops, the stronger will be the differentiation among the behaviors of this resource. The last resource to develop, money, presents a complete differentiation of its behaviors. It seems, therefore, that the degree of differentiation among the behaviors of a given resource is related to the position of this resource in the sequence of resource differentiation.

Differentiation among resources does not mean complete independence; some relationship is likely to remain. An adult may prefer a restaurant where "service is good" (i.e., where love is given in addition to service); children may insist on receiving services from their mothers long after having acquired skills for self-service. These situations suggest that service is not fully differentiated from love. The differentiation between love and status appears to be rather weak in some traditional cultures, as the episode of the Arab student may show. If information, in turn, is related to status, it can be expected that higher status individuals will tend to be regarded as likely sources of information. Some evidence to this effect is provided by studies of imitation in children (Baldwin, 1967, p. 431; Bandura, 1965, p. 9) and possibly also in monkeys (Hall, 1963), and by experiments showing that statements attributed to prestigious individuals are more likely to be accepted (Asch, 1948; Lewis, 1941; Sherif, 1935). Informal observation suggests that wise men are honored and humble ones are assumed to be ignorant.

This sequence of differentiations among classes of resources is identical with the proposed order among them (see Table I). In fact, the order rests on the assumption that the differentiation of a new resource from a preexisting one is never fully completed so that proximal resources are related more than remote ones. Complete differentiation would mean that all the resources are independent of each other. By assuming partial differentiation, we have attempted to link the order to the developmental sequence. Starting from the caring love of the mother, differentiation on the concreteness dimension results in the development of the notion of services (more concrete than love) and of status (less concrete than love). Then the two branches continue to differentiate, along the second dimension, from more to less particularist resources. The least particularist one, money, although differentiating from goods is also close to information, as evidenced by institutional arrangements such as patenting and copyright, permitting the exchange of information for money. The model for the child's differentiation of resources is provided by the institutional structure of his society and transmitted through the parents. In a culture where trade is by barter, neither the child nor his parents will have to differentiate money from goods. Social institutions specialize in the exchange of specific resources, while barring certain others, so that they can be viewed both as channels and constraints to interpersonal communication. Conversely, resource specialization differentiates among institutions of the same society and the degree of differentiation varies for different cultures. To this aspect of social organization we now turn.

INSTITUTIONAL AND CULTURAL CONSTRAINTS

Consider the following situation: the guest is about to leave after having been treated to a very good dinner. What shall he give in exchange? In a private house, he would probably thank the hostess profusely, expressing his pleasure for the pleasant evening (giving love) and his admiration for her cooking skills (giving status). In a restaurant, he will pay the bill and leave a tip on the table for the waitress. It is easy to imagine what would happen if the guest would give money for the meal in a private home or if he would express his pleasure at the restaurant and leave without paying. In both the latter cases, he is likely to find himself in trouble. It appears, therefore, that not every type of exchange is permissible in any given institution; an exchange appropriate to the commercial catering institution may be highly unsuitable for the hospitality institution and vice versa. Moreover, it seems that in each institution certain means of exchange are more typical and significant, although other means may appear as well in interactions within the institution. The exchange money-services appears to be typical of the work institution; the exchange money-information of the school institution, if private, or status-information, if public; money-goods exchange is typical of the trade institution. In the family, love and status appear to be the crucial resources. In these institutional examples, the means exchanged tend to be proximal in the order of resources given in Table I. This may tentatively suggest that each institution will focus on a particular segment of the order. In fact, it is difficult to think of an institution where the crucial resources exchanged are remote from one another in the order, like love and money, goods and status, or services and information.

The family is probably the institution where the widest range of exchange is found, but even here not every exchange is permissible or customary: one is not supposed to give money for a service received in the family. The wife of a colleague of mine asks money for shining her husband's shoes. Her explanation for this seemingly strange request is that shoe shining is not part of the normal duties of a housewife.

Institutional specialization in particular means of exchange seems to be stronger in modern Western society than in more traditional ones (Foa, 1967). There is indeed some evidence suggesting that in traditional societies the difference between one institution and another, in terms of means of exchange, is less pronounced than in the modern western world (Foa and Chemers, 1966; Mitchell and Foa, 1969). A preliminary analysis of critical incidents between Americans and Thais suggests that some of the tension generated in these incidents stemmed from cultural differences about the means of exchange appropriate to a particular institution, usually work. The exchange expected by the Americans did not match the expectation of the Thai. Frequently, the Thai expected to receive status and sometimes also love in situations where giving these resources was not appropriate, according to American culture.

Here is an illustrative episode in which the Thai's expectation of receiving status was not met. Colonel Samuel Holden and three other American staff officers arrived at a conference to talk with the Thai Army Staff about developing the defensive fortifications of Thailand. One of the Thai Staff officers, Lt. Col. Bancha, who a few weeks earlier had been in a short training course conducted by Col. Holden, came up to say "Hello" and exchange pleasantries. The American said "Hello," but remarked that he had little time at the moment and wished to get the meeting started. During the meeting, Col. Holden introduced many U.S. proposals for helping the defensive build-up and the conversation between the Thais and the Americans flowed freely. Only Colonel Bancha failed to participate.

In the following episode, the Thais expected to receive love, but their expectation was not fulfilled. The Thai Government had given an American construction company a contract to enlarge and remodel the national railroad station in Thonburi. Charles Adams was appointed manager to handle the company's business in Bangkok, and Charles recruited a staff of about forty local personnel to handle bookkeeping, records, etc. From the time these employees began their work with the company, Charles found himself having to listen to and advise them on their family affairs and health problems. This took so much of Charles' time that he found it necessary to tell them to stop seeing him about personal affairs that were not the company's business. Soon Charles felt that his employees were not as friendly to him as before and he noticed that they often went to talk to his Thai assistant.

Incidents like these were collected to provide material for training persons of different cultural backgrounds to improve communication. Their usefulness in studying means of exchange is limited since the resources involved are not fully specified in the story. They tend, however, to support the view that facilitations and limitations provided by social institutions for the exchange of certain resources are culturally determined.

EXCHANGE IN PSYCHOTHERAPY

The psychotherapeutic situation can be seen as an institution, in the sense that it provides an opportunity for the exchange of certain resources, while barring certain other ones. Furthermore, resource exchange appears to vary, in theory and perhaps also in practice, for different therapeutic schools. Consider three different schools: the behavioristic, the Rogerian, and the orthodox psychoanalytic. In each of them it might be possible to specify the resources involved in the behavior of the therapist toward the patient, as well as in the behavior of the patient toward the therapist and toward himself. The behavior of the therapist toward himself is not included, since little information about it can be found in the theory of the respective schools, and one is led to presume that it should not be much in evidence in the therapeutic situation. The learning analysis of the therapist, required in psychoanalysis, is indeed meant to free the analyst from concern with his own problem, i.e., to reduce the frequency of his behavior toward himself. On the other hand, the behavior of the patient toward himself appears to be very relevant to psychotherapy. When therapy is behavioristic, for example, the patient is quite likely to be rewarded for doing some service to himself, such as feeding himself, whereas the patient's giving love to self is desirable in client-centered therapy. As already noted, this kind of exchange occurs also between parents and child in training for independence.

SELECTIVITY OF SCHOOLS

Each school appears to prefer certain resources and to exclude certain others. In behavior therapy, the rewards given by the therapist to the patient often appear to be money or tokens and goods, like M & M candies. Love and status seem to be in little use and, according to some reports (Hamblin *et al.*, 1969), giving status or approval has not proved very effective. Punishment, when used, is likely to be in the form of taking away a service, such as mild electrical shock. Information does not seem to play much of a role in behavior therapy. There are apparently no resources that the subject ought to give to the therapist, but he is expected to give himself certain services, such as keeping clean, assuming a certain posture, and the like. Often the behavior rewarded may be toward a third individual and, in this case, most resources can be involved.

In Rogerian therapy, the client is to receive love and status from the therapist and to give these resources to himself. Some results, given later, suggest that this exchange may run into difficulties with schizophrenics in regard to love and with neurotics in regard to status, since the respective correlations between receiving from other and giving to self are rather low in these cases. The sole resource the client is expected to give the therapist is information, talking about himself. The resource exchange of client-centered therapy appears, therefore, to be different from the one of behavior therapy.

Still another picture is presented by orthodox psychoanalysis. Here the therapist is expected to give information to the patient in the form of interpretation of the material (free association, dreams, etc.) supplied by the latter. The therapist appears also likely to take away status from the patient by putting him in a position of inferiority; lying on the couch without being able to see the therapist is indicative in this respect. The analyst should be perceived as a stern and superior father image. It seems also that taking away money from the patient, making him pay for the treatment, is considered a relevant aspect of the psychoanalytic treatment. The therapist is not expected to give love to the patient (counter-transference is indeed discouraged) nor to give goods or services. The administration of services such as shots and other forms of physical treatment may, however, occur irrespective of school when the therapist is a psychiatrist.

In orthodox psychoanalysis, the patient should give information and money to the therapist, as already noted. He is also expected to give him love (transference) and status by recognizing his superior position in the situation. At the same time, the patient is expected to take away status from himself. The existence of defense mechanisms is assumed to lead the patient to rationalize and misinterpret his behavior, thus taking away information from himself, in the terminology adopted here.

TABLE II.

Resource Exchange in Three Psychotherapeutic Schools

Behavior	Resource	School		
		Behavioristic	Rogerian	Orthodox Psychoanalysis
Therapist	Love	?	+	0
to	Status	?	+	-
Patient	Information	0	0	+
	Money	+	0	-
	Goods	+	0	0
	Services	-	0	0
Patient	Love	0	0	+
to	Status	0	0	+
Therapist	Information	0	+	+
	Money	0	0	+
	Goods	0	0	0
	Services	0	0	0
Patient	Love	0	+	0
to	Status	0	+	-
Self	Information	0	+	-
	Money	0	0	0
	Goods	0	0	0
	Services	+	0	0

This attempt to describe three schools of therapy in terms of resource exchange is summarized in Table II. In this table, giving is indicated by a plus sign and taking away by a minus sign. A zero indicates absence of both giving and taking away. No sign has been used to indicate ambivalence or joint occurrence of giving and taking, as we were unable to find prescriptions for it in the theory of the various schools. This does not mean, of course, that ambivalence cannot occur in practice. A question mark has been used when we felt unable to reach even a tentative decision with regard to the use of a particular resource. In Table II, resources are listed in their proposed order as given previously in Table I. It should be remembered, however, that this order is circular so that the first and last resources in the list are also neighbors.

SELECTIVITY AND ORDER

Listing the resources in their order reveals an interesting property: identical signs appear next to each other in the order so that there is no mixing up of different signs. The pluses, minuses, and zeros are grouped together. The sole exception is in the behavior of therapist to patient in psychoanalysis, where the taking of status is separated from the taking of money by a giving of the intervening resource, information. The position of the zeros in the behavior of the patient toward himself for psychoanalysis, and in the behavior of the patient toward the therapist for Rogerian treatment, may give the false impression of deviating from the order. The order is, however, circular, services being closer to love, so that the zeros are actually grouped together.

The grouping of the resources in all three schools, while providing further support for the proposed order of resources, also suggests that in each school similar or neighboring resources are likely to be treated in a similar manner. This manner appears to be different in each school: the profiles of signs in Table II differentiate very well among the schools. For each of the three types of behavior, the profile of signs is always different in the various schools. In fact, the patient behavior toward self with regard to status would be sufficient to differentiate among schools: status is taken away from self in the Freudian, given in the Rogerian, neither given nor taken in the behavioristic school. Another difference among the schools, related to exchange but not appearing in Table II, is the degree to which the behavior of the therapist toward the patient is contingent upon the behavior of the patient toward the therapist, himself, or a third individual. The strictest contingency is likely to be found in behavioristic treatment where reward and punishment administered by the therapist are determined by the behavior of the patient. At the other end, the Rogerian therapist is assumed to keep his behavior independent of the patient's behavior; his giving of love and status is unconditional. Orthodox psychoanalysis probably occupies, in this respect, an intermediate position: the analyst may, for example, modify his behavior if the patient is resistant.

These considerations, tentative as they may be, suggest that the resources exchanged differ in the various schools of psychotherapy and that each school tends to treat similarly resources which are proximal in the order. In this respect, these three schools appear to constitute different institutions: like social institutions, each school prescribes particular exchanges and bars certain others.

In comparing different therapeutic approaches, the strongest contrast is provided by the Rogerian and behavioristic treatments. Love and status are prominent in the former and absent in the latter. Data presented in the next section suggest that deviations in the cognitive organization of mental patients with regard to behaviors dealing with these two resources are likely to impair their ability to exchange love and/or status. For this reason, these resources may not be effective in behavior therapy where the giving of the therapist is strictly contingent upon the response of the patient. Using love and status as rewards would be somewhat like attempting to train a pigeon by rewarding it with dollar bills. In client-centered therapy, on the other hand, the very absence of contingency permits the giving of these resources, hoping to modify the cognitive structure of the patient toward normalcy through such an unconditional giving.

Even if these considerations are speculative, it seems plain that we will have to move in the direction of matching the resource exchanged in the therapeutic situation with the specific exchange problems of various types of patients, so as to assure that each patient receives the exchanges most appropriate for him. A first step toward this goal is to investigate the cognitive organization of exchange behaviors in patients and normals. Some data of this type[2], dealing with exchange of love and status in schizophrenic and neurotic patients as compared to other groups of subjects, are given in the next section.

LOVE AND STATUS IN MENTAL PATIENTS AND OTHER SUBJECTS

Using the Role Behavior Test (Foa, 1966), the perceived exchange of love and status in various positions and various populations of subjects was studied.[3] The positions, populations, and their size are given in Table III.

The data reported here refer to the perceived amount of love and status a significant other in the dyadic pair gives to the subject and the amount of the status and love given by the subject to the other and to himself. Details about the manner in which these

---

[2]Foa, Edna, unpublished research, 1969.

[3]Grant RD-2743-P-68 from the Social and Rehabilitation Service, Department of Health, Education, and Welfare provided partial support for the collection of these data.

TABLE III.

Populations and Positions

Population	Position	Size of Sample
Normal Adult Males (Jerusalem, Israel)	Husband to Wife	633
Normal Adult Females (Jerusalem, Israel)	Wife to Husband	633
Delinquent Boys (Missouri)	Son to Mother	41
	Son to Father	29
Delinquent Girls (Missouri)	Daughter to Father	17
	Daughter to Mother	34
Schizophrenics (Missouri)	Spouse to Spouse	30
Neurotics (Missouri)	Spouse to Spouse	30

data were collected are given elsewhere (Foa, 1966). Here, it may suffice to say that each variable is represented in the test by three scalable short stories about a given behavior. These three items express essentially the same meaning, but with different words and with different degrees of intensity or extremeness. Items belonging to the same variable do not follow in order, but are scattered randomly in the test. The items are semi-projective, i.e., the subject is not asked to state whether he or his partner behave in a given manner, but how often his behavior is similar to the one described in the item. For example, the three stories referring to the husband's giving status to his wife are as follows:

Jack has consideration for his wife and displays respect and esteem toward her.

Dick thinks his wife is very successful and especially esteems her personality and her actions.

Bill is sure that everything his wife does is important and good and there is no limit to the esteem and importance that he attributes to her.

Examples of stories for other behavior are:

Giving status to self: Jack is a husband who esteems himself and relies on himself and on his decisions.

Giving love to self: Dick is a husband who is satisfied with his actions and feels very much at peace with himself.

Taking away status from wife: Jack slightly criticizes his wife's behavior and thinks that she makes a few mistakes.

Taking away love from self: Bill is a husband very dissatisfied with himself and his behavior towards his wife; he rejects and blames himself.

Similar stories were used for the behavior of the wife and for the children-parents positions. After each story, two questions were asked:

    Actual level: Do you behave toward your wife as does the husband in the story? (Almost always, generally, sometimes, seldom, almost never.)

    Ideal level: Do you think a husband should behave as does the husband in the story in relation to his wife?

A scale score was computed for each subject on each variable. This score is derived from the subject's answers on the three items pertaining to a given variable. Scores were then intercorrelated. The correlation coefficients given in the upper half of Table IV indicate the relationship between the amount received from and the amount given to other in each one of the two resources, for each type of population studied. The coefficients in the lower half of the table relate the amount received from other to the amount given to self. The correlations between giving to and receiving from other indicate to what extent there is a mutual exchange in a particular resource. High correlation would suggest that the amount given and the amount received tend to be similar, that a certain balance exists in the exchange.[4] The correlations between receiving from other and giving to self show to what extent the subject's self-acceptance is dependent on the resources received from a significant other. The previous discussion of exchange in childhood and in psychotherapy would suggest a predominance of dependence over mutual exchange in parent-child relations and possibly also in pathological states. The correlations presented in Table IV may provide some answer to this problem.

    1. *Comparison of exchange and dependence.* Comparing the coefficients for exchange, in the upper half of Table IV, with those for dependence, in the lower half of the table, shows that in normal adults there is always more exchange than dependence with regard to both status and love. The predominance of exchange over dependence tends to decrease for delinquent boys and girls in their relation to parents. Dependence, in turn, becomes dominant in schizophrenics for status and in neurotics for love.

    2. *Comparison of love and status.* Exchange and dependence are generally higher for status than for love. This relationship is, however, reversed in the role of a son to mother: here love is predominant, as predicted by Parsons (Parsons and Bales, 1955).

---

[4] The correlations would also be high when there is little or no interaction. The means of the variables indicate, however, that this is not the case for the data presented here.

TABLE IV.

Intercorrelation of Giving and Receiving Status and Love in Various Populations and Family Positions

RECEIVING FROM OTHER

Behavior	Resource	Normal Adult Male — Husband to wife		Normal Adult Female — Wife to husband		Delinquent Boys — Son to mother		Delinquent Boys — Son to father		Delinquent Girls — Daughter to father		Delinquent Girls — Daughter to mother		Schizophrenics — Spouse to spouse		Neurotics — Spouse to spouse	
		Status	Love	Status	Love	Status	Love	Status	Love	Status	Love	Status	Love	Status	Love	Status	Love
Giving to Other	Status	60	55	57	49	39	48	64	41	95	91	74	77	36	17	34	31
	Love	55	53	47	45	39	49	46	47	82	86	63	76	35	18	18	11
Giving to Self	Status	41	30	38	20	47	42	46	33	93	90	68	55	49	12	27	25
	Love	38	22	32	18	39	59	55	48	80	70	56	59	51	15	42	38

Note—Decimal point omitted.

Neurotics are slightly more dependent on love than on status. The opposite is true for schizophrenics.

The exchanges of love for status and of status for love are almost even in normal adults. Boys and girls, on the other hand, are somewhat more likely to give status to mother in exchange for love received than the other way around. The girl also gives status to father in exchange for love. In the son-father relation the contrary happens: the son is more likely to give love in exchange for status than to give status for receiving love. In neurotics, the exchange of status for love appears to predominate, while the contrary, giving love to obtain status, occurs in schizophrenics.

3. *Comparison among groups of subjects.* Mutual exchanges of love and status are lower for patients than for any other group of subjects. Status exchange is also low between son and mother. Dependence is higher for teen-agers than for adults. Among the latter, schizophrenics have high dependence for status and neurotics for love.

Our group of schizophrenics exhibits a low degree of exchange and relatively high dependence for status. Similar results are reported by Eldred and others (1964) in comparing schizophrenics with ward personnel using a different procedure for observation. In their study, schizophrenics were found to have a lower rate of exchange than ward personnel and to be more dependent. It was also found that they are less successful in obtaining resources from the other person and less likely to be resource givers than resource receivers. This similarity of findings on schizophrenics between the two studies is noteworthy in view of the different methods of observation. Our data are based on the patient's self-reporting of family relations; Eldred's data were obtained by the recording of a trained observer. It is well-known that different observers may give diverging accounts of the same social interaction (e.g., Foa, 1966; Mitchell and Foa, 1969). Furthermore, behavior in a hospital ward does not have to be the same as in the family. Yet the characteristics noted on the behavior of the schizophrenic are apparently strong enough to cut across various observation approaches, as well as across different positions of the patient.

THE INTERVIEW: VERBAL BEHAVIOR
AND RESOURCE EXCHANGE

Some of the chapters in this volume deal with verbal behavior and with the analysis of the subject's verbal fluency in various experimental conditions. It is, therefore, pertinent to ask in which way the model presented in this chapter relates to these other studies. Resource exchange is just a particular way of classifying interpersonal communication, i.e., behavior in a social situation. It is obviously not the only possible way, as Longabaugh (1963) has pointed out in discussing the differences between his system and Bales' interaction process analysis. Whatever system of classification one adopts, some information has to be thrown away, while other information, deemed more relevant or important, will be stressed. A good classification system should cover many events with few concepts and lead to meaningful prediction about these events. Within these limitations, resource exchange is equivalent to social communication. A good deal of this behavior is verbal. Indeed, the exchange of information is almost always verbal. Exchange of love and status is often verbal, but not always so. Verbal activity is likely to accompany the exchange of money, goods, and services. It follows that fluency can be taken as a crude index of the extent to which resources are smoothly exchanged in a particular situation. Pauses and other fluency disturbances, on the other hand, may indicate the existence of some problem in the exchange of resources, as, for example, a perceived discrepancy between actual and expected exchange. Productivity may thus be related to both expected and actual levels of exchange, but particularly to the former. This interpretation of speech characteristics is supported by the findings reported by Siegman and Pope in this volume, showing that: (1) A warm interviewer, who *actually* gives love, increases both the productivity and the fluency of the interviewee. (2) A high status interviewer, who may *potentially* give status, increases productivity but not fluency. The differential effect appears to depend on love being actually given, while status is only potentially available. These findings of Siegman and Pope serve also to clarify the fact that in the interview situation the exchange of resources is much less institutionalized than in psychotherapy. It is quite clear that the interviewee is expected to give information. What he should expect to receive is not, however, institutionally prescribed and likely to vary from one interview to another.[5] Giving information to other does not always provide information for self so that, in order to

---

[5]A. W. Siegman, personal communication.

maintain the flow of information, the interviewer should give some resource in exchange. Both money and status, which are neighbors of information in the order of resources, are exchanged for information through status more often than money in interviewing. A well-trained interviewer will convey to the interviewee the feeling that the information he gives is of great interest and importance. At the same time, he will refrain from making status-giving contingent upon the kind of information received by expressed approval or disapproval. Absence of contingency and exchange of status for information make the interview situation similar to Rogerian therapy, though not identical. The interview may focus on different topics depending on its purpose, whereas client-centered therapy is primarily concerned with behavior toward self. In Rogers' therapy, information is exchanged for love and status; in the interview, the resources given in exchange may be money and/or status, but other resources may also be used since the expectation of the interviewee is not institutionalized. This lack of clear expectations about the resources the interviewee is to obtain may explain why Siegman and Pope were able to influence the behavior of the interviewee by manipulating the resources offered by the interviewer. This interpretation is further supported by their finding that a previous "cold" interview reduces the effect of a subsequent "warm" one. The previous cold interview reduces the interviewee's expectation of receiving love so that, when love is actually offered, he is less able to take profit of it. If expectation of what the interviewee should receive had been institutionalized, it is unlikely that a previous single experience of "cold" interview would have had such a drastic effect on the subsequent one. Siegman and Pope also report on the effect of an ambiguous interviewer on the subject: the latter increases productivity but reduces fluency. In the absence of institutionalized expectation, the ambiguity of the interviewer leaves the subject in the dark regarding the resources he may receive. His attempt to determine expectations increases productivity. The absence of actual exchange decreases fluency. Another independent variable, related by Siegman and Pope to speech characteristics, is anxiety. One may think of specific anxiety as an expectation of deprivation in a particular resource, and of free-floating anxiety as an expectation of unspecified deprivation. Increased productivity, as noted by Siegman and Pope under anxiety conditions, may indicate an attempt to secure the resources being threatened. A person who feels inferior may seek to gain status by talking about his "achievements." Thus productivity may relate to exchange expectations while fluency suggests actual exchange. It appears, however, that a more definite answer to these problems would require observation of the specific resources, exchanged or expected in verbal communication, to complement the analysis of formal characteristics of speech given in several papers of this volume.

CONCLUSION

This paper constitutes an attempt toward a theory of interpersonal communication based on the cognitive structure of resource exchange. The structure in the adult is viewed as an image of the institutional structure of the social system acquired in childhood through communication with significant others. Social institutions specialize in the exchange of certain resources, while excluding the exchange of certain others. The extent of specialization may vary from culture to culture, thus influencing the number of institutions and their degree of resource differentiation in each given society. Interpersonal communication seems, however, to require in every culture a certain degree of differentiation below which a society or an individual would cease to be functional. Thus the child has to learn the pattern of differentiation of his society in order to become a resource-exchanging member of it. Interaction with parents and with other persons, including peers, has the double function of providing the child with the resources he needs and with an opportunity to learn resource differentiation through imitation and the experience of differential rewards and punishments for his behavior. Culture is thus viewed as a complex learning program and, conversely, a reinforcement schedule appears to be a miniature culture. If the child fails to learn the differentiations which are culturally appropriate, either because the parents themselves deviate or because of communication problems, the cognitive structure he acquires will deviate from the normal one. Cognitive deviation will create communication problems with normal others, resulting, in turn, in abnormal behavior. Thus specific deviant patterns of over- and under-differentiation may provide a classification of behavior pathologies. Psychotherapy can then be viewed as a technique for changing degrees of differentiation toward normalcy.

The picture of interpersonal communication presented here has drawn heavily on previous research and has attempted some measure of integration. At the same time, it has generated several hypotheses requiring further research. The main ones can be summarized as follows:

1.   In the cognitive structure of the adult, resources are ordered circularly by degree of differentiation, so that the more proximal any two resources are, the less they are differentiated one from another.[6]

2.   The order of resources results from the sequence of resource differentiation in the child, each resource being closest in the order to the other one from which it has been differentiated.

3.   The later a given resource is differentiated, the stronger is the differentiation between behavior toward self and toward other, as well as between behavior of giving and taking for this resource.

4.   The ability to function as an adult is impaired by scarcity of resources in childhood.

5.   Needs, powers, and motives are related in the same order as their respective resources.

6.   Substitution of one resource for another is more likely when these resources are proximal in the order than when they are distal.[6]

7.   Resources exchanged in any given social institution tend to be proximal in the order. The same applies to schools of psychotherapy.

8.   The range of resources exchanged in any social institution varies culturally, being narrower for modern society than for more traditional ones.

Further progress toward a theory of interpersonal communication will require testing these hypotheses, for which only partial and indirect support exists so far. At the same time, one should proceed with the formulation of the theory. The notions presented in this chapter constitute only a partial beginning, dealing mainly with behaviors of giving. An analysis of the "taking" behaviors still remains to be done. If taking away is equivalent to aggression, there might be one type of aggression for each resource, and these types might be related in the same way as are resources. Likewise, frustration may be interpreted as loss of a resource or as failure to receive an expected one. If frustration leads to aggression, it is possible that a frustrated person will tend to take away a resource proximal to the one which had been taken from him. Failure to discuss taking behaviors is clearly a shortcoming of this paper, but certainly not the only one. The classification of resources, for example, may be criticized as being ill-defined and too gross: can services to the person and to his belongings be put in the same class? It may be necessary to subdivide this class, since personal services are closer to love, whereas services to objects will be more related with goods. In the same

---

[6]Empirical support for this hypothesis has been obtained in the meantime.

manner, it may be necessary to subdivide "goods" into "durable" and "consumption," the latter being closer to services.

In spite of its imperfection, we hope that this chapter will contribute to the comprehension of interpersonal communication. The research of the last few decades has produced an amazing amount of findings, but has also led to theoretical fragmentation. The need for organizing the newly gained knowledge is thus clear. This report is presented as a modest attempt in such direction.

References

ASCH, S. E. The doctrine of suggestion, prestige, and imitation in social psychology. *Psychol. Rev.*, 1948, **55**, 250-76.

BALDWIN, A. L. *Theories of Child Development.* Wiley, New York, 1967.

BALES, R. F. *Interaction Process Analysis.* Addison-Wesley, Cambridge, Mass., 1951.

BANDURA, A. Vicarious processes: A case of no-trial learning. In L. Berkowitz (Ed.), *Advances in Experimental Social Psychology,* Vol. 2. Academic Press, New York, 1965. Pp. 1-55.

BANDURA, A. and WALTERS, R. H. *Social Learning and Personality Development.* Holt, Rinehart & Winston, New York, 1963.

BENOIT, E. Status, status types, and status interrelations. In B. J. Biddle and E. J. Thomas (Eds.), *Role Theory: Concepts and Research.* Wiley, New York, 1966. Pp. 77-80.

BIJOU, S. W. and BAER, D. M. *Child Development: A Systematic and Empirical Theory.* Appleton-Century-Crofts, New York, 1961.

BLAU, P. M. *Exchange and Power in Social Life.* Wiley, New York, 1967.

CARTWRIGHT, D. and ZANDER, A. Power and influence in groups: Introduction. In D. Cartwright and A. Zander (Eds.), *Group Dynamics: Research and Theory.* Harper & Row, New York, 1968. Pp. 215-35.

CROWNE, D. P. and MARLOWE, D. *The Approval Motive: Studies in Evaluative Dependence.* Wiley, New York, 1964.

ELDRED, S. H., BELL, N. W., LONGABAUGH, R. and SHERMAN, L. J. Interactional correlates of chronicity in schizophrenia. *Psychiat. Res. Rep. 19,* American Psychiatric Association, December, 1964, 1-12.

ELDRED, S. H., BELL, N. W., SHERMAN, L. J., and LONGABAUGH, R. H. Classification and analysis of interaction patterns on a ward for chronic schizophrenics. *Disord. Communication,* 1964, **42**, 381-6.

FANON, F. *The Wretched of the Earth.* Gove Press, New York, 1963.

FOA, U. G. Cross-cultural similarity and difference in interpersonal behavior. *J. Abnorm. Soc. Psychol.,* 1964, **68**, 517-22.

FOA, U. G. Perception of behavior in reciprocal roles: The ringex model. *Psychol. Monog.,* 1966, **80** (15, Whole No. 623).

FOA, U. G. Differentiation in cross-cultural communication. In L. Thayer (Ed.), *Communication: Concepts and Perspective.* Spartan Books, Washington, 1967. Pp. 135-51.

FOA, U. G. Three kinds of behavioral change. *Psychol. Bull.,* 1968, **70**, 460-73.

FOA, U. G., TRIANDIS, H. C., and KATZ, E. W. Cross-cultural invariance in the differentiation and organization of family roles. *J. Personal. Soc. Psychol.,* 1966, **4**, 316-27.

FOA, U. G. and CHEMERS, M. M. The significance of role behavior differentiation for cross-cultural interaction training. *Internat. J. Psychol.,* 1967, **2**, 45-8.

FRENCH, J. R. P., JR. and RAVEN, B. The bases of social power. In Cartwright and Zander, *op. cit.* Pp. 259-69.

GEWIRTZ, J. L. and BAER, D. M. Deprivation and satiation of social reinforcers as drive conditions. *J. Abnorm. Soc. Psychol.,* 1958, **57**, 165-72.

GOULDNER, A. W. The norm of reciprocity: A preliminary statement. In Biddle and Thomas, *op. cit.* Pp. 136-44.

HALL, K. R. Observational learning in monkeys and apes. *Br. J. Psychol.,* 1963, **54**, 201-26.

HAMBLIN, R. L., BUCKHOLDT, D., BUSHELL, D., ELLIS, D., and FERRITOR, D. Changing the game from "Get the teacher" to "Learn." *Trans-action,* January, 1969, 20-31.

HARLOW, H. F. Mice, monkey, men, and motives. *Psychol. Rev.,* 1953, **60**, 23-32.

HARLOW, H. F. The nature of love. *Amer. Psychol.,* 1958, **13**, 673-85.

HARLOW, H. F. and HARLOW, M. K. Social deprivation in monkeys. *Sci. Amer.,* 1963, **34**, 136-46.

Homans, G. C. *Social behavior: Its elementary forms.* Harcourt, Brace & World, New York, 1961.

Hunt, J. McV. *Intelligence and Experience.* Ronald Press, New York, 1961.

Lewis, H. B. Studies in the principles of judgments and attitudes: IV. The operation of prestige suggestion. *J. Soc. Psychol.,* 1941, **14,** 229-56.

Longabaugh, R. A category system for coding interpersonal behavior as social exchange. *Sociometry,* 1963, **26,** 319-44.

Longabaugh, R. The coding manual: Social and interactional systems in schizophrenics. 1964, mimeographed.

Longabaugh, R. Coding interaction as social exchange: A modified perspective. Harvard Medical School and the McLean Hospital, 1967, mimeographed.

Longabaugh, R., Eldred, S. H., Bell, N. W., and Sherman, L. J. The interactional world of the chronic schizophrenic patient. *Psychiat.,* 1966, **29,** 78-99.

Lorenz, K. *On Aggression.* Harcourt, Brace & World, New York, 1966.

MacKay, D. M. Psychophysics of perceived intensity: A theoretical basis for Fechner's and Stevens' laws. *Sci.,* 1963, **139,** 1213-16.

McClelland, D. C., Atkinson, J. W., Clark, R. A., and Lowell, E. L. *The Achievement Motive.* Appleton-Century-Crofts, New York, 1953.

Miller, G. A., Galanter, E., and Pribram, K. H. *Plans and the Structure of Behavior.* Holt, Rinehart & Winston, New York, 1960.

Mitchell, T. R. and Foa, U. G. Diffusion of the effect of cultural training of the leader in the structure of hetero-cultural task groups. *Austral. J. Psychol.,* 1969, **21,** 31-43.

Parsons, T. *The Social System.* Free Press, Glencoe, Ill., 1951.

Parsons, T. Family structure and the socialization of the child. In T. Parsons and R. F. Bales (Eds.), *Family, Socialization and Interaction Process.* Free Press, Glencoe, Ill., 1955. Pp. 35-131.

Rodgers, D. A. and Ziegler, F. J. Cognitive process and conversion reaction. *J. Nerv. Ment. Dis.,* 1967, **144,** 155-70.

Sears, R. R., Maccoby, E. E., and Levin, H. *Patterns of Child Rearing.* Row & Peterson, Evanston, Ill., 1957.

Sherif, M. An experimental study of stereotypes. *J. Abnorm. Soc. Psychol.,* 1935, **29,** 371-5.

Thibaut, J. W. and Kelley, H. H. *The Social Psychology of Groups.* Wiley, New York, 1959.

Zelditch, M., Jr. Role differentiation in the nuclear family: A comparative study. In Parsons and Bales, *op. cit.* Pp. 307-52.

Author Index

327

Subject Index